STUDIES IN
LATER GREEK COMEDY

by

T. B. L. WEBSTER

MANCHESTER UNIVERSITY PRESS
BARNES & NOBLE INC, NEW YORK

Published by the University of Manchester at
THE UNIVERSITY PRESS
316-324 Oxford Road, Manchester M13 9NR
1953

Second edition 1970

© 1953, 1970 T. B. L. WEBSTER
UK standard book number: 7190 0439 X

U.S.A.
BARNES & NOBLE INC
105 Fifth Avenue, New York, N.Y. 10003

US standard book number: 389 03989 6

To
W. B. A.

ISBN: 071900439-X

Printed in Great Britain by
Butler & Tanner Limited, Frome and London

STUDIES IN
LATER GREEK COMEDY

PLATE I.—GRAVE RELIEF OF ATHENIAN COMIC POET

Lyme Hall, Stockport. From Athens, Kerameikos. About 380 B.C. Reproduced through the kindness of the Town Clerk, Stockport.

PREFACE

THIS book is a companion to *Studies in Menander*. It completes the programme formulated in my first Rylands Lecture (1944), which, with the permission of the Governors of the Rylands Library, is reprinted in an amended form as the first chapter. I cannot pretend that this book with its multitude of footnotes and references makes easy reading, but I hope it may be useful to those who are interested in this important section of Greek literary history ; I have tried to make it more useful as a reference book by adding a chronological table of plays quoted or mentioned and an Index Locorum. I have noted my indebtedness to other scholars when possible, but I am sure that I have unconsciously absorbed much more from them than I have acknowledged and that there is still more of which I have remained unaware ; in particular I wish Professor W. Beare's *Roman Stage* had come out in time for me to make more use of it. I have tried to rationalise my spelling except for those names that are household words in English, but I have undoubtedly left many inconsistencies. The historical sections of Chapters II and III were read to my colleagues in the Greek Department of University College and to Professor A. H. M. Jones, the substance of Chapter V to the Birmingham branch, of Chapter VI to the Southampton branch of the Classical Association, and of Chapter VII to the London Classical Society. The Town Clerk of Stockport, M. Coche de la Ferté, Dr. B. Neutsch, Mr. J. M. Cook, Mr. B. Ashmole, and Professor C. M. Robertson have given me the photographs from which my illustrations are taken. Mrs. D. J. Furley has helped me with the index ; my wife and Dr. V. Ehrenberg read my manuscript and Mr. E. W. Handley my proofs : to them in particular I would express my thanks.

T. B. L. WEBSTER

LONDON, 1950.

v

PREFACE TO THE SECOND EDITION

IT is nineteen years since the first edition of this book went to press. A great deal of work has been done on comedy in this time. Most obviously, our knowledge of Menander has immensely increased. I have, therefore, recast chapter VII, 'Menandreia', so as to give a general account of his art as we can now appreciate it, adding a note of the most important bibliography on particular plays. For the rest of the book 'Addenda and Corrigenda' take some account of publications since the first edition.

T. B. L. WEBSTER

STANFORD, 1969

CONTENTS

Contents

LIST OF ILLUSTRATIONS

ADDENDA AND CORRIGENDA TO THE SECOND EDITION

P. 2. The question of how Plautus adapted his originals will have to
be re-examined now that we have for the first time a considerable
fragment of Menander's *Dis Exapaton* adapted by Plautus for the
Bacchides, cf. E. W. Handley, *Menander and Plautus*, 1968.

P. 3, n. 1. See chapter VII for new references for Menander.

P. 7 f. Date of Aristotle's *Poetics*. The final form, it is true, belongs
to this period, but the first draft was written before he left Athens
the first time in 347. See my *Art and Literature in fourth-century
Athens*, 54 ff.

P. 10 f. Attic vases and a marble relief. On the vases see now A. D.
Trendall, *Phlyax Vases* [2] (abbreviated below as PH), Nos. 2 (Louvre,
rightly dated there 420–10), 6 (Leningrad, should be dated 410–400 ;
the treatment of the eyes of the frontal mask suggests blindness—
could this be Aristophanes, *First Plutus* ?), 7 (Heidelberg, should be
dated on shape in the first quarter of the fourth century and might
be inspired by *Ekklesiazousai*). For the relief, cf. my *Monuments
illustrating Old and Middle Comedy* [2] (abbreviated below as MMC),
AS 1.

P. 13. On the staging of the *Ekklesiazousai* with a single door, cf.
A. M. Dale, *J.H.S.*, 77, 1957, 205 ff., *Collected Papers*, 110 ff.

P. 16. On personifications of Penia and Ploutos see H-J. Newiger,
Metapher und Allegorie, 155 ff. On the Agon see T. Gelzer, *Der
epirrhematische Agon in Aristophanes*, 52 ff.

P. 18. Plato's *Phaon* : cf. A. Giannini, *Dioniso*, 19, 1956, 232 ff. ;
22, 1959, 3 ff. The vases in n. 2 are now *A.R.V.*,[2] 1312/2 ; 1321/9.

P. 20. On Philoxenos' *Kyklops* see now Pickard-Cambridge, *Dithyramb, Tragedy and Comedy*,[2] 45.

P. 27. On Agyrrhios see N. Valmin, *Op. Ath.*, 6, 1965, 171.

P. 29, n. 1. Now *A.R.V.*,[2] 1186/30.

P. 30. On Euboulos 10 see E. K. Borthwick, *C.Q.*, 16, 1966, 107.

P. 41, n. 5. Pickard-Cambridge, *Dithyramb etc.*,[2] pl. 4, No. 15.

P. 45. On Aristogeiton see now R. Sealey, *B.I.C.S.*, 7, 1960, 33.

P. 46. On the fishmongers see D. M. Lewis, *Hesperia*, 28, 1959, 237.

P. 48. On Alexis 116 see W. G. Arnott, *Hermes*, 93, 1965, 303.

P. 52, n. 1. Cf. also Flacelière, *R.E.A.*, 49, 1947, 243 ; explains
pilidion as ' skull-cap '.

P. 57, n. 1. PH, No. 86 ; Bieber, *History*,[2] fig. 494.

P. 60. On Alexis 107 see Taillardat, *R.P.*, 37, 1963, 100.

P. 65. W. G. Arnott, *G.R.B.S.*, 9, 1968, 160 argues that Alexis transferred the word ' parasite' from religious to secular use. On Antiphanes 195 see J. H. Quincey, *Rh. Mus.*, 106, 1963, 96.

P. 65, n. 2. PH, No. 76 ; Bieber, *History*,[2] fig. 509.

P. 66. On the cook see A. Giannini, *Acme*, 13, 1960, 135 ff.

P. 67. Now, of course, the *Dyskolos* is the best example of the one-character comedy of Menander.

P. 68. The comedy of errors presupposes a set with more than one door (cf. above on p. 13) since confusion of persons is impossible if there is also confusion of place. Cf. *Rylands Bulletin*, 42, 1960, 509.

P. 69, n. 2. Cf. above on p. 65, n. 2.

P. 70. Julian was presumably thinking of the final scene of the *Dyskolos* which the Paestan vase anticipates.

P. 71, n. 3. Add M. N. Tod, *B.S.A.*, 8, 1901, 208 ; *Epigraphica*, 12, 1950, 8.

P. 75, n. 3. See also *MMC*,[2] AS 2.

P. 76, n. 1. *MMC*,[2] AT 15–21 ; Bieber, *History*,[2] figs. 192–8.

P. 77, n. 2. PH, Nos. 133 and 83 ; Bieber, *History*,[2] fig. 507. (The bundle on PH 83 may not be a child.)

P. 78, n. 2. Cf. R. Hoistad, *Cynic Hero and Cynic King*, 8 f., on the chronology of Diogenes.

P. 78. Even if the *Poenulus* does go back to an original of Alexis (W. G. Arnott, *Rh. Mus.*, 102, 1959, 252), the original need not belong to this period.

P. 80, n. 5. W. G. Arnott, *C.Q.*, 5, 1955, 210 argues that the passage is a forgery.

P. 85. Euboulos' *Oidipous* may be illustrated by PH No. 115, Oidipous haggling with Kreon and the sphinx in the background, possibly a parody of Euripides *Oidipous*.

P. 85, n. 1. *MMC*,[2] AT 8–14 ; Bieber, *History*,[2] figs. 185–91.

— n. 2. PH, No. 3 ; *A.R.V.*,[2] 1335/34.

P. 86, n. 1. PH, No. 79, Sicilian, *not* South Italian ; Bieber, *History*,[2] fig. 488.

P. 87, n. 1, 3. British Museum F 193, Trendall, *Red-figure vases of Lucania, Campania, Sicily*, 231. An earlier Tarentine vase, Taranto 4600, *Archaeological Reports*, 67, 1956, 62, pl. 5c, adds Hermes so that he may have spoken the prologue in Euripides' play, on which see my *Tragedies of Euripides*, 92 ff. On *Rudens* 86 see O. Skutsch, *Studia Enniana*, 179.

P. 90, n. 4. Cf. now Pickard-Cambridge, *Dithyramb etc.*,[2] 255 ff.

P. 91, n. 3. PH, No. 65 ; Bieber, *History*,[2] fig. 484.

P. 99, n. 3.   Add my *Monuments illustrating New Comedy*[2] (abbreviated below as *MNC*), 5 ff.

P. 100, n. 1.   Cf. my *Hellenistic Poetry and Art*, 9, ff., 124, ff., 183 ff., 199 ff., 242 ff., 265 ff., 280 ff.

P. 101, n. 5.   See N. Valmin, *Op. Ath.*, 6, 1965, 171 ff., on *theorikon*.

P. 103.   Dario del Corno, *Dioniso*, 32, 1962, 136 ff., argues that the *gynaikonomoi* were introduced in 322 by Antipater.

P. 104, n. 2.   On Ophellas, cf. Will, *R.E.A.*, 66, 1964, 320.

P. 110.   The arrival of the *advocati* in the *Poenulus* (522 ff.) has been identified with Alexis (263K).

P. 115.   *Com. Flor.* is now identified as *Aspis*.

P. 117.   It is easy to overrate the seriousness of the philosophical sentiments expressed by Menander's characters, and C. Gaiser's realistic treatment in *A.u.A.*, 13, 1967, 8 ff., is salutary.

P. 119, n. 2.   A fairly complete list of New Comedy illustrations is given in *MNC*. The examples shown in plate IV are *MNC*, AS 10 UT 15, FT 2.

P. 119, n. 3.   Lateran relief : *MNC*, IS 10 ; Bieber, *History*,[2] fig. 317 ; Pickard-Cambridge, *Festivals*,[2] fig. 109. Silver cup : *MNC*, NJ 2.

P. 120, n. 3.   *MNC*, NS 25 ; Bieber, *History*,[2] fig. 324 ; Pickard-Cambridge, *Festivals*,[2] fig. 110.

P. 120, n. 4.   *MNC*, IT 65 ; Bieber, *History*,[2] fig. 587.

P. 120, n. 5.   *MNC*, NP 6 ; Bieber, *History*,[2] fig. 395 ; cf. also the second-century painting in Delos, *MNC*, DP 2, *B.C.H.*, 87, 1963, 869 ff.

P. 120, n. 6.   *MNC*, NP 45 ; Bieber, *History*,[2] fig. 328.

P. 120, n. 7.   *MNC*, NP 14 ; Bieber, *History*,[2] fig. 327.

P. 120, n. 8.   *MNC*, NM 2 ; Bieber, *History*,[2] fig. 346. Probably illustrates Menander's *Theophoroumene*, cf. p. 206.

P. 121, n. 1., *MNC*, NP 13 ; Bieber, *History*,[2] fig. 371.

P. 121, n. 2.   *MNC*, NP 22 ; Bieber, *History*,[2] fig. 770.

P. 121, n. 3.   *MNC*, NP 38 ; Bieber, *History*,[2] fig. 383.

P. 121, n. 4.   *MNC*, NM 1 ; Bieber, *History*,[2] fig. 347. The connection with the *Synaristosai* is proved by the Mytilene mosaic, *MNC*, YM2, cf. p. 208.

P. 121, n. 5.   *MNC*, NP 25.

P. 123.   To Gorgias in the *Georgos*, add now Gorgias in the *Dyskolos*.

P. 124.   To sympathetic soldiers add now Stratophanes in the *Sikyonios*.

P. 125, n. 4.   On Magas, cf. *B.C.H.*, 82, 1958, 571.

P. 128, n. 3.   *Com. Flor.* is now identified as *Aspis*.

P. 130.   Della Corte, *R.I.F.C.*, 1952, 329, connects 124K with *Mercator* 404.

P. 135, n. 1. *MMC*, AT 99, BT 10 ; *MNC*, IS 20.

P. 135, n. 2. *MMC*, AT 21.

Pp. 139, 142. Kassel, *Rh. Mus.*, 105, 1962, 96, suggests neatly *ac nodos* for *agnitus*.

P. 142 f. The very difficult further fragments of the Strobilos play add a considerable cook scene, including a reference to cooks in comedy (Siegmann, *P. Heidelberg*, No. 184 ; cf. also Treu, *Philologus*, 102, 1958, 215, who adds Page, *G.L.P.*, No. 59b).

P. 143, n. 3. *P.S.I.* 1176 (61P) is given by Mette in *Lustrum* 10, 149, to Menander's *Koneiazomenai* (see p. 207).

P. 160, n. 3. Cf. above on p. 70, n. 1.

P. 161, n. 1. *MMC*, AT 34 ; *PH*, No. 132.

P. 168, n. 1. Plautine reminiscence of Ennius is also possible, cf. O. Skutsch, *Studia Enniana*, 179.

P. 173. K. Gaiser, *Poetica*, 4, 1967, 436, suggests that Menander's *Ephesios* was the original of the *Miles Gloriosus* and that ' Periplectomenus ' (cf. 648) was the Ephesian. *Alazon* would then have been an alternative title. Judgment must wait for his full treatment, but it is difficult to conceive of the soldier as one of Menander's latest creations.

P. 176. On *Miles*, 214–232, cf. E. Fraenkel, *Mus. Helv.*, 25, 1968, 231.

P. 237. J. W. B. Barns and H. Lloyd-Jones have published a new study of *Antinoopolis papyri*, No. 15, in *J.H.S.*, 84, 1964, 21 ff. It now appears that p. 61 opened the play with a complete list of characters and that the other side previously read as p. 60 should be p. 62 and that the speaker was not called Kantharos. The play therefore began with the speech of the young husband and then went on with the finding of recognition tokens. As p. 61 is the first page of the play, it becomes more tempting to restore Menander's name as the author. The article gives some new readings.

P. 239. The Schubart papyrus is now said not to be in the same hand but may, of course, still be from the same play.

P. 240. The Ghoran papyrus, 65 P, is accepted as Menander by Mette, *Lustrum*, 10, 1965, 192.

P. 254, n. 1. *PH*, No. 33.

I. FORETHOUGHTS ON LATER GREEK COMEDY

THE series of Greek tragedies produced by Aeschylus, Sophocles, and Euripides are a guide of inestimable value to the changes in the spirit which informs all works of art and thought in the fifth century B.C. Although only a small proportion of their works survive, they form a series which is datable over a period of some eighty years, of works by great literary craftsmen who expressed, even when they did not create, the highest standards of religious, political, and ethical thought. Moreover, the plays can be illustrated by datable sculpture and vases created for the same patrons.

In the fourth century and later the story is more confusing. The chief cause is perhaps the specialisation of the arts. Fourth-century ethical and political thought belongs to the philosophers and not to the poets or artists, and the creative ideas of a generation can no longer be summed up in pairs of names like Aeschylus and Polygnotus or Sophocles and Pheidias. Instead, a number of series survive which have no such obvious cross-connection with each other—dated sculptures, datable Attic and South Italian vases, the Platonic dialogues, the works of Aristotle, Theophrastus, and Epicurus, and the series of dated law court speeches.

The series with which I am concerned here is the series of comedies produced between the beginning of the fourth century and the end of the first quarter of the third century. In the fifth century the Old Comedy of Aristophanes and his predecessors was political in a wide sense ; events were discussed and politicians attacked, and at the same time the sophistic movement was bitterly criticised as responsible for contemporary manners and morals. We shall have to see how far this critical function of comedy continues when Athens no longer holds her dominant position as an imperial state and when the itinerant sophists had given place to established philosophical schools. The old violent abuse certainly becomes much rarer but does not die altogether and we shall find good reason for interpreting many

I

passages of Middle Comedy as political ; in New Comedy the
evidence is slighter.   The philosophical schools are for the most
part treated with tolerant contempt ; their positive influence on
the practice of comedy only becomes apparent in the time of
Menander.   Primarily however we are concerned with Greek
comedies as a series of works of art.   At the beginning and end
of the fourth century we can see poetic personalities and study
individual methods and aims.   For the period between Aristophanes and Menander we have only fragments and therefore
cannot hope to do more than say when particular themes and
techniques can be first detected in the comic repertoire.

The remains of later Greek Comedy consist of the last two plays
by Aristophanes, three plays by Menander, and twenty-seven
plays produced by Terence and Plautus in the Roman period.
These thirty-two plays provide the framework for the history of
later Greek Comedy, into which the mass of short Greek fragments must be fitted.   Further help is afforded by representations
of Greek Comedy in works of art, by ancient writers on literary
criticism and the theatre and by reflections of Greek Comedy in
contemporary or later works.   Finally, because comedy was not
produced as a private performance but at a public festival, the
history of Greek Comedy forms part of the general history of
Greek thought and ideals as known from other works of literature
and art.

At the outset, before even a framework can be constructed,
the problem of the Latin adaptations of Plautus and Terence must
be faced.   Should they be given the same status as originals by
Aristophanes and Menander or should they be treated with as
much care and circumspection as the archaeologist devotes to
Roman copies of Greek statues ?   The archaeologist knows little
about the multitudinous artists who made the Roman copies and
he seldom has first-rate originals with which to compare those
copies.   For the literary historian, however, three original plays
of Menander (and fragments of original plays by the other poets)
survive and the Roman copyists, Plautus and Terence, are
known quantities.   Plautus may elaborate the particular scene to
the detriment of the play as a whole ; he remodels his text to
produce song and dance where there was plain dialogue before ;
he substitutes elaborate metaphor and mythological allusion for
the plain and ' ethical ' language of the original.   But this

colouring and distortion is a recognisable quality for which allowances can be made. Terence is far more faithful to the style and feeling of his originals, and is so honest in his admissions when he has interpolated figures or scenes from alien plays that there is little reason to suspect him of concealing other such interpolations. In the main, Greek parallels can be found for most of the elements in the Latin adaptations although detailed consideration of the faithfulness of the Roman authors in minor points must be reserved for further study.

We have also thousands of Greek fragments [1] of Middle and New Comedy. Some of them are quotations by later writers, selected for a particular purpose ; some of them are random stretches of papyrus texts. The latter are practically confined to New Comedy but are far more valuable for appreciating the technique of the author. While quotations give considerable information about the themes and subject matter of Middle and New Comedy, they never or hardly ever tell us anything about the actual situation on the stage and we can seldom see the threads leading forward or backward from them. The papyrus fragments on the other hand, though maddeningly corrupt and tantalisingly difficult to restore, give us live situations for which we can often suggest beginnings and endings on the analogy of the surviving plays of Menander and the Roman adaptations. A tattered fragment of a painting of known style may tell us more about the whole picture than a carefully excerpted head ; similarly a papyrus fragment of New Comedy can tell us more about the play than a well-preserved philosophical sentiment or list of eatables.

Aristophanes and Menander present the beginning and the summit of the development of later Greek Comedy. The two last plays of Aristophanes, like his earlier plays, are dominated by a single idea and the characters are only sufficiently sketched for the working out of this idea—in the *Ekklesiazousai* the effects of Platonic communism and in the *Ploutos* the effects of making Wealth see. In both plays the young men hardly count, and

---

[1] I give references to Kock, *Comicorum Atticorum Fragmenta* (K), and D. L. Page, *Greek Literary Papyri* (P), wherever possible. For the fragments in Page the index gives cross-references to Demianczuk, *Supplementum Comicum* (D), and Schroeder, *Novae comoediae fragmenta* (S). I have also added in the index references to the forthcoming Teubner Edition of Menander by A. Körte. I am indebted for these to Professor A. Thierfelder.

the old women who behave like hetairai in the *Ekklesiazousai* are caricatures introduced to make amusing episodes. Two character contrasts, however, are fruitful in later comedy, the pair of master and slave in the *Ploutos*, which has ancestors in the *Peace* and the *Frogs*, and the pair of kindly old man and stern old man in both plays, which on our evidence appears now for the first time. But the characters only exist to demonstrate the dominant idea. Seventy years later character drawing is an end of Menander's comedy and character contrast is as essential a means to this end for him as for Sophocles a hundred years before. The contrasts are both within types and across types : youth contrasted with youth but also hetaira contrasted with wife, and slave with master. These contrasts can be seen in the fragmentary originals and amplified from the Latin adaptations. The characters of Menander are individual people sympathetically drawn but besides the individuality of the characters there is a general problem of human behaviour which particularly interests him. It is the Aristotelian problem of nice discrimination between true and false values in choosing a course of action. Apollodoros of Karystos, who started writing about the time of Menander's death, is his successor in this line of comedy but has shifted the emphasis somewhat ; for him the misconceptions of his characters have become a technical device for advancing the action and the real value in which he is most interested seems to be the solidarity of the family. Common to both poets is the sweet sympathy which idealises the braggart soldier Polemon and the hetaira Bacchis.

The other two personalities of whom we can form some idea are older contemporaries of Menander, Philemon and Diphilos. Their comedy is less concerned with sympathetic character drawing and ethics and more with satire and knockabout. But for Philemon friendship is always a real value, and Daemones in Diphilos' *Rudens* behaves in exile with the ' philanthropy ' and discrimination of an educated Athenian. Normally however Philemon seeks to raise laughter rather than smiles and he is a master of the comedy of extemporisation in his intrigues. Diphilos delights in knockabout but also in spectacle. In the *Rudens* he escapes from the conventional ' conversation before two houses ', which is the normal scene of later Greek Comedy, into a wilder world of storm and shipwreck.

The types of comedy which can be thus distinguished serve as a guide both in assigning a position to the other plays of Plautus and in mapping the uncharted territory which separates Menander from Aristophanes. The later development of the . Aristophanic comedy of the dominant idea can be seen in three plays : *Amphitruo, Menaechmi,* and *Persa.* The *Amphitruo* with its small heroic cast, who are, however, completely human in all their actions, and its few scenes is unlike any other play. The dominant idea is the indistinguishability of Amphitruo from Jupiter and Sosias from Mercury and the consequences of these confusions. In default of other evidence the *Amphitruo* should belong to the Middle Comedy. The *Menaechmi* has more scenes and more characters and has lost the heroic garb of the *Amphitruo* ; the ' wimpled ' hetaira and her pert maid, the complaining wife and her muddled father, at least foreshadow the world of Menander ; but the confusions of the twins matter so much more than characters and story that this play, too, is probably based on an original from Middle Comedy. The dominant idea of the *Persa* is the parasite who sells his daughter to obtain food ; the elaborate intrigue looks forward to New Comedy, but the small cast and simple characterisation belong to the period before Menander.

We can examine the numerous Greek fragments of Middle Comedy from the same point of view and we may be able to discover by what time the comedy of satire and intrigue and the comedy of character had begun. In works of decorative art a chronological series can often be established by observing that new decorative elements appear first in a subsidiary field, later occupy the main field, and finally retire to a subsidiary field again when a newcomer has supplanted them as the main theme of the decoration. That the analogy may also hold for Greek Comedy is suggested by the history of the hetaira figure. The hetaira is unknown as a speaking character in the earlier works of Aristophanes but appears as a subsidiary caricature in the closing scenes of the *Ekklesiazousai* ; it is justifiable to assume that she was the dominant figure in the many plays of Middle Comedy named after hetairai ; the idealised hetairai of Menander and Apollodoros are no longer the chief figures of the plays in which they occur.

Four figures which dominated many Middle Comedy plays

but retire into the background of the New Comedy are the soldier, the parasite, the cook, and the philosopher. Antiphanes wrote a comedy called *The Soldier*, in which the braggart soldier described how the King of Cyprus was fanned by doves at dinner; in the surviving plays of New Comedy (not excluding the *Miles*) the soldier is a minor character, except in the *Perikeiromene*, where Polemon is not satirised but idealised. Antiphanes and Alexis both wrote a *Parasite* in which, presumably, the parasite was the central figure, but in New Comedy the parasite retires to the fringe except in the *Phormio*, where again he is idealised. The cook is a minor figure in most of the surviving plays, although in the *Pseudolus* he has a scene to himself in which to describe his art. A glance through the fragments of Middle Comedy shows the paramount importance of food; sometimes the meal itself is described, sometimes a slave describes what he has seen or bought at the market; but often the cook himself talks, and Anaxandrides named his *Nereus* after a famous cook. The philosopher only leaves traces in New Comedy but in Middle Comedy Aristophanes' Sokrates has many descendants: an old man in Antiphanes' *Antaios* is described as 'the Academy itself', and Aristophon wrote both a *Plato* and a *Pythagorean*.

Middle Comedy also provides parallels and ancestry for the *Amphitruo*, the mythological play in which heroic characters appear in modern guise. A large crop of mythological plays appeared at the end of the fifth century and they had their greatest popularity in the first forty years of the fourth century. In Euboulos' *Antiope* Zethos has settled in Thebes because they sell better loaves there, and a Boeotian describes the Boeotian character in the Boeotian dialect. The *Amphitruo* is a further development along the same lines: the heroic characters are completely human in their reactions and the heroic story is merely a convenient excuse for the confusions which are the main theme of the comedy. The influence of tragedy on comedy is a subject which deserves a monograph in itself; three main stages can be distinguished—in the Old Comedy parody of individual tragic lines or at most whole speeches, and occasional introduction of figures from the mythological world of tragedy, in the Middle Comedy parody of tragic stories with the characters thinking and behaving like 'those worse than ourselves', and in the New Comedy inspiration by tragedy. Menander's technique of character contrast recalls Sophocles ; Diphilos was influenced by the *Ion* and the *Iphigenia in Tauris* for his settings in the *Rudens*. The rescue stories which end with a recognition have ancestors in many late Euripidean plays, and Euripides seemed to Aristotle, writing before the New Comedy began, to be the most effective of the tragic authors on the stage.

The beginnings of the new tragi-comedy of Menander and his contemporaries, which differs from the single character play about soldier or hetaira because the portraiture is sympathetic instead of being satirical, can already be seen in Middle Comedy : young men suffer the tortures of love, a son upbraids his father, a slave tells his young master (who has presumably threatened suicide) that no one ever died when he wanted to die. In Antiphanes' *Hydria* the only surviving fragment reads : ' The man of whom I speak saw a hetaira living in his neighbour's house and fell in love with her, an Athenian with no guardian or relations, but had a golden virtuous heart, a true hetaira— the rest spoil that good name by bad behaviour.' The hero of this play was a young man in love with a hetaira of the same breed as Palaestra in the *Rudens* ; we can guess further that she has to be rescued either from a brothel-keeper or from an unwelcome lover and that the hydria which gives the play its name contains gold to help the solution.

The fragments though numerous are disconnected, but the general correctness of the picture can be seen from scanty remarks made by Aristotle. In one place he clearly has in mind the plot of a mythological comedy : ' For in comedy those who have been the worst foes like Orestes and Aegisthus retire as friends at the end, and nobody is killed by anybody.' His insistence that the subjects of comedy are ' worse than present-day men ' agrees with what we have said about caricature and satire, but when he qualifies this later by calling them ' rather trivial people but not really vicious . . . errors and ugliness that do not bring about major pains or destructions ', he is already thinking of the newer character comedy rather than of the older satirical comedy. That the comedy of plot has already appeared in his day is implied by the statement that comic poets construct their plots of prob- able incidents.

It is usually assumed that the *Poetics* was composed soon after Aristotle started teaching in the Lyceum in 334 B.C. At this date, then, according to this testimony, since his theory of comedy like his theory of tragedy is undoubtedly based on existing plays, the mythological comedy and the comedy of satire—and ' worse than present-day men ' implies knockabout as well as satire— were well established and the comedy of plot and the comedy of character had already begun.

The same decade, in which Aristotle wrote the *Poetics*, 340–330, also saw the defeat of Athens at Chaironeia and Lykourgos' attempt to restore morale after the disaster.   Part of this attempt consisted in a revival of fifth-century tragedy outwardly sym-bolised by the erection of statues of the three great tragedians in the theatre of Dionysus and the establishment of their texts. The influence of fifth-century tragedy on New Comedy must be ascribed both to Lykourgos and to Aristotle, to Lykourgos because he established fifth-century tragedy as classical tragedy, and to Aristotle because he founded his theory of drama on the plays of Sophocles and Euripides.   Partly because of Aristotle and partly because of Lykourgos the three poets who created New Comedy to satisfy the needs of the Athenians after Chaironeia went to fifth-century tragedy for their inspiration.

The decade in which Chaironeia falls is as decisive for Greek Comedy as the decade of the Persian wars for Greek Tragedy. Although the beginning of the new can be seen growing under the cloak of the old, the certain progress of the new dates from the crucial decade.   Much of the earlier fourth century is in the straight line of development from the fifth century.   The political and ethical thought of Plato and Isokrates grows naturally out of the thought of Sophocles, Euripides, Protagoras, and Thucydides. The Eirene, which Kephisodotos carved in 373, is the last of a line of draped female figures which can be traced back through Pheidias to the Argive sculptors of the Persian wars.   So too there is no essential break between Old Comedy and the *Ekklesiazousai* and *Ploutos*, and the tradition of Old Comedy survives in the parodies of tragedy, the caricatured philosophers, the loquacious cooks, and the riddling slaves of Middle Comedy. The new thing, which makes Menander's Comedy both possible and necessary, is a new assertion of the value of the individual, not as in the early fifth century as a citizen of an imperial state but as a private individual in a larger whole.   Aristotle laid the foundations in the *Ethics* by propounding the theory of the

Mean and the value of the speculative life : on the foundations the two philosophies of the later Greek world, which are primarily designed to guide the individual's life, Epicureanism and Stoicism, are built ; but by the time these schools were started New Comedy was firmly established.

But the parallel with the beginning of Greek Tragedy may be pursued a little further. The assertion of the value and responsibility of the individual, which for us is first documented by Simonides' skolion to Skopas, in 510 B.C., broke down the archaic conventions of manners and deportment, so that the smiling and conventionally composed archaic statue gradually develops into the solemn and freely composed classical statue and the oratorio of early Aeschylus gradually changes into the character drama of Sophocles. A similar liberation of emotion and revolution in composition can be observed during the fourth century B.C. In the plastic arts, as in the fifth century, the stress on composition comes from the Peloponnese, from the Sikyonian painters and Lysippos in Plato's time ; the liberation of emotion belongs rather to Athenians and Ionians (again as before) and the mile-stones are the pensive Hermes of Praxiteles (younger brother or son of Kephisodotos whose Eirene is still in the fifth-century tradition), the Mausoleum sculptures in the middle of the century, the Tegea heads in the 340's, and in the last third of the century the gentle Tanagra figures, which best illustrate the heroes and heroines of Menander. Enough remains of the poets of Middle Comedy to show that here, too, the new art was gradually growing and that the comedy of intrigue and the comedy of character have their roots in the second third of the fourth century. The change can be summed up in a word ; the citizen of the imperial state has given place to the individual in a free town within a Hellenistic kingdom, and New Comedy expresses the spirit of this new world as surely as Classical Tragedy expressed the spirit of Periclean Athens.

FOR the beginning of the fourth century the last two plays
of Aristophanes are our chief source and our account must
start with them. The *Ekklesiazousai* is named after its chorus,
the women who went to the Assembly, and the play tells how
the women took over power and what happened when they did.
This is a common formula for Old Comedy : a startling idea is
put into practice and the consequences are seen.   In the *Acharnians*
Dikaiopolis makes his private peace and the rest of the play
shows what results it brings to him and others. This is the
Comedy of the dominant idea and we shall be able to trace its
survival through the fourth century.[1] In this period Theopompos' *Stratiotides*, 'women-at-arms', would seem to belong
to the same category, and in Aristophanes' *Gerytades* an embassy
of poets was taken to Hades, perhaps to bring back one of the
dead, like Dionysos in the *Frogs* ; but where only fragments
survive the structure cannot be seen.   The chorus of women who
dressed themselves up as men in the *Ekklesiazousai* (or as soldiers
in the *Stratiotides*) were themselves startling and we can quote
other startling choruses in the tradition of the fifth century :
Aristophanes' *Storks*, Philyllios' *Cities*, Plato's *Islands*, and Strattis'
Makedones, who talked Macedonian and were shown the sights
of Attika (28, 30K).

Two Attic vases and a marble relief from the Kerameikos give
us an idea of what these plays looked like. The relief[2] is the
funeral monument of a comic poet erected in Athens about
380 B.C. ; it may even be the funeral monument of Aristophanes.
Two points concern us here : the poet himself and the masks.
His face is damaged but the deep lines on the forehead, the deep
furrows on either side of the chin, the drooping corners of the
mouth show that for the sculptor the poet was not simply a
jester or a buffoon but a serious and perhaps disillusioned man.
There is no proof that this is Aristophanes but it would be
difficult to imagine the Aristophanes of the last two plays other-

[1] Cf. below, pp. 67, 115 : *Studies in Menander*, 110, 117, 183.
[2] Pl. I : *Essays presented to D. M. Robinson*, 590 ; *J.H.S.*, 1903, pl. XIII.

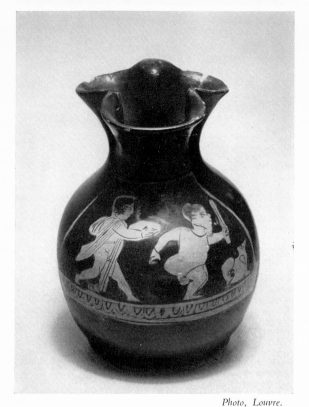

(*a*) COMIC ACTOR WITH COMAST AND DOG
Louvre CA 2938.   Attic oenochoe, early fourth century B.C.

(*b*) COMIC ACTORS
Heidelberg B. 134   Attic bell krater, 370/60 B.C.

PLATE II

wise. The masks represent a slave and an elderly man with full hair and beard ; the old man's expression is differentiated—the left brow is smooth and the right brow raised ; the appropriate side could be turned to the audience, angry and proud, or calm. The old man's mask is not unlike Pollux' description of the Lycomedian who 'suggests interference' ; Blepsidemos is so characterised in the *Ploutos* (335) and the same mask would suit the realistic man who refuses to surrender his goods in the *Ekklesiazousai* (746).

The well-known Attic oenochoe in Leningrad [1] shows that the padded costume with phallos continues in comedy. There are three actors and five masks ; from left to right—(*a*) man with receding hair and perhaps joined brows ; [2] (*b*) an old man, bearded, with hooked nose and raised brows, and a small *polos* on his head which marks him as a god and probably Zeus ; (*c*) an old man with smooth brows and scanty hair and beard ; (*d*) a slave with wild scrubby hair and beard ; and (*e*) a young man with dark hair and short nose. The two old men are the second Pappos ('energetic in expression') and the first Pappos ('his brows are very mild') of Pollux' list. The mild old man would do very well for Chremes in the *Ekklesiazousai* and for Ploutos when he returns with his eyesight restored. The occurrence of Zeus wearing a normal mask shows that Aristophanes' *Ploutos*, though he is a divine or an heroic figure, would not be differentiated as such by his mask ; this is an important point to which we shall return.

An Attic bell krater in Heidelberg [3] may have been painted a year or two after the close of this period but is included here because it gives a good idea of Praxagora and the chorus of the *Ekklesiazousai* when they are clothed as women and no longer wear their beards. The figure on the left is the typical member of a comic female chorus, wearing chiton and embroidered himation and mask with short nose and untidy dark hair. The figure on the right has raised his female mask on to the top of his head, holds a torch in his left hand, and the himation has been pushed

---

[1] Bieber, *History of the Greek Theatre*, fig. 121 ; Pickard-Cambridge, *Dithyramb*, fig. 32 (drawing) ; Bethe, *Griechische Dichtung*, pl. VIII.

[2] The same mask is worn by a padded man on an Attic oenochoe, Louvre CA 2938, here pl. IIA. Cf. G. van Hoorn, *Choes*, no. 854.

[3] Pl. IIB, B.134, Kraiker, pl. 48. Cf. my interpretation in the Festschrift for B. Schweitzer.

off his shoulder. We are shown two moments in the play : on the left a choreut in a quiet dance, on the right a choreut dancing off wildly in the procession at the end of the play.

The figure on the left would not be unlike Praxagora when she comes out at the beginning of the *Ekklesiazousai* to make her prayer to the ' bright eye of the wheeled lamp ' which knows all a woman's secrets. It is a parody of a prayer to the sun in tragic style and metre.[1] At the very beginning we find the violent contrast between heroic style and metre on the one hand, comic costume and realistic content on the other, which is so common in this comedy.[2] The other women then arrive and dress up, and the rehearsal for the Assembly takes place ; this is first-rate comedy leading up to Praxagora's serious account of the evils of contemporary Athens, which will be considered later. The women move off to the Assembly. The next scene in which Blepyros, Praxagora's husband, and his neighbour fail to find their clothes is low comedy of the best kind. Then Chremes returns from the Assembly and reports that the government of Athens has been handed over to the women. There are several points to be noted in this scene. Fraenkel [3] describes it as apparently under the influence of similar scenes in Euripides, and particularly of the famous speech of the messenger in the *Orestes* (866). This is true but the messenger scene does not bear the same relation to tragedy as Praxagora's opening prayer. That is parody for the fun of parody ; here Aristophanes borrows Euripidean technique for his own purpose, a process which we shall see again in later Greek comedy. Chremes himself is not a colourless reporter nor simply scornful like Blepyros ; he believes that it is the citizen's duty to carry out the policy on which the Assembly has decided.

Praxagora and the women return and change back into women's clothing. The following scene in which she makes excuses to Blepyros and hears from him that the women have been put in charge of Athens is again pure comedy. The great

---

[1] Cf. particularly Fraenkel, *Plautinisches im Plautus*, 102, n. 1. I have translated τροχηλάτου ' wheeled ' to try to get the pun : wheel-made lamp and charioteer sun.

[2] For parodies of single lines or short stretches of tragedy cf. 392, 563 : *Plut.* 34, 114, 160, 601, 635, 639, 641, 1127, 1151. In other authors at this time cf. Nikochares 2K ; Alkaios 19K ; Theopompos 3K.

[3] *Greek Poetry and Life*, 261.

debate on communism follows (and will be discussed later) ; it is an agon like the agon between Kleon and the sausage-seller in the *Knights* but reduced to half its old size. Again here Chremes plays a consistent part ; he is the man who forces Blepyros to allow his wife to speak (564) [1] and intervenes certainly twice in the debate (609, 668) to approve the new regulations. At the end (728) he goes in to prepare his possessions for surrender to the common store.

The delightful little scene in which Chremes invites his possessions to come out of doors, and then with his slaves arranges them, recalls Dikaiopolis' Rural Dionysia in the *Acharnians* (241 f.). Then another man comes out, probably rightly called Pheidolos by two manuscripts. Let us pause and look at these names for a moment since we are here between Old Comedy and New. Praxagora, Pheidolos, and Blepyros (' look to the corn ') are significant or speaking names like Lysistrate, Dikaiopolis, or Strepsiades. Chremes, like Chremylos and Karion in the *Ploutos*, are what Aristotle calls ' chance names ' and this is the normal practice of New Comedy except perhaps for braggart soldiers who have character names like Thrasonides in Menander's *Misoumenos* and Polemon in his *Perikeiromene*. Here the new practice is just beginning. The scene between Chremes and Pheidolos is the earliest scene in comedy in which two old men are clearly contrasted, Pheidolos first realistically refusing to contribute to the common store because the Athenians will change their minds, but hurrying off as soon as he hears that there is a free feast, Chremes loyally carrying out his duty to deposit his goods before he receives his reward.

The following scene, in which the old woman and the girl sing rival songs on their roofs and the young man who serenades the girl from the street is caught by the old woman and then nearly torn in pieces by a second and finally by a third old woman, is again low comedy. It has been carefully prepared by one of the rules of the new state (615 f.), which has in fact nothing to do with communism but is merely introduced to make the later scene possible. The three hags must be distinguished by mask and the three old women's masks in Pollux' list will suit them ; the first, who is snub-nosed (940) and thin (1002), presumably wears the ' little housekeeper ' ; the third, who is like a toad and

---

[1] So Wilamowitz, *Lysistrate*, 213.

a monkey (1072, 1101), is the fat woman ; the second by elimination should be the wolfish old woman. The play ends when the servant of Praxagora comes in slightly tipsy to look for Blepyros because he has not yet dined ; she brings dancing girls for him and they dance, while she sings the song of the fantastic dish which will be served at the feast. Then Blepyros, she, the dancing girls and the chorus dance off together to dinner.[1]

It is difficult and perhaps to-day impossible to assess this play. I see no sign of tiredness or age or failing powers ; the dominant idea is good, the construction flawless, the wit brilliant and the humour admirable. Yet there is a change from the fifth-century plays, not only in the development of new themes and the reduction of the lyric element but also in tone ; the experiment is carried through but the result is not so boisterously successful as in the *Acharnians* or the *Peace*. The same may be said of the *Ploutos*, where the experiment is to cure the blindness of wealth, and again the background is the desperate poverty of the early fourth century, which extends even to the farmers.[2] Formally this play like the *Ekklesiazousai* has the agon cut to half its old size, and the lyric element is still further reduced since only the opening chorus has special words written for it and there is nothing to correspond to the love songs and serenade of the *Ekklesiazousai* or the lyric description of the monstrous dish. We have not enough evidence to account for this reduction in the choral element[3] ; we cannot say for certain whether it is due primarily to financial stringency, to lack of inspiration, or to a change in emphasis. Clearly however the emphasis has changed when instead of brilliant lyrics and dances written for the particular play the chorus now sing and dance interludes too trivial to be recorded. After the first chorus the *Ekklesiazousai* has two brief odes of its own and interludes indicated twice (729, 876) ; in the *Ploutos* there were probably interludes after 626, 770, 801, 958, 1096, and 1170. The *Aiolosikon* which was

---

[1] See Wilamowitz and Fraenkel, *loc. cit.* Fraenkel's suggestion that the man who is late for supper but receives this superb reward at the end is Chremes is attractive but seems to me impossible : the ' most blessed mistress ' (1113) of the servant must be Praxagora ; no other woman can be so described ; therefore ' the master ' (1125) must be Blepyros. Nor do I believe that the second half of the play is a refutation of communism (Roos, *Eranos*, xlix, 5).

[2] Cf. Ehrenberg, *People of Aristophanes*, 70, 93.

[3] On this see Maidment, *C.Q.*, 1935, 1 f.

produced after the *Ploutos* is said not to have had choric songs.[1]
We cannot say whether this was the general practice of comic
poets in the fourth century, but the plays which had interesting
choruses—Storks, Islands, Women at Arms, etc.—must surely
have had at least a special parodos.   On the other hand, the
fragments show no metres which could not have been recited by
actors, although this may be due to the chance of survival.

In the *Ekklesiazousai* and the *Ploutos* the chorus are still present
all the time and occasionally intervene in the action.   But even
here there is a difference ; the *Ekklesiazousai* is still their play.
In the *Ploutos* they do not matter, and the emphasis is even more
completely transferred to the characters.   The *Ploutos* opens with
Master and Slave pursuing Ploutos, whom they have followed
from Delphi to Athens.   The situation is not unlike the beginning of the *Peace*, but the brilliant phantasy of feeding the dung-
beetle is gone ; instead, Karion complaining of the madness of
his master is much more like the slave of New Comedy, and
Chremylos wants to know whether, since only injustice prospers,
his only son ought to change his whole life—a question which
was treated fully but much more lightheartedly in the *Clouds* ;
in New Comedy the question has altered—the elderly pair of
brothers in the *Adelphi* do not ask which life shall our sons lead
but how shall we educate them to lead it.   The seizing of
Ploutos is a brief snatch of thug comedy, and then Ploutos (like
the sausage-seller in the *Knights*) is told of his power—comedy
again, covering a statement of the economic basis of civilisation.
Again there is a foretaste of later comedy when he characterises
the miser and the spendthrift as the only two types of men that
he has known (237 f.).

The chorus' opening and only song parodies the *Cyclops* of
Philoxenos of Kythera and therefore had more comic value than
we can appreciate.   The next scene is a contrast of two characters
like the scene between Chremes and Pheidolos in the *Ekklesiazousai* ; here Chremylos is the simple, generous man who has invited
his friends to share his unexpected good fortune, Blepsidemos as
his name implies is the realistic political man who is certain that
wealth can only be got by foul means and offers to bribe the
politicians to prevent legal action.   He is finally convinced and

---

[1] Platonios 5 (Kaibel).   On the interludes in *Ekkl.* and *Ploutos* see E. W.
Handley, *C.Q.*, 1953 (forthcoming).

the two old men then have to meet the terrifying figure of Poverty, who looks like a cross between a Fury from tragedy and a landlady. Her entry and her final departure are pure comedy but she leaves us with an uncomfortable feeling that she has got the best of the argument and that there is more to be said for her unpleasant doctrine of hard work than for the communism propounded by Praxagora in the corresponding scene of the *Ekklesiazousai*. Now Ploutos is taken to the temple of Asklepios to have his blindness cured. A night passes during the interval and then Karion returns with the news that Ploutos has been healed. Here too, as in Chremes' report of the assembly in the *Ekklesiazousai*, the machinery is tragic : Karion first addresses the chorus and the chorus sing for joy, then Chremylos' wife comes out to hear the news like Eurydice in the *Antigone* and then the report is given largely in tragic style with the wife, whom Murray [1] characterises as ' a nice ignorant pious Athenian *hausfrau* ', making frequent incredulous interruptions. In all this scene we are in the borderland between parody of tragedy and adoption of tragic technique, here rather nearer to parody than in the *Ekklesiazousai*. Ploutos himself returns escorted by Chremylos, and Karion reports on the result ; bins and wine jars are full, the pottery has changed into silver and bronze. The experiment is now complete and in the traditional Aristophanic manner we see the effect on various types of character, the just man, the sycophant, the rich old woman and her poor young lover, Hermes and the priest of Zeus. This is all traditional comedy and the play ends with a torchlight procession to establish Ploutos in the back of Athena's temple. The new world is not a world of deceit and scheming but of ' straightforward ways ' (1158), which might bring back to Athens her old prosperity.

Ploutos is a character from mythology and therefore the play belongs to the class of mythological plays, which had become increasingly common in the latter part of the fifth century and remained popular during the first half of the fourth. Even from our fragmentary evidence various kinds of mythological play can be seen. In the *Ploutos* Ploutos himself is a mythological character and the same status must be accorded to his counterpart Penia, but they, as well as Hermes, are plunged into a human

[1] *Aristophanes*, 204.

story, are treated as human beings, and, as the archaeological evidence shows, look like human beings. We need not look for a source in tragedy or other high literature any more than for the part played by Dionysos in the *Frogs* ; similarly in Aristomenes' *Dionysos Asketes* the god appeared as an athlete. Sometimes however a mythological title was given because the prologue was spoken by a mythological figure as later Menander's *Heros* ; we know that Kalligeneia, the nurse of Demeter, spoke the prologue in Aristophanes' *Second Thesmophoriazousai*, and Dorpia was a character and probably the prologue figure of Philyllios' *Herakles* ; the mountain Lykabettos was a character in Theopompos' *Mede* and it is difficult to see what he can have been but a prologue figure (29K). It is likely therefore that Plato's *Hellas* and Theopompos' *Eirene* were also named after the figure who spoke the prologue.

But the majority of mythological plays can be referred to a source even if we cannot say precisely what the source is. They are translations of old stories into the language of comedy. The last two plays of Aristophanes are founded on tragedies. To later scholars the *Kokalos* seemed to bear some relation to New Comedy because it included a rape and recognition and all the other specialities of Menander.[1] This is no doubt exaggerated but must contain a seed of truth. The story is founded on Sophocles' *Kamikoi* ; after the death of Ikaros, Daidalos found refuge with Kokalos, King of Kamikos ; Minos pursued Daidalos and recognised him because he was able to thread a spiral shell. Kokalos was prepared to surrender Daidalos but Daidalos was saved by Kokalos' daughters, who conspired with Daidalos to kill Minos in his bath.[2] We have no evidence as to how Sophocles treated the story, but Aristophanes transferred it to the plane of everyday life as is shown by the references to old women filling themselves up with Thasian wine (350K) and a scene in which two people prepare to check their accounts (348K), which reminds us of Strepsiades at the beginning of the *Clouds*. The rape is presumably the rape of one of Kokalos' daughters by Daidalos, but how this came into the story and whether it was

---

[1] *Life of Aristophanes* : cf. G. Murray, *Aristophanes*, 209 ; Schmid-Stählin, IV, 221.

[2] In Aristophanes, fr. 347K, one of the daughters tells Kokalos that it is time for dinner. The word ἀντανείρειν, ' destroy as a substitute ', fr. 12D, may refer to the conspiracy.

derived from Sophocles we cannot say. In the *Aiolosikon* also, a new edition of an earlier play, parodying Euripides' *Aiolos*, the heroic story is also reduced to the level of ordinary life. Aiolos, the king of the winds, is called Sikon, a common slave name, often given to a cook ; he goes marketing and accounts for his purchases (1-3K) like any other Athenian (e.g. of this period Ephippos, 15K) : one bedroom and one bath tub will be enough for all his daughters (6K).

The formula is followed by many authors.[1] Contemporary and heroic were inextricably mixed, and it is perfectly natural that in Anaxandrides' *Protesilaos* the marriage of the hero should be compared to the marriage of the Athenian soldier Iphikrates with the daughter of the Thracian Kotys in a long passage of anapaestic dimeters which probably formed part of the exodos of the play. Rather more fragments survive of Plato's *Phaon* than of most plays. The story of the young ferryman who ferried Aphrodite and received in return an ointment which made him the most beautiful of men was popular in the early fourth century as is shown by its occurrence on two vases.[2] The two vases belong to the same general group, the group of the Meidias painter ; the earlier may have been painted as early as 420 B.C., the later has been dated into the fourth century but probably belongs to the last years of the fifth. On the earlier, Phaon is reclining in the concealment of a thicket while Aphrodite drives to him in a chariot drawn by Himeros and Pothos. On the other, Phaon looks scornfully on Aphrodite's women, one of whom tries to embrace him. The source may be tragedy or lyric ; the atmosphere is heroic, an idyllic landscape with winged Loves and beautiful women. In Plato's play the story is brought down to the level of everyday life ; the hetaira Lais is mentioned (179K) and an old man is shown in love with a flute girl, to whom he sings a serenade (178K). This gives the milieu. In two longer fragments a woman, who describes herself as *Kourotrophos*,

[1] e.g. Diokles, *Bacchae* ; Alkaios, *Pasiphae* (26K, to the bull ?) ; Theopompos, *Theseus* (note 17, 18K), *Althaia* ; Strattis, *Atalanta* (note 3-7K) ; Philetairos, *Atalanta* (note 3K) ; Plato, *Laios* ; Anaxandrides, *Protesilaos* (note 40-1K), *Io* ; Antiphanes, *Omphale* (note 176-7K) ; Aristomenes, *Admetos*, almost certainly go back to tragic ancestors. Nikophon, *Adonis* ; Plato, *Phaon* ; Anaxandrides, *Herakles*, were founded on well-known stories but we cannot as far as I know be certain that they had been treated in tragedy.

[2] Beazley, *A.R.V.*, 832-3, 833-154 ; add now Agora P10, 270, *A.J.A.*, liv. 320. On the *Phaon* see particularly Wilamowitz, *Sappho u. Simonides*, 36.

'nurse', tells some women, perhaps the chorus, what sacrifices they must make to a whole catalogue of fertility spirits before they can see Phaon (174K). *Kourotrophos* is known as a title of Aphrodite, and as Aphrodite was a character in this play (280/3D), it seems likely that she appeared as the procuress of the male prostitute Phaon. The other long fragment (173K) gives someone reciting from Philoxenos' new cookery book with emphasis on aphrodisiacs ; this is probably Phaon himself. How the Phaon story was connected with the old man who is in love with a flute girl we cannot tell and there is no reason to suppose that the connection was close. But we can at any rate sense the spirit of these mythological plays, even if we cannot fill in the details. It seems likely that the original story provided a tenuous thread on which all sorts of contemporary allusions could be hung and that the only essential in a heroic comedy was that everything should be unheroic except an occasional tragic line in glaring and intentional dissonance with its speaker and surroundings.

The earlier plays deriving from tragedies were probably produced soon after the tragedies which they travestied like the parodies of the *Andromeda* and *Helen* in Aristophanes' *Thesmophoriazousai* : such were probably the *Medea* and *Phoinissai* of Strattis. In the fourth century this may have been possible again when the revival of fifth-century tragedies became an annual event, but the travesties of Sophocles and Euripides in the last two plays of Aristophanes are unlikely to have been inspired by recent production. In two cases however a connection can probably be seen. We shall speak later of Strattis' *Zopyros*, which parodied Spintharos' *Herakles*. Meletos, the accuser of Sokrates, produced his *Oidipodeia* in the same year as Aristophanes' *Storks* (438K) ; Plato's *Laios* was produced about the same time and may have been a travesty of the first play of the *Oidipodeia*. Here may have been satire as well as travesty since Meletos is one of the 'Hades visitors' in Aristophanes' *Gerytades* [1] (149K). Meletos is on the borderline between poetry and politics and we know too little to say which aspect was more important for the poet.

---

[1] The distinction between the younger and the elder Meletos is not entirely clear but it seems likely that here and in the *Frogs* (1302) the younger is meant and in the *Georgoi* (114K) the elder.

Another poem, a dithyramb and not a tragedy, which was quickly imitated by the comic poets, was Philoxenos' *Kyklops*. In this dithyramb Philoxenos told the story of the ninth book of the *Odyssey* with the major alteration that Polyphemos was in love with the sea nymph Galateia. In the surviving fragments Polyphemos serenades Galateia, Odysseus asks what monster this is with whom he has been shut up, and Polyphemos tells Odysseus that he shall be sacrificed because he has sacrificed one of the Cyclops' sheep. It must certainly have been known in Athens at the time of Aristophanes' *Ploutos* because there (290) Karion sings to the chorus as if they were Polyphemos' flock and the chorus answer with a reference to the blinding of Polyphemos. According to the ancient commentator such details as ' threttanelo ' imitating the twanging of the lyre and the Cyclops' bag of vegetables are taken from Philoxenos. In the following pair of verses Karion goes on to the Circe story, but we cannot tell whether this has any reference to Philoxenos, as well as to Philonides and his friends who were victims of a contemporary Circe in Corinth.[1] The stupid and bestial Philonides, whose sons were among the earliest pupils of Isokrates, is mentioned again in Nikochares' *Galateia* (3K) : ' What then are you even worse brought up than Philonides ? ' This is presumably Galateia's view of Polyphemos (cf. 268/2D). In the other fragment Polyphemos offers Galateia a spice box ' wrought by craftsmen's cunning hands [this line a parody of Euripides, *Alc.* 438] with many little pots inside it '. Antiphanes, whose first production was in 388/4 B.C., may have written his *Kyklops* about the same time ; there Polyphemos is making arrangements for his wedding feast and will provide meat and cheese (133K) if his bride provides fish (132).

The dithyramb of Philoxenos must therefore have made a considerable impression in Athens when it was first performed there. Here again there is a problem which cannot be solved. Comedies on this theme could obviously be extremely amusing,

---

[1] Note (a) the *Kyklops* could have contained a forward reference to the Circe story ; (b) *Circe* could have been another dithyramb by Philoxenos ; (c) the Scholiast here equates Circe with Lais and on 179 says that Lais was presented by Dionysios of Syracuse to Philoxenos who brought her to Corinth ; (d) Athenaeus (592e) suggests substituting Nais for Lais as the lover of Philonides in *Pl.*, 179, but there is no reason why Philonides should not have loved two hetairai and no evidence that Nais was a Corinthian.

and Philoxenos himself evidently wrote realistically of Polyphemos and his love affair if we can trust a corrupt passage of
Aristotle.[1] But are there also politics involved here ? It is
certain that Philoxenos was at the court of Dionysios of Syracuse,
that he was imprisoned in the stone quarries, that he escaped and
died at Ephesos in 380/79.[2] The reason for his imprisonment
may have been his criticism of Dionysios' poetry or an intrigue
with Dionysios' hetaira Galateia, and he may have written the
Kyklops in revenge, equating Polyphemos with Dionysios, the
cave with his prison, and himself with Odysseus. The *Kyklops*
was accepted as an allegory of Philoxenos' relations with
Dionysios by Phainias of Eresos (ap. Ath., 6e) in the late fourth
century B.C. This is possible : the *Kyklops* may have had an
autobiographical conclusion like Timotheos' *Persai* and there the
allusion could have been explained. It is also possible that the
equation was first made by the comic poets in Athens and so had
got into the tradition by the time of Aristotle. In either case
the comedies with the Galateia story must almost have been seen
as satires on Dionysios and this political reference will occupy us
again later. There is no evidence of hostility to Philoxenos
himself as there is to Meletos and Kinesias ; he seems rather to
have provided the comic poets with material which they could
readily transpose into their own medium.

Another unsolved problem is the authorship of the *Deipnon*,
which is an elaborate description of a feast in dactylo-epitrite
metre. Modern opinion [3] ascribes it to Philoxenos of Leukas,
largely because Athenaeus identifies his *Deipnon* with the
' new cookery book of Philoxenos ' in Plato's *Phaon* (173K).
Athenaeus, however, when he quotes the *Deipnon* itself (IV,
146 f.), says, ' if in fact it was the poet of Cythera and not the
Leucadian Philoxenos to whom the comic poet Plato referred
in the *Phaon* '. Athenaeus was in doubt as to the authorship,
and the *Deipnon* seems to have been ascribed to Philoxenos of

---

[1] *Poetics*, 1448 a 15. It seems certain that Philoxenos' *Kyklops* must represent
men ' worse than ourselves ', since Aristotle must keep the order which he has
used just above for Homer, etc. The realism may simply consist in the introduction of the love affair or Aristotle may have regarded the *Kyklops* as political
abuse and therefore like Old Comedy.

[2] For references see Pickard-Cambridge, *Dithyramb, etc.*, 61 ff. ; Schmid-
Stählin, IV, 498.

[3] e.g. Wilamowitz, *Textgeschichte*, 85.

Cythera at least as early as Aristotle (fr. 83R). A poem in
dactylo-epitrites is likely to have been written by a lyric poet and
if the evidence of Antiphanes' *Kyklops* is to be trusted, the
Kyklops of Philoxenos of Cythera contained a description of a
projected marriage feast so that there would be no incongruity
in his writing a *Deipnon*. For us the question is unimportant
since Athenaeus is clear that Plato mentioned the *Deipnon* in the
Phaon, and we can probably see two directions in which comedy
took off from the *Deipnon*. In the *Phaon* Plato changes the metre
to pure hexameters which sound more oracular and makes it a
'new cookery book' which is only concerned with aphrodisiacs ; in the *Ekklesiazousai* (1168 f.) Aristophanes parodies the
elaborate compound adjectives of the *Deipnon* by running some
twenty-five words together into a single vast dish. There may
have been many other poems like the *Deipnon* ; for us it is an
interesting orphan, evidence both for the Greek interest in descriptions of feasts at this time and of the comic poets' habit of
basing their extravagances on some other form of existing literature, which we have already noted in their use of tragedy.

Descriptions of marketing, feasting, and food become increasingly common and with them three figures develop into
characters—the cook, the parasite, and the hetaira. Cook and
parasite hardly concern us yet. The hetaira begins to become
important in the early fourth century. Before that only Pherekrates named plays after hetairai : *Korianno*, *Petale*, *Thalatta*.
These are all hetaira names ; whether they were in any real sense
hetaira plays we have not enough evidence to say, but the
Korianno at least had a scene with the hetaira drinking on the
stage and this provided an ancestor for the opening scene of
Menander's *Synaristosai* : a similar scene evidently occurred in
Theopompos' *Feast of Aphrodite*, which was produced early in
the fourth century. Of Pherekrates' plays the *Petale* was produced about 425 and the *Korianno* probably earlier. We cannot
tell the date of Diokles' *Thalatta* or Alkaios' *Palaistra*, and they
may still belong to the fifth century ; but the two plays called
after *Anteia* (Philyllios/Eunikos, Antiphanes), Theopompos'
Nemeas and *Pamphile* and Epikrates' *Antilais* can almost certainly
be dated to the early fourth century. The fragments tell us little
about the plays. It would be fascinating to know more of
Alkaios' *Palaistra* (761/22–3K) where someone swears to keep a

confidence as a man approaches and someone served her lover with another instead of herself. In Antiphanes' *Anteia*, the hetaira complains of her lover's (?) purchases (34K, cf. 35K), and the hetaira's greed is from now on a persistent theme, a greed which is only moderated when old age makes the aged eagle so tame that ' she will eat silver out of your hand'. This is Epikrates' cruel satire on the old Lais in his *Antilais*, a title used also by Kephisodoros, a title perhaps best explained as the name of a hetaira who set up as a rival to Lais. The old women in the *Ploutos* and *Ekklesiazousai* with their make-up, wrinkles, tooth-lessness, and girls' clothing are merciless caricatures of the aged hetaira, just as the youth's description of the girl is an idealisation of the young hetaira (*Ekkl.*, 972) and foreshadows the later development by which the young man in love with a hetaira becomes the hero of the play. These are only minor themes beginning to appear in Aristophanes and in the *Ekklesiazousai* not at first sight consistent with the decree against all *pornai* (718 f.) ; but in fact with the abolition of marriage, free women behave exactly like hetairai. The old woman in the *Ploutos* is perhaps most easily explained as a hetaira who has grown rich by her trade and now buys herself a lover. Aristophanes' view of hetairai is clear from the decree already mentioned, from a line at the end of the *Ekklesiazousai* (1161), ' do not be like evil hetairai who only remember their last lovers', and from the comparison of Lais to Circe, who turns men into swine (*Plut.* 302 f.). This was perhaps the usual line in comedy. Theolyte, a contemporary of Lais, appeared in the *Nemeas* of Theopompos as an old woman who is easily persuaded by a fellow slave to drink (741/32K). Here Theolyte has presumably lost her custom and become the slave of the young and successful hetaira Nemeas, a relationship anticipating that of Scapha and Philemation in the *Mostellaria*.[1] The fragments do not tell us much, but at least a hetaira who gives her name to a play must have a considerable part in it.

Two other plays with personal titles, Strattis' *Kinesias* and Euboulos' *Dionysios*, which are rather in the tradition of Plato's *Hyperbolos*, take us into the realm of politics. We must now ask how far comedy is still political and whether, in so far as it

---

[1] In the *Pamphile* of Theopompos also there is a drunken old woman who seems to be the mother of Pamphile's nurse and a source of gossip (744/40–42).

is political, other comedians take the same view of policy and
politicians as Aristophanes or whether different political allegi-
ances can be traced ; the two complete plays of Aristophanes
in any case provide most of our evidence. Policy cannot be
discussed without politicians and we know more about the comic
poet's view of politicians than of their views of policy. Comedy
is performed before the whole Athenian people and vilification
of the private life of politicians must be calculated to discredit
their policy ; no one presumably believed the Peloponnesian
war originated because two prostitutes were stolen from Aspasia,
but all must have seen that the *Acharnians* was an attack on the
Periclean and post-Periclean policy of aggression.

For this period the political references in comedy can be
grouped round two main events, the early arrangements with
Persia and the formation of the second Athenian confederacy.
I am only concerned to sketch the history in so far as it is echoed
in comedy. The first move was in 396 B.C., when the King of
Persia appointed Konon admiral and sent Timokrates with gold
to spread among those Greeks who were antagonistic to Sparta.
Epikrates and Kephalos at least had long been in favour of an
arrangement with Persia and various embassies were sent,
although Thrasyboulos, Anytos, and Aisimos at first urged
caution. But in 395 B.C. Thrasyboulos consented to an Athenian
alliance with Thebes against Sparta and later with Argos and
Corinth. The campaign against Sparta was pursued with
varying success, but Sparta had always had friends in Athens,
and peace negotiations began in 392 B.C. In 393 Tiribazus had
started negotiations with the Spartan Antalkidas suggesting the
surrender of the Greek cities in Asia Minor to Persia and
the autonomy of the rest of Greece. The Athenians refused the
terms but in the next year negotiations were resumed in Sparta ;
according to Philochorus (ap. Didymos, *in Dem.*, 7) the Athenians
again refused the terms and on the proposal of Kallistratos the
Athenian negotiators including Epikrates and Andokides were
banished, but had fled before their trial opened.

We have several references to this sequence of events in comedy.
The elements on which the comic poets seize are the instability
of Athenian policy, the vacillation of the politicians (particularly
Thrasyboulos and Epikrates), and the use of Persian gold for
bribery. ' The Great King gives himself airs ' because of his

wealth, says Aristophanes in the *Ploutos* (170). In Theopompos'
Mede (740/30), Kallistratos ' once scattered small coins to bewitch
the sons of the Achaeans when he asked for an alliance ; only
he did not bewitch the thin Rhadamanthys until he had given
him a fine drinking cup to dissolve his strength'. Kallistratos
seems to have been credited by the comic poets[1] with introducing the obol pay for the assembly, although according to
Aristotle this was done by his relative Agyrrhios. This may be
the meaning of 'scattered coins' ; the Athenians are called
' sons of Achaeans ' because the statement is in oracular style.
In view of the title the money must be Persian money and the
time before the peace of Antalkidas. The reference should therefore be to the Boeotian alliance of 395 and it seems at least possible
that Rhadamanthys is Thrasyboulos, who seems then for the first
time to have abandoned his cautious foreign policy and sided
with the forward statesmen. The same sequence of events
explains the difficult passage in the *Ekklesiazousai*,[2] in which
Aristophanes telescopes the story. Praxagora complains that the
leaders of the Athenian democracy are bad men (176) and that
their policy has been unstable (193 f.). According to Praxagora,
they said the alliance was essential ; then when it happened they
did not like it and the rhetor who had misled (ἀναπείσας) us ran
away. The poor men liked, the rich men and the farmers disliked a policy of naval aggression. If you have made terms with
the Corinthians you must keep faith with them. It is no good
both regarding the Argives as fools (who urge you against
alliance with Sparta) and Hieronymos (Konon's lieutenant) as
clever. ' Salvation showed her face (perhaps the hope of a
Spartan alliance ?) but Thrasyboulos gives himself airs (?) because
he is not asked to speak.' If the rhetor who ran away is an
allusion to the conduct of the ambassadors of 392 who did not
wait to stand their trial, as it seems to be, then Praxagora means
something like this : Epikrates persuaded you to make the
alliance with Boeotia ; when you did not like it Epikrates started
to play with Sparta ; when you put him on trial for that, he ran
away. So through the whole passage the chief complaint is
clearly against instability and inconsistency as in the later passage
(823 f.), when the people rounded on Euripides for failing to

[1] K., iii/532/697.
[2] Gigante, *Dioniso*, XI, 147 ; Barry, *Ekkl. as Political Satire*, Chicago, 1942.

produce the 500 talents which he had promised from the 2½ per cent. tax ; and the instability is due to the tension between the poor and rich, who have however the farmers on their side. The poverty is real, as can be seen from the pathetic picture of Euaion (408 f.), who appears naked in the assembly and proposes a general distribution of clothing : Blepyros comments that there should also be a general distribution of corn by the rich Nausikydes. The solution is communism in this play, and in the *Ploutos* (1191) the establishment of Wealth in his old home the *opisthodomos* of the goddess

These are fantastic solutions which do not tell us Aristophanes' views of contemporary politics. For that we must look at the personalities mentioned by him and the other comic poets. In Plato's *Ambassadors*, Epikrates and Phormisios have taken many bribes from the king (119, 120K), and both men are also mocked by Aristophanes in the *Ekklesiazousai* [1] (71, 97), and if our interpretation is right, Epikrates by adroit telescoping of the story is represented as a forward-looking politician who had not the courage of his convictions. Scurrilous abuse of Phormisios is carried on by Philetairos' account of his death in a play written thirty or more years later [2] (232/6K). Epikrates, who according to Strattis (714/10) is a cipher, is the man whom Demosthenes describes as ' a man of energy, very useful to the city, one of those who brought the demos back from the Peiraeus and generally a public spirited man ' (XIX, 277). Kephalos, who joined Epikrates in favouring an arrangement with Persia, is remembered by Demosthenes as one of the ' great and glorious statesmen before my time ' (XVIII, 219) and by Aeschines as ' most public spirited ' (III, 194) ; but Plato (185K) calls him ' stinking, a disgraceful disease ' and Praxagora in the *Ekklesiazousai* (248), when asked what she will do if Kephalos abuses her

---

[1] Cf. Plato, 633/122K.

[2] At the time of the *Frogs* (965), Phormisios apparently belonged to the aggressive warmongers, but then joined the moderates grouped round Theramenes (*Ath. Pol.*, 34/3) and after the restoration of the democracy suggested a restricted franchise ' because the Spartans desired it ' (Lysias, XXXIV, *argument*) ; there may be a reminiscence of this in Plato's *Ambassadors* (634/124K), where someone, perhaps Demos, rejoices in outwrestling ' the bearded, ropy-haired, dirty-knuckled, drag-cloak ' ; the fragment is quoted as a commentary on the simplicity of Laconian dress. K. J. Dover, *C.R.*, lxiv, 6, refers it to a Spartan whom he thinks was a character in the play, but neither supposition is necessary or likely.

in the Assembly, says that she will first say that he is mad, then
that he is 'melancholic', and then that he is 'a bad potter but
a good politician'. Thrasyboulos, the great democratic leader
of the revolution, who first advised caution in dealing with
Persia and then in 395 B.C. agreed with the Theban alliance and
finally went to Asia himself in 389 B.C., is called 'pompous and
self-willed' by Strattis (716/17), 'gives himself airs because he
is not asked to speak' in the *Ekklesiazousai* (202), and has apparently diplomatic indigestion when asked to support the Spartans
(356); in the *Ploutos* (550) it is implied that some Athenians
thought him a tyrant. The impression that one gains from
comedy is of a great but unsympathetic figure whose move away
from Sparta is not received with any pleasure.[1] Agyrrhios was
sent out to the Hellespont as strategos on the death of Thrasyboulos in 389/8. In the *Ekklesiazousai* (102, 184) he is effeminate
and everybody regarded him as a low character until he introduced pay for the assembly, and in the *Ploutos* (176) he is 'bursting
with wealth'. Plato's *Demos* (652/185) asks someone to hold
his hand down because he is going to elect Agyrrhios strategos,
and then having done it wants to be sick. No reference to Konon
has survived unless it is justifiable to see one in Plato's *Hellas or
Nesoi*. Poseidon (606/24K) threatens to destroy 'all these
things' unless someone (a man) 'willingly surrenders this sea'.
Mr. K. J. Dover [2] suggests that he may be speaking to Konon
and his Persians after Knidos. Unfortunately we cannot go any
further; it is completely unclear how the chorus of Islands came
in, who is to be pulled up on a rope (21K), or who is 'weak and
feeble' (1D). Timotheos' tower is only just mentioned in the
Ploutos (180). But there are scornful references to Isokrates as

---

[1] Aisimos and Anytos (*Hell. Ox.*, i, 2) had also been critical of the early over-
tures to Persia. In the *Ekklesiazousai* (208), 'Aisimos like public affairs is rolling
downhill' and in fact he later joined Kephalos in making the alliance with
Chios (Tod, *G.H.I.*, no. 118; cf. no. 122). Anytos, who was strategos in
409, when according to Aristotle he invented the method of bribing the jury
to escape condemnation (*Ath. Pol.*, 27/5), was the accuser of Socrates in 399
B.C.; he was a rich man (Plato, *Meno*, 90A) and before the revolution belonged
like Phormisios to the middle party grouped round Theramenes; for comedy
he is the 'cobbler' or the 'shoeman' (Archippos, 685/30; Theopompos,
748/57). Philepsios and Agyrrhios are both named by Demosthenes (xxiv,
134) as good democrats who were put in prison in spite of their services to the
State: Philepsios in the *Ploutos* (177) 'tells stories to get wealth' and according
to Plato (660/217K) is a portentous talker.

[2] *C.R.*, lxiv, 7.

the ' flute-borer ' and to his concubine Lagiska [1] ; the latter must
date from the time of the *Panegyrikos*. Kallias, the son of Hip-
ponikos, who was in command of the Athenian hoplites at
Corinth in 390, is said to be able to contribute very little to the
common fund in the *Ekklesiazousai* (810) ; when he is acting
against Sparta he is caricatured as a spendthrift, as in the *Birds*
(283) a quarter of a century earlier. But he is not mentioned
in the *Ploutos* or in later comedy as far as we know, and he was
the leader of the Athenian embassy to Sparta in 371.

Another reaction to the forward policy of the 'nineties can
perhaps be seen in the treatment of the poet Kinesias. Kinesias'
poetry was parodied by Aristophanes in the *Birds* (1372 f.) and
he is one of the Hades visitors in the *Gerytades* (149K). Strattis
wrote a play called *Kinesias* in which he made fun of Kinesias'
impiety (716/19K) as well as his poetry.[2] His impiety may
account for the allusions to his defiling the shrines of Hekate.[3]
Lysias (fr. 73) adds the information that he abandoned his art
for sycophancy and became rich, and in 393 he proposed a decree
honouring Dionysios of Syracuse,[4] which synchronised with the
unsuccessful embassy sent by Konon to ask Dionysios for an
alliance. It is therefore possible that in the early fourth century
the attacks on Kinesias in comedy are not purely aesthetic.

We have already suggested that allusions to Polyphemos' love
for Galateia must have been interpreted in Athens as satire of the
tyrant Dionysios of Syracuse. In the *Ploutos* (550), Penia complains that the Athenians are so stupid that they cannot distinguish
between Thrasyboulos and Dionysios. She implies that to the
sane Athenian of the 'eighties Dionysios appears to be a dangerous
tyrant. This is just the view which we find later in Euboulos'
Dionysios (written presumably in the 'seventies, since Euboulos
won his first City Victory in 374/2 and Dionysios died in 367) :
he is the typical tyrant who will not listen to serious critics but
treats only jesters and flatterers as free men. It will be remembered that according to one story Philoxenos was imprisoned
because he dared to criticise Dionysios' poetry ; perhaps Philoxenos is the speaker of the difficult fragment (26K) in which

[1] Aristophanes, 700K ; Strattis, 712/3K.
[2] 15K. It seems unlikely that the reference is simply to poetry here. Cf.
Maidment, *C.Q.*, 1935, 9.
[3] *Frogs*, 366 ; cf. *Ekkl.*, 330.   [4] Tod, *G.H.I.*, no. 108.

apparently all that Dionysios has preserved of Euripides is his sigmatism. In Ephippos' *Homoioi* (259/16) someone hopes that his worst enemy may be compelled to learn the dramas of Dionysios. On the other hand, Euboulos' allusion to Prokles who betrayed his city to Dionysios is purely political. Strattis in the *Atalanta* (6K) coined the word ' Dionysio-beard-conflagration' which probably does not allude to his being the grandson of a barber (if indeed he was) but to the well-attested story that he was so terrified of being murdered that he had his hair and beard singed by his daughter and would not allow a barber to touch him. It is tempting to suppose that the same story was used by Strattis in an earlier play, the *Zopyros Perikaiomenos*, in which someone is told to be brave and singe himself like a moustache. Spintharos had written a tragedy or satyr play called *Herakles Perikaiomenos*, which is perhaps reflected on a vase of about 390 B.C.[1] Strattis seems to have travestied this with Zopyros-Dionysios substituted for Herakles. Thus Dionysios seems to have been a figure of fun to the Athenians from the 'nineties till his death, and comedy gave no encouragement to the aggressive politicians who wished to make an alliance with him.[2]

It is fair to say that Comedy shows no more sympathy with the forward policy of the 'nineties and 'eighties than with that of the late fifth century and derides the personal characteristics of the politicians in the traditional way. For the period of the Second Athenian Confederacy we have lost the testimony of Aristophanes, but a few relevant fragments survive. The leading political figure here was Kallistratos, who had accused Andokides and Epikrates and the other ambassadors when they came back from Sparta with peace terms in 392; he was strategos in 378/7 and again in 372; by 371 the Thebans had become more danger-

---

[1] Beazley, *A.R.V.*[2], 1186/30.

[2] Of other men satirised by comedy we know too little to be certain : the blind and thieving Neokleides (*Ekkl.*, 254, 398 ; *Pl.*, 665 ; 725 ; 439K), Pamphilos the thieving sycophant who was probably the unsuccessful strategos of 389/8 (*Plut.*, 174 ; Plato, 604/14K ; *R.E.*, xviii, 331), the stupid and bestial Philonides whose sons were among the earliest pupils of Isokrates (*Plut.*, 179, 303 ; Philyllios, 787/23 ; Theopompos, 734/4 ; Nikochares, 771/3 ; Plato, 618/64 ; *R.E.*, xx, 61), the diseased Laispodias who was strategos at the time of the *Birds* (*Birds*, 1569 ; Strattis, 716/16 ; Theopompos, 744/39), the unwashen Patrokles (*Plutus*, 85 ; 431K ; Isocr., XVIII, 5) and the disgusting Aristyllos (*Ekkl.*, 647 ; *Plut.*, 314 ; 538K ; *G.H.I.*, no. 131).

ous than the Spartans, and Kallistratos spoke in favour of peace with Sparta. The loss of Oropos in 366 was followed by a charge of *prodosia* against Kallistratos, who was, however, acquitted ; he was sentenced to death before 361 and escaped to Thasos. At the time of the Second Confederacy, Kallistratos' chief opponent was Melanopos ; his grandfather, the Laches of Plato's dialogue, belonged to the party of Nikias, but according to Plutarch (*Dem.*, 13) he himself more than once succumbed to bribery. The bribing of Melanopos is certainly referred to in Anaxandrides' *Protesilaos* (151/40K), where he is said to have bought expensive Egyptian ointment to anoint the feet of Kallistratos. (Euboulos also twice mentions Kallistratos, though probably these two passages fall outside our period : in the *Antiope*, in which he contrasts the large meals and good food of the Boeotians with the eloquent Athenians' sustenance of air and hope (167/10, 12), Kallistratos is reckoned among the loose-livers who have run to seed (168/11), as again in the *Sphingokarion* (201/107) where he is also credited with eloquence and versatility.) In the *Protesilaos* (151/41K) someone, presumably Protesilaos, is going to have a much better marriage feast than was given to Iphikrates when he married the daughter of the Thracian Kotys. This dates the passage about 380 B.C., which also suits the flute-player Antigeneidas and the poet Argas who performed at the marriage ; Kephisodotos of Acharnai (who is unknown) sings first of Sparta and then changes his song to seven-gated Thebes, presumably a reference to the Spartan seizure of the Kadmeia in 382 and its liberation in 379 B.C. Anaxandrides may be deriding a poetic description of the marriage of Iphikrates which was then current in Athens. This is suggested by the fact that a character in Ephippos' *Homoioi* (259/16K) prays that if he does something foolish he may be punished by having to learn the dramas of Dionysios and all Demophon composed for Kotys, by listening to Theodoros reciting at dinner and by living next door to Laches (who may be the brother of Melanopos). But we may also detect a slight scorn of Iphikrates and his Thracian experiments. Thus during the early years of the Second Confederacy also it is the aggressive politicians who are the butts of the comic poets and the charges against them are the old charges of bribery and loose-living. If Theopompos' *Eirene* is rightly referred to the peace of 373, it is a cry of joy at the end of military service

(735/7K). A comic poet's view of the Boeotian alliance at the time of the Second Confederacy is perhaps preserved in a list of vices which dwell in Boeotian cities (K., iii/469/337) : ' Dishonesty in Oropos, Jealousy in Tanagra, Violence in Thebes, Greed in Anthedon, Officiousness in Koroneia, Boastfulness in Plataea, Fever in Onchestos, Stupidity in Haliartos.' This certainly sounds like comedy and the reference to Plataea limits the date to the period between the restoration of Plataea in 382 B.C. and its destruction in 373 B.C.

So far we have been concerned with particular policies and politicians. Comedy has also a view of the working of democracy in general and provides us with portraits of the typical official and voter. The most debauched of the young men are the cleverest at speaking in the Assembly (*Ekkl.*, 112). This is a statement in general terms of the particular charges made against Agyrrhios, Kallistratos, and others. When they are poor they serve the city and the people, but as soon as they have enriched themselves from public funds, they plot against the masses and make war on the demos (*Pl.*, 567 ; cf. 30 f.). A particular instance of collusion to cheat the public is given in the *Ploutos* [1] (377 f.) : Blepsidemus assumes that Chremylos' wealth is the result of embezzlement and offers to stop the politicians' mouths with money before the whole city gets to know the truth ; Chremylos answers that he supposes that Blepsidemos will spend 300 drachmae and charge him 1,200 drachmae.[2] On a smaller scale, in the *Storks* (437K), one unjust man, when prosecuted, can find twelve dependants to bear witness for him. A cog in this machine is the sycophant ; he loses everything if wealth is distributed to the virtuous (*Pl.*, 850) and complains that such distribution is manifestly an anti-democratic revolution ; he claims that he is a good patriot (900), who by his prosecutions helps the enforcement of the laws—a claim also made by the speaker of Lysias' speech against the corndealers (xxii. 3). He is the typical townsman whose ideal is *polypragmosyne* and regards a peaceful life as only fit for sheep. He may claim that his object is to support the law but his real motive according to Aristophanes is to gain his own livelihood (*Ekkl.*, 562). His career is made possible by the ordinary citizen's need to make money

---

[1] Cf. Lysias, XXVIII, 9.
[2] Cf. Isocr., XVIII, 9 f., and earlier Ar., *Equ.*, 439.

in the courts or the assembly ; [1] the ordinary citizen has only been persuaded to attend the assembly by the introduction of pay but nevertheless always considers his own private advantage in voting (206). If we ask further what is the result of this wholesale pursuit of self-interest, the comic poets see various symptoms. The motions that are passed in the Assembly are as mad as the plans of drunkards (*Ekkl.*, 137 ; cf. 473 ff.) ; consequently, as Plato says (22K), ' our laws are like the fine webs which spiders weave on the walls '. This excessive complication of legislation has its effect both on the legislative assembly and on the citizen in his private capacity. ' The city ', writes Anaxandrides (162/67K), magnificently parodying Euripides (920N), ' willed it, paying no heed to laws.' Aristophanes expresses the same idea rather differently when he says ' our *arche* now is to be original and to have no respect for what has gone before '.[2] Thus public policy is completely unstable, as we have already seen, and the private citizen disobeys a law which is personally inconvenient to him because there is always a chance that while he delays it may be changed.[3]

Both in the *Ekklesiazousai* and the *Ploutos*, Aristophanes sees the root cause of these evils in the wrong distribution of wealth, for which communism and the curing of Wealth's blindness provide comic solutions. In the *Ekklesiazousai* (452, 564 f.) the result of women's rule will be that there will be no more sycophants, no more prosecutions, and no more revolutions, no more robbery, no more envy of neighbours, no more nakedness or poverty, no more public abuse, no more seizure of goods given as security. The key line here is ' no more nakedness or poverty ' ; crime in private life, corrupt legal and political action, are simply a means of getting out of poverty. Poverty is common in the town and poverty is common now in the country. This is the new thing which distinguishes the last two plays of Aristophanes from his early plays ; there the instability of the democracy, the self-seeking of politicians and officials, the aggressive designs of Athens are pilloried no less unkindly, but if peace can be regained there is simple prosperity to be had in the country.

[1] Cf. *Pl.*, 1166 ; Lysias, XXVII, 2. In 395 the theorikon had been raised to a drachma (K, iii/465/314). On this whole section see Ehrenberg, *People of Aristophanes*, 345 f.

[2] *Ekkl.*, 586, cf. 193, 797 ; Plato, 220K (undated).

[3] *Ekkl.*, 767, 812 f. ; cf. Plato, *Rep.*, 557e.

Now the countrymen, though they are still honest men (*Pl.*, 105, 223) and remember the pride and independence of their ancestors who came to the Assembly without any pay (*Ekkl.*, 276, 292 f.), live a cold and unkind life in the wearing misery of their fields (*Pl.*, 224, 263). The difficult fragment of Theopompos' *Eirene* (1D) : ' Then there was an inscription set up in Delphi : the farmer always hoped for wealth to-morrow, if, as his first need, he escaped starvation ', probably echoes the same hopelessness. In the *Ploutos* (124 f.) the whole of civilisation is interpreted as an attempt to get wealth—religion, the arts and crafts, and public life are directed to this single end. Wealth is the only thing of which one cannot have enough (189) and therefore the man who gets 13 talents tries to get 16 and if he achieves this he wants 40. The just man who uses what he has to help his neighbours, like Kallias in Xenophon's *Symposium* (IV, 1), only loses all he has and no one remembers him (829 f.). The wealth goes to the sacrilegious, the politicians, the sycophants, and the criminals (30 f.). *Penia* (Frugality ?), who appears looking like a cross between a tragic Fury and a lodging-house keeper (415 f.), states the same position from another point of view : if everyone is well off no one will work, there will be no farmers or craftsmen and therefore everyone will have to do everything for themselves ; the rich are physically flabby and given to excesses of every kind ; the poor are physically fit and have learnt *sophrosyne* (557 f.). Here something survives of the contrast between the Old and New Education of the *Clouds*, but it is restated with no reference to education and in economic terms.

Penia is driven off the stage (like the Just Argument in the *Clouds*) and the old men take Ploutos to the temple of Asklepios to recover his sight ; thereafter the just man becomes rich and the sycophant is ruined. This is the solution of Comedy which has no more relevance to real life than the communism of the *Ekklesiazousai*. There is besides the satire on the Athenian democracy and the pure comedy a hint of positive advice : in the *Ploutos*, as we have said, *Penia* describes the men who have *sophrosyne* and a modest competence as ' better in mind and body ' than the rich, and in the *Ekklesiazousai* (441 f.) the women are commended as governors because they are wise and discreet and honest in their dealings with one another. They will not continually pursue new and foolish ideas (215 f.) and their economics will be sound (229 f.). This is Aristophanes' method which we can see in the earlier plays : he states clearly what he dislikes, he provides an unreal but entirely satisfying comic solution, but he leaves behind a suggestion of real practical advice.

We have noticed that whereas in the *Clouds* and the *Frogs* the New Education is largely responsible for contemporary evils, nothing is said about education in these plays. Yet when we examine them in detail we see a considerable number of echoes of Plato's *Republic*. These have long been noticed, especially the close parallels between the communism of the *Ekklesiazousai* and the *Republic*.[1] The differences, as many scholars have pointed out, are fundamental : Plato's communism is a provision to secure the maximum of honesty and efficiency in the governors of his ideal state, Aristophanes' communism is merely a redistribution of wealth over the whole free population. Aristophanes could have achieved his end without reference to Plato, and it seems to me difficult to avoid three conclusions, first that in some form or other the matter of the *Republic* was already known (and this agrees with the evidence of Plato's *Seventh Letter*), secondly that Aristophanes seized on Plato's communism as an admirable comic solution for his quite different problem, and thirdly that Plato's own demand for honesty and technical skill and the education of the Guardians would not meet with Aristophanes' disapproval (since these are the positive qualities that the women show in government), and if anyone were led by the comic representation of communism to find out more about Plato's ideas Aristophanes would not object.

In the *Ploutos* (35) Chremylos has been to ask Apollo whether his son shall change his whole way of life and live the life of injustice—the same question that Socrates puts to Thrasymachos in the first book of the *Republic* (344d). Plato's ' minimum city ' is rejected by Glaukon as a ' city of swine ', just as the old men reject Penia's life of modest competence (*Pl.* 555 ; *Rep.*, 372d). The organisation of Plato's city is based on ' need ' (369c) just as it is ' need ' that makes the artisan work in the

[1] Particularly 416d community of possessions, 457c community of wives, 458cd mating and community of life, 461cd community of children, 464d absence of lawsuits as a result. I think we may therefore stress the meaning of ' philosophic ' in *Ekkl.*, 571. Aristophanes clearly wanted this word which he has introduced at considerable metrical inconvenience.

Ploutos (534). If the craftsmen are rich they will do no work ; if they have nothing, they will not have the tools and materials for their work : thus wealth and poverty are extremes which must be avoided in the ideal city (*Rep.*, 421d). In Aristophanes Penia is similarly a mean between Wealth and Beggary, and she sees exactly the same danger as Plato in craftsmen becoming rich (563 ; 525 f.). Both Plato and Aristophanes draw the contrast between the fat, puffy rich man and the hard, waspish poor man (*Pl.*, 559 ; *Rep.*, 556d, cf. 422d). It is perhaps also worth noticing that the examination of the Sycophant by the Just Man is a Socratic examination and establishes him as unjust by Platonic standards because he is a busybody and meddles in other people's business (902 f.). As in the *Ekklesiazousai*, enough parallels of detail with the *Republic* can be seen to suggest that Aristophanes was at this time not unsympathetic to Platonic teaching. The only other comic fragment of this period which may be relevant is Theopompos' quotation of the *Phaedo* in the *Hedychares* (737/15K : *Phaedo*, 96e). Here we cannot catch the flavour of the allusion. A further fragment (13K)—' you stand in a row a starving chorus of mullets, fed on vegetables like geese '—may well be a reference to the Academy in the mouth of Hedychares and need not represent either the truth or Theopompos' view. Meineke suggested that Hedychares is Plato, but there seems no more justification for this than for his suggestion that the odious Aristyllos is Plato ; Aristyllos need not be explained as a diminutive of Ariston, since his name occurs in an inscription.[1] If Hedychares is not simply a bon viveur or a parasite, the most likely identification for him is Aristippos of Cyrene.

In the first quarter of the fourth century we can see no obvious divergences between Aristophanes and the other comedians. The forward policy of agreement with Persia and attack on Sparta seems to meet with general disapproval and the politicians who favour it are derided as notorious bad characters. The restored democracy like the post-Periclean democracy pursues no stable policy because the motive of politicians and voters alike is self-interest. This is the more intelligible now because of the general impoverishment following the Peloponnesian war ; the countrymen are as poor as the townsmen. The only possible solution is a new kind of politician who is disinterested as well

[1] For references see above, p. 29, n. 2.

D

as skilful. Aristophanes uses his old weapons to hint at this, fantastic, solution which does not entirely conceal a real requirement, comic defeat of an unpopular view which remains nevertheless in the minds of the audience. For us Old Comedy makes its last brilliant bow in the *Ekklesiazousai* and the curtain goes up on mythological comedy in the *Ploutos*. In both, however, political criticism is still strong and in both the decrease of the lyric element throws a new emphasis on the actors and the first beginnings of character comedy appear.

III. GREEK COMEDY, 370–321 B.C.

1. POLITICS AND PHILOSOPHERS

TRADITIONALLY we have been taught that political comedy belongs to the fifth century and yet, as we have seen, although changed, it certainly continues for the first thirty years of the fourth century. After that the picture is less clear, because we have fewer surviving plays, but we have enough political scraps to jolt our complacency. For the period between the death of Aristophanes and the earliest Menander no complete plays survive except the three Latin adaptations, *Persa*, *Menaechmi*, and *Amphitruo*, and these are non-political; it does not follow that their originals had no political allusions since these would have been meaningless to Plautus' audience (and we may be able to see in one place [1] where Plautus substituted a Roman joke for a Greek political allusion). The Greek fragments contain much more that may be political.

As in the first quarter of the century, we can distinguish between direct political allusions, general speculations on political behaviour, and allusions to philosophers who may have some impact on Athenian political life. The first class is the most difficult to deal with because many of the allusions refer to the private life of men whom we may or may not be able to identify as politicians, but we have seen already that in the first quarter of the century denigration of private life was a common form of political satire. That this was still a reality later is proved by an allusion in Isokrates (VIII, 14) to the complete freedom accorded to comic poets to publish the city's evils abroad and by Plato's refusal in the *Laws* (935e) to allow ' a comic poet to ridicule any citizen either by word or by likeness, either in anger or without anger '. The distinction between ' word and likeness ' is probably a distinction between what is said and what is seen, between the words of the play and the characters on the stage.[2] Thus Plato gives evidence (of which we shall find

---

[1] See below, p. 72, on *Menaechmi*.
[2] I am indebted to my wife, Professor D. Tarrant, and Mr. D. J. Furley for the interpretation of this passage.

37

more in the fragments) that public figures might still at the time of the *Laws* be put on the stage by comic poets. Continued criticism is also implied by the distinction between the *aischrologia* or abuse of Old Comedy and the *hyponoia* or allusion of Middle Comedy which Aristotle makes in the *Ethics* [1] (1128 a 22). This evidence shows that comedy was still considered dangerous in the second and third quarters of the fourth century, although for the most part, if we may so interpret Aristotle, its methods had changed from direct assault on the public life of its victims to an indirect attack through their private lives or through allegory. Plato's second distinction ' in anger or without anger ' defines exactly what we want to know. Plato's statement shows that both kinds of ridicule existed in fourth-century comedy, and we have to assume not only the two obvious classes, victims of angry ridicule and victims of good-tempered ridicule, but also that the victims of angry ridicule could also be ridiculed without anger by other poets. To take one instance, we know that Kallimedon the Crab did all he could to help Macedon, and the comic poet Timokles is the most clearly pro-Macedonian of all the comic poets, yet even he ridicules Kallimedon's squint (463/27)—he looks at one person and talks to another. Timokles does not say anything about his passion for fish and it was that rather than the squint on which the other comic poets seized, when they wished to harm him, and it may of course be a kind of insurance to ridicule mildly an unpopular member of your own party.

Sometimes the same personal jokes are made by poets who differ politically. Sometimes a poet ridicules a man of his own political colour. Sometimes the people ridiculed seem to us to have no political colour at all (although here we may be misled by our ignorance). In all such cases the anger, where any anger is felt, is not political. Anger is certainly felt against the proud and exorbitant fishmongers and perhaps against the hetairai, whether they are strong and rich or old and bibulous, perhaps also against Misgolas with his unfortunate passion for male harpists, but not much against the parasites Korydos and Chairephon, or Chairephilos and his sons, who were admitted to the citizenship by Demosthenes between 340 and 330 and

---

[1] See Wehrli, *Motivstudien*, 17. Cf. also Hoistad, *Eranos*, xlix, 20.

evidently tried to cut a dash in Athenian society :[1] they were called the ' mackerel '.

In the years after the peace with Sparta and before the rise of Macedon, Antiphanes, Anaxandrides, and Ephippos make comments on the political situation. In the *Sappho* (95/196) of Antiphanes someone misinterprets Sappho's riddle : ' The creature you mean is a city and the orators are the babies which it feeds inside itself. They shout loud and drag here the spoil from Asia and Thrace to Athens ; they feed themselves and abuse each other while the Demos sits by, hearing nothing and seeing nothing.' This is the old accusation of exploitation by imperialistic politicians and may in particular refer to Timotheos' campaigns of 365/4. The same campaign seems to me likely to have provided the background of the *Soldier or Tychon* (which can be dated rather before 360) : there the soldier (97/202) spent the whole war in Cyprus, where in Paphos he saw the king fanned by doves. This is the first dated instance of the braggart soldier as we know him later in New Comedy, and the allusion is to the luxury of Nikokles. Nikokles was in fact king of Salamis, but Antiphanes has substituted the better-known Paphos. The soldier's tall story makes him a laughing stock and with him the system of foreign campaigns which produced him. So also a slight scorn for the Second Confederacy may be detected in the *Philometor* (108/220) : ' *Metra* [swine's matrix] is the sweetest meat they sell, and Metras the Chiot is the friend of the demos ' —an alliance with Chios had been made in 384 and Chios headed the membership roll of the Second Confederacy. Antiphanes' *Philothebaios* surely, as Meineke suggested, was a caricature of an Athenian who imitated Theban manners and customs ; but in the 'sixties the elderly politician Aristophon, whom Demosthenes [2] includes with Kallistratos, Kephalos, and Thrasyboulos among ' the great and glorious orators before my time ', was notably pro-Theban and we know he was criticised by comedy

---

[1] *Fishmongers :* Antiphanes, 26, 125, 159, 161, 206, 218 ; Amphis, 30 ; Alexis, 16, 125, 200 ; Xenarchos, 7. *Hetairai :* particularly Antiphanes, 26 ; Amphis, 23 ; Anaxilas, 22 ; Timokles, 25. *Misgolas :* Antiphanes, 21 ; Alexis, 3 ; Timokles, 30. *Korydos :* Alexis, 47, 168, 183, 227 ; Kratinos, 8 ; Timokles, 10, 11. *Chairephon :* Antiphanes, 199 ; Nikostratos, 25 ; Alexis, 210, 257 ; Timotheos, 1 ; Timokles, 9 ; also in Apollodoros and Menander. *Chairephilos and his sons :* Antiphanes, 26 ; Alexis, 6, 77, 168, 218 ; Timokles, 14, 17, 21. Cf. also the attack on Timarchos mentioned by Aeschines, I, 157.

[2] xviii, 219.

for his cruel treatment of the people of Ceos after the island revolted in 364.[1] Antiphanes' play may therefore have been directed at the policy of Aristophon.

Anaxandrides, who in the first quarter of the century mocked at the forward policy of Kallistratos and Iphikrates and at Melanopos' subservience to it, has left us three fragments which may be complementary. In a list of nicknames (148/34) from the *Odysseus*, which can be dated on inscriptional evidence between 374 and 357, ' a dirty or slovenly fellow is called *Koniortos* (dust storm) '. Koniortos was the nickname of Euktemon, whom Demosthenes [2] mentions with Polyeuktos and Timokrates as a hireling of Meidias ; Meidias himself was closely connected with Euboulos, the leading politician of the time after the Social War. The threads lead back from Euboulos to Melanopos, because when in 353 Melanopos was accused of keeping prize-money for himself he was saved from immediate payment by a law proposed by Timokrates. In the speech (written for Diodoros) against this Timokrates Demosthenes calls Melanopos ' a wicked villain and a thief' and also accuses him of ' a false embassy to Egypt '.[3] As Anaxandrides ridiculed Melanopos and Euktemon, it seems likely that the Polyeuktos ' who consumed his patrimony ' (156/45) is Polyeuktos the son of Timokrates (who was born before 400 and may have died before this play was written, possibly in the late 'fifties). In Anaxandrides' *Cities* (150/39) an Athenian explains that disparity of customs makes it impossible for him to be an ally of the Egyptians ; at the time of the Satraps' revolt Tachos was aided by Chabrias and Melanopos' False Embassy to Egypt may have had some connection with this ; officially the Athenians appear to have remained neutral because they were at peace with the King of Persia ; Anaxandrides seems to have expressed this official attitude.

Ephippos, whose dislike of the dramas of Dionysios and the praises of Kotys may not have been purely aesthetic,[4] has left a long and difficult fragment (252/5) which is worth interpretation. The play is called *Geryones* and someone, perhaps Herakles, describes how an enormous fish bigger than Crete is prepared for Geryon in a dish (which is the Mediterranean). The people on

[1] Schol. Aesch., I, 64—Hyperides, fr. 40.   [2] xxi, 103, 139.
[3] xxiv, 126-7.   [4] See above, p. 30.

the coasts cut wood and fire it to boil the King's great fish ; they are called Sindoi, Lycians, Mygdoniotai, Kranaoi, and Paphians. The Sindoi are the subjects of the Bosporan rulers, who were several times honoured at Athens during the fourth century for sending corn ; [1] the Kranaoi are the Athenians themselves ; the Mygdoniotai lived between the Axios and Strymon and may here be a metrically more convenient name for the Macedonians. On the top of the water five boats sail to take messages to the rims : ' You are not firing enough, chiefs of Lycia. This part is cold. Stop blowing, Macedonian ruler. Damp down, Celt, or you will burn it.' [2] There are several elements in the picture. First there is the large cauldron, of which many survive, with little figures on the rim ; as Beazley [3] puts it, ' vessels with men or animals stationed at the rim, and looking curiously over it into the liquid '. Here they have the extra function of telling the people below, who are heating the cauldron, to increase or decrease their fire. The ships, which bring them instructions, remind us inevitably and perhaps intentionally of the Salaminia in Aristophanes' *Birds* (146), which may pop up by any seaboard city bringing a summons. This cauldron is Geryon's cooking pot and we are perhaps justified in remembering archaic terra-cottas of satyrs squatting over cooking pots or enormous drinking cups,[4] because they spring from the same sort of imagination. But this cooking pot is as big as the Mediterranean and Geryon must be correspondingly large. Giants were evidently not unknown in Greek carnivals ; a black-figured cup [5] (*c.* 550 B.C.) shows eight men carrying a giant satyr mounted on a phallus pole. Here is part of the inspiration, but in the Ephippus passage there is a definite ratio : as cooking pot is to man, so is Mediterranean to giant, and man to Mediterranean is itself a known scale. The scale recalls to me the comparison of the Mediterranean to a pond in Plato's *Phaedo* (109b) : there Sokrates says that the world is very big, and ' we who live between the pillars of Herakles and the Phasis occupy quite a small part, living round the sea like ants or frogs round a pond '. We have the same

---

[1] Tod, no. 167 : for *Sindoi*, cf. Tod, nos. 115, 171.
[2] Reading with Kaibel after Wilamowitz, 18. ὑποκαίεις, 21. Κέλθ' ὡς.
[3] *J.H.S.*, lx, 49.
[4] Cf., e.g., Payne, *N.C.*, pl. 44, 5, and the Triton brooding over the lamp, Beazley, *loc. cit.*
[5] Nilsson, *Gesch. d. gr. Rel.*, pl. 35/2–3.

sort of ratio (as pond to Mediterranean, so Mediterranean to the whole world) and it seems to me possible that Ephippus was thinking of the *Phaedo* when he wrote this passage.

Meineke dated the *Geryones* to 334 when Alexander received ambassadors from the Celts. This is difficult because Ephippus repeated the passage in the *Peltast* with the addition of four lines (261/19) : ' Such nonsense he talks as he dines and lives amid the applause of the young : he doesn't know arithmetic but proudly trails his cloak.' The story of Geryon has become a yarn in the mouth of the boastful peltast, repeated because it was successful in an earlier play. The Peltast apparently appealed to the doctor Menekrates, who called himself Zeus, and his patient the Argive soldier Nikostratos, who called himself Herakles, as parallels for his own boasting (261/17) ; Nikostratos went to Persia to help Ochus in 344 and Menekrates is connected by anecdotes with Philip and Archidamos. If the Peltast himself, as Kock suggests, is named after the peltasts of Iphikrates, a date before Iphikrates' death in 353 seems likely and it must be remembered that Ephippos won his first Lenaean victory early in the 'sixties and seems to have been producing in the early 'seventies so that a date in the time of Alexander for the *Geryones* is unlikely. The name of Celt did not, as Kock says, first reach Greece when Alexander received their ambassadors in 334. Dionysios of Syracuse sent Celtic mercenaries to help the Spartans in 369.[1] Here they are perhaps in the first place non-Greek dwellers on the western coasts of the Mediterranean corresponding to the Lycians in the east and the Macedonians in the north ; but we may also suggest that Celt is a scornful name for Dionysios himself, who used the Celts. On the other hand, the Lycians are mentioned twice and it is difficult to see how ' chiefs of Lycia ' could have been interesting after their country had been taken over by Maussollos at the end of the Satraps' revolt (366–59), and the passage must have been originally written at a time when it was possible for the Lycians to cause trouble. The whole makes sense as a satiric picture of Athenian foreign policy at a time when Athens was trying to make alliances with Macedon and Dionysios and to embroil the Lycians against Persia. It might in fact fit with the early 'sixties when Kallistratos and Melanopos were acting together, when alliances were actually

[1] Xen., *Hell.*, VII, i, 20 ; cf. *C.A.H.*, VII, 64.

made with Dionysios and with Macedon, and when Athens
probably would not object to causing trouble in the Great King's
dominions : Chabrias had already operated against him in
Egypt in 377 and would do so again in 361.

The rise of Philip of Macedon makes the picture clearer because
it caused a prolonged crisis in which politicians and poets had to
take sides. Quite early we can see pro-Macedonian and anti-
Macedonian poets appearing. When Antiphanes (60/124) speaks
of guests at a subscription party who, like Philip, promise their
money but do not pay, he is probably thinking of Philip's continued unfulfilled promises to give up Amphipolis to Athens.
Chares' victory in 354/3 over Philip's mercenaries who were
commanded by Adaios 'the cock' was celebrated by both
Antiphanes (303) and Herakleides (K., ii/435). But a little before
this the politician Hegesippos, who was nicknamed Krobylos or
'topknot' and was firmly anti-Macedonian, was ridiculed in
comedy 'as ugly in face and having been wrong about Phocis' ; [1]
he had proposed the alliance with Phocis in 355. His great
activity was in the years from 346 onwards when he opposed
the peace of Philokrates and it is probably at this time that a
character in Sotades' *Paralytroumenos* (449/3) remarks 'I am a
sauce to Krobylos. His main meal is Philip but he eats me in
addition.' Sotades is probably sympathetic to Krobylos, as he
calls another play after Charinos, who is known as a pro-
Macedonian orator and an enemy of Demosthenes ; [2] the man
who gives his name to a play is unlikely to be treated sympathetically. Similarly Mnesimachos' *Philippos* (441/7–10) is an
attack on Philip : Philip himself or one of his supporters boasts
that the Macedonians eat swords and drink lighted torches,
recline on shields and breast plates and are wreathed with catapult
shot : 'Is one of the Pharsalians coming to eat up the tables ?'
'No : there is no one.' 'Good. Perhaps they are eating a
roast Achaean city ?' This is a clear allusion to the Achaean
city of Halos which Philip captured in 346 and handed over to
the Pharsalians. Two other characters of this period may be
mentioned here : Philokrates, who was responsible for the peace

[1] Schol. Aesch., III, 118.
[2] Körte suggests the identification in *R.E.*, IIIA, 1206 : perhaps the same
Charinos' speech is a 'stopper from Stilpon' in Sophilos (Kock, ii/547/23,
gives it to Diphilos without reason).

with Philip called after him, appears in a fragment of Euboulos (206/119) as a glutton who eats as much as two or three other men, and Polyeuktos, who acted with Demosthenes and Hegesippos against Philip, gives its title to a play by Heniochos. A fragment from an unknown play of Heniochos (433/5) runs as follows : ' I will tell the names one by one in a moment. Collectively these are all cities who have now been mad for a long time. . . . All this place round here is Olympia, and this tent you must regard as the tent of the envoys there. What are the cities doing here ? They came once to make sacrifices to celebrate their freedom when they had with difficulty got free of tribute. Then after that sacrifice Folly led them astray, feasting them day after day and domineering over them for a long time now. Two women were always there to disturb them. One is called democracy and the other aristocracy and they have often made the cities play the fool.' The earlier moment when the cities celebrated their freedom has been interpreted as the end of the Social War. Now the cities are no longer inflamed by democracy or aristocracy ; some higher reconciling force has been found and the only possible force is Macedon ; therefore it seems right to refer the fragment to the formation of the Corinthian League and to regard Heniochos as a friend of Macedon. As a friend of Macedon, he could reasonably write a play which satirised the anti-Macedonian politician Polyeuktos of Sphettos.

The first references to Demosthenes in comedy are quotations in Antiphanes (89/190) of a phrase from the *First Philippic* and by Anaxandrides (136/3) of a metaphor which he used in the *Second Olynthiac*. Then in 343 Philip offered to give the Athenians the island of Halonnesos which he had taken from the pirates and which they claimed as their own. Demosthenes in the debate early in 342 said that the Athenians did not wish Philip to *give* them the island but to *give* it them *back*. This is quoted with variations by Antiphanes (80/169), Alexis (299/7, 373/209), Anaxilas (265/9), Timokles (460/18). Anaxilas couples it with an oath ' by the earth ', and we know that Antiphanes (128/296) and Timokles (466/38) laughed at Demosthenes for swearing ' by earth, by fountains, by rivers, by springs '. Here we are justified in applying the Platonic distinction between mockery with anger and mockery without anger. We know

nothing of Anaxilas' politics, but we have already quoted
Antiphanes' reference to Philip's failure to keep his promises,
and Alexis mocks at Aristogeiton (373/208), who prosecuted
Hyperides soon after Chaironeia and was himself prosecuted by
Lykourgos, as well as at the pro-Macedonian Kallimedon and at
Philippides, the thin man who was already a joke in Plato's lifetime and still a joke to the young Menander but whom Hyperides
regarded as a dangerous traitor.[1]   There is therefore no reason
to see any political colour when Antiphanes and Alexis laugh
at Demosthenes.   Timokles is different.   In his *Heroes* (457/12)
someone says : ' First Demosthenes will stop being angry with
you.' 'What? Demosthenes?' 'The son of Briareus, who eats
shot and spears, who hates words, who never yet made an
antithesis but has Ares in his eyes.'   Timokles [2] has taken
Mnesimachos' caricature of Philip and turned it into a caricature
of Demosthenes, implying thereby that Demosthenes is a coward,
loves words and made a famous antithesis.   Timokles tells his
audience that all Demosthenes' war talk amounts to nothing.[3]   In
the same play he says that Hermes has come down in kindness to
Aristomedes so that Satyros may no longer call him a thief (51aP).
Satyros is the comic actor, praised by Demosthenes (XIX, 192)
and derided by Aeschines as ' the player of Karion and Xanthias '
(II, 156).   Aristomedes is the son of Aristophon, who, it is
clearly implied in the *Fourth Philippic* (X, 70 ff.), took bribes
from Philip.   He is called a thief again in the later *Ikarioi*
(51bP) and therefore we must suppose that (like Kallimedon)
he was so unpopular that Timokles found it wise to abuse him
in spite of his own Macedonian sympathies.

   Most of what we know about Kallimedon the Crab comes
from the period after Chaironeia, when he worked so energetically
for the Macedonians that he was twice thrown out of Athens
when there was a democratic revolution.   But the story of the
dining club of 60 members whose wit was so famous that Philip
sent them a talent in return for a copy of their jokes [4] shows that
Kallimedon was a well-known figure in Athens before Chaironeia

---

[1] Aristophon, 8, 10 ; Alexis, 2, 89, 144 ; Menander, 365.

[2] See Meerewaldt, *Mnem.*, lv, 287 ; Coppola, *R.F.I.C.*, 1929, 454.

[3] We cannot say whether the terms ' a cheap jack shouting ' and ' bull-roarer's
chatter ' (K., iii/461/294) applied to Demosthenes came from Timokles' pen or
not ; they are certainly in his manner.

[4] Ath., 614 d e.

and that he was already in Philip's pay. Kallimedon himself was called the crab and it seems likely that when Alexis twice gives a list of diners named after food (328/97, Opson, Karabos, Kobios, Semidalis ; 359/168, Karabos, Korydos, Kobion, Kyrebion, Skombros, Semidalis) he is referring to this dining club. Kyrebion in the second list is known as a relation of Aeschines, called Epikrates.[1] Many of the references to Kallimedon are unimportant and need not be recapitulated,[2] but Theophilos calls him a politician (474/4) and Alexis (388/247) makes one character refer to him with obvious irony as ' pugnacious but useful to the city '.

The fish situation seems to have become difficult in Athens about this time, since the fish importers, Chairephilos and his sons, were given the citizenship by Demosthenes and received the indiscriminate mockery of Antiphanes, Alexis, and Timokles. At the same time Aristonikos, who was working with Lykourgos in 334, proposed laws to control the excesses of the fishmongers for which he was warmly congratulated by Alexis (342/125). We can understand that considerable odium was felt for Athenians who made a corner in fish (cf. Antiphanes, 89/190 [3]) and that it would not add to Kallimedon's popularity when Alexis said (316/56) that the fishmongers had decided to set up a bronze statue of him in the fishmarket holding a crab in his hand.

Timokles used this method of discrediting Hyperides in the *Ikarioi* (458/15), in which he describes him as ' a river flowing with fish, bubbling with the soft sounds of sane speech . . . watering the plains of the giver for pay '. Hyperides had been called a glutton years before by Philetairos (230/2) ; that was presumably when he was making his name as the kind of forward-looking politician who would be unacceptable to the son of Aristophanes ; it may be relevant to remember that Hyperides accused Autokles of treachery in 361 and Autokles had been one of the ambassadors who went to Sparta in 371. The reputation for gluttony was particularly damaging when, as Timokles says (16),' famine blazed up '.

The *Ikarioi* has been dated in the neighbourhood of 330

---

[1] Dem., XIX, 287 ; Aesch., II, 150, 152.

[2] Antiphanes, 26, 76 ; Alexis, 112–13, 145, 193, 215 ; Euboulos, 9.

[3] Cf. Alexis, 314/46, 388/247. Cf. also Demosthenes, XIX, 229 (343 B.C.).

because of the mention of Telemachus, whom we know to have
been concerned with securing the Attic corn supply during the
famine years.[1] Telemachos comes three times in Timokles;
here (16) with a heap of beans, in the *Lethe* (21) with a pot of
beans, and in the *Dionysos* (7) he has a pot. As Demosthenes
was corn commissioner in 328, it seems likely that Telemachus
was working with him and that Timokles had no love for
Telemachus. Telemachus' beans are not a call to the Athenians
to return to the simple life as has been suggested, but voting
beans because he is a *demegoros*, an orator who collects or uses
votes in the law courts or elections. The last line of the fragment
from the *Dionysos* is corrupt but it seems to me that the first
word may well be sound : θανατηγὸν means ' murderous ' and
Telemachus' pot is ' murderous ' because he procures condemna-
tions. His likeness to newly bought slaves (in the same fragment) may only consist in the fact that he has a pot ; the newly
bought slave presumably has a pot in which he collects the sweets
poured over his head when he enters the house.[2] Finally, we
have from Timokles (452/4) a list of orators who took gold
from Harpalos in 325/4 : Demosthenes, Moirokles, Demon,
Kallisthenes, and Hyperides.

Timokles is an unsympathetic figure politically but interesting
because he shows us a late flare-up of personal abuse on a considerable scale. What distinguishes the personal abuse of this
period from the preceding period when the poets were con-
sistently anti-imperialist is the clear division into two camps with
the rise of Philip. It is a pity that we have not enough evidence
to clarify this picture. Moreover, some figures were for one
reason or another so outstanding that they were targets for
comedians of both parties. Nevertheless, we are probably
justified in regarding Timokles and Heniochos as pro-Macedonian
at this time and Antiphanes, Mnesimachos, and Alexis as anti-
Macedonian.

More general remarks on the conduct of the city's affairs can
be found in the fragments but it is difficult to know how much
we have lost here by having no complete plays except the Latin
adaptations. It may for instance be chance that we hear less
about poverty and that there is a little sign of return of prosperity
in the country : it is true that someone in Anaxilas (267/16) is

[1] Perhaps cf. also K., iii/460/290.   [2] Cf. Ar., *Plutus*, 768, 789.

' ruined because he is keeping up a place in the country ' but this
sounds like a joke, and Amphis (241/17) calls the country the
' father of life and the disguise of poverty', while someone in
Alexis (403/303) would rather be a farmer than a *strategos*.

On life in the city the girl in Plautus' *Persa* [1] makes an interesting
comment ; she says she cannot tell what Athens is like unless
she knows its morals ; if perfidy, peculation, covetousness, envy,
desire for office, abuse, and perjury are absent, then all is well.
This must come from the original since the terms are so easily
translated into Greek. We can give instances of most of these
vices from the comedy of this period. The peculation, covetousness and abusiveness of the orators appear in the fragment of
Antiphanes (95/196) about their collecting the spoil from Thrace
and Asia, and Nikostratos (228/34) speaks of orators ' run to
seed, ill-tempered, deposed and re-elected '. The strategoi are
difficult to approach but then their pride is excusable, because
unlike the fishmongers to whom they are compared they have
been chosen by the city (Amphis, 244/30 ; Alexis, 303/16), but
they may in fact be merely parasites who act the part of famous
generals with raised eyebrows, ruining men worth a thousand
talents (Alexis, 338/116) ; the passage is difficult but presumably
refers to Athenian generals who served foreign princes like Konon
in Cyprus, Chabrias in Egypt, etc. At the other end of the scale
we have the fluid boundary between slave and citizen : ' Many
are not free to-day, but to-morrow they will be Sounians, and
the day after they use the agora ' (Anaxandrides, 137/4). We
can also perhaps see a change in the character of the Assembly
indicated in the *Menaechmi* (451 f.) : the parasite complains of
the trouble of attending the Assembly when he is asked out to
a meal—' men of leisure ought to be chosen '.[2] There is certainly no sign here of the eagerness to attend the Assembly which
we saw in the *Ekklesiazousai* and there may be a slight hint at
the desirability of restriction.

In the same play Menaechmus himself is late for dinner because
he has had to support a dependant, presumably a metic, in the law
court (594 f.) : ' I have never seen a man more clearly guilty :

---

[1] 554 f., cf. Isocrates, VII, 13.

[2] ' Soon the ekklesiast becomes home fed ' (Antiphanes, 97/200) seems to
mean that the member of the Assembly has to provide his own rations and
should therefore be referred to the time when payment for attending the Assembly
was abolished (322 B.C.). Cf. A. H. M. Jones, *Athens of Demosthenes*, 23.

there were three witnesses to all his wrongdoings,' and he has more to say about perjury, which probably comes from the original. So also the other Menaechmus, when he pretends to be mad, describes the old man as ' a goat who has often in his life destroyed an innocent citizen, by false testimony ' (838). This is paralleled by another vision (madness or dream ?) in Alexis' *Agonis* (298/4) : ' The third here has a rolled wreath of figs. When he was alive, he used to like figs.' He is a sycophant and there are many references to sycophants in this period as before.[1] In the *Persa* (62 f.) the parasite contrasts his life with the life of a sycophant ; he is not prepared to seize other people's goods without any risk to himself ; he is prepared to admit that the sycophant may be a patriotic citizen (the claim which the sycophant in the *Plutus* made for himself) but suggests that he should stand to lose as much as his victim if he does not win the case : exactly the same suggestion is made in a speech by Isaeus [2] for claimants to an estate. There is evidence then for continued corruption, and in Euboulos' *Olbia* (190/74) a universal market is proposed to sell not only flowers, vegetables and meat but also figs, prosecutors, witnesses, lawsuits, balloting urns, water clocks, and laws. A new feature perhaps is a certain sympathy for the difficulties of the rich in a fragment of Antiphanes (99/204) : ' either taxes plunder all his wealth, or he is involved in a suit and ruined, or he is a *strategos* and then condemned, or he is chosen *choregos* and dresses his chorus in gold but wears rags himself, or he is strangled by a trierarchy '. This is exactly the attitude of Isokrates in the *Peace* (124/131), who blames it on the democratic politicians, and in the *Areopagiticus* (54) he also mentions the choruses dressed in gold.

Much of this criticism is traditional and comedy is traditionally conservative in political outlook ; what is not clear (and it may be only ignorance that prevents us from seeing it) is that comedy still had the same sympathetic interest in the small independent citizen whether from country or town as in the time of Aristophanes. At least the new types of character who occupy more space in mid-fourth-century comedy are either outside the citizen body like the slaves, hetairai, pornoboskoi, and probably many of the soldiers and cooks, or are rich or hangers-on of the

---

[1] Antiphanes, 84/179, 125/277 ; Alexis, 339/117, 365/182.
[2] IV/11, cf. Partsch, *Hermes*, xlv, 598.

rich like the parasites. The private life of the upper class in the
city has begun to take a larger place in comedy and their personal
problems (difficulties in love, difficulties of marriage and old age,
the right use of wealth) are expressed in gnomic utterances
which were collected by the anthologists. In one sense this
comedy seems to us at any rate less positive than either Aristophanes or Menander : neither in the fragments nor in the Latin
adaptations can we see positive values put forward even by
implication, whereas Aristophanes opposes the Unjust Argument
by a Just Argument and Euripides by Aeschylus, and Menander
proposes something like the standards of Aristotle's equitable
man. Mockery of parasites, hetairai, and cooks is negative
criticism. Perhaps the continued complaint of corruption in
public life implies a positive demand for cleaner politics, but we
do not hear the demand voiced.

The references to philosophy in the comic poets are of some
interest because they suggest in what way and to what extent
the philosophers were known to the ordinary man. Three
general qualities naturally stand out. The philosophers are
enemies of pleasure and they are unpractical and less innocent
than they seem. According to Anaxandrides (161/61) Eros is
a better educator for life than a sophist ; this is developed in a
fragment of unknown authorship which says that hetairai are
better teachers than sophists (K., iii/431/122) : Aspasia has more
reason to be proud of Perikles than Sokrates of Kritias. A slave
in Amphis (237/6) regards the good to be got from a hetaira as
even more doubtful than Plato's good, but his master evidently
did not share his hesitation in the choice. A line of Alexis
(364/180), ' rather than chatter with Plato alone ', certainly
implies the life of pleasure as an alternative, and though the
parasite in the *Persa* (123) may compare his basic equipment
with that of Diogenes his ideal of life is entirely different.[1]
Plato is accused of making his pupils thinner than Philippides
(Aristophon, 279/8) and he only knows how to frown with his
brows curled proudly into a spiral (Amphis, 239/13). The
Pythagoreans are dirty vegetarians.[2]

The other charge that philosophers are unworldly we know

---

[1] Cf. Alexis, 372/203 (after 310 B.C.), 376/219.
[2] Antiphanes, 67/135, 76/160, 79/168 ; Alexis, 308/27, 370/196, 378/220 ;
Mnesimachos, 436/1.

both from Plato and Isokrates.[1] It was not the complaint made by Aristophanes against the sophists. In the fourth century we meet first a theoretical form of this charge in Anaxandrides (159/54) : ' the people who keep their wisdom to themselves have no one to judge their work (*techne*) and they are disliked. If one thinks one has made a discovery, one should publish it.' Someone is being asked for some knowledge he claims to possess (a cook or an intriguing slave ?) and the request is moulded on Medea's [2] description of the difficulties of the wise man, who is both disliked and appears to the uneducated to be useless. The isolation of the philosopher had therefore already begun in the fifth century, although to Aristophanes the practical danger of the sophist's teaching was much more obvious. The position is put simply in a fragment of Amphis (246/33) : drinkers are better than philosophers : the philosopher's mind, being always concerned with systemisation, is afraid to leap into action because it subjects everything to subtle and detailed examination ; the drinker's mind does not calculate the consequences and does some youthful, hotheaded deed.

We should probably interpret a difficult fragment of Ephippos [3] (257/14) in this sense. Athenaeus introduces the quotation by saying that Ephippos mocked Plato and some of his acquaintances as sycophants for money, at the same time showing that they were lavishly dressed. The fragment describes a young man speaking in the Assembly, and has ancestors in Aristophanes' *Ekklesiazousai* (427) and Euripides' *Orestes* (917). He comes from the Academy and is smitten with a Platonic-Brysonic-Thrasymachean necessity of coin-snatching. Bryson is the Megarian eristic philosopher who was a pupil of Eukleides. Thrasymachos may be the great sophist of *Republic I*, whose rhetorical works are mentioned in the *Phaedrus*, rather than the obscure Thrasymachos of Corinth who taught Stilpon. The young man then, who is a member of the Academy and has learnt there philosophy, eristics and rhetoric, seeks to make money by politics. ' He associates with the art of making money by speaking and cannot say anything that is not well thought out.'

---

[1] e.g. *Republic*, 490e ; Isocrates, XV, 261 f.
[2] E., *Med.*, 294 f. Cf. E., *Hipp.*, 986 ; *Clouds*, 892 ; Thuc., V, 85.
[3] Reading ὑποπλατωνικοβρυσωνοθρασυμαχειοληψικερμάτῳ and ληψιλογομίσθῳ.

E

His hair is neatly cut, his beard is long, his sandals have long and neatly intertwined straps, his cloak is imposingly draped, and he makes a noble figure leaning on his stick. The description recalls two others : the oligarchic man in Theophrastos' *Characters* (XXVI), ' his cloak thrown over his shoulder, his hair cut half length, his hands manicured ', and a fragment of Antiphanes (23/33), ' Who is this old man ? ' ' He looks like a Greek. White cloak, clean good chiton, soft slippers, stick gently swung, short commons. In fact the Academy itself.' [1] But when Ephippos' young man starts to speak he uses the well-known cliché, ' Gentlemen of the Athenian land '.

The fragment gives a picture of the young Academician taking part in politics : this is how Hyperides, Lykourgos, or Phokion would be represented by an unfriendly comic poet and how they would appear to the rank and file of the audience—beautifully dressed, but lacking in force ; this is one side of the common idea that the philospher is the unpractical man. The sycophancy mentioned by Athenaeus in his introduction perhaps means little more than that the Academy does in fact train practical politicians. But eristic used for personal profit was the charge against Sokrates and his pupils in the *Clouds* and the charge recurs in the fourth century. Two fragments mark a connection between the Megarians and Athenian politics. A speech of Charinos is said to be a ' stopper from Stilpon ' (K., ii/547/23) ; Charinos may be the pro-Macedonian politician and it will be remembered that it was in Megara that Kallimedon and the Athenian exiles assembled in 324 when they were hoping for restoration by Alexander. We cannot tell the significance of the unattributed fragment (K., iii/461/294), in which the Megarian Euboulides, ' the eristic with his horned questions, who butts the politicians with pretentious lies, is gone with the cheapjack shouting of Demosthenes '. It is probably primarily an attack on Demosthenes but it also states a direct connection between philosopher and politician. A description of eristic (but without mention of profit) practised by ' thin, starving, figwood sophists in the Lyceum ' occurs in Antiphanes' *Kleophanes* (58/122) ; the Lyceum is mentioned in Isokrates' *Panathenaïkos* (XII, 18, 33) as the home of the common sophists before 339, but in Antiphanes

---

[1] For beards as a mark of the Academy, cf. K., iii/548/796. Cf. also Plato, *Rep.*, 425a, on the whole picture.

their discussions of being and becoming seem to belong rather
to the time of the *Parmenides*. In Kratinos' *Tarantinoi* (291/7) it
is surprising to find the Pythagoreans confounding the ordinary
man with ' antitheses, periods, parallel clauses, digressions, and
the grand style '—in fact with all the machinery of rhetoric.
Again I think the key is in the *Clouds* ; the Pythagoreans in
Tarentum may here be represented as rhetoricians because they
took part in political life.   The charge that the philosophers in private life also pursue personal profit in spite of their pretensions of
asceticism is made both against the Pythagoreans by Aristophon [1]
and against the Cynics by Euboulos (212/139) in a lyric fragment—' unwashen of feet, bedded on the ground, dwellers in the
open, unholy throats, feasters on others' possessions, dish snatchers
of white delicacies '.   The philosopher thus maintains his old
characteristic of an alazon, a pretender, in fourth-century comedy.

References to Plato and the Pythagoreans easily outnumber
references to other philosophers and schools.   We have mentioned the allusion to the Cynics in Euboulos (212/139) and in
the *Persa* (123), to Euboulides (K., iii/461/294) and Stilpon
(K., ii/547/23), and to Metrodoros of Chios in Antiphanes
(108/220) ; Herakleides Pontikos gesticulates wildly with his
hands (Antiphanes 55/113) ; Aristippos of Cyrene has taught a
pupil the art of cookery for a talent (Alexis 311/36) ; Plato's
pupil Hermodoros does a trade in *logoi* (K., iii/456/269).   This
amounts to very little compared with the dozen or so references
to the Pythagoreans and the twenty or so references to Plato.
Some of the references to the Pythagoreans can be dated :
Antiphanes' *Neottis* which mentions Pythagoras himself as a
vegetarian was produced soon after 342 and Alexis' *Tarantinoi*
between 330 and 320 ; possibly Antiphanes' *Korykos* (67/135)
can be dated about 359 ; Mnesimachus' *Alkmaion* (436/1) is
unlikely to have been later than 340.   The other references seem
to fall between 350 and 320.   As two plays by Alexis and
Kratinos are called *Tarantinoi*, it seems likely that in all Western
Pythagoreans were meant and therefore we must assume that at
least the asceticism and vegetarianism of the Western Pythagoreans was sufficiently well known in Athens to be amusing.[2]

[1] 279/9 ; cf. K., iii/457/275.
[2] The Romans erected a statue to Pythagoras as the wisest of the Greeks in
343 B.C.   (Pliny, *N.H.*., xxxiv, 12, 26.)

We have noticed the more general allusions to Plato and the appearance of the Academician in public life. The more particular references to Plato's doctrine of the soul (Alexis, 355/158), the absolute quality of the good (Alexis, 353/152), the distinction between conjecture and knowledge (Kratinos, 292/10), Platonic love (Amphis, 240/15), and Plato's habit of walking up and down while thinking (Alexis 351/147) imply considerable acquaintance with Plato in poet and audience. The diairesis practised in the *Sophist* and the *Politicus* is the subject of a long fragment of Epikrates [1] (287/11), which gives us a picture of the Academy at work. Satirical elements show dependence on the *Clouds* : the absurd pumpkin as an object of research, the young men bowed to the ground, the rude intervention of the Sicilian doctor. But the problem of classifying the pumpkin is the kind of problem which occupied the Academy in Plato's later years, and because the objects were often natural objects led over into Aristotelian biology ; there may even be an echo of the controversy as to whether plants should be classified as animals. The terminology is Platonic. Speusippos and Menedemos are named with Plato as directors of research ; Speusippos succeeded Plato as head of the Academy in 347 and Menedemos of Pyrrha was nearly chosen as Speusippos' successor in 339. The Sicilian doctor regards the young men's discussion as nonsense ; he plays the traditional comic part of *bomolochos*. The doctor usually appears in comedy as a boasting impostor, like the doctor in the *Menaechmi* (885 f.) who rivals Menekrates of Syracuse by claiming to operate on the gods themselves.[2] But here the presence of the Sicilian doctor is evidence of Plato's interest in medicine and perhaps of his particular interest in Philistion of Lokroi, whom he is said to have met at Syracuse. The picture of Plato himself ' very gentle and in no way disturbed ' rings true.

Where we can detect allusions in comedy to particular dialogues of Plato, we may perhaps say that we have evidence of the circulation of Plato's dialogues since the audience were presumably meant to catch the reference. Ophelion. (294/3) speaks of a

---

[1] Cf. also Alexis, 297/1 ; Heniochos, 432/4 ; K., iii/438/149. On the Epikrates fragment see Jaeger, *Aristoteles*, 16, 18 ; *Paideia*, iii, 38 ; Skemp, *C.Q.*, xlii, 65, n. 3.

[2] Cf. Ribbeck, *Alazon*, 15 f. ; Weinreich, *Zeus Menekrates*. Some knowledge of contemporary medical science is implied by Antiphanes, 26/40 ; Alexis, 341/124.

crazy book of Plato as an ingredient in an appetiser, and this implies that books of Plato were well known. Already in the 'seventies Theopompos (737/15) had quoted the *Phaedo*, and we have suggested that Ephippos (252/5) was thinking of the *Phaedo* when he made the Mediterranean the giant's cooking pot. Three passages in Alexis seem to be reminiscences of Plato's dialogues. The description of the strategos as a large-scale parasite and the definition of his activities as a contest in flatteries (338/116) recalls perhaps intentionally the distinction between arts and flatteries in the *Gorgias* (464), where the orators are described as flatterers. When he says that the lover ' must be like a soldier on campaign, ready to bear hardship, made skilful in siege by his passion, creative, violent, energetic, skilled at providing out of poverty, most miserable looking' (382/234), he is remembering Diotima's account of Love as the child of Poverty and Contriving (*Symposium*, 203b). In the *Phaidros* (386/245), a young man has tried to define the nature of love as he walked up from the Peiraeus. Love is neither male nor female, neither divine nor human, neither foolish nor wise, but compacted from every source and carrying many forms within one mould. He ends, ' I don't know what it is but yet it is something like this, and I am near the name.' The subject, the definition by opposites, the hunt for the name, and the fact that the play is called *Phaidros* all suggest that Alexis is thinking of Plato and in particular of the *Symposium* and the *Phaedrus*. This does not amount to very much but perhaps helps to show that the dialogues of Plato had a considerable circulation and that the comic poet could expect his audience to recognise obvious allusions to them.

The philosopher is solemn and uninterested in pleasure ; he may be incapable of dealing with the practical problems of life, or his practice may be quite different from his pretensions. Occasionally we can see threads leading across from philosophy into politics and where this happens the philosopher comes in for the same sort of obloquy as the politician. But on the whole the comic poets are not unfriendly, if slightly contemptuous, of philosophers in general and the Academy in particular. We miss the violent attacks on the New Education which characterised Old Comedy and we must assume that philosophy is accepted as an ingredient in Athenian life. We have not however yet got to the stage when the comic poets themselves draw on the philosophers for problems, sentiments, and technique. For this Aristotle was largely responsible, and we can see the beginning of his influence on comedy in the prologue of Antiphanes' *Poiesis* (90/191) where the difference between tragedy and comedy are stated and the fragment of Timokles (453/6) which justifies tragedy because the man who has seen other's misfortunes bears his own more easily.

2. FORM AND CONTENT

The philosophers in their turn help us a little to appreciate this stretch of comedy for which we have no Greek originals surviving. Comedy according to Plato is appreciated most by adolescents ; in the well-organised state its performance is left to slaves and foreigners, and no poet, whether by word or by likeness, whether in anger or not, may use comedy to attack any citizen.[1] There is nothing new here : it is the old criticism of comedy as a weapon of political abuse which we find repeated in Aristotle [2] with the significant addition that direct abuse was the weapon of the old poets and insinuation the weapon of modern poets ; whether this distinction can be historically justified is doubtful on the evidence that we have been discussing. In the *Republic*, Plato implies that the characters of comedy are low-born cowards, who abuse, mock, and speak evil of one another, sometimes drunk and sometimes sober (395e) ; its laughter is caused by acts which the ordinary man would be ashamed to perform because they might give him the reputation of a *bomolochos* (606c) ; this again corresponds to Aristotle's description of the characters of comedy as ' worse men ' [3] whose errors or ugliness, like the distortion of the comic mask, do not have consequences such as agony or death which belong to tragedy : in the *Eudemian Ethics* [4] he gives as an instance the rustic who does not even yield to moderate and necessary pleasures —we can see something of him in the fragments of the *Rustic* of Antiphanes and Anaxandrides, and we understand from con-

---

[1] *Laws*, 658, 816, 935.
[2] *N.E.*, 1128 a 22 ; cf. for this general line *Poetics*, 1449 b 7 ; *Rhet.*, 1384 b 10 ; *Pol.*, 1336 b 20.
[3] *Poetics*, 1448 a 17 ; 1449 a 32.   [4] 1230 b 19.

temporary monuments the painless distorted ugliness of the comic mask and costume. Another comic type is mentioned in the *Philebus* (47e–50d) where Plato discusses the psychological reaction of the audience to comedy and finds that we laugh at people who think they are richer, more beautiful, more efficient (*arete*) than they are in fact; he is clearly thinking of the braggarts of the comic stage, the soldiers, doctors, cooks, etc., for whom we have abundant evidence in this period.

Aristotle takes us further in the *Poetics*. In one place (1453 a 36) he clearly has in mind the plot of a mythological comedy : ' for in comedy those who have been the worst foes like Orestes and Aigisthos retire as friends at the end and nobody is killed by anybody '. This is a comic reversal of the traditional story, of which we find traces in the fragments. Tereus seems to have been a henpecked husband in Anaxandrides' *Tereus* (156/45) and the title *Odysseus the Weaver* by Alexis suggests that he instead of Penelope wove the winding sheet. The finest instance, which may well come from Attic comedy, is a scene on a Paestan vase of about 350 B.C.,[1] where Cassandra belabours Ajax as he clings in terror to the statue of Athena. The possibilities of this kind of comedy are enormous and there must have been far more examples than we can detect.

The other important statement about comedy in Aristotle [2] contrasts it with history and with tragedy because it is a combination of probable incidents to which chance names are added. Such a comedy by definition is neither political (in the sense that it has no contemporaries as characters) nor mythological because mythological comedy like tragedy ' keeps to historical names '. Moreover, it is composed of probable incidents, or, as Aristotle has said just above, ' a man of a certain quality performs actions or speaks words of the same quality according to probability '. The phrase ' probable incidents ' further excludes what we have called the comedy of the dominant idea at least in its Aristophanic form : the *Ekklesiazousai* has chance names (if we may include significant names like Praxagora under this head) but most of the incidents cannot be called probable. We must therefore assume that by the time Aristotle wrote the *Poetics* (in the early 'thirties, probably) there was a comedy with clearly marked imaginary characters in which the incidents followed each other in a prob-

[1] Rome : Villa Giulia, Bieber, *H.T.*, figs. 366–7.   [2] 1451 b 11.

able sequence as in a tragedy : to this sort of comedy (and possibly to this passage in the *Poetics*) Antiphanes seems to allude in
the *Poiesis* when he says ' comic poets must invent everything,
new names, previous dispositions, the present position, the end,
the beginning '. Menander's comedy fulfils these conditions,
and if it is justifiable to date the original of the *Persa* between
341 and 338 [1] we have there the kind of comedy of which
Aristotle is thinking. The action is closely related to the quality
of the characters, the inventiveness of the slave, and the greed
of the parasite.

The position then is this. We know Aristophanes and we
know Menander. From Plato and Aristotle we learn that
comedy continues to be satirical and political (and this we have
seen to be true) as well as mythological, that comedy represents
braggarts and people who have not the normal emotions, and
that by the early 'thirties at any rate comedy can consist of probable incidents related to character. Of course we must remember
that neither Plato nor Aristotle is writing a complete account of
comedy or even giving a complete theory of comedy ; even in
the *Poetics* comedy only comes in as an illustration where it is
needed. Logically as we have said the comedy of chance names
and probable incidents excludes the comedy of the dominant
idea, mythological comedy, and political comedy (in its widest
sense) ; practically there was no such hard and fast line. Once
probable incidents related to character had become part of
comedy, they would be found in all kinds of comedy and we
have in fact seen the beginning in the scenes between the two old
men in the *Ekklesiazousai* and *Ploutos*. But Aristotle's statement
gives valuable pointers to a gradual change from historical
characters to invented characters and to a kind of plot construction
approximating to tragedy. Our task is to find evidence for this
in the fragments and the few Attic works of art which represent
comedy. If we can see traces of such characters and situations
in the fragments, then we can use the three Latin plays whose
originals can be dated to this period to give us some idea of what
complete plays in the last twenty years before Menander were
like.

One preliminary question affects all kinds of comedy and that
is the status of the chorus. In the *Ploutos*, as we have said, the

---

[1] See below, p. 78.

chorus have a special opening song but otherwise no songs are recorded for them but only the intervals where they would sing : they are present all through the action and take part in the dialogue.[1] In Menander the arrival of the chorus may be mentioned and the intervals are marked, but they have no songs written for them and they take no part in the dialogue ; there is no certain evidence of their continued presence during the action. In sketching the background of Menander [2] I suggested that our scanty evidence showed traces at least as late as the 'thirties of a chorus which did more than sing interludes, and that the dramatic use of the chorus may have lasted longer in mythological comedy and political comedy than in the comedy of everyday life. For our purpose here we need more detail and precision than were relevant there. Let us start with the instances which are normally quoted. We must, I think, exclude Timokles' *Orestautokleides* (462/25) : there is no reason to suppose that the hetaira-furies sleeping round the hero also formed the chorus : all that is certain is that someone parodied the speech of the priestess in the *Eumenides*. In the fragment of Heniochos (433/5),[3] which has been quoted above for its political implications, the Cities probably formed the chorus ; that is, in 338 a play may still have a special chorus and it seems reasonable to suppose that a special chorus had at least one special song. A papyrus fragment (48P) almost certainly gives evidence of the chorus taking part in the action : a refugee appeals to ' you, men ' and they answer ' we who are present here ' ; the natural explanation is that they are a chorus of local inhabitants (who possibly gave their name to the play) ; the fragment is undated but the tone suggests an intrigue comedy not too early in the century. Shortly before 345, according to Aeschines (I, 157), the comic actor Parmenon in a comedy at the rural Dionysia at Kollytos spoke anapaests to the chorus in which he mentioned ' great prostitutes like Timarchos'. There is no reason to suppose that practice at Kollytos differed from practice at Athens. The phrase makes an anapaestic dimeter, a metre commonly

---

[1] Plato, *Laws*, 816 d, is evidence for comic songs and dances at the time that it was written but not for special song and dance for special plays nor for the presence of the chorus during the dialogue. Cf. also Theophrastos, *Char.*, vi, 3.

[2] *Studies*, 181 f., with references to Maidment, *C.Q.*, 1935, 13 f. ; Pickard-Cambridge, *Theatre of Dionysos*, 160 f.

[3] Cf. above, p. 44.

occurring in the fragments and used both for long descriptions of food and for satire, e.g. the Geryon fragment of Ephippos (252/5) and the description of the Academy by Epikrates (287/11) which we have discussed. We cannot however argue from the fact that the chorus were addressed in anapaests in the Kollytos play to the presence or active participation of the chorus in other plays which are known to have contained anapaestic dimeters ; the Epikrates fragment might be a dialogue between an actor and the leader of the chorus, but it might equally well be a dialogue between two actors. There are however two fragments in anapaestic dimeters in which a reference to the chorus has been seen : in Mnesimachos' *Hippotrophos* (437/4) a slave is told by his master to summon the young men to a feast and, as Mr. Maidment says, ' they would presumably return with him in much the same way as the chorus comes on behind Karion in the *Ploutos* ', whether singing a special song or not ; the play must be earlier than Menander's *Kolax* which quotes it and the only dated fragment of Mnesimachus belongs to the late 'forties. In the *Dodonis* of Antiphanes (48/91) someone, parodying the dithyrambic style, asks where the crowd of Ionians come from : the play cannot be dated but here clearly anticipates the formula used in Menander for the arrival of the chorus ; it implies however a closer connection between actor and chorus in the sense that the chorus are strange and interesting-looking people ; so perhaps also the fragment in iambics of Alexis' *Kouris* (333/107), where someone, probably a parasite in the tradition of Epicharmus (35), sees a *Komos* of young bloods arriving and hopes that he may escape them when they are in their cups. The reference (in the *Kouris*) to Timokles (333/108) suggests a date between 345 and 310 ; if however we give some weight to the liveliness and particularity of the description, we can push this back before 314, since at that date the announcement has already become a formula in Menander's *Perikeiromene* (71) ; the elaborate announcement of the *Dodonis* should be earlier still and it is tempting to ascribe it to the earlier Antiphanes and date before 331. A fragment of Antidotos' *Protochoros* (410/2) has a unique reference by a parasite to the chorus after their entry : ' you stand in your place and listen to me. From my early youth . . .' In the Kollytos fragment we seem to have the type—abuse of chorus before they dance ; this form is very clear in the *Trophonios* of Alexis

(383/237),[1] where the chorus are told in Eupolideans not to behave entirely as Boeotians but to strip themselves (and dance) ; the play can be dated 360/50. Two invocations in iambics in Euboulos may perhaps be addressed to the chorus—in the *Ankylion* (165/3) ' come, women, dance the night through ' and in the *Amaltheia* (166/8) ' put the wine skin in the middle and leap upon it '.

Another possible clue is metre, but this must be used with caution. We have already noted the relevance of Eupolideans and have found it necessary to exclude anapaestic dimeters. We must of course exclude iambic trimeters and tetrameters, trochaic tetrameters, and dactylic hexameters. A long passage about fish in Axionikos' *Phileuripides* (413/4) is a mixture of anapaestic dimeters and lyric metres, presumably recitative by an actor, parodying Euripides.[2] An Aeolic fragment of Nikostratos (221/7) may well be an actor's solo. But two fragments of Anaxilas' *Kirke* (dated before 350) seem to belong to a chorus of Odysseus' companions, who have been transformed into animals. In the first (266/12) the dactylo-epitrites followed by a cretic tetrameter should be choral, and therefore the aeolics of fr. 13 are likely also to be choral. The scene is set near Circe's palace and Odysseus arrives and is warned what may happen to himself and the rest of his crew ; this should then be a first chorus. The other evidence comes from Euboulos : the fragment in dactylic hexameters with ithyphallics about the Cynics (212/139) seems to be choral ; we may perhaps doubt about the fragment of the *Echo* (176/35), but there can be little doubt about the paeonic fragment of the *Titthai* (204/112), or the largely dactylic fragments of the *Stephanopolides* (199/104–5), which sound like the entrance song of the Garland-sellers.

The *Stephanopolides* was produced 350/20. We have Latin fragments of Naevius' *Corollaria* [3] as well as the Greek fragments and we can see a little of the plot. A *lena* does not want her daughter to fall hopelessly in love because if she goes on living (marriage is death) she will be more profitable to her mother (IR). Two Greek fragments seem to come from a conversation between the leader of the Garland-sellers and the *lena* and her

---

[1] The lone Eupolidean from Alexis' *Sikyonios* (undated) may belong to a similar context.

[2] For scansion, cf. Wilamowitz, *G.V.*, 410.   [3] Ribbeck, 12.

daughter : in the first (99K) they discuss what wreaths they will have ; in the second the leader of the Garland-sellers, whose prices the *lena* has no doubt tried to beat down, says at least she and her friends do not use excessive make-up like the prostitutes. The lover is accused by a slave of being excessively timorous (101K, VIR). He has a rival (IIIR), who gets friends by extravagant entertainment (IIR), and asks his slave to anoint his chin and beard with perfume (100K). The great interest of these fragments is the conjunction of the typical characters of New Comedy—*lena*, girl, lover, rival, slave—with a named chorus of the old type.

The *Stephanopolides* is named after its chorus like the majority of the plays of Aristophanes. The fact that the number of plural titles decreases startlingly in the first half of the fourth century is some measure of the change of emphasis from chorus to actors. Unfortunately plural titles by themselves are no evidence of an interesting chorus : we must always remember that the *Frogs* was not named after its chorus, that Menander's *Imbrians* was called after two men and his *Synaristosai* after three women. It seems likely, however, that the description of military life from Antiphanes' *Knights* (54/109) is a description of the chorus by its leader ; it is tempting to say the same of a fragment of the *Skythai* (97/201), a late play of 320/10 ; ' all wearing tunics and trousers '. Alexis' *Gynaikokratia* is not named after its chorus but certainly had a female chorus, who are instructed to ' sit there beside the end block of seats ' (312/41). Probably many other plural titles in fact belong to choruses but we cannot go further safely.

To sum up this discussion. If the *Skythai* is accepted, an interesting chorus is possible, even after 320, but can certainly be traced down to 338, the date of the Heniochos fragment. Euboulos' *Stephanopolides* gives the last clear case of a special song for a chorus, and it is their opening song. Here also the chorus take part in the dialogue ; the Kollytos fragment brings us to approximately the same date, but we have no other evidence that is certainly later. The *Stephanopolides* nevertheless had situations which can be paralleled from New Comedy and can reasonably be called a play of intrigue. In the nature of things we cannot see traces of the chorus losing its hold in the dialogue, but we have no reason to disbelieve the testimony of the Latin adapta-

tions to its absence, and some slight confirmation is afforded by
the gradual growth of the Menander formula for introducing
the chorus and by the apparent absence of a mask for the chorus
from the Aixone relief of 340.[1]

Let us next consider the change from historical characters to
characters of fiction. Aristotle's statement is an over-simplifica-
tion but we may find that it contains a general truth which is
useful as a signpost. In considering the political background of
comedy we have noticed several times that plays have been
named after contemporaries, e.g. Plato, Philonides, Philip,
Polyeuktos, and we must assume that they were characters in the
plays named after them, and Plato's phrase ' comedy by likeness ' [2]
is best interpreted in this way. Timokles' *Orestautokleides* can
be dated in the early 'twenties and is named after a contemporary,
and the practice was sometimes revived in New Comedy ; [3] it
continued all through this period, and so far Aristotle is inexact.
A particular case of considerable interest is the hetaira. We
noticed that at the end of the preceding period living hetairai
were sometimes put on the stage and sometimes satirised without
being put on the stage. Satire of living hetairai by name certainly continues through this period ; old men remember their
former flames (Anaxandrides, 138/9) or someone warns a young
hetaira of the fate in store for her (Philetairos, 232/9) or a
pedagogue or father tells a young man of the dangers of hetairai
(Anaxilas, 269/22 ; cf. also Alexis, 329/98) or the young man
himself contrasts the rich hetaira with the girl he loves (Amphis,
242/23). I think we can also see different kinds of hetairai on
the stage. First, it is reasonable to suppose that the contemporary
rich hetaira continues to be a character and that plays such as
Euboulos' *Plangon* and *Nannion* and Timokles' *Neaira* are
examples : [4] we can see a description of Malthake's behaviour to
her lovers in a fragment of Antiphanes' *Malthake* (71/148).
Secondly, the type rich and greedy hetaira appears as a character ;
a pale example is Erotium in the *Menaechmi* and a famous example
in New Comedy is Menander's Thais. Thirdly, a new type
appears as a heroine, the young girl who is called a ' true hetaira '
(Antiphanes 103/212) or a ' modest hetaira ' (Euboulos, 178/42).
She is the heroine of the new intrigue or recognition play, to

[1] Cf. below, p. 75.   [2] *Laws*, 935e, cf. above, p. 37.
[3] See below, p. 109.   [4] Perhaps cf. also Ephippos, 254/6.

which we shall return later. The names for these fictional
hetairai were taken from historical though not necessarily contemporary hetairai : Alexis' *Agonis* was a recognition play and
Suidas tells us that Agonis was the name of a hetaira. The young
hetaira brings with her into comedy her owner, *leno* or *lena* ;
the *lena* may be her mother as in Euboulos' *Stephanopolides*,
which has been quoted above.[1] The *leno* appears soon after the
middle of the century in Euboulos' *Pornoboskos*.[2]

The braggart soldier [3] also starts as an historical character with
Lamachos in the *Acharnians*. Historical examples existed in the
fourth century and were mentioned by comedy, Nikostratos the
Argive Herakles and Adaios the Cock of Philip.[4] Philip himself
was the braggart soldier of Mnesimachos' comedy and perhaps
himself boasts that they eat swords and drink lighted torches,
recline on shields and breast plates and are wreathed with catapult
shot. Otherwise we know no names but can deduce from the
fact that Antiphanes, Alexis, and Xenarchos all called their plays
Soldier that their heroes were fictional. Antiphanes' hero tells
the story of the King of Cyprus being fanned by doves (97/202)
and evidently has a parasite, since the philosophy that the only
safe human possession is food in the mouth (98/204) must be a
parasite's philosophy : this is the first instance of the *alazon-kolax*
relationship. A similar story is told in Alexis' *Eisoikizomenos*
(318/62) and should also be the story of a soldier. The only
fragment of Alexis' *Stratiotes* is difficult to interpret (373/209) :
someone brings back a borrowed child which the owner refuses
to accept. The implications are obscure but an anticipation of
the *Truculentus* where the hetaira borrows a child so as to extract
more money from the devoted soldier seems possible.

The parasite has a history which goes back to Epicharmos
but as far as we know he only becomes a stock character in the
fourth century.[5] The reason may be the shift of interest from
politics to the private life of the city. He is the reverse of Aristotle's rustic in that his pleasures bear no relation to moderation

---

[1] Cf. also Epikrates, 285/9.

[2] Cf. also Euboulos, 67K ; Antiphanes, 168K ; Alexis, 2K ; undated Xenarchos, 4K ; Anaxilas, *Hyakinthos or Pornoboskos*, and 48P. He has an ancestor
in Skiron in Euripides, fr. 675N² (interpreted by Schmid-Stählin, III, 626).

[3] Cf. Ribbeck, *Alazon*, 28 f.   [4] Cf. above, p. 42 f.

[5] On parasites in fifth-century comedy, see Ehrenberg, *People of Aristophanes*,
242.

ɔr necessity. There were plenty of parasites in Athens ; we hear in comedy of Moschion, Philokrates, Chairephon, Korydos, Gryllion, and others, and Plato in the *Phaedrus* (240b) speaks of the flatterer as a ' monster and a great evil '. Moschion gave his name to a play by Kallikrates, and here we can perhaps see a parallel development to the use of hetaira names for fictitious characters ; Moschion entered comedy as an historical parasite and his name became the common name for the wild young man about town. They also had their counterparts in political life in the Athenian generals who were parasitic on foreign princes (Alexis, 338/116). We cannot date any parasite earlier in comedy than the parasite in Antiphanes' *Soldier* (365/60), who expresses the philosophy of *carpe diem*, reaffirmed with an allusion to Pythagorean philosophy in Alexis' *Tarentines* (377/219). Alexis' *Parasite* is dated 360/50, and in the same decade a parasite of Anaxandrides (139/10) traced the art back to Palamedes and Rhadamanthys. Sometimes he is simply spoken of as a disaster to his friends like a youth in Alexis (364/175) and the weevil flatterers of an unknown play of Anaxilas (274/33). On the other hand, in two fragments of Antiphanes (94/195) and Aristophon (277/4) we find the parasite who is prepared to serve his friend in any necessity, such as breaking down doors, climbing walls, or giving testimony. These fragments are unfortunately not dated but we have no reason to suppose that Aristophon went on writing into the New Comedy period. They seem therefore to anticipate Gnathon in Menander's *Kolax* and Phormio in Apollodoros' play.[1] This is not unlikely as the Kolax mask which we associate with this type of parasite can be seen on a Paestan vase of about 350 where two friends join to rob an old man.[2]

The audience of Greek Comedy had always enjoyed hearing about food and drink and this interest can be traced back beyond Aristophanes. We have seen how lengthy descriptions of food had even got into lyric poetry in the early fourth century and had then been parodied in comedy. A comedy which represents a world of rich soldiers on leave, hetairai, and parasites is sure to be concerned with food. A glance through the fragments of Middle Comedy shows the paramount importance of food ;

[1] See *Studies in Menander*, 75 : below, p. 227.
[2] Bieber, *H.T.*, fig. 373.

sometimes the meal itself is described, sometimes a character describes what he has seen or bought at the market, particularly the offences of the proud and exorbitant fishmongers ; [1] but often the cook himself talks.   Nereus, a famous cook, gave his name to a play about 350/40 by Anaxandrides (145/30) in which he is hailed, by identification with his mythical namesake, in tragic style as ' first inventor of the costly cut of the Glaukos' front and of the blameless tunny and other food from the wet sea '. A cook in Axionikos (414/8) is of the same date.   Alexis' *Ponera* is earlier and probably a little before 360 : there the cook comes out and soliloquises on the right treatment for the twopenny-worth of fish which he has.   In the *Lebes* (340–30) the cook, who is described by Athenaeus as a ' scrubby sort of citizen ', gives an elaborate scientific explanation of why his treatment of burnt fish will be successful and is rewarded by the remark ' How like a great doctor, Glaukias.'   Glaukias was a contemporary doctor : I think that Glaukias is not the name of the cook, but the name of the doctor is used as a compliment to him—' well cured, Hippocrates ! '   In the *Milesia* (351/149) the cook philo-sophises about the need for the guests to come in time, and his partner reckons him to be a sophist ; he goes on, ' You are in position, my fire is burning, already countless hounds of Hephaistos bound lightly up to heaven ; for them birth and death are bound together by an unseen law of necessity.'   The cook is now firmly established as a loquacious and pompous charlatan and many variations can be played on the theme.

In all these typical characters that we have examined except the *leno* and *lena*, we have seen both historical contemporaries and invented personalities : we cannot say on our evidence which comes first because our sources are so scrappy ; in the case of hetairai it certainly looks as if historical hetairai came first ; for soldiers, parasites and cooks the evidence points the other way but may be misleading.   At the same time we find plays named after character types—*Soldier*, *Parasite*, and *Leno*—and we may assume that in such plays the typical character had an important part.   They occurred occasionally in Old Comedy, but there the large lyric element must have hindered the full development of the character.   In our period we can distinguish three kinds, the

---

[1] On fishmongers see above, p. 38 f.   Many references to feasting in Prehn, *Quaestiones Plautinae*, 12 : a selection in *Studies in Menander*, 163, n. 2.

purely professional title which tells us nothing about moral character—*Pilot, Goldsmith*—secondly, professional titles which have a certain ethical colour—arrogance or hedonism or shamelessness : [1] the third kind gives a purely ethical label—*Korinthiastes, Hermit, Pot-belly, Busybody, Friend-lover, Rejoicer over Neighbours' Misfortunes.* In this last kind particularly it is legitimate to see the ancestor of the one-character comedy of Menander of which the best surviving example is the *Apistos* (Plautus' *Aulularia*).

There is then a general truth in Aristotle's statement about chance names. He has picked on one of the characteristics of Middle as distinct from Old Comedy. Stock characters have been developed, and though they may have originated in historical persons and may even at this date be given historical labels, they are now generally given imaginary labels and combined in a plot composed of incidents which display but also derive from their particular characteristics. They can be included in the older-fashioned comedy of the dominant idea and they influence the characterisation of the heroes and heroines of mythological comedy, but the new form of comedy which is devised for them is the comedy of intrigue.

3. Comedy of the Dominant Idea

We have used the phrase Comedy of the Dominant Idea to describe the typical Old Comedy in which a startling idea is put into practice and its consequences are seen. In this period some titles suggest the old formula, particularly the *Gynaikokratia* of Amphis and Alexis and the *Pythagorizousa* of Kratinos. A particular theme of this kind is the comedy of errors. In the *Frogs* a special variant of it is used for the Aiakos scene, and in New Comedy it is again used for particular scenes, e.g. in Menander's *Synaristosai* and in the *Captivi*.[2] After Aristophanes, however, a number of poets seem to have used the theme for the organisation of the whole play. Two examples in Plautus, *Menaechmi* and *Amphitruo*, derive from originals in our period. *Menaechmi* we can now consider and reserve *Amphitruo* as our only example of

---

[1] Examples of arrogance are *Soldier, Peltast, Doctor, Lyre-player, Pankratiast,* and *Poet*, of hedonism, *Rustic* and *Parasite*, and of shamelessness *Leno*.

[2] Cf. *Studies in Menander*, 94, 111, 129, 149, 177. On the *Captivi* see below, p. 145 ff.

a complete mythological comedy. It is unfortunate that titles cannot always tell us whether a play is a comedy of errors or not. ' Brothers ' need not be twins and ' Twins ' need not be of the same sex. ' Likes ' do suggest a comedy of errors and Ephippos' *Homoioi* was produced before 370. Antiphanes' *Didymai* was produced in 360/50 and twins of the same sex must have given rise to errors ; the alternative title *Flute-Girl* suggests that there was a lost twin in the establishment of a *leno* : this is the one certain comedy of errors before the original of the *Menaechmi*.

The *Menaechmi*, like the *Amphitruo* and the *Persa*, and unlike the other plays of Plautus, has little characterisation and little moralising. The story consists of a series of errors, eleven in all, seven involving the visiting Menaechmus and four involving the resident Menaechmus. The poet assumes identical twins who except for the *palla* wear identical costume although one is at home and the other a traveller : if this assumption is granted, as soon as the travelling twin is brought to the same spot as the resident twin the confusion follows naturally. The characters are slightly drawn ; the travelling twin is, as Legrand [1] has seen, bolder and more direct than his brother ; the complaining wife and her muddled old father, the hetaira and her pert maid, the two slaves, the parasite, and the doctor are drawn clearly enough to sustain their parts but are not further elaborated. The only other pair of brothers at about the same age as these is the pair in Menander's *First Adelphoi* (*Stichus*). The resident Menaechmus' relation to Erotium (a youngish husband with a hetaira) seems to be unique in comedy ; he has nothing to do either with the boy in love with a hetaira or with the elderly lovers of the *Mercator*, *Casina*, and *Asinaria*. Peniculus is a traditional parasite like the later Gelasimus in the *First Adelphoi* (*Stichus*) but is more successful than he. The doctor only appears here in the surviving plays, but we know him from fragments. [2]

The play is neatly constructed so that the series of errors leads from one to another : the cloak which the resident Menaechmus steals from his wife to give to his mistress holds the series together —Menaechmus I appears wearing it (146) like Blepyros in

---

[1] *New Greek Comedy*, 183.

[2] Antiphanes, 208K ; Euboulos, 83 ; Alexis, 112, 142 ; Aristophon, *Iatros*, etc. Cf. Ribbeck, *Alazon*, 15 f. The list of diseases from a comedy which Kock ascribes to the first half of the fourth century (III, 472/344) is presumably the boasting of a doctor.

Aristophanes' *Ekklesiazousai* (317 f.) and gives it to Erotium (203), she gives it to Menaechmus II (426), he is seen with it by Peniculus (466) who reports to the wife (562), the wife then charges Menaechmus I with having stolen it (645) and he asks for it back from Erotium (678), then the wife sees Menaechmus II carrying it (705). Another thread of a rather different kind which holds the errors together is the idea of madness (198, 373, 505 f., 633), which culminates in the scene where Menaechmus II feigns madness (831).

The mad scene, like the later and slighter scenes in the *Mercator* (931 f.) and *Captivi* (547 f.), is founded on tragedy, and elements of it can be seen in the four surviving plays of Euripides in which madness occurs. The change in eyes and colour is a common symptom (e.g. *H.F.*, 932). Dionysos' summons to hunt in the forest (835) recalls the *Bacchae* (1079 f., 1107, 1146) and the image of hunting recurs in the *Herakles* and the *Iphigeneia* (*H.F.*, 897 ; *I.T.*, 282). The appeal to Apollo and his oracle (840) recalls the *Orestes* (260, 269). The command to burn out the wife's eyes with flaming torches (840) is the reverse of Orestes' fear of the fire-breathing fury (*I.T.*, 288). The attack on the old man reminds us of the *Herakles* (855 with *H.F.*, 993 f. ; 864 with *H.F.*, 947, 1001) ; finally Menaechmus pretends that he, like Herakles, is forcibly stopped by a god.

The sequel to the mad scene is the attempted arrest of Menaechmus I and his rescue (990 ff.). This is one of the rare occasions in which a respectable poor man is treated with violence. Slaves were beaten up through the whole history of comedy. The *leno* is maltreated in Diphilos, in a papyrus fragment [1] and at the end of the *Persa*. The disreputable old man in the *Casina* (Diphilos again) and the soldier in the *Miles* (possibly Diphilos) are special cases and should not, I think, be used as pointers to Diphilos as the author of the original of the *Menaechmi*. Probably if we had more Middle Comedy we should have more scenes of this kind ; the parasite's fears of a beating by drunkards (Alexis, 333/107) may have been realised in some comedy and Antiphanes describes a fight in a comedy of the mid-fourth century (58/119–20). It may also be that the Paestan vase (mid-fourth century) [2] on which an old man Charinos defends his money chest against two thugs, Gymnilos and Kotilos, while his slave

[1] 48P.   [2] Bieber, *H.T.*, fig. 373 ; Trendall, *Paestan Pottery*, no. 31.

Karion looks on helplessly is based on Attic comedy ; a passage
of Julian speaks of miserly old men being dragged forcibly on to
the stage in comedy.[1]   This kind of knockabout seems to me
more in the spirit of Middle Comedy than New.

It may also be a mark of early date that there are two unrealities
of time : the wife sends her slave to summon her father and he
arrives twelve lines later (736/748) ; this cannot have been otherwise in the original since the whole point of the scene is that the
old man should arrive and find Menaechmus II still there.   In
just the same way the old man goes away and returns with his
slaves while Menaechmus I remains on the stage (956/990) : here
Plautus masks the gap by a long *canticum* by Messenio but only
the end of this is likely to derive from the original.   The convention of New Comedy (except for an instance in Diphilos) [2]
is that people have houses either on the stage or so far off that
an act end is needed to cover their going and coming ; here we
have a convention much more like that of Aristophanes, who
fits journey-times to his own convenience, and the action is
speeded because the poet must avoid a break at these points.
On the other hand, the late return of Peniculus (446) and
Menaechmus I (571) are carefully explained ; as they have
arranged to return for supper, some reason must be given for
their delay, which is necessary for the construction of the series
of errors, and the reasons are neatly parallel : Peniculus is delayed
by a meeting of the Assembly and Menaechmus by helping a
friend in legal difficulties.   In both, Plautus has undoubtedly
enlarged the original but there is every reason to suppose that in
the original also both poor man and rich man gave a ' public '
reason for delaying their ' private ' enjoyment.

Fraenkel [3] has pointed out the close connection between
Menaechmus' explanation and the similar complaint of Lysidamus
in the *Casina* (563 f.), and suggests that the Diphilos version is
earlier.   This depends on the dating of the original of the
Menaechmi.   There are several reasons for supposing it to belong
to Middle rather than New Comedy or at least for putting it
very early in New Comedy—the slight characterisation, the
absence of moralising, the very obvious parody of tragedy in the
mad scene, the violent seizure of Menaichmus I, and the disregard
for reality of time.   The two arguments which have been used

[1] K., iii/464/308.   [2] Cf. below, p. 167.   [3] *Pl. Pl.*, 160.

to justify late dating do not bear inspection. The list of Sicilian kings is clearly a Plautine [1] addition, and Hiero II cannot be used for dating. Cylindrus is a slave cook, and Athenaeus (658 f.) is quoted for the statement that slave cooks are only found in Poseidippos. It is difficult to be certain how he should be interpreted but he cannot be used for ascribing the original of the *Menaechmi* to Poseidippos. We have evidence of the household slave as a cook in the Latin adaptations of New Comedy [2] and before that in the Greek originals of Old Comedy ; [3] this covers Cylindrus, who is a household slave. The reference to Poseidippos may refer to slaves who could be hired in the agora as in a fragment of Poseidippos (23K), but even then the ' only ' cannot stand since the cook in the *Epitrepontes* is called Karion and Karion is a slave name (e.g. in Aristophanes' *Plutus*). Neither kings nor cooks help us for the *Menaechmi*. A possible indication of date may however be seen in Peniculus' remark : *contionem mediam me immersi miser* (448). Fraenkel interprets *contionem mediam* as a meeting of the *ekklesia* ; Peniculus as a poor man is unlikely to have belonged to the classes which could attend the *ekklesia* during the years of restricted franchise ; [4] this suggests a date before 322 or after 307. Stylistically the former seems more probable.

Although in the prologue the story is said to be not Attic but Sicilian, this does not imply a Sicilian author or a Sicilian title ; the natural interpretation is that the two chief characters are Sicilian and not Athenian. The original title must surely have suggested the errors ; *Didymoi, Homoioi, Adelphoi* are possibilities. Many of the plays with these titles can be excluded because the fragments reveal sentiments, scenes, or characters which have no place in the *Menaechmi*.[5] There remain four possibilities :

[1] Fraenkel, *op. cit.*, 368, n. 1.
[2] e.g. *Ad.*, 376, 420 f. ; *Andr.*, 30, 171 ; *Truc.*, 615.
[3] Ar., *Eq.*, 418 : perhaps also Philyllios, fr. 10K. *Mageiroi* occur also in the inscriptions of manumitted slaves which are dated about 330 B.C. (I.G., ii², (2.1), 1553–74, 1576–8).
[4] Aristotle (*N.E.*, 1125 a 2) describes flatterers as *thetikoi* and *tapeinoi*. The words have, I think, a social as well as an ethical meaning.
[5] e.g. *Didymoi* of Antiphanes, Alexis, Aristophon, Xenarchos, Euphron ; *Homoioi* of Poseidippos, Antiphanes, Ephippos ; *Adelphoi* of Philemon, Apollodoros, Hegesippos, Euphron. Philemon has been suggested as author by Kunst, *Szenische Studien*, 170, but the parallels with the *Mercator* are not convincing and Philemon's *Adelphoi* had a *leno* for whom there is no place in *Menaechmi*.

(*a*) an unknown play by Diphilos ; (*b*) the *Didymoi* of Anaxandrides ; (*c*) the *Adelphoi* of Alexis ; (*d*) an unknown play by an unknown author.　We have already noticed the parallel between Menaechmus' explanation of his late arrival and the similar speech in the *Casina*, Diphilos' *Kleroumenoi*, as well as the unreality of time and the violent seizure of Menaechmus I for which parallels were noted in Diphilos.　In his edition of the *Rudens*, Marx mentions, besides minor verbal parallels which carry no weight, the likeness of *Men.*, 894, with Diphilos, 98K ; but it is scarcely credible that Plautus has flattened a vivid phrase meaning ' I will give him back to you either cured or dead ' into ' I promise on my honour that he shall be healthy.'　The strongest argument against Diphilos is that this play shows neither the clear opposition of good and bad nor the climax technique which seems characteristic of that poet.　Of Anaxandrides' *Didymoi* a single word survives, *bretas*, used of a fool : of this no echo survives in the *Menaechmi*, but it ought perhaps to be noted that an old man in an unknown play of Anaxandrides (56K) warns his daughter of the difficulties of divorce and this is just the attitude of the old man in the *Menaechmi* (763 f.).　More important, however, is the fact that we know no Latin adaptation of Anaxandrides.

The *Adelphoi* of Alexis survives in a single fragment (7K) : ' Have I given anything to these women ? Tell me.' ' No (I suppose you would say that), you took it as a security and gave it back.' ' Given / given back ' was a famous antithesis used in the Halonnesos debate and dates Alexis' play soon after 342 B.C. It is possible that we have the Plautine version in *Menaechmi*, 653 f. MEN. *egon dedi ?* MA. *tu, tu istic inquam.* PE. *vin adferri noctuam, quae ' tu tu ' usque dicat tibi ? nam nos iam defessi sumus.* MEN. *per Iovem deosque omnis adiuro, uxor (satin hoc est tibi ?), non dedisse.* The point of the antithesis would be lost on a Roman audience which did not know the Greek allusion.　Plautus therefore substituted a Roman joke ; the joke must be Roman because the night owl says *tu tu* and not σύ σύ.　The original may have run :

MEN.: ' Have I given anything to these women [Erotium and her maid, cf. 1061, *pessumae*] ? '

WIFE (*or* PARASITE) : ' No, I suppose you would say that you took it as a security and gave it back.'

MEN.: ' By Zeus and all the gods I swear, wife [does this satisfy you ?], that I did not give it.'

PARASITE : ' No, rather I swear that we speak true.'

MEN. : ' It was not a present, it was a loan.'

Alexis was popular with Roman translators ; he is mentioned with Menander, Poseidippos and Apollodoros by Aulus Gellius (*N.A.*, II, 23), and seems to have provided originals for Caecilius, Turpilius, and Naevius as well as perhaps for Plautus' *Fugitivi*. It is therefore not unlikely that Alexis' *Adelphoi* was the original of the *Menaechmi*. It is of course chance that we happen to know that Euripides' *Orestes* was acted in 341/0 and his *Iphigenia* in 342/1, both sources for the mad scene in the *Menaechmi* ; it also appears likely that not very much later a memorial was set up to Euripides on which the poet was represented with the mask of Herakles in his hand. Thus a mad scene which parodied the mad scenes of Euripidean tragedy would seem to be appropriate in a comedy produced soon after 342. We have in fact a trace of such a mad scene in the Greek fragments of Alexis. The *Agonis or Hippiskos* was produced in 340/30. *Hippiskos* is part of a garment and should therefore be a recognition token ; the young man tries to persuade the *leno* to give up the girl by a display of wealth (2K). He seems also to feign madness : ' Mother, I beg you do not brandish Misgolas at me. I am not a citharode ' (3K). ' Here is a third with a rolled garland of figs. But he used to like such things when he was alive ' (4K). In the former fragment the parody of the *Orestes* is obvious. The young man pretends to see visions and his visions of furies and the dead are mixed with fourth-century Athens. The same mixture occurs in the *Menaechmi* (835 f.) : *euhoe atque euhoe, Bromie, etc. . . . qui saepe aetate in sua perdidit civem innocentem falso testimonio.*

It is therefore worth while to go a little further and consider how far we can find parallels in Alexis for the *Menaechmi*. Here we cannot expect to find exact correspondence and the question which we are asking is rather whether we can find cross connections [1] enough to enable us to say that it is not inherently

---

[1] It will be simplest to put these down as a catalogue : *Menaechmi*, 79 f. : the form of speech here, a long general introduction coming finally to the present point (96), derives from tragedy but is also common in Alexis (20, 30, 45, 182, 245K). 110 f. : criticism of wives is a commonplace of comedy ; Alexis has three examples (92, 146, 262K). 198 : Menaechmus refuses to dance, cf. Alexis, 222K. 208 f. : a marketing scene occurs in Alexis, 15/18K. 226 : returned traveller's dislike of the sea, cf. Alexis, 76, 211K. 330 : this rather

improbable that Alexis wrote the original of the *Menaechmi*. It is not of course claimed that any of these instances (even the phraseology of the cook) is peculiar to Alexis ; they belong to the common stock of Middle Comedy ; the point is rather that Alexis and the *Menaechmi* make a similar use of the common stock and in some interesting instances, e.g. the use of a general introduction (20, 45, 182, 245K), the phraseology of the cook (149K), the description of hetairai (98K), the fragments of Alexis are roughly contemporary or even earlier than the date suggested for the original of the *Menaechmi*. It seems therefore justifiable to regard the *Menaechmi* as deriving from a comedy written about 340, perhaps Alexis' *Adelphoi*.

4. INTRIGUE AND RECOGNITION PLAYS

A number of fragments point forward to the intrigue and recognition plays which are so common in New Comedy, and the original of the *Persa* was a rather special kind of intrigue play belonging to this period. The essential elements are a lover, a girl, a hindrance, and a helper. The purpose of the intrigue is to get the girl for the lover : in the course of it she may be recognised as the daughter of a citizen and then presumably the play ends with a wedding as in New Comedy. She may herself be a rich hetaira or a poor hetaira or the daughter of a citizen who has been brought up in freedom. The hindrances may be a *leno* or a *lena* or the father of the lover or a rival or more than one of these. The helpers may be the slave of the lover or the nurse of the girl. In Euboulos' *Stephanopolides*, as we have seen, a timid lover is in love with the daughter of a *lena* and is faced with an extravagant rival.[1] In his *Pamphilos* the slave of the

pompous phrase of Cylindrus ' the violence of Vulcan,' is paralleled by a cook in Alexis (149K, 16)—' Already a pack of Hephaistos' hounds leaps lightly up to heaven '. 338 f. : Messenio's description of the behaviour of *meretrices* (cf. above, 258 f., the vices of Epidamnus) is a counterpart to the longer description of the beautification of hetairai in Alexis' *Isostasion* (98K, 340/30 B.C., cf. also 49, 165K), and Messenio's view of his master (438 f.) may perhaps be compared with Alexis, 36K (360/50 B.C.). 351 : Erotium's opening instructions can be compared with Alexis, 111, 250K. 469 f. : Peniculus' complaints can be compared with Alexis, 195, 201/2K. 885 f. : the doctor occurs also in Alexis, 216K.

[1] His *Kampylion* also has complaining lover (178/41), modest hetaira (42), and drunken old woman—*lena* ?—(43). With the lover, cf. Alexis, 386/245.

lover bribes the nurse of the girl with wine, and as the girl is called *parthenos* she is presumably the daughter of a citizen (192/80-82). The love affair with a greedy hetaira can be seen in Alexis' *Demetrios* : the statement ' I am not under oath ' made by a woman can only be a rich hetaira defending her faithlessness to the young man ; he has apparently cheated his father of a talent of silver on her behalf, and the father flies into a fury with a slave who has presumably been the young man's helper.[1] Perhaps the slave is not an entirely willing helper ; when he hands over his purchases to the women (315/49) he sounds remarkably like the indignant slave in the *Truculentus* ; the pretty comparison of the mellowing and souring of human nature with wine (313/45) suggests that the father is philosophical about his sons escapades but marries him off safely at the end.

The chief types of comic love affair are thus well established before the beginning of the New Comedy.[2] A marble slab found in 1941 [3] celebrates the production of a comedy in the Attic deme of Aixone most probably in the year 340 B.C. Aixone has produced a number of inscriptions celebrating its local dramatic festival, but this is unique in having five masks in low relief, which presumably represent the cast. They are a bearded old man, an oldish woman with straggly unkempt hair and longish nose (this seems to me to correspond better with the concubine mask than with any other in Pollux' list), a slave, a youth with raised brows and wild hair, a girl with short hair tied in some sort of knot at the bottom. These masks not only show us what comedy looked like in 340 B.C. but suggest an intrigue play. The young man is in love with the girl and gets her when the slave in the middle has intrigued to help him. Further we cannot go because we do not know the relation of the old pair on the left to each other or to the young pair on the right. Father of the youth and mother of the girl possibly but other combinations are conceivable. Similarly we cannot be

---

[1] Ribbeck, 87, XIV ; XVI ; XIII. For the stern father at this time, cf. Antiphanes, 26/40 ; Anaxandrides, 159/53 ; Mnesimachus, 436/3 (undated).

[2] Other examples are Euboulos' *Pornoboskos* (194/88) : *leno* and young hetaira ; Alexis' *Kouris* (334/107-8), town and country sons and parasite ; Antiphanes' *Neottis* (79/168-9), young hetaira and her brother (a slave ?) ; *Leno* ; Amphis' *Kouris* (242/23), young hetaira ; Anaxilas' *Neottis* (269/21-2), young hetaira : warning against rich hetairai.

[3] Pl. III : I have discussed the date in *J.H.S.*, lxxi, 222, n. 7.

certain of the details but we seem to have the cast of an intrigue comedy in a set of terracottas from an Attic grave which can be dated before but probably not very long before 348 B.C.[1] Here we have a seated slave with his chin pillared on his hand, thinking out an intrigue. Presumably an old man in a felt hat and a skin cloak is his master. A seated man with a purse suggests that money was diverted from its rightful owner as in the *Persa*, *Truculentus*, and *Asinaria*. A fat, clean-shaven man with a wreath on his head is probably a parasite. A bearded man standing with crossed legs is probably the lover, as the young lead of comedy was normally bearded at this time. There remain the young woman and the elderly woman who is perhaps her mother; she seems to wear the concubine's mask as on the Aixone relief. We cannot be certain of the details, but the girl and the excogitating slave make it certain that this was an intrigue comedy. The man with a purse (possibly a bailiff) and the farmer's clothes of the old man strongly suggest that the method of the intrigue was diversion of agricultural money. Otherwise except for the *Persa* we have little evidence : it is probable that the girl in Alexis' *Mandragorizomene* took mandragora to escape from *leno* or rival lover, and it is possible that the 'heir' in the Berlin papyrus[2] is not really an heir ; a death may have been feigned to help him to get control of the girl who is in the possession of the *leno*.

Two other themes are common in New Comedy plays of this general type : recognitions leading to marriage and babies sometimes exposed and sometimes not. In the plays of which we have been speaking we cannot be certain whether a recognition took place or not. But we have five probable cases of recognition. Alexis' *Agonis* has an alternative title *Hippiskos*, which means a garment. The natural deduction is that Agonis was a young hetaira who was recognised as the daughter of a citizen by a piece of cloth preserved from the time when she was exposed or kidnapped. The fragments show her lover trying to impress the *leno* by a display of silver and perhaps then trying to frighten him by pretending to be mad (297/2–4). In Euboulos' *Neottis* (188/69) an old man says : 'I hate inscribed cups more than anything. And yet how like this is to the one my son had when he vanished.' This sounds like a recognition token by which

[1] Bieber, *H.T.*, figs. 129–35.　　　　[2] 48P.

PLATE III.—MARBLE RELIEF CELEBRATING PRODUCTION OF COMEDY AT AIXONE

Athens. From Aixone. Probably 340 B.C.

the son would be recognised ; it does not preclude the possibility that Neottis was also recognised. Antiphanes' *Flute Girl
or Twins*, as has already been suggested, must almost have been
a recognition play. In his *Hydria* (103/212) the youth is in love
with ' a hetaira, living in a neighbouring house, an Athenian,
without guardian or relations, golden-hearted '. It seems very
likely that she was recognised and possible that the hydria contained recognition tokens as well as dowry. Finally in Alexis'
Olynthia a noble girl is living in a poor household (356/162).
She must surely be loved by a young Athenian and it is tempting
to suppose that she is recognised. Similar titles are the *Amprakiotis* and *Samia* of Anaxandrides, the *Boiotis* of Theophilos, and
the *Milesia* of Alexis.

Suidas tells us that Anaxandrides was the first to introduce
love affairs and the rape of maidens. One method of reconciling
this with the similar statement in the Life of Aristophanes about
the *Kokalos* [1] is to suppose that Aristophanes introduced the
theme from tragedy into mythological comedy and Anaxandrides took the further step of transferring it into the comedy of
everyday life. The only traces in the fragments are the baby in
Alexis' *Stratiotes* and the title of Kratinos' *Pseudhypobolimaios*,
which must almost mean a suppositious child subsequently recognised as belonging to the family. Two South Italian vases [2] may
be quoted here, but we cannot tell that they do not represent
mythological comedy : on one an elderly man views with
astonishment a baby lying on the ground, on another a young
man gives a baby to a woman. The evidence is sufficient to
confirm Suidas' statement about Anaxandrides, and we may
therefore suppose that the *Kanephoros* and *Phialephoros* of
Anaxandrides and the *Kalathephoroi* of Euboulos anticipated the
New Comedy plays with similar titles in which the girl was first
observed by her lover at a festival.

The kind of play which we have been discussing is the kind of
play of which Aristotle was thinking when he spoke of a probable
combination of incidents with the addition of chance names.
The further question which must be considered later is the
relation of this kind of comedy to tragedy. For the moment,
however, let us remember the distance which the obscene comic
costume puts between comedy and tragedy and the prevailing

[1] Cf. above, p. 17.   [2] *Jb.*, 1886, 299, n ; Bieber, *H.T.*, fig. 385.

tone of earthy realism and knockabout which the retention of that comic costume implies. The one intrigue comedy of this period which we know in a complete, albeit an adapted, form is the original of Plautus' *Persa*.

The essential passage [1] for dating the *Persa* is the story invented by Toxilus (498) : his master, the Athenian Timarchides, is in Persia and the Persians have captured a city in Arabia ; a Persian friend of Timarchides arrives in Athens with an Arabian girl to sell. No doubt is thrown on the plausibility of this story. The *leno* Dordalus is not tricked because he is ignorant of current affairs but because the situation is sufficiently plausible for him to accept it as real. The Persians must have still been an independent power when this play was written, and the bottom date therefore is 334. Dordalus has a considerable part and a *leno* does not, as far as I know, appear as a character in comedy earlier than two plays of Euboulos which can be dated respectively 350/40 (67K) and 350/30 (88K). Three passages of the *Persa* make the dating a little more precise : Athens could hardly be called *fortunatae atque opiparae* (549) in the years immediately after Chaeronea ; *cynicus egens* (123) may be an allusion to Diogenes, who did not arrive in Athens much before 340 B.C. ; [2] a journey to Eretria (322) would perhaps be unlikely between 343 and 341 B.C. when Eretria was in the hands of Philip's friend Kleitarchos.[3] The probable limits therefore seem to be 341- 338 B.C. Chronologically, Nausikrates' *Persis* is possible since he won his first Lenaean victory in the early 'fifties, and the fragment about lions in Attica (296/3) might possibly in the original have belonged to the riddling dialogue with the girl. It is perfectly possible that Plautus translated an original by a little-known poet since we have the certainly attested example of Demophilos' *Onagos*. We cannot be certain about the author but we must accept the bottom date of 334 and probably 338 B.C.

This date excludes the three chief poets of New Comedy and makes the *Persa* an example of Middle Comedy about twenty years before our earliest surviving Menander. It is therefore of considerable interest as evidence of Middle Comedy in its later

---

[1] See Wilamowitz, *Kl. Schr.*, i, 227 ; Hueffner, *op. cit.*, 70 ; Maidment, C.Q., 1935, 15, n. 8.
[2] Leo, *Hermes*, xli, 1906, 441 ff. ; Dudley, *History of Cynicism*, 23.
[3] *C.A.H.*, VI. 248, 253.

stages and some attempt must be made to recapture the flavour of the original and relate it to earlier and later comedy. The story is simple : a slave, Toxilus, is in love with a girl owned by a *leno*, brothel-keeper Dordalus ; another slave, Sagaristio, who has been sent to buy oxen for his master, gives him this money to buy the girl ; Toxilus persuades a parasite Saturio to lend him his daughter, who is dressed up as an Arabian captive and sold to Dordalus ; Saturio then reclaims his daughter and the play ends with the slaves feasting and discomfiture for Dordalus. That a brothel-keeper should be tricked out of one of his girls is satisfying to any audience of any period but otherwise there is no general moral in this play, although there are patches of moralising in the parasite's first speech and in the two scenes with his daughter. Nor is there much characterisation ; the slaves are clever, the brothel-keeper shameless, the parasite sacrifices his daughter for a good meal, the daughter is impossibly full of wise-cracks, but these colours are all superficial ; the characters of the *Pseudolus*, which borrows much of the structure of the *Persa*, are drawn much more fully and are interesting in themselves ; in the *Persa* the situations in each particular scene are more interesting than the characters ; in the *Pseudolus* (and the other plays of the same general type, *Kolax*, *Poenulus*, and *Curculio*) the interest lies rather in the characters as they appear in the successive situations in the play and not chiefly in the situations themselves. The most striking parallels with New Comedy, however, are with the *Pseudolus*, where we find again four elements of the *Persa* story : a message of distress sent by the girl to her lover, preliminary meeting with the brothel-keeper and abuse of him, a letter brought to the brothel-keeper, and the tricking of the brothel-keeper by a disguise. The diversion of farming money to other purposes recurs in the *Truculentus* and the *Asinaria*. As we are certain that the original of the *Persa* is much earlier than any of these plays, we also know that the original of the *Persa* was not a late and desiccated copy but an early outline or diagram, which was later developed into a three-dimensional picture by the poets of New Comedy.

The Athenian audience would presumably find the intrigue exciting, and by the intrigue I mean the disguising of the girl and Sagaristio and the tricking of Dordalus. In addition there are two ' witty conceptions ', as Aristophanes calls them, in this play : the parasite selling his daughter for food, for which there is an obvious ancestor in the Megarian selling his daughters in the *Acharnians*, and the slave buying his own mistress.   As the slave buys his mistress for nothing, no economic impossibility is involved (and we know in any case from pseudo-Xenophon that rich slaves were not unknown in Athens so that the idea would not seem hopelessly extravagant).[1]   As the master is in Asia, we have no need to ask what will happen when he returns. But the play remains unique among Greek comedies in having a slave intriguing for himself and not for his young master.   We know very little about the slave comedy as distinct from the slave in comedy, and this again gives the *Persa* a special value. We can see a formal ancestor in the *Knights* of Aristophanes ; there three of the characters are slaves (Nikias, Demosthenes, and Kleon) and the sausage-seller belongs possibly to a lower social stratum than the parasite of the *Persa*.   But the *Knights* is political allegory as perhaps also the *Deserters* of Pherekrates and *Helots* of Eupolis, which presumably had choruses of slaves. We know nothing of Theopompos' *Paides* or Plato's *Paidarion* but the titles may indicate slave comedy.   In the early fourth century Karion in the *Ploutos* is a stage further on the road which leads from Xanthias in the *Frogs* to New Comedy, and the slave is felt to be so important that his mask is one of the two represented on the grave relief of a comic poet who died in the early fourth century.[2]   Slaves must also have been important in Antiphanes' *Dyspratos* and *Drapetagogos*, but these titles almost imply the presence of masters as well.   Slave revels we know from paintings of Middle Comedy [3] and New Comedy [4] and from the closing scenes of Menander's *First Adelphoi* (*Stichus*).[5] The slave lover occurs again in Menander's *Heros*, but is speedily made to give up his claim.   Let us try to sum up this evidence. Slave scenes were always popular in Greek comedy.   In the *Knights* (and perhaps in other plays) they occupy a considerable

---

[1] In an inscription of about 330 B.C., *I.G.*, ii (2, i), 1566, l. 33 ; 1570, l. 79, two *demosioi* (public slaves) manumit two slaves. In Aeschines, I, 54, a public slave Pittakos is described as rich and maintained Timarchos for some time. For the fifth century cf. Ehrenberg, *People of Aristophanes*, 184 ff.

[2] Pl. I.   [3] Bieber, *H.T.*, fig. 378.

[4] Bieber, *H.T.*, fig. 228 ; Simon, *Comicae Tabellae*, 145.

[5] According to Sotion in Alexis' *Asotodidaskalos* (306/25) a slave Xanthias encouraged his fellow slaves to lead a life of pleasure : Athenaeus doubts the genuineness of the play.

space but are used for political allegory. In New Comedy they are still popular as episodes, e.g. Onesimos, Daos, and Syriskos in the *Epitrepontes*, Grumio and Tranio in the *Mostellaria*, but in so far as the slave takes an important part in the action he acts for his master and not for himself. The *Persa* has ordinary scenes of slave-banter particularly between Sophoclidisca and Paegnium, which may have been extended by Plautus but could perfectly well have existed in the original (a hierarchy below stairs is attested for Athens by the relations between the Paphlagonian and the other two slaves in the *Knights*), but the striking novelty is that the hero is a slave and intrigues for himself and not for his master.

The parasite, Saturio, introduces himself in a monologue (53 f.) which belongs to a tradition going back to Epicharmus, and Toxilus secures his goodwill by elaborate preparations for a meal, which are in the tradition of Middle Comedy.[1] He is presumably the parasite of Toxilus' master and therefore like Gelasimus in Menander's *First Adelphi* (*Stichus*) is having a thin time while his host is in Asia. It is however interesting that he contrasts himself with the sycophant (62) and compares himself with the Cynic philosopher[2] (123). The sycophant like the parasite lives at somebody else's expense and therefore his life also is open to the idler like Saturio, but Saturio regards him as purely destructive whereas the parasite at least gives pleasure with his fund of Attic stories[3] (395).

Saturio is unique among parasites in having a daughter. Almost her first words (341) are a quotation from Sophocles' *Electra* (597) and she goes on to echo Haemon in the *Antigone* (635, 718) ;[4] her whole conversation with her father consists of a string of high moral sentiments, neatly rounded and probably ultimately derived from Greek tragedy. The situation is comic, and in the original the tragic quotations of this impossibly virtuous girl must have been laughable. But there is a faint reminiscence of this scene in New Comedy when the young man, again like Haemon in the *Antigone*, uses philosophy to persuade his father to help him in his love affair (e.g. in Menander's

[1] See *Studies in Menander*, 163 ; Prehn, *Quaestiones Plautinae*, 12.
[2] Cf. Leo, *Pl. F.*[1], 110.
[3] ' Attic, *not* Sicilian.' Pollux lists a ' Sicilian ' among his parasite masks.
[4] 383 f. may also be a reminiscence of Sophocles if, as I think, *Amphitruo*, 839 f., is based on Sophocles' *Alkmene*, cf. below, p. 88.

Dyskolos, 128K).[1]   The same high tone is struck again when the girl is questioned by Sagaristio and Dordalus (549 ff.), and when she is asked her father's name, she quotes Orestes' answer to Iphigenia in the *Iphigenia in Tauris* (499) : ' rightly we should be called Unfortunate '. The sentiments are not used for characterisation as in the later more sparing use of New Comedy. This girl is as unreal and has the same sort of unreality as the doll in the Tales of Hoffmann.   The ancestry of this style leads back to the oraclemonger of the *Birds*, but nearer examples can be found in the riddling cook of Euboulos' *Sphingokarion* (201/107) and the riddling Sappho of Antiphanes' *Sappho* (95/196), both of which were produced twenty to thirty years before the *Persa*.

Here then we have the intrigue comedy at an early stage.   In its later developments in New Comedy, this intrigue becomes merely the machinery by which the characters are displayed and the interest lies in the characters themselves and some positive value which is being put forward.   At this stage the intrigue itself is exciting ; the parasite, his daughter, and the slaves are amusing ; the brothel-keeper as usual is shameless.   The play is good fun and that is enough.

5. Mythological Comedy

In the early part of the fourth century comic poets made use of high poetry and particularly tragedy in various ways : parody of tragic lines or diction purely to raise laughter, borrowing of tragic technique, introduction of heroic figures into an everyday context, use of heroic figures to speak prologues, and translation of tragic plots into comic idiom. Most of these survive into our period, but I only know one instance of the introduction of a lone heroic figure into an everyday context like Ploutos and Penia in the *Ploutos* or, as we must suppose, Dionysos in the *Dionysos Asketes* of Aristomenes. The single instance is the *Orestautokleides* of Timokles, and we cannot say how far this is analogous : we only know that the homosexualist Autokleides is described as surrounded by furious hetairai like Orestes surrounded by the Furies in the prologue of the *Eumenides*.

Parody of tragic lines continues : perhaps the most satisfactory

[1] Cf. also 383 f. with *Aul.*, 239 ; *Adelph.*, 345.

is the line of Anaxandrides (162/67) : ' it was the will of the
city which pays no heed to laws ' ; Anaxandrides has substituted *polis* for *physis* in a famous line of Euripides' *Auge*
(920N) ; but we may also notice a pleasant perversion by
Antiphanes (112/231) of Haimon's wisdom in the *Antigone*
(712 f.) : ' Tell me what is life. Drinking, say I. You see
beside the winter torrents all the trees that get wet night and
day are tall and beautiful. But those that resist, because they
have some thirst and drought, perish roots and all.' Presumably
this is part of a parasite's speech. Similar in kind is the wisdom
of the girl in the *Persa* which we have already quoted. In the
Agonis of Alexis and the mad scene of the *Menaechmi*, elements
are taken from the mad scenes of Euripides. That is part of the
fun, particularly the mixture of tragedy and contemporary
Athens in the line (298/3) : ' Mother, I beseech you, don't set
Misgolas on me.' But at the same time the comic poet has
borrowed the idea of a mad scene from tragedy, and parody
shades over into borrowing of technique.

Borrowing of technique is difficult to trace in the fragments.
One special instance, the prologue figure, is clear, where it gives
the play its title. The only god is Timokles' *Dionysos*, but a
god perhaps spoke the prologue of Antiphanes' *Aiolos* (17/18),
Ganymedes (40/73), and the epilogue of his *Thamyras* (52/105) ;
these plays are undated, but in view of the scanty number of
mythological comedies in New Comedy are probably the work
of the earlier Antiphanes. Antiphanes' *Tychon* (if it is not the
name of the soldier), Euboulos' *Orthanes*, and Timokles' *Konisalos*
(undated) are named after fertility spirits, who presumably spoke
the prologue. Antiphanes' *Knoithideus* and *Arkas* (or *Arkadia*)
are local personifications, another such perhaps spoke the prologue speech of Heniochos' *Cities* (?) ; Dithyrambos (Amphis)
and Hybris (Anaxandrides) are known as names of satyrs and
they may have appeared in that form. Anteros (Anaxandrides)
is clearly modelled on Eros. Echo (Euboulos), Pannychis
(Euboulos and Alexis), Lethe (Timokles), and Poiesis (Antiphanes) belong to the general class of Nymphs. In all these
cases there was probably a prologue speech modelled on the
divine prologues of Euripidean tragedy.[1] We have no means

[1] We cannot tell who spoke the paratragic prologue of Anaxandrides' *Nereus*
(145/30).

G

of tracing whether the prologue speech was ever, as later in
Menander, preceded by a dramatic scene.

It is natural to ask whether borrowing of technique in the
non-mythological comedies is direct or through the medium of
mythological comedy, whether for instance the slave intriguer
comes direct from such plays as Sophocles' *Elektra* or Euripides'
Ion or through the medium of a mythological comedy.   But the
question is perhaps academic since most of the poets of Middle
Comedy wrote mythological as well as non-mythological
comedy and were therefore steeped in Greek tragedy.   The
change in form to what Aristotle calls a system of probable
incidents, the shrinking of the lyric element, the growth of
clearly defined character types all show comedy approximating
to tragedy ;   we cannot see the details but we can be certain
of the development.   At the same time the actual incidents of
the love comedy, rape, intrigue, recognition, etc., are incidents
which had been already dramatised in tragedy, particularly by
Euripides.   If, however, we survey the titles of mythological
comedy, we cannot see that tragedies of this particular type in
any way predominate as models.   In fact, the only titles which
seem to me certainly to belong here as possible models for the
love comedy are Antiphanes' *Aiolos*, Anaxandrides' *Helen*,
Euboulos' *Auge*, *Danae*, *Ion*, *Phoinix*.   All are presumably based
on tragedies by Euripides with the same titles, and these contained rapes, recognitions, and intrigues.   It is interesting that
we do not find among our Middle Comedy parodies some of
the plays which most obviously inspired scenes in New Comedy
such as Euripides' *Alope*, *Skyrioi*, *Melanippe Desmotis*, and
Sophocles' *Tyro*.   Perhaps the development was something like
this.   Parody in the early stages of mythological comedy brought
into comedy situations from tragedy which could be developed
in the idiom of non-mythological comedy, and as non-mythological comedy advanced further towards probable plots and
detailed character drawing more and more of such situations
were borrowed direct from tragedy.   In time this kind of
comedy, which was gradually developing into New Comedy,
outshone mythological comedy, which still depended for its
effect on the contrast between the comic costume and everyday
sentiments on the one hand and on the other the heroic names
and atmosphere of its heroes.

The decline of mythological comedy during our period is remarkable. In the first half of the fourth century something between a third and a half of the dated plays have mythological titles but between 350 and 320 B.C. the proportion falls to a tenth. This strongly suggests that the desire for probable incidents and chance names killed the old type of mythological comedy, however strongly the new type of comedy may itself be inspired by tragedy. From numerous fragments of mythological comedy we can see that the formula has not been changed ; the tragic story is transferred to the lowest level of contemporary life. Pelops is an Oriental complaining of the small meals in Athens ; in his country the Great King was given a whole roast camel (Antiphanes, 81/172). Dolon is so fat that he cannot tie his shoes up and he never had to wash up because he always licked the plates clean (Euboulos, 175/30). Oidipous is apparently a parasite and curses all who give subscription feasts (Euboulos, 189/72 ; cf. S.O.T., 233 f.). Prokris' hound lies on a Milesian rug under a fine cloak ; its food is mixed with goose milk and its feet are rubbed with myrrh from Megallos (Euboulos, 195/90). Athamas says that a hetaira is much better disposed to a man than his wife (Amphis, 236/1). Herakles, asked to choose a book from Linos' library, finds Simos' cookery book (Alexis, 345/135). These are sufficient examples to give the atmosphere. These people we recognise in another set of terracottas [1] found in the same grave as those discussed above. Only the presence of Herakles shows that these little figures belong to a mythological comedy, and Herakles is the fat, greedy, goggling-eyed monster, whom we know already from a fifth-century representation of comedy.[2] The rest of the cast consists of a nurse with a baby, a young woman, a weeping old man in a felt cap or *pilos*, a seated slave, a slave marketing, and a slave with a large pot on his head. The conjunction of the baby with Herakles suggests very strongly that this is the Auge story. In the only fragment of Euboulos' *Auge* someone is warned not to be too late for a magnificent feast, perhaps the old man from the country who is presumably Aleos. We may therefore have the cast of Euboulos' *Auge* in these terracottas and an illustration of the same play can probably be seen

[1] Bieber, *H.T.*, figs. 122-8.
[2] e.g. Pfuhl, *MuZ.*, fig. 572 ; Beazley, *A.R.V.*, 848/22.

on a South Italian vase of the third quarter of the fourth century.[1]

It is probable that after the middle of the century the farce became less broad and all-pervading, and this seems to have happened by the time of the original of the *Amphitruo*, which, as will be seen, may be dated soon after 331. Although it is so late and therefore to some extent untypical of the bulk of the mythological plays which belong early in this period, it is worth examining at some length because it survives complete.

As far as we know, Plautus always used Greek comedy as his source and therefore it is unlikely that in this single case he went direct to Greek tragedy, as has been suggested.[2] We have therefore a double problem; what was the immediate source of Plautus and what was the source of his immediate source? The problem is difficult but worth considering because only here can we see in any detail how a comic poet treated his mythological sources.

The story of Zeus and Alkmene is told by Apollodorus (II, iv, 8). Zeus impersonates Amphitryon, lies with Alkmene, tells her the story of the battle and triples the length of the night. Amphitryon arrives, asks his wife why she does not welcome him, and she tells him that he had come the night before and slept with her. The same story is repeated with little variation by Hyginus (XXIX). So far it agrees with the *Amphitruo*. A detail can be added from Charon of Lampsacus (Athenaeus, 475c); he saw in Sparta the golden cup given by Zeus to Alkmene when he impersonated Amphitryon; the cup therefore had come into the story by the early fifth century B.C. In Apollodorus, Amphitryon learns the truth from Teiresias; Alkmene bears two sons, and Herakles is already eight months old when he strangles the snakes. In the *Amphitruo* the story is telescoped : the twins are born the night after the long night, the snakes arrive as soon as the twins are born and Amphitruo then proposes to consult Teiresias after the birth. The arrival of the snakes immediately after the birth of Herakles and the visit to Teiresias agree with Pindar (*Nem.*, I, 35 f.) ; in Theocritus (XXIV), Herakles is ten months old when he strangles the snakes, and it is Alkmene who summons Teiresias.

---

[1] Bieber, *H.T.*, fig. 358. For other South Italian vases with scenes from mythological comedy cf. *C.Q.*, xlii, 20 f.　　[2] Caldera, *R.F.I.C.*, xxv, 145.

There is one other important element in the story which appears in no literary version but on two vases, one Paestan and one Campanian,[1] both belonging to the third quarter of the fourth century B.C. : Alkmene has taken refuge on an altar, Amphitryon and Antenor have piled wood round it and propose to set fire to it : Zeus sends the Clouds [2] to extinguish the conflagration. The Paestan vase includes, if I interpret the mind of the painter aright, a detail which is otherwise only known from Pindar (*Isthm.*, VII, 5), the golden rain which heralded Zeus' first arrival. The vases are likely to derive from tragedy since Python, the painter of the Paestan vase, painted several other tragic scenes. The *Alkmene* of Euripides has been generally accepted as a source [3] because Plautus in the *Rudens* (86) mentions a famous storm in the *Alkmene* of Euripides. The conclusion is confirmed by a fragment of Euripides' play (90N) : ' How did you come to think of using a torch ? ' This formula could not be applied to someone using a torch for a normal purpose, for instance to Hermes guiding Zeus on his nocturnal adventure (as apparently in Plato's *Nyx Makra*, 84–5K). It must be a reprimand to someone misusing a torch, and the natural explanation is that someone chides Amphitryon after he has lit the fire round Alkmene. We need not suppose that the scene was acted on the stage, the smoke may have been seen coming from the palace as in the *Bacchae* (596 f.) and perhaps in the *Phaethon* (781N). The reprimand may have been quoted by a messenger reporting the action which the vase-painters have illustrated ; the nearest parallel for such a reprimand is perhaps Peleus' opening words in the *Andromache* (547 f.) and for quotation in a messenger speech Ion's questioning of the old man who tried to poison him (*Ion*, 1210 f.). We cannot tell much more about Euripides' *Alkmene* except that complaints about the power of wealth (95/6N) suggest that Amphitryon found Alkmene pregnant and believed that some rich man was responsible. A fragment about the duty of slaves to please their masters (93N) expresses a sentiment which is repeated by Sosia in the *Amphitruo* (958, cf. 557) ; but it is too general to build on, and such sentiments are common

---

[1] British Museum, F 149 and 193 ; CV, IV a, pl. 1, and pl. 6,7. Trendall, *Paestan Pottery*, 56.
[2] Beazley, *E.V.P.*, 105.
[3] e.g. Wilamowitz, *Herakles*, I, 54 ; Séchan, *Étude sur la tragédie Grecque*, 244.

in Plautine slaves. The burning of Alkmene does not appear in Plautus but this does not by itself prove that the earlier part of Plautus' play is not based on Euripides. On the other hand, it is incredible that Apollodorus and Hyginus should have omitted this striking episode if their stories were based on Euripides, and the Apollodorus version, in which Amphitryon learns the truth from Teiresias, seems to exclude the burning. As the earlier part of Apollodorus/Hyginus agrees with the *Amphitruo* and as we have no evidence for the appeal to Teiresias in Euripides' play, we should probably assume another tragic source. It seems likely that the essential difference between Euripides' play and the other tragedy, which we may reasonably ascribe to Sophocles as he is the most famous tragic writer on this theme, was that in Sophocles Amphitryon returned at the end of the Long Night in which Herakles was conceived, while in Euripides he returned only when Alkmene was already pregnant. We may then suppose further that in Sophocles, as in Apollodorus, Amphitryon learned the truth from Teiresias and the birth and strangling of the snakes were prophecies, but that in Euripides the birth took place after the burning of Alkmene and the snakes arrived immediately.

If this is true, Plautus' original combined the two tragedies [1] into a chronologically impossible but therefore amusing whole. To appreciate the further changes, we must examine the *Amphitruo* in greater detail. The prologue is spoken by Mercurius, and Hermes may well have spoken the prologue in the tragic original. Mercurius calls the play a *tragicomedia* (54 f.) : it cannot be a comedy because it has gods and kings but a slave also has a part, and therefore the mixed name is necessary. This implies the Aristotelian distinction between the better men represented in tragedy and the worse men represented in comedy, but the distinction was already made at least implicitly in the fifth century. The term *tragicomedia* is not known in Greek and is perhaps impossible as a Greek formation, but *Komoidotragoidia* is recorded as a title of plays by Alkaios and Anaxandrides ; there is nothing to be learnt from the fragments of these and it is difficult to see how they would differ from the ordinary mythological comedy, which was itself a translation of heroic

---

[1] This is, I think, the answer to the difficulties raised by Kakridis, *Rh. Mus.*, lvii, 463.

life into everyday terms. Here (62) Mercurius mentions the addition of a slave as the essential comic element ; this is true but an understatement. What the comic poet did is clear. He found in the tragedy the doubling of Zeus and Amphitryon, but it seems unlikely that in tragedy Zeus appeared on the stage in the guise of Amphitryon. He brings both on the stage and doubles Hermes with Sosias, thus making the whole comedy of errors possible, as well as the arbitration between Zeus and Amphitryon. The cup forms an additional element of mystification :[1] we do not know whether the cup given by Zeus to Alkmene was traditionally the cup taken by Amphitryon from Pterelaos, but certainly the comic poet has made an increased use of it so that it performs the same kind of function as the stolen cloak in the *Menaechmi*. It is perhaps likely that in Sophocles also the cup originally belonged to Pterelaos and was used by Alkmene to prove the truth of her assertions that Amphitryon had visited her the night before ; it may even be that a slave arrived and announced its disappearance like the messenger who announces the disappearance of Helen in Euripides' play (*Hel.*, 597). Then the comic poet has added chiefly the mystification of Sosias when Hermes describes the cup (418). The audience is carefully prepared for the comedy of errors itself : Zeus is identical with Amphitryon and appears therefore as an elderly general (121, 1072) ; Hermes is identical with Sosias and appears as a bearded slave (124, 444). Hermes is distinguished by little wings in his hat (143), as commonly on works of art, and Zeus by a golden band round his hair (144), which shows under his hat.[2]

The ' first deception ' is the scene in which Hermes frightens Sosias away from the house on the ground that he is himself a better Sosias and proves his identity because he knows details of Pterelaos' cup and Amphitryon's ring and of Sosias' own behaviour during the battle. It is a parody of tragic recognition scenes and the comic poet was perhaps inspired by the use of the golden cup to establish Alkmene's identity. There are two other elements in this scene : thug comedy and the report of the

[1] Referred to in the prologue, 138 ; by Sosias, 260 ; quoted by Hermes as a means of recognition, 418 ; presented by Zeus to Alkmene, 534 ; absent from Sosias' luggage, 773 f.

[2] For a hairband showing under a petasos, cf. Pfuhl, *MuZ.*, figs, 424, 598. For Sosias' lantern (149, 341) cf. Epikrates, 285/8K.

battle. Hermes' violent treatment of Sosias (369 f.) is carefully prepared by Sosias' timorous entry (153) and his description of his own conduct in the battle (198, cf. 427). The thug comedy is traditional and the softening-up process (296 f.) has been compared to similar scenes in Diphilos.[1] Sosias' opening [2] recalls Epicharmus' parasite (153, with Epicharmos, fr. 34/5) who fears that the police will beat him on the way home. During the battle [3] he stayed in his tent like Theophrastos' coward (*Char.*, XXV, 4) or Stasimus in the *Trinummus* (726) : the ultimate source may be Thersites' attempt to escape the hunt of the Calydonian boar (*Schol.*, *IC.* B212). But he tells the story as if he had been in the battle himself ; and the telling is a rehearsal for a later recital to Alkmene ; [4] only thus can the poet tell the story because Sosias is not allowed to meet Alkmene, and the story evidently interested him and his public, not as a piece of comic parody but as a magnificent description in itself. Plautus may have expanded and to some extent Romanised his original ; it seems for instance hardly likely that a Greek poet would have left Hermes on the stage during this long narrative which is not addressed to him. But we can assume that the story belongs to the Greek original ; in fact, considerable likeness has been seen with the messenger speech of Euripides' *Herakleidai* (799 f.) in which also the preparations for the battle and the clash of the two armies are described at length, and we may suppose that in the tragic original the story ended in a duel between Amphitryon and Pterelaos, just as in the *Herakleidai* the general mêlée gives place to Iolaos' pursuit of Eurystheus. The exciting new thing, which made the story worth retelling for the comic poet, must have been the cavalry charge from the right wing which brought Amphitryon the victory. These tactics first became prominent in the time of Epameinondas and it may be relevant to remember that Epameinondas was a Theban and Amphitryon was operating from Thebes. We do in fact know of a famous picture in Athens in which the Athenian

---

[1] See below, p. 160 f. Cf. also K., iii/432/125. Palmer notes parallel of 358 with E., *Bacch.*, 968.   [2] Cf. Fraenkel, *op. cit.*, 181 ff.

[3] On the battle scene see Fraenkel, *op. cit.*, 349 f., and more recently Riess, C.Q., XXXV, 155 f. ; Guillemin, *Humanitas*, X, 42 ; Janne, *Révue Belge*, 1933, 515 ; Halkin, *Antiquité Classique*, 1948, 297.

[4] The parallel to Epicharmos, 99 (Kaibel), has been shown to be an illusion by Stanford, *C.P.*, xlv, 167.

cavalry were shown routing the Theban cavalry and the most prominent figures on either side were, according to Pausanias, Gryllos the son of Xenophon and Epameinondas. This was Euphranor's picture of the battle of Mantineia (362 B.C.), which occupied the long wall of a stoa in the Kerameikos at Athens. The picture made the tactics familiar, but in that battle the Theban was unsuccessful and in any case Epameinondas was not an heroic figure nor were his opponents. The only fourth-century encounter in which a cavalry charge decided the issue between figures of heroic scale was the encounter of Alexander and the Great King as depicted in the Alexander mosaic, an accurate copy of a painting which dates from Alexander's time.[1] In default of other evidence this dates the original of the *Amphitruo* soon after 331 B.C.

The next scene is the farewell scene between Zeus and Alkmene.[2] The farewell scene is comedy. It is unlikely that Sophocles brought Zeus on the stage as Alkmene's lover, but a line of Plato's *Nyx Makra* may be evidence for an earlier comic version of the scene : ' it is absurd that my husband does not worry about me at all ' (624/83K—*Amph.* 508). Here Zeus has a touch of the braggart soldier (504 f.), and Hermes plays the slave who assists his master in love : in an earlier comedy, which is illustrated on a Paestan vase [3] of about 350 B.C., Hermes with a lamp guides Zeus, who carries a ladder with which to climb to Alkmene's window.

After the dawn, which Zeus now commands to end the long night and which probably marks an act division in the original, Amphitryon arrives with Sosias. The master disbelieves the slave's story that he has been chased away by his double. This is the common scene of angry master and frightened slave which we know from fifth-century tragedy, e.g. Kreon and the guard in the *Antigone*, as well as fourth-century comedy : Plautus has undoubtedly expanded it. Then Alkmene comes out ; she speaks of the divine rule that pleasure should be accompanied by grief and of her present experience of this ; sentiment and arrangement recall Deianeira's opening speech in the *Trachiniai*

---

[1] Cf. Rumpf, *J.H.S.*, lxvii, 15.

[2] Leo, *Pl. F.*[1], 202, believes that the prologue speech of Mercurius comes from the original ; it may however have been lengthened by Plautus.

[3] Vatican, 121 ; Bieber, *H.T.*, fig. 368 ; Trendall, *P.P.*, no. 48.

and the Sophoclean Alkmene may not have spoken very differently. The basis of the scene between Amphitryon and Alkmene is also Sophoclean, as is shown by its echo in Apollodorus ; but Amphitryon, like Zeus before him, behaves with the pomposity of the braggart soldier (676). Sosias is added by the comic poet and plays the traditional part of *bomolochos* ; [1] in the tragedy, as has been suggested already, an attendant may have announced the disappearance of the golden cup. At the end of this scene Amphitryon does not seek Teiresias, as in the tragedy, but Naukrates, a relative of Alkmene who may prove the truth of Amphitryon's story ; his unheroic name shows that he belongs to comedy rather than to tragedy.

Alkmene's speech (882), when she comes out again,[2] opens with a variant of the common tragic theme—' I will tell my misery to the open air '.[3] It would be interesting to know if Sophocles' Alkmene also threatened to leave Amphitryon when he doubted her loyalty. If so, a tragic ancestor is provided for the scene in the *Menaechmi* (780 ff.) where the wife threatens to leave her husband, and for the various other *apoleipousai* of comedy. Zeus in the character of Amphitryon pacifies her by saying that his conduct in the preceding scene had merely been designed to test her loyalty and clinches this unconvincing fiction, for which the only analogy known to me is in the test devised by Antipho in Menander's *First Adelphoi* (*Stichus*, 126), by resounding sentiments on the instability of human relationship which are near enough to well-known passages of the *Ajax* (678 f.) and *Oedipus Coloneus* (607 ff.) to' claim a Sophoclean ancestry. At the end Sosias is sent to fetch Blepharo, the pilot of Amphitryon's ship ; this is merely preparation for the arbitration scene which comes later. Zeus then summons Hermes and returns indoors with Alkmene. Hermes enters as a running slave. There may be some Plautine expansion here, but the running slave is a Greek invention since we see a very early stage in the arrival of the messenger in the *Birds* (1122),[4] and

---

[1] Cf. Pickard-Cambridge, *Dithyramb, etc.*,[2] 174.

[2] In his preceding speech (861 f.) Juppiter has announced the further course of the play ; it may or may not derive from Plautus' original but must stand or fall with the earlier speech of Mercury (463 f.).

[3] Cf. Page on Euripides, *Medea*, 57.

[4] Prehn, *Q.Pl.*, 17, interprets Klearchos, fr. 1 (K., ii, 408), as the arrival of a *servus currens*. The Strobilus fragment also seems to be this (64P3).

here the Greek poet clearly wanted to contrast the speedy entry of Hermes with the immediately following entry of Amphitryon, who comes on wearied after a fruitless search. Hermes then puts on a wreath [1] and climbs to the roof to act the drunk slave. It is one of the very few scenes in comedy where the roof is actually used, although it is several times mentioned as a possible place for entry or spying.[2] Amphitryon returns, having failed to find Naukrates anywhere in the city ; a close parallel for his description of his wanderings can be found in the speech of Demeas in Menander's *Second Adelphoi* (713 f.), when he returns from the fool's errand on which he has been sent by Syrus ; such wanderings of a deceived father are part of the stock in trade of comedy.[3] Amphitryon then finds himself kept from his own door by Hermes playing the drunk Sosias on his roof. In its main idea the scene is parallel to the earlier scene in which Hermes scared Sosias from the door. The end of this scene, which was probably greatly expanded by Plautus, is lost in the gap of three hundred lines.

The second Argument tells us that Amphitruo and Juppiter accuse each other as adulterers and Blepharo is chosen to arbitrate but cannot tell which is Amphitruo. The end of this is preserved (1035, with fr. XIX). The interpretation of the nineteen fragments surviving from the gap is extremely difficult since naturally the speakers are not indicated. Lindsay is undoubtedly right in assigning I–VI to the preceding scene between Hermes and Amphitryon. The words : ' You swore that you were joking when you said to me . . .' (fr. VII), can only be spoken by Alkmene to Amphitryon while she is still unaware that Zeus is not Amphitryon. Therefore Zeus at this moment must have left her and she is not surprised to find Amphitryon outside : is this perhaps what Zeus meant when, before Amphitryon returned, he asked Hermes to help him when he sacrificed to himself (983) ? If Zeus ostensibly leaves Alkmene to sacrifice and

---

[1] His winged *petasos* (which is necessary to distinguish him from the human Sosias) probably hangs on his back.

[2] Cf. Dalman, *de aedibus scaenicis*, 62 ; Fraenkel in *Greek Poetry and Life*, 264.

[3] The close parallel of this passage with the *Epidicus* (197 f.), when the running slave claims to have looked for his master in the same places, may perhaps suggest that the running slave comes first as a type and that the errant father is later modelled on him as a kind of slow motion version of the same theme ; this seems likely in itself but is too much to build on the likeness of two passages in Plautus.

Hermes tells Amphitryon that he is going to help his master sacrifice, Amphitryon is left alone outside the house and hammers on the door ; Alkmene opens it and is not astonished to find him there, but then discovers that he still regards her as unfaithful to him. Presumably after that Zeus finds Amphitryon with Alkmene (frs. XV, XVI) ; Alkmene is sent in, then Blepharo arrives and the arbitration takes place.

Blepharo departs because he cannot decide. Zeus goes in because Alkmene is going to give birth. Amphitryon is left alone on the stage and decides to force his way into the house ; Bromia comes out to announce the birth. Nothing in our text (except Bromia's description, 1072) suggests that the thunderclap which announces the birth and strikes Amphitryon to the ground separates Amphitryon's decision to enter the house from the entrance of Bromia. With Bromia's account of the birth of the twins we are back in the world of tragedy and, as we have already suggested, Euripidean tragedy. The atmosphere can reasonably be called Euripidean : Amphitryon hammers on the door like Jason in the *Medea* (1317) ; the thunderclap which strikes Amphitryon to the ground reminds us of the scene in the *Herakles* where Herakles is smitten by Athena ; the voice of Zeus answering Alkmene's prayer (1063) recalls the voice of Dionysos answering Agave in the *Bacchae* (1079) ; Bromia criticises her master during her recital (1085 f.) rather as the messenger criticises Pentheus' assumptions about the immorality of the maenads ; and finally Zeus appears like an Euripidean *deus ex machina* to prevent Amphitryon consulting Teiresias.

Let us try to get some total impression of this curious play. It has a pleasing clarity of structure : a prologue, then the timorous entry of Sosias, the battle story, and the frightening of Sosias by his double ; then two corresponding sequences of three scenes —Zeus' farewell to Alkmene, Amphitryon/Sosias, Amphitryon's greeting of Alkmene, followed by Zeus' explanations to Alkmene, Hermes' mockery of Amphitryon, Amphitryon's attack on Alkmene ; this leads to Amphitryon's encounter with his double, the arbitration, and Amphitryon's attempt to break into his house followed by the thunderclap, Bromia's recital, and the epiphany of Zeus. We cannot tell with any certainty how the act breaks occurred in the original ; presumably after the prologue, since Hermes can hardly have stayed on the stage for the battle recital, then perhaps at Sosias' departure (462), since it would be a pity to break the sequence of three scenes, then certainly at Amphitryon's departure to fetch Naukrates (860). It seems possible that there is another break after the second scene between Alkmene and Amphitryon ; Amphitryon may go in with Alkmene, then he comes out again with Zeus : after that no break is possible. However this may be, the careful balancing of four main groups of scenes, the earlier Sosias scenes with his battle story, the two main groups of three scenes each, and the final scenes with Bromia's recital, is, as we shall see, not unlike the structure of the *Casina*.

We have already noticed a parallel between the softening up of Sosias and scenes by Diphilos,[1] and some minor verbal correspondences with Diphilos have also been detected.[2] The one possible indication of date, the allusion to Alexander in the battle recital, makes it perfectly possible that this is early Diphilos and of Diphilos' titles three at least must be mythological. We have detected various cross-references to New Comedy but far fewer to Middle Comedy ; there is no elaborate description of food, and though Hermes behaves like an ordinary slave and Zeus has a touch of the braggart soldier, this is much milder caricature of divine and heroic life than Middle Comedy fragments lead us to expect.[3] This also seems reasonable in a play probably produced in the early 'twenties less than ten years before Menander's first production. The two early Greek comedies on this theme, Archippos' *Amphitryon* and Plato's *Long Night*, cannot be considered ; the whole tone of the *Amphitruo* is not the tone of Old Comedy or early Middle Comedy. Philemon's *Night* has been suggested as the original by Dietze,[4] but none of the parallels which he notes are convincing and nothing in the *Amphitruo* really agrees with the picture of Philemon's art which can be drawn from the other plays ; it may be asked whether a play called *Night* did not certainly have Night as the prologue figure ;[5] if this is so, Philemon's *Night* can be

---

[1] See above, p. 90.
[2] Marx, *Rudens*, 318. Tredennick, *Cambridge University Reporter*, 1941, adds *Amph.*, 307 = *Rud.*, 708.
[3] See above, p. 85.
[4] *De Philemone comico.* He compares fr. 96K with *Amph.*, 170 f. ; *Merc.*, 1015 ff., with *Amph.*, 993 ff. ; *Trin.*, 1013 ff., with *Amph.*, 180 ff.
[5] For Night as a prologue figure cf. *C.A.F.*, III, 553/819.

excluded as the original of the *Amphitruo*. Rhinthon's *Amphitryon* is possible as far as date goes, but can also be excluded : in the only fragment (1 Kaibel) we are told that Rhinthon used the word πάνος in its Messapian meaning of loaf ; it sounds as if someone, probably a slave, is deliberately misunderstanding the Euripidean account of the burning of Alkmene, in which this word was used in its normal meaning of torch (90N). As far as we can form any idea of Rhinthon from the scanty fragments, he seems to have revived, or continued since it had never entirely vanished, the Middle Comedy tradition of transposing a Euripidean tragedy into the terms of low life. The original of Plautus' play, as we have seen, had comparatively little of this kind of humour and did not introduce the burning of Alkmene from Euripides' play.

Diphilos remains as a possible author, but the possibility cannot at present be converted into a probability. It is however highly probable that we should regard the *Amphitruo* as dependent on a Greek comedy written soon after 331. We have a very late stage in the development of the mythological comedy. The representation of Hermes as a slave and Zeus as an elderly soldier has become slightly self-conscious. Alkmene retains so much of her tragic colouring that it is not a long step from her to Pamphile in the *Epitrepontes* ; we can see here how parody of tragedy fades into the comedy of manners. The two balancing messenger speeches—the description of the battle and of Herakles' birth—are great dramatic narratives but have no specific comic value except perhaps that they are incongruous in the mouths of the frightened slaves who speak them. In the comedy scenes three strains appear which have already been noted before this date in non-mythological comedy—comedy of errors, deception, and knockabout. The play is well constructed and proceeds through a series of scenes which have each an individual value to the climax when Amphitryon is struck down by thunder as he tries to break into his own house ; then the denouement follows quickly. The myth is accepted without criticism and the consequences are drawn ; there is no political reference, no moral commentary, and no study of character. The characters are transposed from their divine or heroic sphere to the level of everyday life but they do not sink below that to the level of farce. Their level is nearer the level of Menander than the level of Aristophanes. The two gods retain their divine power, and the comedy of errors and the deceptions result from their use of it, and they are in no fear of discovery. This distinguishes the play from the others where errors and deceptions are either unintentional or the result of human intentions. It is perhaps this added piquancy which has made the play wear so well.

IV. NEW COMEDY

1. INTRODUCTION

AGAIN for the period after 321 B.C. we have Greek originals, not whole comedies but fragmentary papyrus texts of varying lengths. We have also abundant quotations in Greek authors, particularly of the more philosophical passages. All the Latin adaptations of Greek comedies except the three dealt with in the last section derive from New Comedy originals ; in addition to the complete plays of Plautus and Terence, a considerable number of Latin fragments survive which can sometimes be referred to their Greek originals. The majority of the Greek poets must remain little more than names to us since they are only represented in brief and often unrevealing quotations, but four, Menander, Philemon, Diphilos, and Apollodoros, can be apprehended as individual artists. Menander I have studied in some detail already, and he only appears here as a background figure, a known value to whom other poets can be related ; the other three poets will occupy much of our attention. If we can form some idea of all these four as artistic personalities, we shall be able to see the considerable number of unidentified but interesting papyrus fragments and the unattributed plays of Plautus (*Captivi, Curculio, Epidicus, Miles, Pseudolus,* and *Truculentus*) in some relation to them even where caution forbids a definite attribution.

I have treated the plays of Plautus and Terence as adaptations of earlier Greek originals not as specimens of Graeco-Roman drama of the late third and early second century, because I am primarily concerned with Greek comedy of the fourth century and believe that the colouring and distortion of the Roman dramatists are recognisable qualities for which we can make sufficient allowances to enable us to draw a generally truthful picture of the Greek originals. There may be considerable disagreement about points of detail but the main characteristics of Plautine adaptation were fixed by Professor E. Fraenkel's *Plautinisches im Plautus*, and Terence is generally admitted to have been faithful except where he has himself marked his divergences.

It is natural to us to think of Menander as Greek and Plautus as Latin and we are in danger of overemphasising the differences and forgetting that the Roman poets were translating and adapting Greek drama which was being acted in their own day and which they could see for themselves. Only twenty years separates the death of Philemon from the first performance of Livius Andronicus in Rome, and our scanty records show that the plays of Menander and his contemporaries were continually revived in Athens ; we have inscriptional records of revivals in 250/1,[1] 208, 193, 185, 183, 181, 169, 167, 160, 155 B.C.[2] Moreover, study of the representations of New Comedy [3]—Gnathia vases of the early third century, terracottas from Myrina and elsewhere, masks in varied materials from many places in the Graeco-Roman world, frescoes, mosaics, reliefs and finally the ninth-century illustrations of Terence—shows that the types of masks and costumes remained fixed from the late fourth century well into the Christian period. The diffusion of these monuments—to quote obvious examples, Athens, Corinth, Delos, Myrina, Larisa, Amisos, Pergamon, Palermo, Herculaneum, Pompeii, Corneto, Ostia—proves that the external appearance at least of Menander's comedy must have been well known all over the Graeco-Roman world for a long time. We can therefore say that late-fourth-century comedy became a classic in two senses. Texts survived and were read widely, and plays were revived and translated into Latin for acting, but in addition Menander and his contemporaries fixed not only the external appearance of comedy but also, as far as we can judge from the titles and surviving fragments, the type of comedy for succeeding generations. We shall have rather more to say about this when we discuss the form and content of New Comedy, but we probably have an example of this later derivative comedy in the *Asinaria*, adapted from the *Onagos* of Demophilos, who may very well have been a contemporary of Plautus ; similarly the *Asotos* of Caecilius may have been adapted from Timostratos, who produced a play at Athens in 189/8 B.C.[4] The wide diffusion of New Comedy which is suggested by the spread of the illustrative material is confirmed by our knowledge of performances outside

---

[1] *Hesperia*, VII, 116, no. 22. [2] *I.G.*[2], 2323.
[3] Cf. *Rylands Bulletin*, XXXII, 97 ; *J.H.S.*, lxxi, 222 f.
[4] *I.G.*, 2323 ; Wilhelm, *Urkunden*, 356.

Athens. Dr. Pickard-Cambridge's admirable discussion [1] of
these can be briefly summarised : we hear of comedy at Alexandria in the late third century, Delphi in the third, second, and
first century, Delos in the third century and early second century,
Boeotia in the first century, Magnesia in the first century B.C.
At the same time the considerable building and rebuilding of
theatres in the Hellenistic age must have been intended for performance of comedy as well as of tragedy and satyr plays : the
obvious examples (excluding the places already mentioned) are
Priene, Sikyon, Eretria, Ephesos, Pleuron in Aetolia, Oropos,
Segesta, and Pompeii. Thus Attic comedy of the late fourth
century set the style for succeeding comedy and in company with
later comedy was produced and read over the Graeco-Roman
world in the Hellenistic age, but the great creative period was the
last quarter of the fourth century and the first quarter of the
third.

2. POLITICAL BACKGROUND

Four poets are known to us. In view of the international
future of New Comedy it is interesting that only one of them,
Menander, was an Athenian by birth ; Diphilos came from
Sinope on the Black Sea, Philemon from Syracuse in the West,
Apollodoros from Karystos in Euboea. [2] Philemon and Apollodoros themselves and Diphilos' brother became Athenian citizens,
and whatever their origin their art is in the tradition of Attic
comedy. Yet although we can see again and again that this or
that element derives from earlier comedy or tragedy, this is a
new art which quickly became international and had something
of the same sort of universal appeal as the cinema and the detective
story. [3] It was not conceived as international any more than
earlier comedy or fifth-century tragedy. Three reasons perhaps
may be given for the swift spread of New Comedy ; it was good,
it was non-political, and it expressed the thoughts of the educated
class in their language. We must first interpret the last two
statements before we consider the art of New Comedy in general
and in particular of Philemon, Diphilos, and Apollodoros.

[1] *Theatre of Dionysus*, 240 f.
[2] See below, pp. 125, 152, 225, for discussion of their birthplace, etc.
[3] Cf. Ehrenberg, *People of Aristophanes*, 42, n. 1.

Although New Comedy quickly became international, Philemon's excursion to Egypt is the only evidence that the great poets wrote for anybody but Athenians. Menander wrote between three and four plays a year and they cannot all have been produced at the Dionysia and the Lenaia in Athens, since it seems impossible that every year he produced two plays at one or both of these festivals. We cannot however argue from this that he wrote for other Greek cities, since we know that comedies were performed during the fourth century in Attica itself at the local theatres of Peiraieus, Anagyrous, Rhamnous, Aixone, and Acharnai,[1] and these local theatres may have been used for first productions as well as revivals. We must therefore suppose that Menander as much as Aristophanes wrote for Athens. How far had Athens itself changed? According to Rostovtzeff [2] the public of Menander and his fellow-dramatists preferred not to be reminded of the grave and melancholy topic of politics when they sought recreation, aesthetic impressions, and amusement.

The audience itself may have changed in character, but it is difficult to know what exactly was the effect of the restriction of the franchise in 322 B.C. and the slighter restriction under Demetrios of Phaleron in 317 B.C. Historians are not decided whether there was a considerable exodus from Athens in 322 B.C. or not.[3] It seems however certain that there were plenty of disfranchised within easy reach to make the counter-revolution after the death of Antipater; a proportion of these must have been again disfranchised by Demetrios of Phaleron; and Diodorus tells us that in 310/9 many Athenians listened eagerly to Ophellas' proposals for an expedition to Carthage. The right to buy tickets for the theatre and the right to receive the theorikon belonged to citizens.[4] There is no reason to suppose that the citizens deprived of the right of voting and holding office were also deprived of the right of buying theatre tickets; the theorikon itself however may have been abolished [5] and this would exclude the poorer citizens; on the other hand, entertainment by the

[1] The evidence, inscriptional except for Peiraieus, is given by Vitucci in *Dioniso*, VII, 210, 312. [2] *S.E.H.*, 1120.
[3] Contrast, e.g., Ferguson, *Hell. Ath.*, 26; *C.A.H.*, VI, 460; Gomme, *Population of Athens*, 19.
[4] The essential texts are Theophrastos, *Char.*, IX, 5, and Dem., xliv, 37.
[5] This is assumed by Ferguson, *Hell. Ath.*, 58, 73, and Schwahn, *R.E.*, s.v. *theorikon*, but I have failed to find any direct evidence.

agonothetes may have sometimes provided a substitute.[1] In any case the richer citizens counted for more than the poorer citizens because they now had all the political power, and in this sense the audience was certainly different in character. The change cannot be assessed with any degree of accuracy, but it would probably be fair to say that the change of audience and atmosphere in the years from 322 to 307 (excluding the break 319–317) made it easier for Menander to develop character comedy into something more subtle and more serious than it had been before, so that by 307 it was firmly established and could advance further on the same lines. Middle Comedy had already become increasingly interested in the town life of the upper class and the change to New Comedy is essentially an acceleration of this process, which had already been started before the character of the audience had changed.[2]

A few harmless references to contemporary private citizens occur in early Menander,[3] and this kind of joke did not entirely die ; much later in the third century Phoenikides mentions Chairippos the glutton by name. It is more important to try and discover how far public events influenced comedy.[4] Menander's *Epitrepontes* has no reference to public events at all, but in the *Samia* the heroine was presumably driven out with the Athenian cleruchs in 322, as also the Bacchises in the *Dis Exapaton* and the hetairai in Diphilos' *Theseus* (50K). The event is still a memory some eighteen years later at the time of the production of the *Eunuch* (107). There is no question of criticism here ; the evacuation itself is not mentioned, but mention of a woman who had left Samos must have recalled the evacuation to the audience and so given the play contemporary reality. This kind of neutral reference to external events is naturally common.[5]

---

[1] e.g. Philippides, *I.G.*, II², 657 = Syll.³, 374.

[2] On the general trend in Athenian society see Ehrenberg, *op. cit.*, 371 f.

[3] Cf. *Studies in Menander*, 103 f. The reference to Dionysios of Herakleia as a glutton of international reputation (Menander, 21/3K) belongs essentially to the same class. Telesias who gave his name to Diphilos' play is probably a contemporary parasite and Synoris a contemporary hetaira (see below, pp. 153 ff.).

[4] It is unfortunate that the one reference to the battle of Lamia in Menander (52K) is so corrupt as to be unintelligible ; the reference is certain and the verse sounds like a criticism of someone who ran away from Lamia.

[5] Cf., e.g., the various references to Lemnos (which allow us to date these plays to periods when Lemnos was controlled by the Athenians), to Aetolia in the *Pseudolus*, to Leukas in the *Leukadia*, to Ambracia in the *Stichus*, to Rhodes

Political abuse was however still possible ; we know that Archedikos abused the democratic politician Demochares but this presumably from the safe shelter of Antipater's patronage.[1]

Demetrios of Phaleron ruled Athens from 317 to 307. The *gynaikonomoi*, who were established to inquire into private extravagance and enforce the new sumptuary laws, were naturally butts for the comic poets.[2] Timokles (465/32K), wanting to show a party feasting on the stage, makes a character suggest that the doors should be opened in order that the *gynaikonomos* may count the guests : ' It would be better if he made a list of the houses of the dinnerless.' Here we seem to have a criticism ; Demetrios is more interested in checking the extravagance of the rich than in helping the poor. Diphilos (549/32K) puts a parody of this institution in Corinth : the rich man is allowed to be extravagant ; the poor man who is extravagant is fined or put in prison ; thus criminals, sycophants, and perjurers are ' cleaned up '. Menander has an interesting reference to the *gynaikonomoi* in the *Apistos* (*Aul.*, 504) ; the rich Megadorus, who proposes to marry a poor girl in accordance with the best Peripatetic principles for promoting *homonoia*, delivers a long tirade against the extravagance of rich women and is told that he ought to be a *gynaikonomos* ; this does not imply approval—the whole question is shown to be entirely academic because the young lovers have answered their own problem in their own way.

Two events during the period of Demetrios' rule made sufficient stir to be recorded by comedy. Menander seems to refer twice (*Perik.*, 91 ; *Aspis*, 74K) to the murder of Polyperchon's son Alexandros. He is not named, but the reference to the manager of armies murdered by his mercenaries in the *Perikeiromene* would be easy to recognise. It is possible that the Corinthian setting of this play, and the Sikyonian setting of the *Synaristosai* and *Sikyonios*, and the reference to Corinth in the *Georgos*, are all a compliment to Polyperchon who had promised to restore Samos to Athens. The ' miseries of Corinth ' were still remembered some sixteen years later when Menander wrote

in the *Thesauros* and *Eunuch*, to Andros in the *Andria*, to Thebes in the *Epidicus*, to Aetolia and Elis in the *Captivi*, to Lemnos in the *Phormio* and Imbros in the *Hekyra*.

[1] III, 278/4K. Polybios apparently doubts the whole incident.
[2] e.g. Philemon, *Most.*, 941 ; Menander, 272K.

the *Heautontimoroumenos* (96, 629). At the time of the *Perikeiromene* (282), ' the miseries of Corinth ' in the War of the Coalition is part of ' the fine crop of misery ' which is afflicting all the Greeks. It is surely right to see a similar view of the same moment in a fragment of Apollodoros of Gela's *Grammateidopoios* (281/5K) ; [1] in which someone (perhaps a prologue figure ?) complains of the ' boorish Fortune ' which allows Greeks to fight and kill each other when they might enjoy life. Exactly the same tone is heard in a papyrus fragment (63/15P), which Professor Page translates : ' Grant us peace, Almighty God, at last, an end to suffering and misfortune ! ' Thus the comic poets state openly that Greece is afflicted with the misery of civil war and the misery of internal distress during the time of Demetrios of Phaleron.

From their misery many Greeks sought escape in Ophellas' expedition against Carthage, which seemed to promise a new and rich land to inhabit, ' since Greece had been weakened and humbled by continuous wars and the rivalries of the Diadochoi ' (Diodoros, XX, 40).[2] Diodoros says that Ophellas was willingly received in Athens because of his marriage with Euthydike, daughter of Miltiades, and ' his other efforts ' on her behalf. Apollodoros of Gela (287/24) speaks of the parasite Chairephon attending Ophellas' marriage. It was therefore a famous event, memorable for comedy. The ' other efforts ' of Ophellas may have included the offering of land to Athenian immigrants. It is very tempting to connect the setting of the *Rudens* with this : Daemones is an Athenian exiled in Cyrene not because of any crime, political or other, but because he lost a fortune through kindness in saving others though it embarrassed himself (36 f.). It sounds very much as if he had lost his citizen rights through the restriction of the franchise and had been accepted by Ophellas in Cyrene. It would be too rash to go further and suggest that the traitor from Akragas has any connection with Agathokles, who persuaded Ophellas to undertake the expedition against Carthage which led to Ophellas' death. But it seems likely that

[1] Capps, *A.J.P.*, 1900, 50, convincingly attributes this fragment to Apollodoros of Gela.

[2] We cannot say whether Alexis' *Karchedonios* fits in this context. Menander's *Karchedonios* (Plautus' *Poenulus*) must be earlier if Professor Westlake is right in saying that the Aetolians cannot have been in favour at Athens under Demetrios of Phaleron (*C.R.*, lxiii, 90). On Ophellas, see Ehrenberg, *R.F.I.C.*, lxvi, 144 f.

Diphilos wrote the play when Ophellas was well known in Athens and certain that he is criticising the rule of Demetrios of Phaleron for driving out of Athens some of those who lived most truly by the Athenian ideal.

The capture of Athens by Demetrios Poliorketes in 307 nearly brought disaster to Menander. He was, according to Diogenes Laertius (V. 79), nearly condemned for the sole reason that he was a friend of Demetrios of Phaleron ; but he was saved by Telesphoros, a cousin of Demetrios Poliorketes.[1] That Menander was a friend of Demetrios of Phaleron was a natural conclusion since they were both pupils of Theophrastos, and Menander's plays were steeped in Peripatetic philosophy ; that Menander approved uncritically of the legislation of the dictator seems unlikely from the evidence quoted above. In fact, Menander and Theophrastos were too precious to be sacrificed whatever their relations to the tyrant. A fragment of Alexis' *Hippeus* (327/94) echoes the popular reaction against the philosopher : 'Is this the Academy of Xenokrates? May the gods bless Demetrios and the law-givers for sending those who claim to give young men the power of argument to hell out of Attica.' Meineke was no doubt right in supposing these to be the words of an angry father whose son has been corrupted by philosophy. Xenokrates had been dead seven years, but he had been a member of the embassy to Antipater in 322 B.C. ; we have noticed earlier that the Academy was accused of teaching rhetoric.[2] The Peripatetics are not mentioned, perhaps because Theophrastos had already fled. When Demochares defended Sophokles, who had proposed this law expelling the philosophers, he also attacked the Academy as a training ground for tyrants.[3] Alexis' sympathies earlier seem to have been with the democrats and against Macedon, and this praise of Demetrios like the slightly later demand for libations to Antigonos, Demetrios and Phila is in keeping,[4] but surely verges on flattery.

---

[1] Telesphoros should undoubtedly be identified with Antigonos' naval commander (Beloch, III, I, 126, n. 3) and therefore Demetrios in Diogenes Laertius must be Poliorketes.

[2] Cf. above, p. 51.

[3] Ath., 509. Ferguson, *Hell. Ath.*, 106. It is difficult to be certain how much of the passage in Athenaeus goes back to Demochares' speech but there is no doubt about the references to Euaion of Lampsakos and Timaios (Timolaos) of Kyzikos, both listed as Academicians by Diogenes Laertius (III, 46).

[4] 336/111K. See Ferguson, *Hell. Ath.*, 114, n. 7.

It is not my purpose to draw a detailed picture of Athens during this most complicated period ; [1] for comedy the salient events are these. Demetrios Poliorketes spent the winter of 304/3 in Athens, living in the Parthenon with Lamia and other hetairai. In the spring of 302 the calendar was so rearranged that Demetrios could be initiated into the mysteries. Then came the Second Coalition of Cassander, Ptolemy, and Seleukos against Antigonos and Demetrios, which ended with the defeat and death of Antigonos at Ipsos in 301. The politician who had been responsible for the excessive flattery of Demetrios was Stratokles, and he was now attacked by the comic poet Philippides, who was possibly already writing in the 'thirties [2] and won a victory both at the Lenaia and the Dionysia in the time of Demetrios of Phaleron. He accused Stratokles of tampering with the calendar, turning the Parthenon into a brothel and giving a man the honours due to a god (308/25K), and possibly it was he who called Lamia ' capture of a city' (463/303K). Plutarch quotes another line (310/31K) : ' You can hardly kiss her when she turns her head away ', which if correctly quoted proves that Philippides actually brought Stratokles on the stage. Here then is political abuse in the old manner.[3] Philippides also says ' this [Stratokles' policy], not comedy, destroys democracy ' ; this seems to imply that Stratokles had accused the comic poets of destroying democracy and perhaps that some restriction had been placed on comedy in the preceding years, which might explain the excessive flattery of the Alexis fragment quoted above. The comedy of Philippides was' presumably produced at the next festival after the initiation of Demetrios, i.e. early in 301. Philippides then left Athens and stayed with Lysimachos of Thrace, with whom he arranged for the burial of Athenian dead and disposal of prisoners after Ipsos ; he also persuaded Lysimachos to make other gifts to Athens during this time.[4] Presumably as a friend of Lysimachos, he was not in sympathy with Lachares, the tool of Cassander, who was apparently the leading spirit of the new government. We also hear that ' Menander wrote his *Imbrians* in the archonship of Nikokles

---

[1] See Ferguson, *Hell. Ath.*, 122 f., brought up to date by *C.P.*, xxiv, 1 f.

[2] Cf. *C.Q.*, 1952, 21.

[3] This alone seems to me sufficient to rule out Elderkin's interpretation of the *Curculio* as indirect satire of Demetrios Poliorketes (see below, p. 217).

[4] See *I.G.*, II², 657 = Syll.³, 374.

(302/1) and gave it for production for the Dionysia but it was not produced because of Lachares the tyrant.'[1] There is no reason to suppose that Menander wrote a political play and it is hard to understand this prohibition unless, as we have suggested, Menander had been recognisably out of sympathy with Demetrios of Phaleron, whose relationship with Cassander Lachares sought to imitate. The only mention of Lachares in comedy occurs in a fragment of Demetrios' *Areopagite* (357/1K), which was clearly written after Demetrios Poliorketes had besieged and taken Athens in 294. A cook claims that he was sauce-maker to Seleukos and first served 'Royal Soup' to the Siceliot Agathokles (who called himself king in 304):

'My greatest achievement I have not mentioned. One Lachares was feasting his friends at the time of the famine and I refreshed them by serving capers.'

B.: 'At that time Lachares stripped Athena without any provocation. You are provoking me enough to make me strip you now.'

The cook is a fool and expects to be employed in Athens although he prides himself on having cooked for tyrants: it might still be remembered that Agathokles murdered Ophellas in Africa in 309. Lachares then according to the comic poet behaved as a typical tyrant and feasted his friends when most Athenians were starving (it is astonishing that the fragment is quoted as evidence that 'Lachares set a worthy example of unselfishness, and cheerfully shared the privations of his troops'[2]); the gold from the Athena Parthenos was a legitimate expedient but provided an obvious joke for comedians.[3] The sense of the whole passage is that Lachares was a tyrant and thanks to Demetrios Poliorketes we are rid of him. Nevertheless, immediately after the battle of Ipsos there was a moment of optimism and peace, which is twice reflected in comedy.[4]

Seleukos is mentioned with Agathokles and Lachares, and at this time Seleukos had quarrelled with Demetrios. Seven other references to Seleukos have survived. They do not tell us much except that Seleukos was a known person. He had sent the Athenians a tiger, perhaps after his Indian campaign, and it

---

[1] *Periochai*, 115. [2] Ferguson, *Hell. Ath.*, 133.
[3] On this see Homer A. Thompson, *Harvard Studies*, Supplt., Vol. I, 183 f.
[4] *Heautontimoroumenos*, 194; *Truculentus*, 75.

becomes a symbol of unintelligent brutality.[1]   He had a flatterer
called Phormion, who probably provided Apollodoros with the
name of a parasite in two plays.   He is immensely rich and
fortunes can be recouped in his kingdom.[2]   His soldiers strut the
stage in vanity and meet with disaster.[3]   The references probably
all date from the years between 304 and 294 B.C.   The *Miles
Gloriosus* is the most interesting.   This soldier of Seleukos claims
to have defeated Demetrios Poliorketes (15) and the play must
therefore have been produced at a time when Demetrios was
not ruling Athens, which also explains Pleusicles' embassy to
the Aetolians, Demetrios' enemies.   In Pyrgopolinices' desire
for any pretty woman that he sees we may perhaps find a
reflection of Demetrios' love affairs far clearer than that which
has been discovered in the *Curculio*, and the play is certainly
a satire on the kind of soldier who admired Demetrios as his
ideal.[4]

With the return of Demetrios the flattery started again, and
Antiphanes mentions Demeter and Demetrios together as ' the
holy goddess and the dearest king ' in terms that recall the well-
known ithyphallic hymn.[5]   For the rest of our period there is
not much to record.   We know that Philippides returned from
exile at the time when Athens broke with Demetrios and was
much concerned in negotiations with Lysimachos, but no trace
of this has survived in the comic fragments.   In 288/7 he was
agonothetes and spent largely of his private fortune in entertaining
the Athenians during the contests, for which he was rewarded
with a gold crown and a bronze statue in the theatre.[6]   The
secret treaty which Demetrios' son Antigonos made with
Pyrrhos about 286 B.C. is twice mentioned in comedy as the kind
of news retailed by gossips.[7]   In the early 'seventies Alexis'
Hypobolimaios (244K) contained a toast to Ptolemy Philadelphos,

---

[1] Alexis, 372/204 ; Philemon, 490/47.

[2] Antiphanes, 88/187K ; Philemon/Plautus, *Trinummus*.

[3] *Miles* and possibly *Truculentus*.   The sense and text of K., iii/498/450, is
unclear to me ; all that is certain is that Dionysios referred to Seleukos in a
comedy and mentioned someone who could not move because of a damaged
knee.

[4] The title of Diphilos' *Hairesiteiches* must be a parody of Demetrios' sobriquet
Poliorketes.

[5] Antiphanes, 44/81K.   Cf. Ehrenberg, *Aspects*, 185.

[6] *I.G.*, II², 657 = Syll.³, 374.

[7] Phoenikides, 333/1 ; Adesp., 473/347 K.

Arsinoe, and Homonoia, and this reflects the contemporary
attitude to Egypt ; probably Philemon went to Alexandria about
this same time. Poseidippos wrote an *Arsinoe*, but we know
nothing of its contents and cannot tell whether the queen
appeared on the stage or spoke the prologue to justify the title.[1]
A reference to Nikomedes of Bithynia by a cook in a comedy of
Euphron is only interesting as showing the extent of Athenian
knowledge.

Thus the statement that New Comedy is non-political needs
a little modification. Direct abuse in the old manner is still
possible when conditions allow it, and there is a little evidence
that both Stratokles and Lachares somehow restricted the
production of comedy. Direct flattery is also not unknown.
We can also see more general criticism of the restrictive legislation of Demetrios of Phaleron and its effects on the poorer
Athenians, and in the *Miles* an unsympathetic portrait of the
amorous soldier which could hardly fail to recall the behaviour
of Demetrios Poliorketes. General views on politics are rarely
expressed, and are confined to remarks on the disastrous results of
flattery whether of a king or of the Athenian people, the unre-
liability of politicians, the ability of the rich to buy witnesses,
and the power of slander.[2] City life means behaving like a
monkey if one is to survive ; a life of *apragmosyne* is best, and in
practice that means living in the country.[3] The remedy for
present political troubles is good character rather than excessive
eloquence in politicians, and education of the young, who are
corrupted in youth and become political criminals.[4] Political
office is seldom mentioned except to lend reality to a character :
thus Pleusicles in the *Miles* has been an ambassador, Demipho
in the *Synaristosai* (*Cistellaria*) has been away all day because he
has been sitting on the *boule* : to be an Areopagite implied a
certain severity and strictness of character as we see from several

---

[1] On the general situation see *C.A.H.*, VII, 706. An even later instance of
' comedy by name' is Epinikos' *Mnesiptolemos* (330/IK), in which M. who
was the historian of Antiochos III (241–187 B.C.) appeared on the stage, parodying
his own style.

[2] Flattery : Diphilos, 547/24, 572/97 ; Menander, *Kolax*, 87 f. Politicians :
Diphilos, 573/101. Wealth : Philemon, 495/65 ; Menander, 537K. Slander :
Menander, 88K.

[3] *Apragmosyne* : Apollodoros, 288/1K. The country : Diphilos, 570/89K ;
Philemon, 496/71 ; Menander, 466K ; Adesp., 434/133, 480/382.

[4] Menander, 578K ; Apollodoros, 291/13.

passages.[1] This does not amount to very much when we remember Aristophanes, *Knights* and *Acharnians*. Occasionally, as we have seen, political satire does still occur but the majority of the political references in New Comedy have only the purpose of giving contemporary reality to the play.

3. COMEDY AND THE PHILOSOPHERS

Primarily New Comedy is concerned with private life and with the private life of the educated. Rostovtzeff[2] however makes an overstatement when he says that ' they [the poets of New Comedy] were not interested in the psychology of the lower classes as such '. The figures of slaves are only ' semi-conventional' to the same degree as their masters : Daos in Menander's *Heros*, Onesimos in the *Epitrepontes*, Grumio in the *Mostellaria* (Philemon), Davos in the *Phormio* (Apollodoros), Gripus in the *Rudens* (Diphilos) are completely individual and studied with great sympathy.[3] So also are such figures as the poor *advocati* in the *Poenulus* (Menander) and the considerable number of poor girls and their relatives in Menander.[4] The social scale of New Comedy probably does not differ from the social scale of Aristophanes ; the difference between Strepsiades of the *Clouds* (the obvious instance because the *Clouds* also deals primarily with a problem of private life) and Demeas of the *Samia* is not class or wealth but education, or in other words familiarity with classical tragedy and the ideas of the philosophers.

During the period of New Comedy the schools of Aristotle and Plato continued, the Cynics continued, and the new schools of Epikouros and the Stoics were started. The philosophers touch comedy in three ways. They are part of Athenian life ; they are known by name and have individual and general characteristics which come up in conversation. Secondly their views are known and have coloured the general tone of conversation in Athens ; not only citizens but cooks and slaves have picked up at least a smattering of the jargon. Thirdly the comic poets themselves live in this atmosphere and are affected by it,

---

[1] Menander, *Fab. Inc.*, 11 ; perhaps also *Epidicus*, 292, 522. Demetrios named a comedy *Areopagite*.

[2] *S.E.H.*, 1133-4.

[3] Cf. below on slave apologies (p. 244).   Add D. 314/24 = 68P, 301/15 = 70P.

[4] Cf. *Studies*, 60 f.

although we only know for certain of two actual adherents of the philosophical schools—Menander was a pupil of Theophrastos and Baton was a pupil of Arkesilaos, who was head of the Academy in the middle of the third century B.C.

In general, philosophers still have the same characteristics as before, they are pale ascetics, they are unpractical, they are really out for private gain : the enlightenment that philosophy brings may be the bogus enthusiasm of a pupil.[1] A hetaira who lived with a philosopher discovered that his scorn for money only meant that she was not paid.[2] Philosophy makes a man useless as the head of a household, but for that very reason he needs a wife to look after him.[3] This general and traditional attitude naturally colours the remarks made about particular philosophers. The Academy according to Alexis only trains young men in Rhetoric.[3a] The Cynics are dirty beggars : Menander knows Monimos' doctrine that the whole of conceptual knowledge is illusion ; Krates wears a thick cloak in summer and a thin cloak in winter ; his wife wore the same clothes as he did ; and his daughter was given to a man in trial marriage for thirty days.[4] The Stoic Zeno appears as an ascetic ;[5] Epikouros naturally is devoted to pleasure and particularly the pleasure of eating. Epikouros unlike the destitute Diogenes has a wealth of barley cake. When a father complains to an elderly slave that his son has been corrupted, the slave says that according to Epikouros the good is pleasure and pleasure can only be achieved by a riotous life, and in fact the philosophers[6] who seek wisdom as if it were a runaway slave (presumably the Stoics) are the most accomplished gluttons when they get a chance ; Baton, who wrote this, was himself an Academic philosopher and in some comedy made a personal attack on Kleanthes, the head of the Stoic school ; for this he was for a time excluded from the Academy. The most elaborate exposition of Epicureanism is given by a cook in the *Syntrophoi* of Damoxenos (349/2) : he has been a pupil

---

[1] References for Menander, cf. *Studies*, 196. Add Philemon, 496/71 ; Anaxippos, 296/1, 299/4 ; Baton, 326/2.

[2] Phoinikides, 334/4.

[3] Adesp., 430/119. Contrast Theophrastos on matrimony (cf. *Studies*, 214).
[3a] Alexis, 327/94.

[4] Philemon, 523/146 ; Menander, 249K (see Dudley, *History of Cynicism*, 56) ; 117–18K. Cf. also Adesp., 431/120.

[5] Philemon, 502/85 ; Poseidippos, 340/15 ; Adesp, 460/285.

[6] Hegesippos, 314/2 ; Adesp., 432/127 ; Baton, 328/5, 330/8.

of Epikouros : a cook must have read all Demokritos and the Kanon of Epikouros ; he must know the significance of the different seasons and the peculiar characteristics of all ingredients ; he does not do the work but stands by and conducts the symphony ; ' Epikouros intensified pleasure, he chewed carefully, he alone knew the nature of good, whereas the men in the Stoa continually seek it without knowing what it is.' [1]

In the later period of Middle Comedy general reflections on general subjects were noticeable. To judge from the number of such general reflections in the fragments (and they were collected as energetically by later anthologists as descriptions of food by Athenaeus and rare words by grammarians) they became increasingly popular in New Comedy. To call them quotations from philosophers is inexact. They have perhaps three sources : traditional views, tragedy, and technical philosophy. The three often cannot be sorted out because by the time of New Comedy they are inextricably intermingled. For instance, the traditional view of the badness of women had become a theme in comedy long before New Comedy and from there had passed into Theophrastos' Golden Book on Marriage ; Aristotelian ethics drew on tragedy largely for examples, because classical tragedy was by that time recognised as a repository of quotable wisdom. These sentiments are expressed by the comic poets in a high style which admits easily of quotation from high poetry ; thus in a fragment of Theognetos (364/1) a quotation from a Stoic is swiftly succeeded by a parody of a line in Philoxenos' *Kyklops* and a quotation of half a line from the *Medea*. In some cases however, even where the wisdom is traditional, we feel that it has been reformed by the philosophers, and suspect that the poet had a passage from a philosopher in mind when he gave it this particular expression. For Menander in particular we can suppose a very close acquaintance with Peripatetic ethics.[2] There are passages in the other poets also where we can see the same sort of ideas, e.g. the contrast between false and true modesty, justice, and wisdom in three passages from Philemon,[3] the

---

[1] Some of the terminology is meant to parody Epicurean uses : καταπυκνοῦν, μεταβολαί, ἰδιότης, συμφωνία. With the criticism of the Stoa at the end, cf. Theognetos, 364/1. The long account of Lakydes (Arkesilaos' successor at the Academy) and his slaves (Adesp., 418/103) probably does not derive from comedy, cf. *R.E.*, s.v. Lakydes.

[2] Cf. *Studies*, 198 f.   [3] Philemon, 479/5 ; 507/94K ; *Trinummus*, 367.

comparison of men with animals in Philemon and Apollodoros,[1] the nice distinction between ἁμαρτάνειν and ὑβρίζειν in Philippides (309/26), and the characterisation of Periplectomenus in the *Miles Gloriosus* (627 ff.). We cannot tell whether such passages are directly dependent on Menander, but in spite of some close parallels in phraseology with him it seems more likely that Peripatetic ideas were very generally known in Athens in the late fourth and early third century and had spread beyond the confines of the school. We shall see more of this when we come to discuss the individual poets. On the other hand, much less can be said with any confidence to be Stoic or Epicurean. An Epicurean echo has been seen in a fragment of Alexis,[2] where someone exemplifies the traditional view that all subjects of inquiry yield to the persistent searcher [3] by the example of eclipses and the motions of the heavenly bodies : here it seems likely that Alexis meant his audience to see the reference. Stoic echoes are even harder to detect, since much of Stoic ethics was a hardening of the old Greek rules of *Sophrosyne*. Richard Heinze said in a course of lectures (for the notes of which I am indebted to the kindness of Professor Andreas Rumpf) that the *Trinummus* was full of views which could be described as Stoic, and he was no doubt thinking particularly of the dialogues between Philto, Lysiteles, and Lesbonicus : but it is equally true that the character of Lesbonicus is described in terms derived from the Aristotelian *asotos*. In fact, Epicureans and Stoics develop different sides of Peripatetic ethics and it is often safer to say, particularly for the surviving plays, of which only the *Asinaria* comes from an original later than the first quarter of the third century, that a particular view is philosophical than that it is specifically Epicurean or Stoic.

4. Form and Content

The influence of philosophy on the poets themselves can only be assessed in general terms : some points of detail will appear later in the discussion on individual poets. Aristotle's statement

---

[1] Philemon, 478/3 ; 504/89 ; 507/93. Apollodoros, 58P.
[2] Alexis, 309/30, interpreted by Bignone, *R.F.I.C.*, 1924, 174, who compares particularly Epicurus, II, 96 f.
[3] Cf. Philemon, 488/37 ; Menander/Terence, *Heaut.*, 675.

in the *Poetics* (1451 b 11) that comedy is a combination of probable incidents to which chance names are added can be applied to New Comedy with much less reservation than to Middle Comedy. Theophrastos' definition (Kaibel *C.G.F.*, 57) is based on Aristotle : tragedy is a ' reversal of heroic prosperity ', comedy is a ' change in private affairs involving no disaster '. It is perhaps unwise to say that the close parallel between the definitions implies also an approximation of comedy to tragedy in form such as we in fact see occurring. What is however significant is the implied new description of the characters of comedy as ordinary citizens. Aristotle had described the characters of comedy as worse than ourselves ; the new description of the incidents of comedy as ' private affairs ' implies that the element of satire and caricature has become much less obvious. Aristotle's description is a brilliant penetration into the latent possibilities of the most advanced practice of his time. Menander saw the possibilities and developed them, and they became the common practice of his contemporaries and successors.

Comedy is a ' combination of probable incidents ' ; the important word is ' probable ' and it can be interpreted in three ways. In the first place it means that the incidents of the plot arise out of one another in a probable sequence. In this sense ' probable ' refers to the technique of plot-construction, to the unity of action and the preparation and motivation of exits and entrances. I have tried to show that the *Epitrepontes* in particular has the Desis–Lysis form prescribed by Aristotle for unitary action in drama.[1] We shall see later that Philemon, as far as we can judge from the Roman adaptations, sometimes elaborates particular scenes further than their place in the economy of the plot justifies, whereas Diphilos has a very strong formal sense of his own, which leads him to build up his plays as a series of climaxes and oppositions.

Secondly ' probable ' is interpreted as ' the sort of things which would happen ' or, as we might say, the sort of things which do happen every day. We have seen in discussing politics that the chief point of many of the political allusions in New Comedy is simply to give a realistic contemporary reference. The realities of time and place are also carefully observed ; we shall find extraordinarily few instances where the relation between

[1] *Studies*, 178 f.

real time and acted time is disregarded ; normally act ends are carefully arranged to cover journeys to harbour or market-place and distant journeys are no longer undertaken within the limits of the play.

It follows that the comedy of the dominant idea has become rare. Traces of it survive : the *Casina* (Diphilos' *Kleroumenoi*) obviously belongs to this class ; the more extravagant intrigues— the feigned deaths in the *Heauton Penthon* (= *Com. Flor.*) of Menander, the hiring of the sycophant in the *Trinummus*, the wall comedy and the final tricking of the soldier in the *Miles*— are clearly in the same line of descent, but in New Comedy the use of the dominant idea is different : it does not form the basis of the play's structure but only dominates an amusing scene or two.

It follows also that mythological comedy has little place now ; mythology travestied in the old way would be discordant, mythology untravestied belonged to tragedy. Very few mytho-logical titles can be found in New Comedy ; we cannot be certain that Philemon's *Myrmidons* and *Palamedes*, Diphilos' *Danaides*, *Herakles*, *Theseus*, and *Peliades* belong to New Comedy in the strict sense of plays written after 321 ; Apollodoros of Karystos and Philippides are both credited with an *Amphiareos* ; Euphron wrote a *Muses* and an *Assembly of the Gods*. Otherwise the only seeming mythological titles are probably the names of prologue figures. The gluttonous Herakles or the amorous Zeus would not fit in this world. Instead tragedy continued a source for quotation, to stress the solemnity of an occasion (often for purely comic effect), a repository of classical wisdom to which characters can relate their own position, and a source of situations which the comic poet can translate into his own idiom and use for his own purposes. There is no travesty in the old sense of an heroic character on the stage speaking everyday words, but a human character may for a brief space dramatise himself as an heroic character, as Alcesimarchus plays Aias in the *Synaristosai*,[1] and this seems to me the probable explanation of titles like the *Pseudherakles* of Menander and the *Pseudaias* of Apollodoros of Gela.

Thirdly, ' probable ' can be used in the sense of ' suitable to the character in this particular situation '. As Aristotle says, ' a man

---

[1] Cf. *Studies*, 160.

I

of a certain quality performs actions or speaks words of the same quality according to probability'. Most of the characters of New Comedy are naturalistically drawn. We may doubt whether Periplectomenus in the *Miles* (627 f.) or Charinus in the *Mercator* (11 f.) should describe their characters at quite such length (even when allowances have been made for Plautine expansion), but this kind of presentation is part of the convention of ancient drama as a whole and particularly of tragedy, a convention from which only Menander and Apollodoros to some extent broke away. The old men, the young men, the women and the slaves are all recognisable as belonging to the real world and in the main thinking and acting as they would in the real world. To this world also belong soldiers, cooks, and parasites. But these are stock figures of Middle Comedy and in some scenes at any rate are exaggerated out of all proportion—the cook of the *Pseudolus* is the one example that we can see in its context but the fragments provide many more, and both cooks and parasites can be traced into the second century.[1] A soldier in Damoxenos (348/1) has a cup which is the work of Alkon (a mythical artist) and was given him by Adaios, who died in 354/3 ; this is wild exaggeration since Damoxenos was a contemporary of Epikouros and seems to have won his first victory after 280. Possibly Damoxenos has taken over a passage from an earlier play ; we have a clear example of this in Straton's cook, who repeats in a slightly expanded form the speech of Philemon's cook.[2] Many of the soldiers, parasites, and cooks are stock figures and nearer to farce than comedy, but this of course does not prevent the comic poet from individualising a particular soldier, cook, or parasite when it suits his plot.

We have already mentioned the self-portrait of Periplectomenus in the *Miles* (627 f.) and the description of Lesbonicus in the *Trinummus* (333) as instances in which the comic poet describes characters in philosophical terms, and we have to reckon with constant interaction between Peripatetic ethics and comedy from the time of Aristotle. Theophrastos' *Characters* and *On Matrimony* in particular both take from comedy and give to comedy ; we should probably find many more cross echoes if

---

[1] e.g. Nikomachos, 386/1 ; Kriton, 354/3. Athenion (369/1, cook) has been dated to the first century, *R.E.*, s.v. Juba.

[2] See below, p. 145.

we had his *Erotikos, On Pleasure, On Drunkenness,* and *On Flattery.*
The more important question to decide is how far we can say
that the comic poet was influenced by the philosophers in his
presentation of characters. On the technique of presentation the
philosophers as far as we know had little of importance to say.
Aristotle's chapter on characters in the *Poetics* hardly amounts to
more than listing various aspects in which the speeches of
characters should fall within the bounds of probability, and these
bounds the comic poets observe on the whole ; Theophrastos'
Characters gives a number of minor external behaviours which
suggest a character of a particular type, and we can sometimes
see this kind of description in comedy. Aristotle's definition of
the tragic hero[1] as 'a man who is neither outstanding in excellence
and justice nor brought into misfortune by badness and vicious-
ness but by an error' (in the technical Aristotelian sense) does
penetrate through external behaviour to the idea of an underlying personality. In a general sense, of course, *mutatis mutandis*
the description can be applied to the character and fate of many
comic heroes from the time of Strepsiades and might be applied
to Demipho in the *Mercator* and Lysidamus in the *Casina.* The
characters of Menander and of Apollodoros however stand
out convincingly as complete and individual portraits ; in
Philemon, as we have said, speeches may be overcoloured to
get a particular effect in a particular scene.

Philemon is philosophical because it is the fashion. Menander's
problems are the problems of Peripatetic ethics : the right assessment of errors or mistakes due to anger, drunkenness, or ignorance (and to make the emphasis entirely clear the prologue may
be spoken by Anger, Drunkenness, Ignorance, or Scrutiny, i.e.
by a philosophical abstraction personified), the possibility of
education, the possibility of penetrating through fictitious values
to real values, which leads to the sympathetic portrayal of
figures hitherto satirically treated by comedy, the soldier in the
Perikeiromene, the rich hetaira in the *Eunuch,* and probably the
flatterer in the *Kolax* (for him, however, we noted an anticipation
in Middle Comedy). As far as we can see, only Apollodoros
developed this kind of comedy further. No doubt we should
find more examples if more New Comedy survived ; the nice
distinction between ἁμαρτία and ὕβρις in a fragment of an un-

[1] *Poetics*, 1453 a 8.

known play of Philippides (309/26) is just the sort of distinction
that Pataikos makes in the *Perikeiromene*, but we cannot tell how
important this was in the play as a whole.   Machon, who produced in Alexandria, wrote a play called *Ignorance* and it is
reasonable to suppose that it was called after the prologue figure.
In Apollodoros, as we know him from Terence's *Phormio* and
Hecyra, we find again the sympathetic treatment of the flatterer
and the rich hetaira and for the first time the sympathetic treatment of the mother-in-law.   In both plays but particularly in
the *Hecyra* the misconceptions of the characters about each other
are an important element : for this many parallels can be found
in Menander, and the arrival at a true assessment is very much the
concern of Aristotle's equitable man.

Philosophy is part of the atmosphere of educated Athens.   In
some comedies it is a superficial colouring but in others it is
essential.   It is tempting to suppose that a chronological sequence
can be traced and that boisterous satire gradually yields to a more
serious and sympathetic comedy.   For Menander himself this is
probably true, but it must be remembered that though we can
date the *Samia* and the *Perikeiromene* early, we have no considerable Greek fragments which can be dated late ; on the other
hand, we can date the *Heautontimoroumenos* late and we know
that the *Andria* was less boisterous than the earlier *Perinthia*.   The
same contrast can be seen between Philemon's *Phasma* = *Mostellaria* (317/07) and *Thesauros* = *Trinummus* (after 300), but unfortunately we have no solid evidence for dating the original of the
Emporos = *Mercator*.   On this criterion we should naturally
expect that Diphilos' *Kleroumenoi* (*Casina*) is earlier than the
original of the *Rudens*, but we have no certain means of dating
the *Casina*.   The two Apollodoros plays which carry on the
serious tone of Menander can be dated well into the third century.
But we must remember that the *Miles*, which has very strong
elements of satire and knockabout, cannot be dated before the
beginning of the third century, and the stock figure of the cook
as we have said can be traced down to at least the second century
and becomes more and more preposterous as he goes on ; if the
Asinaria is really an adaptation of a contemporary original, that
original was certainly not a philosophic comedy.   We can
therefore only say that our evidence suggests that the most
philosophical plays belong to the last years of the fourth and the

(a) DELICATE YOUTH   *Photo, British Museum.*

Marble, British Museum 2440.

Photo, University College.

(b) FLATTERER

Terracotta, University College, London, G.A. 90.

Photo, British Museum.

(c) LITTLE HOUSEKEEPER

Terracotta, British Museum C. 749.

PLATE IV.—MASKS OF NEW COMEDY

early years of the third century. On the other hand, we can see a boundary between Middle and New Comedy, although many elements of Middle Comedy survive and some years elapse before the strong form or the philosophical tone of the *Epitrepontes* and *Heautontimoroumenos* are achieved. In particular, the characterisation is far more detailed and penetrating even in the earliest plays like the *Samia* and in the most rollicking plays like the *Casina* than in the *Persa* or *Menaechmi*.

5. COSTUME AND MASKS

The change of tone was accompanied by a change of costume. The padding in front and behind was dropped. The short garment stopping at the hips worn by male characters gave way to long chiton down to the ankles for free men and short chiton reaching nearly to the knee for slaves. Soldiers presumably also wore this short chiton, except when they put on civilian clothes like Polemon after the beginning of the *Perikeiromene* (58, 164). The phallos if still worn was not normally visible ; it could still be seen on occasions just as obscene jokes could still be made on occasions.[1] But normally the characters of New Comedy were dressed like the average Athenian of the day, and so it was natural to expect them to behave and speak like the average Athenian of the day. A great many monuments illustrating the actors of New Comedy survive and they include masks in various materials, statuettes of single figures, and associations of figures in paintings and reliefs.[2] With the new costumes certain new masks come in, notably the two masks normally used for fathers and four of the masks used for young men. Two of these masks appear on the well-known relief[3] on which Menander is represented studying the masks of the speaking characters in some particular scene. We must not conclude from this that he

[1] *Rudens*, 429, seems to me certain ; Prehn, *Quaestiones Plautinae*, 79, adds other instances.

[2] The most convenient collection of illustrations is in Bieber, *History of the Greek Theatre*, and in Pickard-Cambridge, *Dramatic Festivals* (forthcoming) ; cf. also Simon, *Comicae Tabellae*, and Webster, *Rylands Bulletin*, XXXII, 97. Pl. IV shows three typical masks of New Comedy.

[3] Rome, Lateran. Bieber, *H.T.*, fig. 223 ; Robert, *Masken*, fig. 96 ; Pickard-Cambridge, *Festivals*, fig. 93. On a silver cup in the Louvre (Schefold, *Bildnisse*, 166/2 ; *Mon. Piot.*, 1899) the skeleton of Menander holds the mask of the *Agroikos* as described by Pollux.

invented the new masks and costumes, but we can at least be
sure that they were introduced in his lifetime. We have, as far
as I know, no more precise lower limit for the change than this ;
the list of New Comedy masks in Pollux seems to be based on
an Alexandrian scholar of the third century and the original of
the Dioskourides mosaics with the comedy scenes can be dated
to about 280 ;[1] but most of the illustrative material is later.
The upper limit is given by the Aixone relief probably to be
dated 340.[2]

The reliefs and pictures in particular give us some idea of what
New Comedy looked like. We can very seldom say that we
have an illustration of a preserved scene but we can very often
point to scenes in existing comedy of the same type as the scenes
represented. A young man dances drunkenly, supported by
his slave, his father is restrained from attacking him by an
elderly friend ;[3] a rough parallel is afforded by the scene in the
Heautontimoroumenos (1045), where Menedemus restrains Chremes
from attacking Clitipho. A slave has taken refuge on an altar
and his master flies at him with a stick while an elderly friend
looks on ;[4] Tranio at the end of the *Mostellaria* or Daos in the
papyrus fragment of the *Perinthia* come to mind. An old slave
rushes on and addresses the audience while a young man and a
hetaira overhear in horror ;[5] the news may be that the youth's
father has returned from abroad as in the *Mostellaria*. An old
slave disapprovingly watches a younger slave embracing a flute-
player ;[6] the old slave reminds us of Grumio in the *Mostellaria*
and the slave revels recall the end of the *Stichus*. An old man
leaves a young wife, presumably his daughter, in fury ;[7] her
slave overhears ; the *Epitrepontes* and the *Stichus* provide parallels.
A youth with a drum and a youth with clappers dance in the
street while a hetaira plays the flute ;[8] this recalls various passages

---

[1] Rumpf, *J.H.S.*, lxvii, 16.   [2] Cf. above, p. 75.

[3] Bieber, *H.T.*, fig. 252 ; Pickard-Cambridge, *Theatre*, fig. 77 ; *Festivals*,
fig. 94.

[4] Bieber, *H.T.*, fig. 425 ; Pickard-Cambridge, *Theatre*, figs. 78–9.

[5] Bieber, *H.T.*, fig. 238 ; Simon, *Comicae Tabellae*, no. 1 ; Pickard-Cambridge,
Festivals, fig. 97.

[6] Bieber, *H.T.*, fig. 228 ; Simon, no. 5.

[7] Bieber, *H.T.*, fig. 229 ; Simon, no. 7 ; Pickard-Cambridge, *Festivals*,
fig. 101.

[8] Bieber, *H.T.*, fig. 239 ; Simon, no. 8 ; Pickard-Cambridge, *Theatre*, fig. 85 ;
Pfuhl, *MuZ.*, fig. 684.

—Diniarchus is called tympanotriba in the *Truculentus* (611) ; Callidamates arrives with a flute girl in the *Mostellaria* (310 f.). A slave ingratiates himself with a soldier slave ; [1] this might well be an illustration of the Harpax scene of the *Pseudolus* (594). A slave watches through the door as his young master walks by night, as in the prologue of the *Curculio*.[2] A hetaira sends a slave marketing,[3] a scene which we know from the *Menaechmi* (in the *Bacchides* and *Truculentus* the young man's slave returns with his purchases to the hetaira). Finally two pictures may be illustrations of Menander's *Synaristosai* (*Cistellaria*), first the opening scene of Gymnasium, Selenium, and the *lena* drinking wine together [4] and secondly the scene where the *lena* and Gymnasium are seen leaving the house by the slave Lampadio.[5]

These pictures show us a different world from the padded, obscene, goggling-eyed figures of Attic and South Italian vases of the early fourth century. This is not only due to the change of costume but also to the masks. In fact, we can trace a gradual approach to naturalism in the masks if we take the Leningrad oenochoe, the New York terracottas, the Aixone relief, and the New Comedy pictures as successive stages ; the change is most noticeable in the old men and younger men and least noticeable in the women and the slaves. The slaves' masks and the old women remain distorted caricatures ; the younger women's masks seem to have come in during the Middle Comedy and never to have been much distorted.

For the old men and the young men of New Comedy six important new masks were introduced.[6] We can see three possible reasons, fashion, distinction, and characterisation. In the early fourth century shaving is a sign of effeminacy or wildness ; in the late fourth century it is the normal fashion for young men, following the example of Alexander.[7] By the time of Menander

---

[1] Bieber, *H.T.*, fig. 237 ; Simon, no. 14 ; Pickard-Cambridge, *Festivals*, fig. 98 ; Rumpf in *Mimus und Logos*, 163.

[2] Robert, *Masken*, figs. 54 and 61 ; Simon, no. 16.

[3] Bieber, *H.T.*, fig. 243 ; Simon, no. 6 ; Pickard-Cambridge, *Festivals*, fig. 96.

[4] Bieber, *H.T.*, fig. 242 ; Simon, no. 20 ; Pickard-Cambridge, *Theatre*, fig. 86 ; *Festivals*, fig. 95. Pfuhl, *MuZ.*, fig. 685.

[5] Robert, *Masken*, fig. 88 ; Simon, no. 19.

[6] The *Eikonikos* was also new and was apparently used for rich foreigners (cf. Simon, *op. cit.*, 94).

[7] Chrysippos, ap. Ath., 565 b, quoting Alexis, 264K.

not only the rake and the soldier but also the sober young man is clean shaven. At the same time I think it is possible that someone (perhaps Menander, since he was particularly interested in the relations of father and son) saw that it helped the audience if the male members of a household could be recognised and that an easy way of distinguishing households was by hair-dressing. The frame-work was already provided for three such households distinguished by rolled hair, wavy hair, and curly hair. Rolled hair can be seen on earlier slave masks and possibly on the mask of a rustic youth : New Comedy adds the leading old man (as father) and three young men, the *panchrestos*, dark youth, and delicate youth. Wavy hair appeared earlier on slaves and wild young men (perhaps including soldiers from the time of Alexander) ; now the old man is added. Curly hair had already been worn by old men and by slaves ; the young man is new. Thus the new masks make it possible to distinguish fathers, sons, and slaves of three households by their hairdressing ; and on the Naples relief already quoted father, son, and slave all have wavy hair ; the elderly friend who restrains the father has a roll of hair. There is nothing in the monuments to contradict this theory and it is possible to allot masks to the plays in accordance with it.[1] Its convenience is clear. Three households cover the normal needs of comedy and the only apparent breach of the principle is the admission of a soldier and/or his servant as well as a wavy-haired young man and/or old màn (*Perikeiromene, Epidicus, Pseudolus, Truculentus*), but costume and attributes of the soldier would keep the distinction clear.

A third reason for the introduction of new masks may be characterisation. This is not of course new. Some of the masks in Pollux' list which go back beyond New Comedy have character labels such as ' fierce in expression, rather bad-tempered, displaying interference', and the possibility of mixed characteristics is given by the double-sided masks which can be traced back to the fifth century.[2] Character masks are not new in principle, though the characterisation may be subtler now and the result is further removed from grotesque caricature, as we can see by comparing the new pair of fathers as they appear in the Naples relief with the old pair of mild and angry old men

---

[1] Cf. *Rylands Bulletin*, XXXII, 107 f.
[2] Cf. Rumpf, *A.J.A.*, lv, 8.

on the Leningrad oenochoe. The two new old men give two basic types; an energetic old man who can however be calm (only one eyebrow is raised) and a normally calm old man who may be subject to fits of anger. The four new young masks show the need to differentiate between youths by age and character as well as household. The curly-haired youth was perhaps chiefly needed as the son of the curly-haired household; Philocrates in the *Captivi* is a certain instance because he is so described (647), and in this play four young men's masks are needed for the two brothers (the elder Philopolemus and the younger Tyndarus), Philocrates, and the irresponsible Aristophontes. The other new masks for young men make it possible for the leading old man to have four different kinds of sons—the admirable youth who is high-spirited and athletic (Plesidippus in the *Rudens* is fixed by description, 314), the dark youth who is younger and more interested in philosophy than athletics (Charisios in the *Epitrepontes* is a probable example), the delicate youth who is the youngest (e.g. the youth in Menander's *Phasma*), and the rustic, whose age is unspecified, with dark skin, snub nose and flat lips (the legitimate son of the *Hypobolimaios*; Gorgias in Menander's *Heros* and *Georgos*).

We can therefore truthfully say that the new masks do distinguish character types, particularly among the young men for whom with the addition of the wavy-haired masks of the soldier and the rake there are now seven masks available. The whole range of 44 masks in Pollux' list (or 40 if we exclude those which do not seem to have survived into the New Comedy period) makes a repertoire which is very adequate for the needs of New Comedy. The evidence of the monuments suggests that the types remained extraordinarily fixed. This, however, raises a question. The rustic mask with physical characteristics like the bad horse of the *Phaedrus* myth (253d), which are interpreted by the *Physiognomonica* as indicative of cowardice and sensuality, was clearly invented for a rustic boy, whose pleasures, unlike Aristotle's rustic,[1] exceed all moderation or necessity. This suits Ctesipho in the *Adelphi* well enough and Strabax in the *Truculentus* even better. It does not suit that admirably moral youth Gorgias of the *Georgos*. But the question is not confined to rustics. Menander and Apollodoros took various

[1] *E.E.*, 1230 b 19.

characters who were normally objects of satire on the comic stage and made sympathetic studies of them—the soldier, the flatterer, the rich hetaira, and the stepmother. Did they have special masks? We have no evidence that they did. Then perhaps we can say that we have here a special instance of the contrast between conventional and real values which Menander so much desired to emphasise. Not only in the opinion of all the characters (even of her lover at times) but also in her appearance to them and to the audience, Thais in the *Eunuch* is the greedy, fickle, rich hetaira : in spite of all this, Menander shows that she is very human and has higher ideals than anyone else in the play.

V. PHILEMON AND HIS COMEDY

IT is more difficult to form an estimate of Philemon's comedy than of Menander's comedy because a considerable body of connected Menander has survived on papyrus which enables us to check the accuracy of the Latin translation and to guess the probable contexts of the unconnected fragments known to us by quotation. Whether the few papyri which have been attributed to Philemon have been rightly attributed can only be decided when we have formed an estimate of his comedy from the Greek quotations and the three Latin plays, *Mercator*, *Mostellaria*,[1] and *Trinummus*, for which he certainly provided the originals, but the papyri do not add much to our knowledge.

The little that is known about his life can be briefly stated.[2] He was born between 365 and 360 and he died in 264 or 263. He came either from Syracuse or from Soloi in Cyprus: Syracuse seems more likely because of the known interest of the West in Attic comedy, and the chief comic poet of the generation before, Alexis, came from Thourioi. Philemon had become an Athenian citizen by 307/6.[3] Unlike Menander, Philemon apparently accepted an invitation to visit Egypt. On the way back he was shipwrecked off Cyrene, and Magas, the King of Cyrene, refrained from killing him although Philemon had jested at his ignorance in a play.[4] The date of these events is uncertain; Magas probably captured Cyrene in 308 but the abuse is more likely to belong to the later period when he had revolted from Ptolemy Philadelphos (274).[5] The *Panegyris*, of which two fragments survive, was presumably written in Alexandria. The fragments of the *Panegyris* (58, 59K) have sometimes been connected with Theokritos' *Adoniazousai* and this may give a bottom

---

[1] *Mostellaria* must be a *Phasma*. Menander's *Phasma* is known; Theognetos' has the alternative title *Philargyros*. The surviving Greek fragment of Philemon's *Phasma*, 84K, could belong to the context of 315 or 956; the Latin poet as so often has left out the particularity of the Greek. *Most.*, 1149, *Si amicus Diphilus aut Philemoni es*, I take with Terzaghi, *La Mostellaria*, 1949, to be a *Plautine* joke. So also Fuchs, *Mus. Helv.*, vi, 106, n. 4.

[2] See Körte's article in *R.E.*   [3] *I.G.*, II², 3073, 4266.

[4] Fr. 144 K.   [5] *C.A.H.*, VII, 704.

date : [1] both ' Has the King made this road for you only ? ' and
' An Egyptian has made my cloak dirty ' bring us right into the
atmosphere of Gorgo and Praxinoe.

Philemon won his first victory at the Greater Dionysia in
327 B.C.[2] and at the Lenaia not before 320 ; he comes next in
the list after Menander and won three victories of which one
was in 307/6 B.C.[3] There is no reason to doubt the statement of
the anonymous writer on comedy that he began to write before
328. This statement should also mean that Philemon did not
produce before 332 since the writer is reckoning in Olympiads.
Modern scholars have dated the *Lithoglyphos* before 340 but in
fact this is unnecessary. The fragment of the *Lithoglyphos* (50P)
mentions Aristomedes, who is also named by Timokles in the
Heroes (51P) and the *Ikarians* (51P). There is good reason to
date the *Heroes* soon after 340 B.C. and the *Ikarians* about 330 ; [4]
we must therefore suppose that Aristomedes was a butt for comic
poets for ten years or more and the *Lithoglyphos* need not have
been produced before 330. Meineke [5] believed that Philemon's
first play was the *Hypobolimaios* because Clement calls it a variation on Aristophanes' *Kokalos*, but there seems no sound reason
for the early dating. We can extract a few other dates from
the fragments : [6] *Babylonios*, 326/4 (16K), *Metion* 330/20 (42K),
Philosophoi soon after 314 (85K), *Neaira* after 304 [7] (47K). If
the *novus praefectus* of *Mostellaria* 941 is the *gynaikonomos* of
Demetrios of Phaleron, the *Phasma* can be dated 317/07.[8] The
references to Seleucia in the *Trinummus* help to date the original,
the *Thesauros* : Plautus evidently understood a country rather
than a town, but the town may have been named in the original.
Although the sycophant evidently thinks of Seleucia on the
Tigris (founded in 312 B.C.), Charmides is more likely to have
sought wealth in the Western Seleucia, which was founded about

---

[1] Perhaps about 272 (Gow, *Theocritus*, 265).

[2] *Marmor Parium* : Tod, *G.H.I.*, ii, 310.

[3] Wilhelm, *Urkunden*, 210 ; *I.G.*, II[2], 3073,

[4] Cf. *C.Q.*, 1952, 20. Philemon, 190K, refers to the statue of Astydamas
erected after his tragic victory in 340. But if Photios' reading is right, the
reference is to a past event.

[5] *Men. Phil.*, xlv.   [6] Cf. *C.Q.*, 1952, 19 f.

[7] Ferguson, *Hell. Ath.*, 69, notes that this tiger was probably captured in
India, i.e. in 304. There is no reason to date early because Seleukos' royal
title is omitted.

[8] So Ferguson, *op. cit.*, 45, n. 2.

300 B.C. ; he speaks at length of his sea journey but says nothing about travels on land ; Hueffner's date [1] early in the third century seems therefore likely. The feel of the *Emporos* (*Mercator*) is early, but there is little to go on.[2]

The Greek quotations give us a little knowledge about his comedy. The *Myrmidons* and *Palamedes* must have been mythological comedies ; the *Nyx* may have been a version of the Amphitryon story, but Nyx herself must in any case have been the prologue figure,[3] and therefore her name gives no guide to the contents. Very few contemporary references survive, and they are like those in early Menander : the allusion to Magas' illiteracy alone has some bite in it (144K) ; Kallimedon the Crab (42K), Aristomedes the thief (50P), the self-praise of Astydamas the tragedian (190K), Seleukos' tiger (47K), the asceticism of Zeno (85K) and the self-torture of Krates (146K) are stock comic allusions.[4] The *Neaira* and *Euripos* [5] must have been hetaira plays like Menander's *Thais* and many Middle Comedies. The *Hypobolimaios* must have been a recognition play if it was like Aristophanes' *Kokalos*. Four other titles may suggest recognition plays : *Encheiridion* (the little dagger), the *Ring*, the *Sard*, and *Pterugion*.[6] But the *Ring* and the *Sard* may rather be signet rings used to sign documents as in the *Pseudolus*, and a quite different explanation has been suggested for the *Pterugion*.[7] But the *Pterugion* in any case introduces a *leno* (66K) who objects to

---

[1] Hueffner, *De Plauti com. quaest. chron.*, 61

[2] Dietze, *De Philemone comico*, 15, dates 315–307 but on no sufficient evidence. Possibly the *capra* of the dream (229) is an allusion to Αἰγίδιον = Nannion (still alive after 320).

[3] Night is attested as a character in comedy by Choricius (*C.A.F.*, III, 553/819). The evidence for the *Graces* seems too weak to accept. The *Heroes* is not certainly mythological ; they might be a club of rowdies.

[4] *Pyrrhos* as a title is more likely to be Redheaded Slave than the King.

[5] On *Euripos* as a hetaira name see Lucas, *Rh. Mus.*, 1938, 188 and below, p. 148. Neaira cannot have been Demosthenes' Neaira, who must have been born soon after 400 since she saw Lysias (d. 378 B.C.).

[6] Assuming that πτερύγιον is a bit of a garment like πτέρυξ in *Epitr.*, 228 ; Aristophanes, 325K, etc.

[7] Rappisarda, *Filemone Comico*, 90 (developing Dietze, 33), quotes Polybius (xxvii, 9, 4) for the meaning ' decoration for valour ' and equates this with the *Cornicula* of Plautus. The original of the *Cornicula* must have been written between 307 and 283 (fr. II, i.e. between the date of Demetrios being hailed King in Athens and his death). The combined fragments give us a young man in love with a hetaira in the possession of a *leno* and complaining of his poverty (65, 66K ; *Cornicula*, V) and a soldier successfully tricked by the young

possible clients falling in love with married women (cf. Xenarchos, 4K). A *leno* appears also in the *Adelphoi* (4K) and shows
the realism of thought and disjointedness of style which characterises his kind in Greek comedy.[1]

The cook in a fragment of the *Stratiotes* (79K), who claims that
if he is given proper materials he can turn the diners into gods
and make corpses live, is own brother to the cook in the *Pseudolus*,
who promises that those who eat his dishes will live two hundred
years (829) and offers to rejuvenate Ballio as Medea rejuvenated
Pelias [2] (868). Like the nurse in the *Medea* (57 f.) the cook in
the *Stratiotes* comes out because 'Desire has entered me to tell
earth and heaven—how I prepared the food.' The tragic
reminiscence here shows the pomposity of the cook, and so is
parallel to the tragic diction which Tranio gives to the ghost in
the *Mostellaria* (497). *Ego transmarinus hospes sum diapontius. hic
habito, haec mihi dedita est habitatio.* These uses are comparable to
the flood of tragic quotation with which the slave in Menander's
Heauton Penthon announces the feigned death of Chaireas.[3] The
mad scene in the *Mercator* (930 f.) with its reminiscences of the
mad scenes of tragedy is essentially similar in technique. Another
fragment (119K) reads : 'What right have you to free speech ?
Do you talk among men as though you were a man ? Do you
walk about and breathe the same air as the rest, being the kind
of man you are ?' This recalls Euripides' *Andromache* (590) :
'Are you among men, you villain, son of villains, how should
you count in the tale of men ?' In Philemon perhaps a young
man addresses a *leno* and the tragic reminiscence increases the
force of his abuse. This amplification by tragic reminiscence is
found several times in the *Trinummus* ; for instance, Lesbonicus'
scibam ut esse me deceret, facere non quibam miser (657) recalls
Euripides, *Hippolytus*, 380 : τὰ χρήστ᾽ ἐπιστάμεσθα καὶ γιγνώσκο-
μεν, οὐκ ἐκπονοῦμεν δ᾽, and Lesbonicus tries to give his peccadilloes

man's slave (*Cornicula*, I–III) ; in fact, a play on the same lines as the *Pseudolus*.
This remains, however, highly speculative as the word for a decoration is *corni-
culum* ; *cornicula* should mean a ' crow ', and this is an equally possible meaning
for Plautus' title. The soldier may have been pecked by others.

[1] Dietze, *op. cit.*, 34, adds *Harpazomene* (14K), but this is not certain, though
attractive.

[2] Fraenkel, *Pl. in Pl.*, 82, thinks that this is Plautine because the mythology
is wrong, but the cook may get his mythology wrong : J. Tierney, *P.R.I.A.*,
L, 28, compares Anaxandrides, 34K.

[3] Cf. *Studies in Menander*, 156.

a tragic stature.[1] Earlier in the *Trinummus* (304 f.) the scene between Lysiteles and Philto seems to be a reminiscence of the scene between Haemon and Creon in the *Antigone*, but the general impression made by the fragments and the Plautine adaptations is that Philemon, in spite of the admiration for Euripides expressed in a fragment,[2] is less indebted to the tragedians for incidents and technique than Menander and less varied in his use of verbal reminiscence.

The cook in the *Stratiotes* uses an amusing image to describe the effect of his cooking : ' It was just like when a bird snatches something too big to gulp down. She runs round in circles guarding it and tries to gulp it down, and the other birds pursue. It was the same. The first of them discovered how sweet the dish was, leapt up and ran away in circles with the dish in his hands, and they pursued hot foot. You could shout for joy. Some snatched something, some got nothing.' There are in the fragments other instances of similes which are worked out at length (e.g. 28, 75, 88K), and therefore it seems probable that, although Plautus has undoubtedly added a great deal of elaboration and expansion, the long comparison between the soul and a house in the *Mostellaria* (91 f.) comes from the original.[3] A minor point of style in the fragment of the *Stratiotes* is perhaps also characteristic of Philemon ; although the repetitions from the images to the compared ' snatches snatched . . . pursues pursued ' point the parallel, the repetitions within each half, ' gulped down ' and ' dish ', are less elegant, but can be matched in other fragments, e.g. 46K : ' it is an even worse ill than feeling ill to have to tell all visitors how one feels when one feels ill '.[4] This shows up even in the translations, e.g. *Merc.*, 695 f., *sed coquos, quasi in mari solet hortator remiges hortarier, ita hortabatur.*[5] The style has a certain flat-footedness here which may be

---

[1] Cf. also 199 f. with, e.g., *Ant.*, 295, 672 f. ; 617 f. with Eumaios in the *Odyssey* ; 490 f. with E., *Suppl.*, 549, and Homer, *Iliad*, ix, 319, 409.

[2] Page, fr. 50b : ' Euripides says so, who alone is eloquent ', cf. 130K, which however may not be Philemon.

[3] Cf. also *Trinummus*, 28-33. Note that Demetrios of Phaleron (123W) compared the care needed for each man and each company of an army to the care needed for each brick and each room of a house. Wehrli quotes Xen., *Mem.*, III, i, 7 f., when the right arrangement of materials in a house is compared to the right arrangement of the strong and weak parts of an army.

[4] Cf. 5, 7, 22, 23, 53, 69, 73, 106K.

[5] Cf. also *Most.*, 251 ; *Trin.*, 28-33, 1110-12.

intentionally comic, but does not so far as I know appear in Menander.

Let us now look at the Plautine plays which show us Philemon on a larger scale. No Greek fragment survives of the *Emporos*, which Plautus translated as *Mercator*. At the beginning the young hero Charinus tells his story to the audience.[1] Like Clinias in the *Heautontimoroumenos* he had yielded to his father Demipho's reproaches and gone abroad to make a fortune ; unlike Clinias, he had forgotten his first love and fallen for a girl in Rhodes whom he has bought and brought home. The father's rise from poverty as a rustic to comparative wealth as a merchant is described at some length. Charinus also describes the nature of his own love : *insomnia, aerumna, error, terror, et fuga* : *ineptia, stultitiaque adeo et temeritast, incogitantia excors, inmodestia, petulantia et cupiditas, malivolentia* ; *inerit etiam aviditas, desidia, iniuria, inopia, contumelia et dispendium, multiloquium, parumloquium.* Then the slave Acanthio arrives with the news that the father Demipho has found the girl on the ship and made advances to her—this goat-like quality in a severe father we know also from Menander, e.g. the father of Alcesimarchus in the *Cistellaria* and Nicobulus in the *Bacchides*. Plautus has expanded this scene, but the best parts, the arrival of the panting old pedagogue, the dialogue in which he tortures Charinus, and Charinus' explanation (195), ' in vain did I escape from the storms of the sea. I thought that I was safe on land but I see that savage waves are carrying me on to the rocks,' must be Philemon.

The second act begins with Demipho's description of his dream. The menagerie is Greek : she-goat, monkey, and he-goat. Plautus' *capra* translates the Greek *aix* or *aigidion*, which was the nickname of the hetaira Nannion ; *haedus* is naturally the mate of *capra* ; the monkey, *pithekos*, is masculine in Greek and may be chosen, as Enk suggests, because Lysimachus behaves first as a friend and then as an enemy ; the lengthy description again seems to me characteristic of Philemon.[2] Demipho then

---

[1] Like Palaestrio in the *Miles* (79) and like Demosthenes in Aristophanes' *Knights* (36). With Charinus' preliminary criticism of other prologues, cf. Page, fr. 60. Dietze, *op. cit.*, 56, compares *Merc.*, 40, with Philemon, 34K.

[2] I see no reason for supposing the dream to be Plautine invention : Fraenkel's objection (*op. cit.*, 198 f.) is countered by Enk with a comparison to Euripides, *I.T.*, 42 f. I do not feel certain that the dream does not belong to an earlier entrance of Demipho, possibly at the beginning of the play.

confesses his passion to his old neighbour Lysimachus and the old
men indulge in polite commonplaces : ' although I am busy I
am never too busy to help a friend ', ' it is human to fall in love
and it is human to forgive '.[1] Lysimachus' entry is neatly con-
trived ; he comes out because he is sending his slave to the
country to tell his wife that he has business in town ; as we know
that wives are jealous we expect her to pursue him.[2]

The unhappy Charinus then arrives to do battle with Demipho.
Demipho wins the first round by establishing that the girl is not
the right type to be his wife's servant. Charinus suggests selling
her back to her previous owner. Demipho says he has a client
who will buy her. Charinus also has a client. Demipho's client
will pay any price. Charinus says ' she is not for sale '. Demipho
finally marches off to the harbour to get the girl sold to his friend
Lysimachus, who will house her. The comedy of this scene lies
in the absence of preconceived plan. Each follows the other's
movements regardless of whether he contradicts his own former
statements. The act ends when Eutychus, the son of Lysimachus,
has promised Charinus to go to the harbour and get hold of
the girl.[3]

The chief point of the next scene is the comedy of errors (the
girl Pasicompsa talks of Charinus while Lysimachus means
Demipho), but it also gives a picture of Pasicompsa as genuinely
in love with Charinus. Demipho then explains the philosophy
of having a good time in old age after his strenuous youth
(544 f.),[4] Lysimachus persuades him to come to the market place
and hire a cook. Eutychus returns to tell Charinus that the girl
has been sold, and Charinus threatens to go into exile.

At the beginning of the fourth act, Dorippa, Lysimachus' wife,
returns from the country and finds Pasicompsa whom she assumes
to be Lysimachus' mistress. The hobbling gait of her old maid
Syra is traditional comedy,[5] but her prayer to Apollo is pleasant
realism. We should have expected Lysimachus, Demipho, and
the cook to return at the same moment, but Philemon delays

---

[1] 287, cf. *Heautontimoroumenos*, 77 ; 319, cf. *Adelphi*, 101 f.
[2] For a similar neat motivation, cf. *Mostellaria*, 690.
[3] Two points of interest in this scene : 477, Eutychus has overheard the
preceding scene and thus repetition is saved ; 481, is Charinus' forgetfulness
characteristic of his lovelorn state ?
[4] Alexis, fr. 235, may be an old man's statement of the same philosophy.
[5] Cf. Sophrone in Menander's *Eunuch* and *Epitrepontes*.

Demipho till the next act (957) and the cook to the next
scene [1] (741). By this means Philemon can show two stages in
Lysimachus' discomfiture and twice display his slowness in argument ; it takes him 28 lines to evolve the fiction that Pasicompsa's
presence is explained by an arbitration (732 : *immo iam scio : de
istac sum iudex captus*) and 43 lines to think up an explanation for
the cook, which he is then not allowed to give (783). He is less
nimble than Charinus and Demipho but the underlying comedy
is the same.

The fifth act begins (817) with the return of Syra,[2] who had
been sent to fetch Dorippa's father to bring about a divorce.
The theme is only introduced in order that Eutychus may meet
Syra outside the house and learn that Pasicompsa is inside.
While he goes to verify this, Syra expatiates on the misery of
women in words that recall Euripides' *Medea*,[3] and Charinus
comes out prepared for exile with chlamys, sword-belt, sword,
and lekythos ; *egomet mihi comes, calator, equos, agaso, armiger*
(852). He is a familiar figure whom we know well in several
versions. The earliest is Orestes in the *Choephori* (675) :
στείχοντα δ᾽ αὐτόφορτον οἰκείᾳ σαγῇ. The next is probably a
parody of a tragic hero in Antiphanes' *Athamas* (16K) : χλαμύ-
δα καὶ λόγχην ἔχων, ἀξυνακόλουθος, ξηρός, αὐτολήκυθος. Diphilos
provides a soldier who looks like ' a walking junkshop ' (55K).[4]
Then Menander provides two parallels : Moschion at the end
of the very early *Samia* (313 f.) and Alcesimarchus in the early
Synaristosai (*Cist.*, 284 ff.). In Menander this is good comedy
but also good psychology, the wayward stormy Alcesimarchus
finally carries off his bride by force, Moschion's proposal is a
piece of braggadocio which he fears may not come off : ' supposing he is angry and let me go . . . I shall be too ridiculous
if I have to come back again ! ' But in the *Mercator* Charinus'
equipment is not character drawing but preparation for the scene

---

[1] This is covered by Lysimachus (698) : *eum demiror non venire* ; cf. Menander
at *Eunuch*, 735 (*Studies in Menander*, 73).

[2] There must be an act break between Syra's departure (788) and her return
(803), but no act break is necessary while Eutychus goes into the house (816–42).
Kunst, *Studien*, 143, points out that if Dorippa's father had appeared he would
have been the only *avus adulescentis* in comedy.

[3] Leo, *Pl. F.*[1], 107, cf. E., *Med.*, 184 ff., 230 ff.

[4] Illustrated by a terracotta actor of Middle Comedy in the British Museum
(C.238, Pickard-Cambridge, *Festivals*, fig. 123). Cf. the description of Euripides'
Telephos in the *Acharnians*.

of rich comedy in which, while Eutychus tries to inform him that Pasicompsa is in Lysimachus' house, he pretends to ride round Greece looking for her (931 f.) : the parody of the messenger speech in Euripides' *Hercules Furens* (942 f.) is obvious. The play ends with Demipho's return and admission of folly.

The *Mercator* is good comedy. No very serious satire is intended even of the old fool who falls in love with his son's mistress. The love of Charinus and Pasicompsa is genuine, but Charinus' tantrums are exaggerated to make him the subject of laughter. The play is competently constructed as we have seen, but Philemon is more interested in the comedy of the individual scene or situation (even of the individual phrase) than in building a climax such for instance as the intrigue in Menander's *Dis Exapaton* (Plautus' *Bacchides*) or the battle between husband and wife in Diphilos' *Kleroumenoi* (Plautus' *Casina*).

The *Mostellaria* has obvious similarities with the *Mercator*. The motivation is equally neat,[1] and imagery is used in much the same way.[2] The son, Philolaches, is again in love with a hetaira and indulges in a long speech of self-recrimination like Charinus. Here the father instead of the son returns from abroad. Again the final solution is brought about by the son's friend. Philematium, as appears from the scene with Scapha, is genuinely in love with Philolaches, as Pasicompsa with Charinus. Although much in this long scene has been added by Plautus[3] and some elements are traditional (e.g. the washing and dressing[4] and the comparison with painted old hetairai[5]), the characterisation of Philematium as the ' youthful little hetaira who does not use make-up ' (to quote Pollux' description of her mask) must be Philemon. But the justification of their love is in no sense the object of the comedy as in Menander's plays of Social Criticism. The centre of the comedy is a battle of wits of the same kind as those between Demipho and Charinus and between Lysimachus, Dorippa, and the cook in the *Mercator*. Here, too, the slave Tranio has no preconceived plan but trusts to his invention as

[1] e.g. Grumio, 62 ; return of Theoropides, 547 ; entry of Simo, 690 ; Calli- damates' slave, 933 ; return of Simo, 998. In general on the parallels between the three plays which derive from Philemon, see Kunst, *Studien*, 142 f.

[2] Note how the house image of Philolaches' soliloquy is taken up by the house theme in the central scenes : cf. Demipho's dream and the *hircus* in *Merc.*, 272.

[3] Cf. Fraenkel, *op. cit.*, 177 f ; Fuchs, *Mus. Helv.*, 6, 105.

[4] Cf. *Poenulus*, 205 ff.   [5] Cf. Euboulos, 98K (350/40).

each situation has to be met. He promises to keep the father Theoropides away from the house and first invents the ghost story. He makes up as he goes along (486) :

' We all went to bed. We went to sleep. I had forgotten to put out the light. And he suddenly gave a loud cry.'

THEOROPIDES : ' Who ? Was it my son ? '

TRANIO : ' Quiet. Only listen to me. He said it came to him as he slept, dead.'

The forgotten light would make sense if Tranio had gone to put it out and then seen the ghost, but he abandons that idea and prefers the dream story. Then he is faced with both the moneylender (who had provided the money with which Philolaches had bought Philematium) and Theoropides again. His first offer to the moneylender (592) is pure bluff. He then has the brilliant idea of telling Theoropides that Philolaches has borrowed the money as a deposit to pay for a new house (637). This disposes of the moneylender, but Theoropides wants to know where the house is. Tranio rashly indicates the house next door. Theoropides wants to see it. Tranio says that there are women inside who may not want to be disturbed.[1] He then has to find a way of persuading the neighbour Simo to show Theoropides his house and, having first persuaded him to keep quiet about Philolaches' carousals, tells him that Theoropides is thinking of building on to his own house and wants to inspect Simo's architecture ; he prevents Theoropides from asking awkward questions by emphasising Simo's distress at having to give up his house (810). This is not the planning of a master intriguer but a desperate attempt to meet every situation as it arises. Plautus, just as in the *Bacchides* he increased the part of Chrysalus, who really was a master intriguer in the original, has tried to convert Tranio into a master intriguer by the insertion of three monologues which are out of character (409 f., 775 f., 1041 f.).[2]

The two early scenes with the drunk Callidamates[3] and Tranio's

[1] Note how neatly Simo gives the lie to this unintentionally : 808, Theoropides : *at enim mulieres.* Simo : *cave tu ullam flocci faxis mulierem.*

[2] The boy with the key (425) is only introduced to give Tranio the chance of a monologue ; 775 f. starts with the typically Plautine *Alexandrum magnum atque Agathoclem* ; 1041 f. The typically Plautine military simile *eduxi omnem legionem—manuplaris meos.* Tranio must have announced the escape but without the triumph element.

[3] Cf. Alexis, 87, 244, 301K ; Antiphanes, 199K ; Ephippos, 25K ; Diphilos, 46K.

asylum at the end are rich comedy of the same kind as Charinus' mad scene in the *Mercator*. The asylum scene is worth a moment's attention : Tranio, realising that Theoropides has learnt the truth from Simo, takes refuge on the altar (1094), a traditional scene which we know from statuettes of Middle Comedy period as well as from other plays.[1] When Theoropides asks him to come over and give some advice, he refuses : *nimio plus sapio sedens*. Again we are reminded of terracotta statuettes of seated slaves with their chins pillared on their hands (*os columnatum*).[2] Theoropides then goes up and tells Tranio to look at him ; Sonnenschein says, ' Theoropides assumes an amiable expression of countenance to persuade Tranio that he has nothing to fear ' ; this is both attractive and possible if Theoropides wears a mask with one gloomy and one cheerful side like the mask of the leading old man described by Pollux. Theoropides then threatens to burn him off the altar (cf. Menander's *Perinthia* [3]), but Callidamates arrives in time to save him. Here Philemon shows himself a master of traditional boisterous comedy, making full use of the possibilities of the Greek stage.

In the *Trinummus* also the father returns from abroad and the reconciliation is effected by the son's friend (Apuleius [4] notes *sodalis opitulator* as one of Philemon's stock characters). Two scenes have something of the joyous opportunism of the central scenes of the other two plays ; one is the scene in which Stasimus successfully warns Philto off the one remaining field, which Lesbonicus proposed to make his sister's dowry (523 f.) : ' first of all when the land is ploughed, the oxen die at each fifth furrow . . . There is an outlet of Acheron in our field. Then the grapes hang rotten before they get ripe. . . . Next when elsewhere the crop is very heavy, this field produces only a third of what you have sown. . . . No one has ever owned this field without disaster, some have gone into exile, some are dead, and others have hanged themselves.' The other is the charming scene (861 f.) in which the man who has been hired to bring

---

[1] e.g. Bieber, *H.T.*, fig. 231 (Vatican), 232 (B.M.), 220 (B.M.), and terracottas in B.M. C90, D322 (Cat., pl. XXXIV), and one in the City of Stoke Museum and Art Gallery (*Rylands Bulletin*, XXXII, pl. II, fig. 6, and Pickard-Cambridge, *Festivals*, figs. 130–2).

[2] e.g. Bieber, *H.T.*, fig. 135 (New York).

[3] Cf. Ar., *Thesm.*, 725 ; Strattis, *Zopyros Perikaiomenos* ; South Italian vase, *C.V.A.*, Italy, 745.   [4] *Florida*, XVI.

Lesbonicus forged letters from Charmides meets Charmides himself. The scene in which Lesbonicus and Stasimus do their accounts (402 f.) is traditional comedy and the theme can be traced back to Aristophanes' *Clouds*.[1]

The play, however, differs from the other two in having a much larger amount of moralising and, as we have noted already, a large amount of tragic reminiscence. The proportion of moral discussion to comic scenes has been altered. Moralising in the *Mercator* is practically confined to Charinus' opening soliloquy. It bulks rather larger in the *Mostellaria* because it occupies three of the four scenes in the first act. The play starts with the old country slave Grumio, whom Leo justly compares to Eumaios in the *Odyssey*, abusing Tranio for the life led by Philolaches in his father's absence ; this is followed by Philolaches' soliloquy and Philematium's dialogue with Scapha, both of which can reasonably be described as moralising, but from then on we have pure comedy. The *Trinummus* is packed with moralising. The scene in the first act between two old men, Megaronides and Callicles, begins (after traditional complaints about the badness of Callicles' wife [2]) with Megaronides' uninformed criticism of Callicles : it is slander based on false assumption owing to ignorance of the facts ; the same false assumption is made later by the slave Stasimus, who also believes that Callicles has bought Lesbonicus' house for his own profit (617 f.) and for a moment persuades Charmides himself of this (1081 ff.). Stasimus is finally convinced *hic meo ero amicus solus firmus restitit neque demutavit animum de firma fide* (1110). Two ideas are present here, the wickedness of basing judgements on false assumption and the goodness of friendship. The former idea, which is the theme of Apelles' famous picture of Slander and occurs frequently in Menander in the form of a contrast between conventional and true judgements,[3] only concerns Callicles ; the latter is also one theme in the scenes between the two young men Lesbonicus and Lysiteles (as also between the two young men in the *Mercator* and *Mostellaria*).

Lysiteles' opening soliloquy introduces the contrast between

---

[1] Cf. *C.Q.*, xlii, 26.

[2] For this theme in Philemon, cf. below, p. 138, n. 1.

[3] Cf. *Studies in Menander*, 117 f., and above, p. 117. Dietze, *op. cit.*, 36, compares with this passage *Pseud.*, 427.

the life of love and the life of ambition (like the corresponding soliloquies of Charinus and Philolaches) ; this recurs in the lengthy dialogue between Lysiteles and his father Philto—Philto says that a man must not give way to his own *animus* (305 f.), here ἐπιθυμία rather than θυμός. Lysiteles answers : *sarta tecta tua praecepta usque habui mea modestia* (σωφροσύνη). They then discuss Lesbonicus, who has lost his money through *comitas*, i.e. he is the kind of ἄσωτος who gives too much because he has no standards in giving. As Aristotle [1] says, ' he is much better than the illiberal man, he is easily cured both by growing up and by lack of money, and he may easily move towards the mean.' We are reminded of Micio's theory of education in Menander's *Second Adelphoi*, but Philemon is not interested in the educational problem as such. Lysiteles urges his father to let him marry Lesbonicus' sister without a dowry and suggests that it is shameful if they do not use their wealth to help their friends : again Menander provides the text in the *Dyskolos* (128K), ' a certain friend is better than concealed wealth which you keep underground '.[2] Lysiteles finally persuades his father to see Lesbonicus and arrange the match. Philto reluctantly agrees (392) : *non optima haec sunt neque ut ego aequam censeo ; verum meliora sunt quam quae deterruma.* When he sees Lesbonicus, his generosity in waiving the dowry stings Lesbonicus to offer his one remaining piece of land as dowry, although this probably means going to the wars for himself (595 f.). The opposition between pleasure and ambition is raised again in the dialogue between the two young men (627 f.).

This ends in deadlock because Lesbonicus is resolved to give his sister a dowry since otherwise he will be giving her *in concubinatum* rather than *in matrimonium*, and Lysiteles is resolved not to accept the dowry. Lysiteles' motive is the desire to help his friend. Lesbonicus' generosity is the unwise generosity of the prodigal. His phraseology is interesting because it shows clearly the difference of status between the παλλακή and the γαμετή. It is this change of status that Menander achieves for his heroines (Glykera in the *Perikeiromene*, Selenium in the *Cistellaria*, etc.)

---

[1] *N.E.*, 1121 a 19. Cf. *Studies in Menander*, 66, and Diphilos' characterisation of Daemones in the *Rudens*, below, p. 160.

[2] In Menander the argument is based on the uncertainty of wealth, a theme which Philto uses in arguing with Lesbonicus (490 f.), where he reminds us of another fragment of Menander, 538K.

by discovering their parents. But whereas Menander uses these means to give a love match the social status of a marriage of convenience, Lysiteles' marriage is purely a marriage of convenience and nothing could be more cynical than the pairing off of Lesbonicus and the daughter of Callicles at the end (1183) :

LESBONICUS : *ego ducam, pater, et eam et si quam aliam iubebis.*

CHARMIDES : *quamquam tibi succensui, miseria una uni quidem hominist adfatim.*

CALLICLES : *immo huic parumst, nam si pro peccatis centum ducat uxores, parumst.*

Even Clitipho in Menander's *Heautontimoroumenos* was given some choice when it was decided that he should be reformed by marriage. Such methods of choosing brides result in the unhappy marriages to which all three plays bear witness.[1] Philemon, unlike Menander, accepted the Greek convention ; marriage was normally unpleasant, love of a hetaira was normally demoralising. It is true that in the *Mercator* and *Mostellaria* both Charinus and Philolaches seem genuinely to love and be loved, but no provision is made for the future of Pasicompsa and Philematium, and they may suffer the fate of Scapha (*Most.*, 200), who had also given herself to a single lover : *qui pol me, ubi aetate hoc caput colorem commutavit, reliquit deseruitque me.* Nevertheless, the genuine affection of Pasicompsa and Philematium may account for a story in Athenaeus : [2] 'Philemon was in love with a hetaira and called her good in the course of a play ; Menander wrote against this on the ground that no hetaira was good.' Suess[3] suggested that Menander's play was the *Thais* ; Philemon must in that case have written a play with a good hetaira before Menander's *Thais* and she was presumably a girl like Pasicompsa and Philematium. There is no reason to suppose that Philemon ever gave a sympathetic portrait of the independent hetaira like Thais in Menander's *Eunuch* or Bacchis in Apollodoros' *Hecyra*. The *Mercator* and the *Mostellaria* are primarily concerned with knockabout opportunism, and the only young feminine characters that Apuleius mentions in his description of Philemon's comedy are *amica illudens* and *meretrices procaces*. The love affairs of the three plays translated by Plautus belong to Apuleius' *tuti errores, concessi amores*. Apuleius begins

---

[1] In this play 51 ff. ; *Most.*, 696 f. ; *Merc.*, 667 f. ; 132, 196, 198K.
[2] XIII, 594 (Kock, Philemon, fr. 215).   [3] *Rh. Mus.*, 1910, 449.

this sentence *rarae apud illum corruptelae*, which points in the same direction, since in Menander βιασμοὶ παρθένων are common and were all a stage in a genuine love story. A similar brief summary of Menander's comedy by Manilius (V, 473/4) starts with *ardentis iuvenes raptasque in amore puellas* and Plutarch (ap. Stobaeus, 63, 34) speaks of ἔρως as the cement of his plays. We cannot say that Philemon never wrote this kind of comedy ; if we compare his *rarae corruptelae* with *agnitus lucide explicatos* it seems likely that he occasionally did, although the *Captivi* proves that other kinds of recognition scene are possible, and the *Truculentus* shows that seduction need not imply love in New Comedy ; but if Philemon's *Hypobolimaios* was modelled on Aristophanes' *Kokalos* it must have contained both rape and recognition.

Nevertheless, where Philemon talks about friendship,[1] he appears to be perfectly serious, and it is difficult to see how the other moralising scenes can have been intended primarily as comedy, nor is there any reason to suppose that Plautus has seriously increased the moralising element. Enough moralising fragments of Philemon remain to justify Jachmann's view [2] that the moralising is due to Philemon rather than to Plautus. Whether he is also right in saying that the urge to moralise came to him not from within but from without, in fact from Menander, is not so clear. We have noticed that particularly in the *Trinummus* Philemon reminds us of Menander, but always, or nearly always, the contrast is stronger than the resemblance.[3] Philemon and Menander were catering for the same audiences, and the demands of the audience seem to me a more likely reason for Philemon's moralising than the practice of a not at the time outstandingly successful rival.

Moreover, since each of the plays contains a certain amount of moralising, we cannot tell whether such moralising fragments as have survived belong to plays with isolated moralising scenes like the *Mercator* and *Mostellaria* or to plays with a predominantly moral tone like the *Trinummus* : we cannot therefore say whether

[1] Cf. Zucker, *Ber. Sächs. Ak.*, xcviii, 1 f.
[2] *Plautinisches u. Attisches*, 226 f.
[3] Cf. in addition to the instances noted above : 10K with Menander, 550K ; 21K with Menander, 441K ; 31K with *Epitr.*, 36 ; 65K with Menander, 537K ; 90K, 93K, with Menander, 534K ; 96K, with Menander, 281K ; *Merc.*, 319, with *Ad.*, 117 f. ; *Trin.*, 451, with *Aul.*, 227 ; *Cist.*, 493.

the *Trinummus* was alone or whether there were other plays
like it or, if there were other plays like it, whether they belonged
to some particular period in Philemon's life or not.   One point
suggests that the *Trinummus* is a special play, or let us say rather
a play of a special kind : the prologue spoken by Luxury and
Poverty.   The closing lines are, of course, Plautine, but there
is no reason to suppose that Plautus has invented the prologue
figures although he has invented their Roman names (8–9) and
may have shortened their speeches.   We have one other beginning of a Philemon prologue spoken by a god [1] (91K) : 'I am
he, from whom no single being can keep no single action hid
nor future action nor past action, neither god nor man,—I am
Air, who may also be called Zeus.   I, as is the function of a
god, am everywhere, here in Athens, in Patrai, in Sicily, in all
cities, in all houses, among you all.   There is no place where
Air is not.   He who is everywhere, knows everything of necessity being everywhere.'   The ancestry of the *Trinummus* figures
is twofold.   *Penia* in Aristophanes' *Plutus* is a similar terrifying
figure ; the other ancestor is Euripides' *Hercules Furens* (822),
where Iris sends Lyssa into the house of Herakles, just as Luxury
sends Poverty into the empty house of Lesbonicus.   It is pedantic
to say that Poverty has been in Lesbonicus' house for a long
time ; he is now at a new crisis because he has spent all the
money received from the sale of his father's house (402).   I
think it possible that Luxury did not say much more in Philemon
than she does in Plautus and that her presence is a kind of adver-
tisement that this is a solemn play about a rake's progress.   We
have perhaps a trace of another comedy in which two female
abstractions appeared in the prologue.   Chorikios says (*C.A.F.*,
III, 553/819) : 'If I were a professional comic poet, I would
introduce day and night in the guise of women, as night is introduced by one of the comic poets, and I would make day abuse
night.'   Chorikios may be inventing but on the other hand he
may know of a comedy in which two female abstractions abused
one another.

The form of the moralising is however the same in the *Trinummus* as in the other plays and fragments.   To judge the fragments
is of course unsafe, as the Menander fragments show : if the
Bacchides had not been preserved, who would have guessed that

[1] Cf. also Night, if the conjecture stated above (p. 127) is right.

' whom the gods love die young ' was a slave's jest ? But we
have justifiably noticed in Philemon a certain flatness of form
caused by the near repetition of words which are unemphatic.
Jachmann [1] adds the charge that Philemon's moralising is second-
hand, but this is not in itself serious, since the philosophers to a
lesser degree, the tragedians to a greater degree, and behind
them Homer, contained a stock of coined wisdom on which
the poets of the New Comedy were expected to draw. What
is more serious is that Philemon's moralising is not particularly well adapted to his characters or situations. Menander's
moralising is generally called forth by the particular situation in
which the character finds himself at the moment : in the *Samia*,
Demeas' nice assessment of how he should act arises from his
misapprehension that Chrysis is the mother of Moschion's baby,
and in the *Epitrepontes* Charisios' self-reproach arises from overhearing Pamphile's loyal refusal to leave him. But why must
Charinus soliloquise at such length at the beginning of the
Mercator on the *vitia amoris* when he has bought himself a hetaira
whom he genuinely loves from the profits of successful foreign
trade ? Or why does Lysiteles in the *Trinummus* discuss so long
the disadvantages of being in love and the advantages of work
and ambition, when there is no sign that such a level-headed
young man has ever felt any temptation at all ? The answer
must be that this was good theatre ; the audience liked to hear
such sentiments. Their elaboration falls under the head of
dianoia in Aristotle's definition : [2] *dianoia* is the ability to say
what is inherent in the theme and what is suitable. Taken by
themselves, Charinus or Philto's speeches are admirable disserta-
tions on the dilemma of youth and fulfil the Aristotelian demand.
The audience must have accepted them at their face value, as
they accepted, for example, the debate on the relative advantages of hoplites and bowmen in Euripides' *Hercules Furens*.
Menander's moralising fulfils the further conditions that it is
in character and is called forth by a crisis which would con-
ceivably have had this effect. It would, however, be unfair to
judge Philemon by the standards of Menander because his purpose
was different.

Let us now try to sum up our knowledge about Philemon
so that we may have some criteria for attributing further works

---

[1] *Op. cit.*, 229.　　　　　　　　　　[2] *Poetics*, 1450 b 4.

to him. Apuleius' characterisation will help to show what we know and what we do not know. *Reperias tamen apud ipsum multos sales* (that we readily agree), *argumenta lepide inflexa* (we have noticed his neat construction and motivation), *agnitus lucide explicatos* (of this we have little evidence), *personas rebus competentes, sententias vitae congruentes* (this we should accept with the reservations expressed above), *ioca non infra soccum, seria non usque ad coturnum. Rarae apud illum corruptelae, tuti errores, concessi amores.* Then comes the list of characters : *leno perjurus* we know from Greek fragments ; *amator fervidus* describes Charinus and Philolaches ; *servulus callidus* Tranio (with reservations) ; *uxor inhibens* Dorippa ; *sodalis opitulator* Eutychus, Callidamates, and Lysiteles ; *miles proeliator* occurred in the *Babylonian*, and in the *Ptoche* (70K) ; Theoropides at least may be reckoned under the heading of *parentes tenaces*.[1] We cannot trace *mater indulgens, patruus obiurgator, parasiti edaces*, or *meretrices procaces* in the text of the plays, but the titles *Zomion, Pareision*, and *Sikelikos* indicate the presence of a parasite and *Euripos, Mystis*, and *Neaira* seem to have been called after hetairai. *Amica illudens* in post-Augustan Latin may perhaps mean a mistress who wastes her lover's property, and this description would fit Philematium of the *Mostellaria*, however virtuous she may be. We can add to what Apuleius tells us further characters, a love of imagery, a certain flatness of style, and above all the opportunism of his comedy scenes.

The papyri add something to the picture. The fragment attributed by Blass belongs to a group which all seem to come from the same play.[2] Blass' further identification with the original of the *Aulularia* (developed by Kuiper[3] without the attribution to Philemon) is impossible if only because the colloquy of two male slaves[4] has no place in the *Aulularia*. Page summarises the argument : (1) a slave Strobilus has been commanded by his young master to make a great effort to obtain for him the company of a young woman. The slave has fulfilled his mission to the best of his ability, he has found her lodging, but not yet conversed with her. (2) Strobilus reproaches his master for estranging himself from his father through his passion for the young woman. (3), (4) Strobilus has discovered great

---

[1] Dietze, *op. cit.*, 55, adds 77K.   [2] 64P.
[3] *Mnemosyne, Suppl.*, 1940.   [4] Heidelberg 180 = Page, no. 64 (5).

abundance of treasure. His master enters and hears what the slave has found (into this context the Philemon fragment (189K) ' You are Kroisos, Midas, and Tantalos ' fits beautifully, as Blass says—the papyrus only possesses the first five letters of Kroisos). (5) Strobilus converses with another slave, Daos, who offers to assist him in some enterprise or difficulty. To this we can add the fact that the youth's father was called Demeas,[1] and that the play was written for performance in Egypt, since the word *nomarchos*, only known as title of an Egyptian official, occurs in the first fragment.[2] This does not necessarily mean, as Page following Schroeder appears to believe, that it is the humble work of an obscure poet, since we may be practically certain that Philemon wrote his *Panegyris* for performance in Egypt. But the gain for Philemon is slight : it was obviously a play with an intrigue and contained an amusing version of the *servus currens*, who rushes in to announce his discovery of wealth and enlightens his master as to the source of the treasure by riddling on the name of the place where he found it : Acanthio makes a similar elaborate entry and prolonged explanation in the *Mercator* (111 f.).

The other fragment is attributed by Körte [3] on the strength of the unduly long image of seafaring (10 f.), which recalls a fragment of Philemon's *Ephebe* (28K), and of the phrase ' you fasten the blame on fortune ', which recurs in a fragment attributed by Stobaeus to Philemon.[4] Laches has a son Moschion and a daughter by a different mother. He has sent C. to arrange a marriage between them (26). The fragment opens with the slave Megas [5] making up his mind not to desert Moschion, and reminding himself of the difficulties that sailors meet and surmount. The slave's monologue runs : ' You go in and don't have any fears. So he is inside. You must rouse yourself now, Megas, to some purpose. You must be a man and not leave Moschion in the lurch. I want to, I really want to, but I've

[1] Flind. Petr. 4 = 26D.

[2] 64 (1)P. It is possible, as Page notes (cf. also Körte, *Archiv*, XIV, no. 966), that this fragment does not belong with the rest.

[3] 61P = *P.S.I.*, X, 1176 ; Körte, *Hermes*, 1937, lxxii 73 f. I follow Maas in *P.S.I.*, X, xvii f. Theiler, *Hermes*, 1938, 288, notes parallels with *Epidicus*, 81, 101 ff., and *Pseudolus*, 394, 410.

[4] Quoted by Kock as Menander, fr. 1083K.

[5] Megas appears to be a proper name. I do not think ἀνὴρ μέγας would mean ' a hero ' as Page takes it.

fallen into such an unexpected sea of trouble and I am frightened. I've long been worried that fortune may decide against me. You are a coward, by Athena, you are a coward. I see : you shirk trouble and fasten the blame on fortune. Sailors, don't you see, often have everything against them. Storm, wind, rain, waves, lightning, hail, thunder, seasickness, shipwreck, darkness. Yet each waits for hope and doesn't despair of the future. One seizes the ropes, and watches the sail, another prays to the Samothracian gods to help the pilot, hauls at the sheets. . . . You must yourself show some courage.' In the fragment of the *Ephebe* (28K) someone says to a Laches that sailors have the advantage that their storms end after a crisis but his troubles go on for ever. Laches is a common name in Greek comedy and need not be identified with the Laches of the papyrus fragment but it must be admitted that Megas (or someone else) might very well pick up the image in the papyrus and use it in conversation with Laches : it is therefore possible that the papyrus fragment belongs to Philemon's *Ephebe*. In the papyrus the slave goes when he sees Laches arrive, and C. complains that Laches has misused him by sending him to arrange the marriage. The opening words sound more like the continuation of a conversation already started than the first meeting between two characters who have not seen each other for some time :

' I have been ill-used, Laches, more than anyone ever before.'

LACHES : ' Do not say that.'

C. presumably stands in the same kind of relationship to Laches as Callicles to Charmides in the *Trinummus* and has been given a similar thankless task of looking after the unruly son. The speech of the slave has been compared by Maas to Stasimus' monologue in the *Trinummus* (717 f.), when Lesbonicus leaves him and goes off to discuss his sister's dowry with Lysiteles : there Stasimus pictures to himself the miseries of military life which seem to him his certain future and like the slave in the papyrus addresses himself : *Stasime, restas solus.* In the *Mostellaria* also (407 f.) Tranio soliloquises briefly when he sends Philolaches back to his party and waits for the arrival of Theoropides ; the dismissal of Philolaches at the beginning and the arrival of Theoropides at the end of the soliloquy correspond exactly to the situation in the papyrus. Of these slave monologues the papyrus fragment alone has the lengthy image of

sailors but this in itself seems to be good Philemon. The parallel
with the *Mostellaria* suggests a little more : Laches in the papyrus
has returned from abroad and makes his first entry with C.,
who, we may assume, has been to the harbour to meet him.
It is therefore likely that as in the *Mostellaria* the crisis which
causes the slave's discomfiture is the news of the father's arrival.
The slave is the hesitant slave of Philemon like Tranio in the
Mostellaria and not the self-confident rogue of Menander's *Dis
Exapaton*. His monologue, as interpreted by Maas, is a valuable
addition to our knowledge of Philemon and of the slave apology.

Another possible attribution may be mentioned briefly.
Athenaeus quotes a long fragment in which an old man complains
of the Homeric language used by a cook, whom he calls ' a male
Sphinx ' because he sets him such riddles. Athenaeus quotes the
first four lines as by Philemon (123K) and a version of 47 lines
as by Straton. A papyrus [1] gives a new version omitting about
twelve of the lines quoted by Athenaeus. The editors have
pointed out that the additional lines in Athenaeus are all, or
nearly all, interpolations deliberately inserted to ' improve ' the
piece. Page suggests that they are actor interpolations, but it
is also possible that the papyrus version is Philemon and the
Athenaeus version Philemon improved by Straton.

It is probable that the works of Plautus contain other adaptations from Philemon, and he has been credited with the originals
of the *Amphitruo*, *Captivi*, *Menaechmi*, *Miles*, *Pseudolus*, and
Truculentus. For none of these is there either external evidence
or certain translation of a preserved fragment of Philemon.
Most of the attributions have been made on likenesses to passages
in the three Plautine adaptations of Philemon and this is a
risky proceeding : Plautus had after all a style of his own and
repetitions of single words or pairs of words mean little. Moreover, seen through the glass of adaptation Menander's Greek and
Philemon's Greek is apt to look alike, and we have already
noticed close correspondence between even the Greek fragments
of the two poets. Of the six plays mentioned *Amphitruo* and
Menaechmi have nothing to do with Philemon, *Captivi* and
Truculentus seem to me very probable attributions and *Miles* and
Pseudolus are more likely to belong to other poets.

The case for the *Captivi* is strong and must be taken seriously.

[1] Page, no. 57.

Other poets have been suggested. The parallels with Anaxandrides [1] and Diphilos [2] are too slight to mean anything. The parallel with Alexis' *Thebaioi* (90K) is more striking : ' What is his family ? ' ' Rich : These they all say are well-born. No one sees a poor Eupatrid.' In the *Captivi* (277) we read : *Quo de genere natust illi Philocrates ? Polyplusio : quod genus illist unum pollens atque honoratissimum.* It seems certain that one of the two passages inspired the other but equally certain that Plautus is not translating Alexis. Christ's [3] theory that Poseidippos wrote the original of the *Captivi* rests on two assumptions : that the play was written for the new theatre built at Pleuron in Aetolia during the second half of the third century and that the *Menaechmi*, with which Christ finds affinities, goes back to an original by Poseidippos. There is no need to assume that a play about Aetolians was written for Aetolia : the *Carthaginian* of Menander was not written for Carthage, and the likeness of the opening scenes to the *Menaechmi* rests on the traditional language of the parasite, who says much the same thing always, nor in fact is there any reason to believe that the *Menaechmi* was written by Poseidippos. [4] The dating of the original depends on the probability that the war between Elis and Aetolia is contemporary. Their friendship was traditional and it was partially broken on two occasions : in 314 and in 280. [5] The latter seems more suitable as on that occasion men from Elis invaded Aetolia and this would give Hegio a better chance of obtaining captives. Moreover, the *Captivi* has nothing of the gaiety which we associate with the earliest phase of New Comedy.

The arguments for Dietze's identification with Philemon's *Aetolian* may be stated as follows. In the first place the *Captivi* has a general likeness to the *Trinummus* in that it is predominantly serious and has no love interest at all and the theme of friendship —the friendship of Philocrates and Tyndarus but also Hegio's love for his children—runs right through the play. Secondly, the parasite is an external element introduced to make comic

---

[1] *Capt.*, 636, with Anaxandrides, 59K.
[2] See Marx, *Rudens*, 317.   [3] *Arch. f. lat. lex.*, XII, 1902, 283.
[4] See above, p. 71. Wilhelm, *Urkunden*, 246, suggests *Lytroumenos* as a title, but the two plays which we know with this name were produced after the *Captivi*.
[5] On 314 B.C. cf. *C.A.H.*, VI, 486 ; Hueffner, *op. cit.*, 42 ; on 280 B.C. cf. *C.A.H.*, VII, 99 ; Dietze, *op. cit.*, 18 f., suggests 271 as a possibility.

relief with his traditional entrances complaining of his hunger (69 f., 461 f.) and then as a *servus currens* (768 f.), just as in the *Trinummus* the intrigue with the sycophant provides comic relief. It is, however, more significant that the central scene of comedy where Tyndarus is confronted with Aristophontes depends for its humour on Tyndarus' improvisation just as the central scene of the *Mostellaria* depends on Tranio's improvisations. Let us look at this scene. Tyndarus is faced with Aristophontes, who knows his identity. He first pretends that Aristophontes is mad. The signs of madness which he notes in Aristophontes are, like the signs of Charinus' madness in the *Mercator*, drawn from tragedy.[1] Then as Aristophontes proceeds to interrogate him, Tyndarus suggests that he is a jealous ne'er-do-weel, and then when Aristophontes says he can contain himself no longer, Tyndarus again returns to the charge of madness. When Aristophontes tries to speak to Hegio alone, Tyndarus makes a last desperate attempt to call him off. Hegio, who has been as completely deceived as Theoropides by Tranio in the *Mostellaria*, is finally convinced by Aristophontes' description of Philocrates, which is as circumstantial as the description of the old man in the *Mercator* (638). This scene has the kind of comedy which we have learnt to expect from Philemon, and therefore the slighter indications of neat preparation [2] and flatness [3] of style may be given some weight. Lindsay notes the correspondence between *di nos quasi pilas homines habent* (22) and *di ludos faciunt hominibus* in the *Mercator* (225), and the pretty simile of the snails hiding in summer and living on their own juice if there is no dew (80 f.) may be compared with a fragment possibly by Philemon (114K) in which the snail is congratulated on being able to move its house to avoid a bad neighbour. We can at least say that the attribution to Philemon is probable, and we gain thereby another play with the same general tone as the *Trinummus*. We also gain illustrations of two more phrases in Apuleius' description of Philemon, the *agnitus lucide explicatos* and *parasiti edaces*.

Dietze suggested that the *Truculentus* was derived from the *Babylonian* of Philemon because Stratophanes is a Babylonian

---

[1] Fraenkel, *op. cit.*, 76, regards 562, *Alcumeus atque Orestes et Lycurgus*, as a Plautine addition, but note its likeness to 189K, ' Kroisos and Midas and Tantalos '.

[2] e.g. 126, 192, 449, 496, 751. [3] e.g. 78 f., 255, 461.

soldier. If so, Plautus has omitted to translate the two lines preserved from the *Babylonian* (16K) : 'You shall be queen of Babylon, if all goes well. You know Pythionike and Harpalos.' Dietze argued that this was an Athenian allusion which the Roman poet might well have dropped. Fraenkel, however, suggested that these lines belong to a *lena's* advice to a young hetaira, like Scapha's advice to Philematium in the *Mostellaria*, and this seems more likely than that they are a promise made by a soldier to his mistress. Even if they could be a promise, there is no room for such a promise in the *Truculentus*. Another serious objection is the date : the allusion to Pythionike dates the *Babylonian* between 326 and 324 B.C.,[1] and we should therefore have to assume that in all the passages of the *Truculentus* where a likeness to Menander has been seen Menander is the borrower ; Hueffner's date (299/7) [2] would suit this much better. Hans Lucas [3] proposed an alternative title *Euripos* which he believes to be a hetaira name recalled by the phrase *meretricem ego item esse reor, mare ut est* (*Truc.*, 565, cf. also 350) ; the surviving fragment of the *Euripos* (25K), 'he has a blanket and a skin bag', would be a description of the rustic youth or his slave. A hetaira name is obviously right for this title, and we must remember that Licinius Imbrex' *Neaira* (35R), which is more likely to be based on Philemon than on Timokles, provides an exact parallel to Stratophanes' greeting of Phronesium (*Truc.*, 515).[4] The affinities which Marx [5] notes with Diphilos are too slight to be considered. I have examined elsewhere [6] the considerable number of parallels with Menander and came reluctantly to the conclusion : ' On the other hand it may be argued that the tone is not Menander : there is a complete absence of sympathy and no statement of positive values, the style is harder and more antithetic, the self-characterisation in the mono-

---

[1] Cf. *C.Q.*, 1952, 19.

[2] Hueffner, *op. cit.*, 31, accepted by Dietze, *op. cit.*, 43 : *victis hostibus* (75) should be compared with *Heautont.*, 194.

[3] *Rh. Mus.*, 1938, 188. I do not feel entirely happy about the use of a masculine word for a feminine character but *Euripos* apparently appears in a Byzantine poem as a hetaira. It seems to me possible that *Euripos* is felt as an adjective of two terminations.

[4] So Dietze, *op. cit.*, 43. Fraenkel regards this as Roman, *op. cit.*, 96, but I am not certain that Ares Aphrodite is impossible for a braggart soldier.

[5] *Rudens*, 366.

[6] *Studies in Menander*, 152. Add also *Truc.*, 170, with *Cist.*, 80.

logues is more direct and artless than in Menander. I do not
therefore feel certain that the original was by Menander.' The
monologues are certainly a pointer towards Philemon. In
particular, Diniarchus' opening soliloquy on the disadvantages of
being in love is like the soliloquies of Charinus, Philolaches, and
Lysiteles ; Astaphium (210 f.), Phronesium (449 f.), Stratophanes
(482 f.), Strabax (645 f.), all describe themselves and their intentions for the benefit of the spectators like Demipho in the
Mercator (225 f.) or Simo in the *Mostellaria* (690 f.). The scene
between Astaphium and Diniarchus is a scene of extemporising
comedy in which Astaphium shows no regard for consistency.
Diniarchus (114) overhears her saying that she is going to fetch
a man (Strabax, as subsequently appears) ; she tells Diniarchus
that she is going to fetch a midwife (130) ; she then leads him
away from the dangerous subject ; when he says that he has still
an estate to lose, she changes her tone and asks him to come in
(175), and then embarks on the safe subject of Phronesium's baby
about which Diniarchus already knows. Here again we may
see the hand of Philemon. The other indications are slighter :
the long simile of fishing is certainly in his manner.[1] The preparation for subsequent scenes is carefully made.[2] Astaphium
(270 f.) and Diniarchus (609 f.) are described in detail like the
old man in the *Mercator* (638). The first scene (256 f.) between
Astaphium and Truculentus has analogies with the scene between
Tranio and Grumio in the *Mostellaria*. Callicles' interrogation
of the old woman is carried out in the same spirit as Charmides'
interrogation of the sycophant in the *Mostellaria* (as also Hegio's
interrogation of Stalagmus in the *Captivi*).

There is, however, a further point which has a bearing on the
question of authorship. It is inconceivable from all we know of
Menander's methods that he would have made no use of the
irony of the moment when Phronesium tells Diniarchus about
the baby which she has borrowed and which is in fact his own
son. On the other hand, we have seen that Philemon is more
concerned with the effect of a single scene than with the play
as a whole, and might therefore omit to tell the audience of the
identity of the baby because the baby only interests him in the
first scene as a demonstration of Phronesium's disloyalty to

[1] 35 f. ; cf. 170, 252, 867 f.
[2] e.g. 197/322 ; 317/669 ; 420/633 ; 428/551.

Stratophanes and in the later scene of Callicles' interrogation he wants the surprise of Diniarchus' sudden recollection of his past misdemeanour (773). Unfortunately we have also to reckon with the possibility that the prologue speech in which, as normally in Menander, a deity would have announced the past history, has been, as so often by the Roman adapter, suppressed. Against this, however, may be set the fact that the *Truculentus* has a prólogue speech, and though we have instances of suppressed prologue speeches, and possibly in the *Trinummus* of a shortened prologue speech, we have no instance where Plautus has suppressed an essential fact in a prologue speech.

This is a heartless play in which even Stratophanes is too much of a caricature to win much sympathy, and the marriage of Diniarchus is arranged at the end no less cynically than the marriage of Lesbonicus at the end of the *Trinummus*. It is joyous comedy if we accept its conventions, but they are conventions which we should not expect Menander to accept. On balance the *Truculentus* seems to me slightly more like Philemon than Menander ; if it is Philemon, it gives us two more of Apuleius' characters ; a perfect example of the *meretrix procax* [1] in Phronesium, and a possible example of the *patruus obiurgator* in Callicles, who is a relation of Diniarchus (771). If it is Philemon, then it belongs nearer the *Mercator* than any other play.

Philemon wrote for the same audiences as Menander and was often successful in competitions with him. The tradition that Menander was a pupil of Theophrastos is confirmed by the constant cross-references to Peripatetic philosophy that can be found in his works. Menander went beyond Aristotle in his conception of a dramatic personality, and his people always think and speak in character ; Philemon sometimes at any rate elaborates their sentiments beyond what the occasion requires, nor is he as careful as Menander to create situations in which they may naturally describe themselves. Menander always, except perhaps in the *Dis Exapaton*, lets us see some real value which is more important than the conventional values of Athenian comedy. Philemon may be said to proclaim one real value, the value of friendship, but otherwise his moralising does not go beyond

[1] Menander's *Thais* was undoubtedly *procax* like Bacchis in the *Heautontimoroumenos* (227) but Ovid (*Amor.*, I, 5, 15) uses *blanda* to describe the typical hetaira of Menander.

the polite commonplaces of Athenian society. Philemon is a caricaturist, if not a satirist. The extravagances of the lover, the hunger of the parasite, the avarice of the hetaira, the folly of the old dotard, the boasting of the soldier, the inconsistencies of the frightened slave are the stuff of his comedy and we are meant to laugh at his characters rather than with them. Most of the material is traditional and if we had more Middle Comedy we should be able to assess this traditional element better. The mythical characters have gone except in a very few plays, but comedy of everyday life had been written long before Philemon. The obscene jokes have largely gone because they would not suit the audience of πεπαιδευμένοι. The speeches probably have more ἦθος and more διάνοια than Middle Comedy in the sense in which Aristotle uses those words in the *Poetics*. The construction is probably more consciously neat than the plots of Middle Comedy. But Philemon's comedy is still essentially a comedy of caricature ; within its bounds it is first-rate and little better can have been written in this vein than the scene in which Demipho and his son manœuvre to get possession of the same girl or than Tranio's repeated attempts to conceal from Theoropides how his son has been behaving in his absence. If Menander is the comedian of character, Philemon is the comedian of extemporisation.

VI. DIPHILOS AND HIS COMEDY

DIPHILOS came from Sinope on the Black Sea, the opposite end of the Greek world to Philemon. He died at Smyrna but was buried in Athens. The tombstone [1] of Diphilos, his father, and his brother Diodoros is important for his chronology : it was erected in Athens for the father, Dion of Sinope, before the sumptuary laws of Demetrios of Phaleron were passed, i.e. before 317–07. The second burial was Diphilos, who is called ' son of Dion, from Sinope ', and third Diodoros, who is described as ' son of Dion ' but not as ' from Sinope ' ; he therefore was presumably an Athenian citizen when he died. According to Wilhelm the writing of the third entry is not later than the first third or at the very latest belongs to the middle of the third century, i.e. 275–50. The other known dates for Diodoros are in the early third century.[2] Diphilos therefore died at latest in the early third century and his father came to Athens before 317–07. The other certain date that we have for Diphilos is the Lenaian inscription from which it appears that he won a Lenaian victory later than Menander, Philemon, and Apollodoros and therefore at earliest in 318. We can trace him rather earlier because various anecdotes connect him with the hetaira Gnathaina, who was old in the early 'twenties and at the height of her power in the early 'thirties ; [3] he may therefore have been born between 360 and 350 and have come to Athens at latest soon after 340.

Such dates as we can extract from his plays fall in the last quarter of the fourth century and agree with the statement of the anonymous writer on comedy [4] that he was a contemporary of Menander. Wilamowitz [5] says that the earliest of the few chronological references in the Greek fragments is the mention

---

[1] I.G., II², 10321 ; see Wilhelm, *Urkunden*, 59 f.

[2] I.G., 2319 ; B.C.H., VII, 105–7 ; interpreted by Dittmer, *Didascaliae*, 22, and Wilhelm, *loc. cit.*

[3] See my article in C.Q., 1952, 13. Athenaeus, 583 f., presumably refers to an early unsuccessful production of Diphilos. Athenaeus, 243 f., connects him with Chairephon who is named in comedies from about 325/10.

[4] 18 (Kaibel, p. 10).   [5] *Schiedsgericht*, 166, n. 1.

of the flute-player Timotheos in the *Synoris* (77K) ; we know
that he was a favourite of Alexander and went back to the time
of Philip ; the *Synoris* must therefore be an early play but need
not be dated long before 320. The *Amastris* [1] has been connected
with the queen of Heraclea Pontica, which would date the play
in the late fourth or very early third century, but it is at least
equally likely that it was named after the wife of Xerxes
and mother of Artaxerxes, since in this play Diphilos called
Themistokles' daughter ' an Athenian stranger ' (10K). This
may of course, as Marigo suggests, have been an historical
allusion, but the earlier Amastris, as portrayed by Herodotus,[2]
could certainly be made the subject of comedy, and Themistokles
arrived at the Persian court soon after the palace revolution which
replaced Xerxes by Artaxerxes.[3] Diphilos' *Tithraustes* may have
been an historical play ; his *Sappho* played tricks with history
as he made Archilochos and Hipponax her lovers (70K). The
Amastris then cannot be used for dating : the fragment of the
Gamos (23K), which mentions Stilpon and Charinos, is ascribed
by the manuscripts of Diogenes Laertius to Sophilos and not to
Diphilos, and there seems to be no valid reason to doubt the
ascription. The remaining fragment of Diphilos' *Gamos* (24K)
with its description of the evils done by flatterers is extremely
like a passage in Menander's *Kolax* (85 f.) and may possibly be
contemporary (312 or soon after) ; similarly the close parallel
between a fragment of the *Apoleipousa* (19K) and Menander's
Perinthia (395K) may suggest a similar date. A fragment of the
Enagismata (38K) which mentions Ktesippos, son of Chabrias, has
been equated with a fragment of Menander's *Orge* (363K) produced in 321. Marigo [4] suggests that Diphilos refers to the first
building of Chabrias' monument and dates to 345 B.C., but this
is unnecessary, as ' may sometime be completed ' can refer to
a rebuilding after Ktesippos had started to sell the stones ;
Ktesippos was trierarch in 334/3 [5] and was presumably still
prosperous then : this provides an upper limit for the play.
The reference to the Samian girls in the *Theseus* (50K) may date
this play soon after the expulsion of the Athenian cleruchs in

---

[1] Cf. Marigo, *Studi Italiani*, XV, 1907, 400.

[2] Hdt., VII, 114 ; IX, 109.

[3] The recently published Gyges fragment (*P.B.A.*, XXXV) is a comparable
phenomenon : for very strict versification in comedy cf. Pap. Giessen, 152.

[4] *Op. cit.*, 379.   [5] See *R.E.*, VIIA, 106 ff.

322. Of the Roman adaptations neither the *Casina*[1] nor the *Vidularia* provide any ground for dating their originals. For the *Rudens* slight indications remain. Marx[2] dated it after the fall of Acragas in 255 but this is too late on the evidence for Diphilos' life adduced above : Hueffner's[3] dating (303/289) is certainly possible, though it is perhaps not necessary to go quite so late. The connection of Agathokles with Ophellas of Cyrene in 311/09 and his attack on Acragas in 308 B.C. may have suggested coupling the *leno* and Charmides of Acragas in a play set in Cyrene. Ophellas was well known in Athens because he had taken Euthydike, the daughter of Miltiades, to Cyrene.[4] Hueffner is probably right in saying that the suggestion that Ampelisca may have been born in Thebes (746) implies that the rebuilding of Thebes in 316 B.C. has already taken place, and there is some ground for suggesting that the original of the *Rudens* was influenced by Menander's *Leucadia*, perhaps produced soon after 314.[5] It is also possible that the Attic swallows of Daemones' dream (604) were suggested by the *Perikeiromene* (278), which was produced in 314 B.C. or soon after. The indications seem therefore to favour a date in the last ten years of the fourth century. We have in fact no literary evidence for Diphilos in the third century.[6]

The titles of Diphilos' plays do not tell us much. Three plays, as we have seen, may well take their names from historical characters : *Sappho*, *Amastris*, *Tithraustes*—but the fragments tell us nothing. *Danaides* and *Peliades* must have been mythological comedies ;[7] the *Herakles* and *Theseus* may have been, although both heroes are conceivable as prologue figures ; *Anagyros*, *Hekate*, and *Heros* are likely to have been named after prologue figures. The fragments suggest that these plays were in the Middle Comedy tradition and that the main point was the con-

---

[1] Skutsch, *Hermes*, xxxix, 303, dates soon after 323 B.C. on 328 f., but these lines may be Plautine.

[2] *W. Sitzb.*, cxl, Abh. 8, 76, n. 1.   [3] *De Pl. Ex. Att.*, 67.

[4] Ferguson, *Hell. Ath.*, 111. See above, p. 111.

[5] *Studies in Menander*, 57, n. 2, with references. The reference to Stratonicus (932) also demands an early date, since Stratonikos, who was born about 390 (see *C.Q.*, 1952, 17), should be a recent memory, if not still alive.

[6] The reference in the *Mostellaria* (1149) is probably Plautine ; in any case *Most.* cannot be dated on l. 775 to third century (Fraenkel, *Pl. Pl.*, 17).

[7] See above, p. 95 f., for the possibility that the *Amphitruo* goes back to an original by Diphilos.

trast between heroic names and everyday behaviour. In the
Herakles (46) one character is already drunk and another has had
twelve breakfasts. In the *Peliades* (64) a meal is described with
an enormous fish. In general the Middle Comedy tradition of
describing food and drink, feasts and drinking parties, seems to
survive more strongly in Diphilos than in either Philemon or
Menander ; [1] I count 23 such fragments [2] out of Diphilos' 132
as against 7 out of over 200 in Philemon and 11 out of over 1,000
in Menander, and the descriptions in Diphilos are longer and
more detailed. The *Lemniai* (54) and *Theseus* (49) both mention
hungry slaves : otherwise only two fragments refer to slaves and
they are the slaves of cooks (18, 43) : the Latin comedies however
show us how Diphilos treated slaves, and the *Chrysochoos* (84)
evidently included a spying slave like Sceledrus in the *Miles*.

Athenaeus tells us that in the *Theseus* (50) ' Diphilos says that
three Samian girls were asking riddles at the festival of Adonis.
Someone proposed the riddle " what is the strongest of all
things " and they answered in turn iron, bronze, and sex.' The
Samian girls probably belong to Athenian cleruchs expelled from
Samos in 322, like Thais' mother in Menander's *Eunuch*.[3] There
is no reason therefore to assume with Marigo [4] that the scene was
in Samos. Riddling, as he rightly remarks, was common in
Middle Comedy, e.g. Sappho asked riddles in Antiphanes' play,
which can be dated 370/60. The girls are presumably hetairai.[5]
We may ask whether Athenaeus refers to an actual scene or a
narrative speech in the *Theseus*. The cook in the *Zographos* (43)
ends ' where I am taking you now is a brothel, a hetaira lavishly
celebrating the Adonis festival with other girls ' and the natural
assumption is that the brothel is one of the houses on the stage
(as for instance also in Diphilos' *Synapothneskontes*).[6] Therefore
such a scene in the *Theseus* is perfectly possible. There are however two difficulties, first the way in which Athenaeus begins :
' Diphilos says that ' instead of ' Diphilos introduced three girls ',
and secondly the active infinitive ' *proposed* to them the riddle '.
If this was a stage scene the three hetairai would take the three
speaking parts and there should be no further character. If,

---

[1] See *Studies in Menander*, 163 f. ; Prehn., *Quaestiones Plautinae*, 11 f.

[2] 1, 3, 6, 14, 17, 18, 20, 26, 32, 33, 34, 43, 44, 46, 54, 56, 58, 64, 66, 69, 79, 90,
96K.

[3] Cf. *Studies in Menander*, 103. [4] *Loc. cit.*, 420.

[5] Cf. Coppola, *R.I.F.C.*, 1929, 177. [6] See below, p. 160.

however, it was a narrative speech, it might run ' I proposed them a riddle ', which would account for the absence of subject in Athenaeus' report. In either case the play dealt with low-life in Athens and Theseus' heroic name contrasted with his unheroic surroundings.

All four plays which we know from Roman adaptations are recognition plays. We could not have guessed this from the titles *Kleroumenoi* (*Casina*) or *Synapothneskontes* (*Adelphi*, II, 1) [1] but perhaps the *Schedia* (*Vidularia*) might have suggested it. None of the other titles are suggestive, but a fragment of the *Syntrophoi* (72K) which mentions ' swaddling clothes ' might come from a recognition play and the *Syntrophoi* may be a pair like Ptolemocrates and Tyndarus in the *Captivi*. The *Chrysochoos* must have been an intrigue play if not a recognition play ; the beauty who could be seen by looking down the chimney must have been rescued. Marigo [2] rightly interprets 93K as an appeal by a son to a stern father : ' Should I seem to be more eloquent than you my father, I am wronging myself and I have lost my piety, since I am paining my father and do not love him.' I am inclined to think also that the tirade against Ktesippos in the *Enagismata* (38) comes from a speech by an angry father to his prodigal son. Here then we have various traces of the love theme as we know it also from the *Rudens* and from Menander. The old fool in love is the subject of the *Casina*, and, if Marigo [3] is right, of the *Apoleipousa* [4] (17–19) and of the *Balaneion* (20). In the *Apoleipousa* the cook is hired by an *old* man for a wedding feast (17) and says that his cooking is calculated to titivate the palates of *old* guests (18/5), which means that the marriage feast is for the old man himself and not for his son. His young bride presumably deserts him, and I suspect that it is her young lover who is told to clear out (19), though the precise interpretation of this fragment and its twin in Menander's *Perinthia* (395K) is doubtful.

Other titles show us the soldier, the parasite, and the hetaira, all characters which survive from Middle Comedy into New

---

[1] *Ad.*, 193, seems to me to imply a recognition play (cf. *Studies in Menander*, 87 f.).

[2] *Op. cit.*, 436.   [3] *Op. cit.*, 404–6.

[4] As there appears to be no instance of an aorist participle as a title and three other plays are called *Apoleipousa*, I have no doubt that this is to be preferred to *Apolipousa*.

Comedy. The *Hairesiteiches* (Capturer of Walls, a name which might well parody Demetrios' title of Poliorketes) was later remodelled as the *Eunuch or Soldier*, a title which suggests the influence of Menander's *Eunuch* ; the *Mainomenos* (55K) includes a description of the soldier who looks like ' a walking junk shop ' ; but we do not know anything more than this about Diphilos' soldiers. Three plays are named after parasites, *Aplestos* (insatiable), *Parasite*, and *Telesias*, who may, as Marigo [1] suggests, be an historical character. The name character of the *Parasite* (60) develops a Euripidean theme : ' I am overcome by need and my accursed belly, the source of all evil ' (fr. 907N). ' The belly is an all purpose vessel : you can carry loaves in a bag but not porridge or you will lose it. You put loaves in a basket but not pease-pudding, wine into a bottle but not crab. But into this damned belly you can put everything however they disagree with one another.' The speech of course belongs to the long tradition of parasite monologues and parasites are always realists. This quizzical realism is perhaps characteristic of Diphilos ; it recurs in another fragment where the parasite (61) watches the smoke from the kitchen fire to decide what sort of a dinner he is going to have. In Pollux' list of masks the third parasite mask is the Sicilian, and Dr. Simon [2] has suggested that the ' fat man with rolls of Sicilian lard ' of Diphilos (119K) probably wore this mask. There is no trace of the later parasite whose primary object is to help the young hero.[3] Hetaira and parasite occur together in the *Synoris* (73/5) where the parasite plays dice with the hetaira and again shamelessly parodies Euripides,[4] ending ' I am not concerned with the play but the sense ', and the hetaira and her maid (?) mock the parasite for his bad manners. We have already mentioned the hetairai in the *Theseus*, the *Balaneion*, and the *Zographos*. They may be independent hetairai, and the *Synoris* is named after a real hetaira, who is known to Athenaeus (XIII, 583e). The *leno* does however occur in a fragment (87), as well as in the *Rudens* and the Diphilos scene in the *Adelphi*, and says that his is the most disastrous trade ; he would rather be a hawker ' than support these women ' ; ' *these* women '

---

[1] *Op. cit.*, 434.
[2] *Comicae tabellae*, 54.
[3] Cf. *Studies in Menander*, 113, and above, p. 118.
[4] 73K, 7 = E., fr. 187N, 9 = *I.T.*, 535.

suggests a parade of hetairai like that in the *Pseudolus*[1] (133 f.). Professor Tredennick[2] has pointed out that the *lenones* in the *Adelphi* and *Rudens* are more like the villains of melodrama than any that survive in other plays by other authors. Other characters, which are known from Middle Comedy, are the doctor (98K), the bad wife (91K), the fishmonger (66K), and the cook (17, 18, 43, 90K).

The cook is played down in Menander but Philemon provides at least one superb fragment (79K), which has been discussed above. Philemon's cook gives a prolonged description of a single banquet with an elaborate image to show the banqueters' enthusiasm. Diphilos' cooks are different in temperament and in style. Philemon's cook is an *alazon*, a braggart ; Diphilos' cooks are realists ; one (17–18K) wants to know the nationality of the guests so that he can suit their tastes, another (43) explains to his kitchen hand that he has a list of all kinds of clients good and bad and he then describes the unprofitable sea-captain, the profitable Byzantine financier, very briefly the profitable young rake, and at length the unprofitable subscription party, and finally very briefly the hetairai for whom he is now going to cook.[3] The style is swift and vivid with asyndeton and towards the end quotation in direct speech. The same speed of style and the same selection of significant detail can be seen in the other two long fragments, the description of the fishmonger (66K) and the discussion of extravagant buying in Corinth[4] (32K) : ' You have forced our city on to vegetables. We fight for parsley as if it were the Isthmia. A hare comes in ; you immediately seize it. You and your friends don't allow us to see a partridge or a thrush, even on the wing.'

The same vividness marks Diphilos' imagery. He does not use the extended images which are characteristic of Philemon but brief startling similes or metaphors. The bad wife (91K) has ' never been kissed even by her father. Even the dog won't take bread from her. She is so black that she makes the room dark.' ' Fortune (107) is a wine-mixer who pours in one good thing

---

[1] So Marx on *Rudens*, 1348 ; Marigo, however (*op. cit.*, 481), ascribes 87K to the original of the *Rudens* and thinks that it should come in at *Rudens*, 1383.
[2] *Cambridge University Reporter*, May 1941.
[3] Cf. Dionysios, K., II/423/2 ; Anaxippos, III/297/1.
[4] Cf. Antiphanes, 89/190.

at the bottom and empties three bad ones on top of it.'[1] His moralising, to judge from the fragments, is also brief. Although Clement of Alexandria said that he was 'very full of gnomes',[2] the fragments[3] show nothing of the originality or depths of Menander nor the obvious relation to contemporary philosophy. On the other hand the phrasing is conciser and more pointed than the moralising fragments of Philemon. It is perhaps unwise to look for any kind of political bias in the fragments.[4] Anti-Macedonian spirit can be seen in a fragment (97K) : 'to be a courtier seems to me the job of either an exile or a starveling or a villain'. It is then tempting to suggest that the discussion of extravagant buying (32K) is a criticism of the sumptuary laws of Demetrios of Phaleron, and the Corinthian setting provides a safe though transparent cover. If this is true, the flattery which has even got under the skin of the populace is presumably flattery of the Macedonians (24K) and the politicians whose oaths are no more valid than a hetaira's are pro-Macedonian (101K). In the scene from Diphilos in the *Adelphi* the *leno* appeals to Athenian *isonomia* (183) and accuses 'Aeschinus' of behaving like a tyrant (175).

The *Casina* has no political reference, but it is possible to see at any rate a political ideal in the *Rudens*. The theodicy of the *Rudens* has perhaps been overstressed :[5] it is true that Arcturus claims to be a minister of Zeus and punish the wicked (prologue), that Palaestra mentions her outstanding piety (190) and the impiety of the *leno* (198), that Daemones and Palaestra are rewarded for their piety and the two villains suffer the discomfiture of shipwreck and considerable loss of property. But, as in the plays of Menander,[6] the theodicy is conventional background to the two types of character represented in varying degrees by Daemones, the priestess, Palaestra, Ampelisca, Trachalio on the one side and by Labrax, Charmides, Gripus, and Sceparnio on the other. The reason for mentioning this

---

[1] Cf. also 33/4, 74, 83, 89 (discussed by Wilamowitz, *Kl. Schr.*, I, 438/1)·
[2] *Strom.* [3] e.g. 4, 24, 45, 48, 83, 88, 94, 99, 105, 106K.
[4] Marigo, *op. cit.*, 386 f. Marigo has noted the references to Charinos (23K), Phaidimos (38K), and Timotheos (77K) as satirical, and it is possible that they are slightly tinged with politics ; Timotheos was a favourite of Alexander ; Charinos was pro-Macedonian but as we have seen this fragment probably belongs to Sophilos rather than Diphilos ; if Phaidimos was the son of Xenophon he was certainly also pro-Macedonian.
[5] e.g. by Marx in his edition.   [6] Cf. *Studies in Menander*, 199 f.

here is that the contrast is a contrast of social and political behaviour and not merely of ethics or religion. Charmides is a traitor (50) ; Labrax has no care for the sanctity of oaths (1373). Daemones however stands for an ideal of civilised conduct which is peculiarly Athenian. He is generous of his poverty to all who visit the temple of Aphrodite (a conscious contrast to Euclio in the *Aulularia* and Theophrastos' mistrustful man).[1] Trachalio's appeal to the Cyrenaeans to see that the rule of law and not the rule of force is upheld (621) is in fact an appeal to the Athenian Daemones, who answers him and upholds the law of the sanctity of suppliants (724). In his two decisions against Gripus he shows the nice discrimination of Aristotle's equitable man in deciding cases which are not entirely covered by the law ; the second decision (1355 f.) is a masterpiece : Labrax must pay because he has sworn to pay, but the money is used half to free Ampelisca and half to free Gripus. There is perhaps a further point as we have suggested : Daemones seems to be one of those who lost his citizen rights through the restriction of the franchise by Antipater in 322 or Demetrios of Phaleron in 317 B.C. Diphilos then is saying that the Macedonian rule has driven out some of those who live most truly by the Athenian ideal.

The scene from the *Synapothneskontes* in the *Adelphi* (155–196a) is valuable because Terence claims to have translated Diphilos word for word (11) and it gives us the movement of the stage which the fragments cannot give. It is a scene of violent action. 'Aeschinus' and Parmeno have seized the girl from the *leno's* house and the *leno* tries to prevent them transferring her to their own house. Verbal correspondences have been noticed particularly with the *Rudens*,[2] and the use of physical violence on the *leno* (173 f.) is paralleled both in the *Rudens* (804 f.) and in the battle of the slaves and the beating of Olympio and Lysidamus in the *Casina* (404 f., 930 ff.). This thug-comedy is a legacy from Aristophanes (e.g. *Frogs*, 605 f.) and is also illustrated by a Paestan vase of the mid-fourth century,[3] in which an old man is beaten up on his money-chest. 'Aeschinus' demands of Parmeno (170) : 'Take care that you never move

---

[1] 133 : contrast *Aul.*, 90 ff., and Theophrastos, *Characters*, XVIII, 7.

[2] On this see Marigo, *op. cit.*, 508 f. ; Drexler, *Philologus Suppt.*, XXVI, 1 f. ; Beare, *R. Phil.*, 1940, 31 f. ; Tredennick, *loc. cit.*

[3] Bieber, *H.T.*, fig. 373 ; cf. *C.Q.*, xlii, 26.

your eyes from my eyes so that, if I nod, your fist may be at
once on his jaw'; this shows a complete mastery of stage
technique. Professor Tredennick has pointed out similar careful
setting of a tableau twice in the *Rudens* (688/91, 807).

The *Kleroumenoi*, the original of Plautus' *Casina*, was probably
an early play because it shows its Middle Comedy ancestry so
clearly. We have already mentioned the beating of Olympio
and Lysidamus : the battle of the slaves (404 f.) is paralleled by
an Attic terracotta and a Campanian [1] vase. The elaborate
description of food with the characterisation of the fish, when
Olympio goes marketing (490 ff.), recalls many Middle Comedy
fragments as well as fragments of Diphilos himself, which have
already been noted. For other scenes we can only see an ancestry
in Aristophanes because our Middle Comedy material is so
scrappy. Thus for us the *Thesmophoriazusae* provides a parallel
for the dressing up of Chalinus and the resulting misunderstandings (the riddling we have already noticed in Diphilos), the
Lysistrata for the withholding of the old man from his beloved
and the *Peace* and the *Birds* for the marriage song.[2] It seems to
me at least possible that a fragment of Alkaios comes from an
account of a similar substitution in his *Palaistra* (23K) : ' She
anointed and shut up X with him instead of herself, and he did
not know '.[3] Thus all these elements are Greek and there is no
reason to ascribe them to Plautus. Diphilos has therefore made
a large use of traditional elements from Middle Comedy in
this play.

Other points can be paralleled from the Greek fragments which
have already been examined : imagery is brief—Chalinus will
stick to Olympio like a shadow (92), Lysidamus is like a hunts-
man because he spends days and nights with a bitch (319).
Moralising is rare and short : Olympio before the drawing of
lots says that ' all men rely on the gods but I have seen many
deceived who rely on the gods ' (348). When he draws the right.

[1] Bieber, *H.T.*, fig. 86, 382.
[2] Cf. particularly 911 with *Thesm.*, 639–48 ; 616 ff. with *Lysistrata*, 845 ff. ;
798 ff. with *Peace* and *Birds*. Cf. Wehrli, *Motivstudien*, 21 ; Suess, *Rh. Mus.*,
1910, 458 f.
[3] F. Skutsch (*Rh. Mus.*, 1900, 283 f.) notes a parallel also in Ovid, *Fasti*, ii,
303 ff., which Ovid ascribes to *peregrinae Musae*, i.e. not Plautus. Prehn, *Q. Pl.*,
80, suggests also a parallel with the version of the Pelops story in which Pelops
steals the *ius primae noctis* from Myrtilus, but this cannot, as far as I know, be
traced in drama.

lot, he says that he has won because of his ancestral piety (418), and yet the outcome proves the truth of his first statement at least in the sense that a wrong reliance on the gods will lead to deception. Tragic reminiscence is difficult to trace through the Latin, but there is no sign of anything remarkable here; the allusion to Temenos in the drawing of lots (385, 398) and the echo of the entry of the Phrygian (E., *Orestes*) in Pardalisca's entry (621) are the most obvious instances. The pungent realism with emphasis on significant details which characterises the Greek fragments is seen again in Olympio's description of what he will do to Chalinus (118 f.), Cleustrata's description of her husband (144 ff.), and Lysidamus' joyous entry (217 ff.).

Without for the moment raising the various difficult problems of the *Casina* we can see certain elements of Diphilos' technique on a large scale. His sense of stage effect is obvious as in the scene from the *Synapothneskontes*: it is very clear in the scene of drawing of lots, which gives its name to the play, but also in the marriage procession and in the frightened entries of Pardalisca, Olympio, and Lysidamus in the later scenes. The first act introduces the characters: the contrast between Olympio and Chalinus is not the normal contrast between country slave and town slave as Philemon gives it in the opening scene of the *Mostellaria*, because our sympathy is with Chalinus rather than with the savage Olympio. Chalinus' own desires are not emphasised or later developed; it is tempting to say that Menander saw the problem of Chalinus and developed it in the *Heros* but we do not know enough to assert a definite relationship. Cleustrata is shown by her scene with Myrrhina to be not only an injured but a harsh wife. It is not clear whether Plautus has suppressed a scene in the first act which characterised Lysidamus:[1] he presents himself admirably when he first appears (217) and perhaps nothing more is necessary.

With Lysidamus' appearance at the beginning of the second act[2] all is ready for the battle between the two determined protagonists, Lysidamus and Cleustrata. The main steps are the drawing of lots, the three delays, the marriage, and the sequel. Each part works up to a climax: thus the test of Chalinus (II, 4) and the test of Olympio (II, 5) precede the drawing of the lots

[1] So, for instance, Marigo, *op. cit.*, 490.
[2] The first act must end at 215: all before is exposition, all after is story.

(II, 6). This part is concluded by Lysidamus' plan to put Casina in the neighbouring house [1] (II, 7, 8, III, 1), which is overheard by Chalinus and thus forms the basis of the delaying action. The delaying action again has three stages ; Cleustrata refuses the help of Myrrhina (III, 2), Cleustrata promotes a quarrel between Lysidamus and Alcesimus (III, 3, 4), Pardalisca reports that Casina has gone mad (III, 5, 6). The marriage scenes again work up through the account of further delays (IV, 1, 2), the singing of the marriage song (IV, 3) to the transference of the bride (IV, 4). Finally the sequel is divided between Olympio and Lysidamus.

This is a very carefully conceived and organised action, in which the impatience and resource of Lysidamus is pitted against the resolve and resource of Cleustrata and after long seeming success is finally defeated. This is the driving force all through, though the light may shift on to different minor figures, now Olympio, now Chalinus, now Pardalisca, and, as Fraenkel [2] has pointed out, a theme like the madness of Casina is dropped as soon as it has done its job ; it has no further effect on the action. Straightforward movement of the action was obviously Diphilos' aim and must be taken into consideration in assessing what is Diphilos and what Plautus. The main problem centres on the question of the recognition. Casina is the exposed daughter of the neighbour Myrrhina ; Myrrhina could presumably discover this if she visited Casina in Cleustrata's house and the old slave who is ill at the beginning of the play (37) can confirm it ; when it is confirmed, Casina can marry Euthnicus, who has been rusticated by his father (62). It is possible to imagine a play that would realise these possibilities and follow the rules which seem to be observable in Menander's plot construction. Suggestions have been made along these lines. [3] Myrrhina in Plautus does in fact visit Cleustrata and is much more sympathetic than in her first appearance. She could then have discovered the truth, seen the old slave, and Euthynicus himself may have arrived to plot the final deception. This would all have happened in the third act. At the end, the marriage could have been arranged. The major objection seems to be the inevitable slow-

---

[1] The second act ends when Lysidamus goes to the forum (526) ; he returns in the next act as normally.

[2] *Pl. Pl.*, 303.　　　　[3] Fraenkel, *Pl. Pl.*, 298 ff. ; Marigo, *op. cit.*, 499.

ing up of the action and the incompatibility of the sentiments
(Euthynicus' love for Casina, Myrrhina's recovery of her long-
lost daughter) with the kind of comedy which dominates the
play. If this is granted, then we may also note that the sick-
ness of the slave seems to belong to the Greek original,[1] that
Plautus' reference to himself (65) does not necessarily prove that
Euthynicus arrived in the course of the original,[2] that a recognition of Casina in the third act is excluded by *reperietur* (1013) in
the last scene and that probably the last scenes show a good deal
of thickening up by Plautus ;[3] no scene need have more than
three actors. Fraenkel [4] has shown that Diphilos could leave a
great deal to his audience to supply ; he gave enough time for
Lysidamus to tell Cleustrata to receive Myrrhina and for
Lysidamus to tell Alcesimus to send Myrrhina, and left his
audience to assume the rest. So too the brief announcement
that Casina will be recognised and will marry Euthynicus may
well be Diphilos. A brief scene of formal recognition and an
announcement of the betrothal is of course possible, but what is
certain is that the emphasis in Diphilos was not on the recovery
of a lost daughter or on the love affair of Casina and Euthynicus
but on the battle between Lysidamus and Cleustrata, and the
proof of this is the straightforward movement of the action which
must derive from Diphilos.

The play inevitably invites comparison with Philemon's
Emporos. They have in common the rivalry between father and
son and the father's use of his neighbour to provide a rendezvous.
There the likeness ends. Diphilos portrays in detail the present
state of the old man in love ; Philemon gives the background,
since we hear far more about the past history of Demipho than
about the actual course of his amour ; Euthynicus does not
appear in Diphilos' play, whereas Charinus describes at length the
nature of his love. The *Mercator* is a series of pictures : Charinus
in love, Demipho in love, Charinus' extemporisation in battle
with Demipho, Lysimachus' extemporisation in battle with his
wife, Charinus' mad scene. In Diphilos the action is more con-
centrated and moves by stages over its three great peaks, the
drawing of lots, the madness of Casina, and the marriage and its

---

[1] Skutsch, *Rh. Mus.*, 1900, 283 ff.   [2] Skutsch, *loc. cit.*
[3] I do not feel certain that Myrrhina appeared in the last scenes ; in 687 *haec*
may be Casina.   [4] *Op. cit.*, 304.

sequel. Neither play has any moral intention except in so far as they satirise the follies of the old. Both are concerned primarily to raise laughter but the means are different. We laugh at the reckless extemporisation of Charinus, Demipho, and Lysimachus in Philemon, in Diphilos we laugh rather at the shifts to which single-minded determination drives Lysidamus and Cleustrata.

The *Rudens* [1] has the same essential structure as the *Casina* and shows much of the same technique and some detailed correspondences, but the atmosphere is entirely different because of the very strong flavour of Menander and Euripides. The *Casina* is wanton, joyous comedy ; the *Rudens* has plenty of comedy of the same kind (the parallel between the thug-comedy in the *Rudens*, *Casina*, and the Diphilos scene of the *Adelphi* has already been mentioned), but through the comedy Diphilos is asserting a definite value in the portrait of Daemones as I have tried to indicate above. Again the mainspring of the action is a battle between two opposed parties, and the campaign has various stages : the reception of the girls in the temple, the arrival of Labrax at the temple, the protection of the girls by Daemones and the trial of the *leno*, the recognition of Palaestra, and finally the freeing of Ampelisca. The action is more complicated than in the *Casina* because Plesidippus has to have a part in it as well as Daemones, whereas in the *Casina* Cleustrata acts for Euthynicus all the way through : moreover, there is a double object, not only the liberation of both girls but also the recognition of Palaestra ; whereas in the *Casina* the recognition theme is kept in the background because it would have been alien to the spirit of the play, here it is an additional means of displaying the characters of Daemones, Labrax, Trachalio, and Gripus. The actual interweaving of the two themes of liberation and recognition is masterly : Palaestra worries about her recognition tokens as soon as she has been received in the temple (388) ; Daemones dreams of an attack on Athenian swallows (604) ; Trachalio says that Palaestra is an Athenian (739) when he persuades Daemones to protect the girl from Labrax. Thus when Plesidippus takes

---

[1] *Anasozomenoi*, *Epitrope*, *Pera* have been suggested as the name of the original. Perhaps *Pera* is most likely, but we only have some 50 titles out of 100 plays by Diphilos. *Anasozomenoi* seems to imply return home rather than rescue from the sea (cf. Wilhelm, *Urkunden*, 76, 246).

Labrax off to justice, the audience are ready for the recognition story which starts with Gripus and his basket, but Gripus' discontent is the link which ties on the final chapter of the liberation story consisting of two sections, struggle (V, 2) and arbitration (V, 3), parallel to the two sections of the recognition story (IV, 3 ; IV, 4).

As in the *Casina*, the first act gives the atmosphere (here a romantic atmosphere of star, storm, sea, country, and temple) and presents the characters (Labrax [1] and Charmides are sufficiently described by Arcturus and the girls). Then the action goes forward in chapters with the beginning and end and sometimes the middle (e.g. Ampelisca's sight of the *leno*, II, 4 ; the altar scene, III, 4, and the recognition, IV, 4) clearly marked : thus the song (?) of the fishermen, Daemones' dream, the arrival of Gripus,[2] and the return of Labrax all make striking beginnings. As in the *Casina* full weight is given to the minor characters by suppressing the major characters through part of the action ; in fact, neither Daemones nor Plesidippus nor Palaestra appear in the second act, the girls are silent all through the third act,[3] and Labrax does not appear in the first or fourth act. The rustic Sceparnio, the pert Ampelisca, the compassionate priestess, the essentially noble Trachalio, the odious Charmides, and the hardbitten Gripus thus have space to display their characters, which have their independent value while at the same time contributing to the movement of the action : the charming scene between Sceparnio and Ampelisca (II, 4) is justified because it leads to Ampelisca's seeing the *leno* on the shore and then to Sceparnio's surly though to us sympathetic refusal of Charmides' appeal for help. As a character Sceparnio has something in common with Olympio of the *Casina* and Trachalio with Chalinus, and here again as in Menander's *Epitrepontes* the comparison is in favour of the town slave.

The movement is necessarily slower than in the *Casina* (and has been slowed still more by Plautus' elaboration),[4] but again

---

[1] Palaestra's arrival and reception (185 f.) seems to me to belong to the exposition and not to the action ; therefore the traditional act division after 290 is right (contrast Jachmann, *Plautinisches*, 98). The way from shore to temple is very short, as we can see in Act III.

[2] Therefore I am inclined to believe that IV, 1, is Plautine.

[3] III, 3, I take to be an insertion by Plautus.

[4] See particularly Jachmann, *op. cit.*, and Fraenkel, *op. cit.*, on this.

we can see where Diphilos has left things to the imagination of the audience or has admitted improbabilities to secure the kind of movement that he requires. It is unclear and does not matter what happens to Plesidippus between his hasty departure and his return (159, 839). The rejection of Charmides, a pause between acts, and Daemones' dream separate Labrax' entry into the temple from Trachalio's appeal for help (570, 615) : the assessment of Charmides by Sceparnio helps us to assess his companion Labrax and Daemones' dream prepares Daemones' future action and the recognition. The removal of the girls from the statue of Aphrodite inside the temple to the altar outside (707) is pure stage convenience. So also is the fact that Trachalio returns so quickly with Plesidippus (775, 839) ; only Plesidippus can remove Labrax and thus release the girls from the altar ; until both happen the act cannot end ; yet Trachalio's errand should be covered by an act end ; instead Diphilos introduces the club tableau (III, 5) to mask the lapse of time. Plesidippus is a relation of Daemones : the only importance of this is that it makes it easy and natural for Daemones to give him his daughter ; Daemones knows this in the fourth act (1198, 1213) ; whether Palaestra or Trachalio told him Plesidippus' family name does not matter ; there is not the smallest justification for assuming that Plautus has cut out a recognition scene between Daemones and Plesidippus ; we have had enough instances of Diphilos' compendiary technique.

Diphilos' love of spectacle is even clearer in this play than in the *Casina* ; the prologue figure Arcturus, the tiling of the broken roof, the brilliant account of the shipwreck (it is of course nonsense to suggest that the actual shipwreck was seen on the stage), the searching of the girls for each other, the fishermen, the dripping old villains, the dream, the altar scene, the club tableau, Gripus with his basket are all spectacular in word or actual stage effect. A remnant of the descriptions of food and drink can be seen in the fishermen's list of fish (297) and Labrax' list of cups (1319). The pungent realism of Olympio's opening scene recurs in the words of the two country slaves Sceparnio and Gripus. Gnomes [1] in this play are more frequent but still brief, except for the moralising of Arcturus in the prologue and Daemones' moral

---

[1] e.g. 185, 290, 400, 975.

parable to Gripus (1235 ff.). Tragic reminiscence [1] is much easier to detect in this play than in the *Casina*, and tragic reminiscence which is not only simple quotation with or without parody of the kind that can be observed in the fragments [2] but the echoing with or without parody of a situation in a tragedy. This sort of reminiscence is not obvious in Philemon but is common in Menander.[3] In this play it is probably justifiable to see something of the atmosphere of the *Ion* in the opening, of Tecmessa's search in Sophocles' *Ajax* in the entry of Palaestra and Ampelisca, of the *Helen* in the behaviour of the priestess, of the *Stheneboea* in the arrival of the fishermen, of the *Iphigenia in Tauris* in Daemones' dream, and of the *Andromache* in the altar scene, which is essentially different from the altar scene of Menander's *Perinthia* and the comic tradition descending (for us) from the *Thesmophoriazousai*. Gripus fishes up the recognition tokens as the satyrs fish up the chest in the *Diktyoulkoi*. The first arbitration of Daemones has affinities with the arbitration in Euripides' *Alope*. We can see perhaps several rather different elements in these reminiscences, first the recapture of tragic atmosphere in the opening scenes, secondly the heightening of tone of a comic scene by tragic reminiscence (most obvious in the entry of Palaestra), thirdly the transference of tragic situations into comedy either with the tragic scene consciously in the background as in the altar scene or with complete translation into the idiom of comedy as in the arbitration scene.

For all these techniques parallels can be seen in Menander and for three of the reminiscences in the *Rudens* a parallel in Menander is known—the *Leucadia* for the opening scenes, the *Halieis* (14K) for the fishermen, and the *Epitrepontes* for the arbitration ; it is therefore tempting to suppose that in this more extended use of tragic reminiscence Diphilos was following Menander, but the question of priority is extremely difficult to establish and in the case of the arbitration even both poets may have borrowed direct from Euripides and the common details (e.g. the arbitrator's firm dealing with interruptions) may come from the common original. The fact that Diphilos has gone further away from

---

[1] See on this subject Marx, Marigo, Coppola, *op. cit.* ; Wehrli, *Motivstudien*, 120 f.

[2] e.g. 9 with E., fr. 506N., 160 with E., *I.T.*, 270 f. ; 400 with Euripidean doxologies ; 1144 with S., *El.*, 1165 ; 1335 f. with *I.T.*, 743.

[3] Cf. *Studies in Menander*, 161.

the original (the arbitrator is not the grandfather but the father of the girl, Gripus does not know at the beginning that recognition tokens are involved at all, Gripus and Trachalio are not shepherds but a fisherman and a town slave) does not necessarily prove that he is adapting Menander ; Menander may later have gone back closer to Euripides for the particular purpose of the *Epitrepontes*. It is, however, clear that Menander was strongly influenced by tragedy from his earliest period whereas neither the *Casina* nor the fragments of Diphilos show such influence to the same degree.

The fragmentary *Vidularia* (Diphilos' *Schedia*) [1] adds little to our knowledge. The likeness to the *Rudens* is obvious ; here too there is a shipwreck (fr. I, 72) and the scene is near a shrine of Venus [2] (fr. IV) ; the old man Dinia is generous to the young stranger Nicodemus like Daemones ; a box of recognition tokens is discovered in the sea by a fisherman Cacistus, who is caught by a slave and persuaded to deposit them with Gorgines, the fisherman who is housing Nicodemus ; in the course of their recovery Dinia discovers that Nicodemus is his son, just as Daemones discovers his daughter.

The details are obscure. The scene showed the houses of Gorgines and Dinia and a shrine of Venus in a myrtle thicket. The Plautine prologue was very short and cannot have given the pre-history.[3] Then a slave, whose name is restored as Aspasius, starts the play with a *sententia*. In the gap of 190 lines Nicodemus certainly sought shelter with Gorgines (54) and possibly, as Marigo suggests, met Cacistus. When the text resumes he is asking for work from Dinia. After another gap of 150 lines Cacistus and the slave are depositing the box of tokens with Gorgines ; the slave departs ; Cacistus soliloquises ; Dinia and Nicodemus come out of Dinia's house while Cacistus watches them, and Dinia prepares to lend Nicodemus a mina. The struggle between Cacistus and the slave has evidently immediately preceded this ; the corresponding scene in the *Rudens* takes 140 lines (905/1045) but the scene here may have been cut much shorter. Cacistus is a fisherman (fr. VII) ; his soliloquy (62 f.)

---

[1] Marx, in his edition of the *Rudens*, 271 f., rejects the attribution to Diphilos, but in view of the title and the parallels noted by Marigo, *op. cit.*, 525 f. ; Jachmann, *op. cit.*, 26 f. ; Coppola, *R.F.I.C.*, 1929, 175, etc., this seems unjustifiable.
[2] Cf. Thiele, *Hermes*, xlviii, 522 f.　　　　　[3] Cf. Leo, *Pl. F.*[1], 197.

shows that he does not know Gorgines or Dinia : he does, however, recognise Nicodemus, and one possibility is that he is acting for Nicodemus, if Nicodemus has already met him and told him that the box is lost in the shipwreck ; in any case the money Nicodemus borrows may be a reward for the discoverer of the box ; the sum is much too small to be the price of a hetaira. What does the box itself contain ?

The fragments give us a clue : in fr. XVII someone who must be Nicodemus says ' this is my country and this is my father and that man is the father of Soteris '.   This is the announcement of a double recognition which has recently happened, and three people are present : Nicodemus, Dinia, and Gorgines.   This suggests that the box contains Soteris' tokens, which Gorgines can identify, and was sealed by the ring of Nicodemus, which Dinia recognises as having been his own (fr. XIV) ; Nicodemus establishes his claim on the box by describing the seal (fr. XI) and this proves to Dinia that Nicodemus is his lost son (80, 86). As the recognition is double, both Gorgines and Dinia are needed ; therefore the box is deposited with Gorgines instead of with Dinia, who plays the part of Daemones in the *Rudens*. But we still have not accounted for the struggle.   Whether Cacistus is acting for Nicodemus or not in getting hold of the box, what reason has the slave for trying to remove it from him ? No one can contend a fisherman's claim to his catch unless like Trachalio in the *Rudens* he has a superior claim.   The interested parties are Gorgines (if he already suspects that Soteris is his daughter), Nicodemus, Soteris herself, and whoever at the moment is in charge of Soteris.   The slave says nothing in the surviving passage ; the opening speech belongs to Cacistus because it is echoed in Cacistus' soliloquy : Cacistus asks *hicine vos habitatis*, which should mean Gorgines *and* the slave.   The slave then at the moment lives with Gorgines ; there is no reason to suppose that Gorgines already had suspicions about Soteris and it seems therefore likely that the slave belongs to Nicodemus and like him is lodging with Gorgines.   He is acting for Nicodemus and Cacistus is acting for himself and trying to make money out of the tokens.

The scene between Cacistus and the slave on the analogy of the *Rudens* starts an act, which finishes with the recognition scene ; the act starts at the earliest at l. 250 and at the latest at l. 340

according to the length that we give to the struggle. In the
Rudens Act II starts at l. 290 and Act III at l. 593 ; in the *Casina*
Act II probably starts at l. 217 and Act III at l. 530. The struggle
and recognition cannot therefore be the fourth act as in the
Rudens ; but it must be either the second or the third act. We
do not know how much Plautus may have shortened the
beginning of Diphilos' play and therefore we cannot exclude the
possibility of this being a third act ; on the other hand, it is also
possible that the play began with brief Plautine prologue, slave
scene, divine prologue. But in any case it is clear that, whereas
in the *Rudens* the main action of·the liberation story is over before
the main action of the recognition story, here the main action
of the recognition is over early. The rest is guesswork : there
must have been another side to this play ; Gorgines and Dinia
are the white side, there must also have been a black side of which
Cacistus, like Gripus in the *Rudens*, is part. The suggestion that
Aul. fr. vii *sed leno egreditur foras, hinc ex occulto sermonatus sublegam*
may belong to the *Vidularia* since it cannot belong to the *Aulularia*
is attractive. A *leno* would provide ·the black side of the picture,
and it is at least possible that the *leno* captured Soteris, who may
have become separated from Nicodemus in the shipwreck. The
play must have been like the *Rudens* but had an essential difference
in structure in that the liberation story followed the recognition
story.

In general we can say that Diphilos' comedy is rooted in
Middle Comedy and derives from there its delight in feasting,
drinking, and riddling. Spectacle with tableaux and violent
action plays a large part, and pungent realism with vivid imagery
and sparing use of apt gnomes marks the speeches. The two plays
which we have are constructed as a progressive action between
two opposed characters round which the minor characters are
grouped, and the speed of action is more important to the poet
than complete exposition and complete adherence to probability.
Many of the stock characters of Middle Comedy appear but
we can trace also New Comedy themes. There is however no
evidence that the particular problems of human relationships
which Menander treated in his plays of Reconciliation and Social
Criticism were also problems for Diphilos, but in the *Rudens*,
while he borrows much of the technique of tragic reminiscence
from the younger poet, he also very gently through the medium

of comedy asserts a positive value, the old Athenian ideal of Daemones (compassion and discrimination), a value which the new Athens with its sharper distinctions of rich and poor was likely to lose.

There is one papyrus fragment [1] where we see a character like Daemones in the *Rudens* and Dinia in the *Vidularia*. Here Demeas provides a young man and his slave with money and provisions. Most of the situation is unclear ; but the relationship between Demeas and the young man recalls the two Diphilos plays. The young man does not belong to the place and from his comment seems not to have had any previous connection with Demeas : ' Demeas seems to be a real Greek in character but Tyche makes no distinction in whom she treats badly.' This is a common enough idea, the use of ' Greek ' as a term of moral approbation has been compared with Pataikos in the *Perikeiromene* (430) and the blindness of Fortune is a commonplace. But here at any rate it suggests that Demeas like Daemones is a poor man—so poor that he has to borrow a basket to have his loaves fetched but not so poor that he has no slave. His very genuine prayer for peace also fits the character of Daemones. It is at least possible that Demeas, like Daemones, is living in exile and that his present city is at war with his home, from which the young man also comes. The young man takes refuge with Demeas and this gives him the right of asylum for a day. Demeas is prepared to give him both money and provisions for his journey.

The story is obscure. This short scene of 38 lines is clearly not the first meeting of Demeas and the young man. After an earlier meeting Demeas sent his slave marketing and his slave has returned ; the earlier meeting must then have been in a previous act. The young man and his slave have been discussing the situation before Demeas comes out. The young man wants to take away ' these women ', who resolve themselves into ' this woman ' and an ' old woman '. Demeas evidently objects to the scheme. When Demeas has gone in, the young man remarks on his character. Then someone talks back at his wife, apparently abusing her for not bringing a child out of the house, and then says something about an old woman, who apparently has brought the child here (36–8). The old woman must surely be the old

[1] P63 (= D21 ; S1). Early third century B.C.

woman with the girl whom the young man wants to take away.
Therefore the speaker can hardly be Demeas and must be his
neighbour ; he will then be the father of the girl and the child,
her child by the young man, and the old man wants to expose
it ; the scene is not unlike the scene in the *Samia* (202 f.) where
Nikeratos similarly discovers his daughter's child. How the play
continues we cannot say ; it is not even certain whether the
young man overhears this or not, though this seems hardly
possible as both the old man and his wife seem to be on the stage.[1]

The only ground for ascribing this fragment to Diphilos is the
relationship between Demeas and the youth, a relationship for
which the only close parallels are in the *Rudens* and the *Vidularia* ;
a rather different form in the *Miles* we have yet to discuss.
Therefore the ascription can only be rated as a possibility ; the
parallel however, is interesting. Another possibility which we
have already discussed is the *Amphitruo* ;[2] there besides minor
verbal correspondences and thug comedy, the careful structure
with a first and last group of scenes each with a splendid messenger speech balanced about two main groups of three scenes
each recalls the composition of the *Casina*. A third possible
ascription is the original of the *Miles Gloriosus*.

The soldier who gives his name to the play is serving Seleukos
(75, etc.) who was king from 306 to 281. The period can perhaps be shortened ; the soldier has fought victoriously against the
grandson of Neptune (15), which seems to allude to Demetrios
Poliorketes' claim to be son of Poseidon ; whether grandson
is to be taken literally or not, i.e. whether the reference is to
Demetrios or his son, the allusion is impossible before the death
of the elder Antigonos and unlikely long after the death of
Demetrios, i.e. before 301 or after 286. A date soon after the
Battle of Ipsos is perhaps most likely ; then Seleukos' Indian campaign (25) would be a recent memory, and an Athenian might
well in those years have gone on an embassy to Naupactus
(102). A date in the first ten years of the third century would
also fit the curious cross-connections with Menander's *Second
Adelphoi*, which is probably one of his later plays.[3]

---

[1] Prof. E. G. Turner tells me that the correct reading in 43 is τὸν and not
τὴν.   [2] See above, p. 95.
[3] See *Studies in Menander*, 106, for dating of *Second Adelphoi* ; see below for
cross-connections with *Miles*. See Dietze, *De Philemone Comico*, 41 f., for
dating of *Miles*.

The *Miles* has given cause for much discussion and has certainly been greatly extended by Plautus. The older view that it has been put together from two originals, a braggart soldier, to which most of Acts I, III, IV, and V of the Plautine play belong, and a wall comedy, which occupies Act II, has been successfully refuted in the recent papers [1] of Drexler and Tierney, and the case need not be re-argued in detail. We may therefore assume that Plautus has followed the main lines of the original, but at the same time the argument for contamination shows that the poet of the original emphasised the individual scenes rather than the structure of the whole. The *Miles* lives in the mind as a series of tableaux, of which the most striking are the opening picture of the soldier and his parasite, the wall comedy, Periplectomenus' apologia, the deception of the soldier, the escape of the lovers, and the punishment of the soldier.

At the beginning the soldier appears with his parasite. The scene is in a tradition which we can trace back through the Bias/Strouthias scene of the *Kolax* [2] to Antiphanes' *Stratiotes* (rather before 360).[3] The shield so bright that it blinds the enemy, the sword longing for its feast of blood are traditional, probably also the casualty list, which has an obvious affinity with the tour of conquest in the *Curculio*. The imaginary beauty to which all women succumb is perhaps a new trait ; the soldier's desire for any pretty woman that he sees and his complete disregard for present commitments is in the forefront of the picture and brings him to well-deserved discomfiture at the end. The surviving plays show us the soldier as a genuine lover (*Perikeiromene, Misoumenos*), the soldier as the unsuccessful rival of the genuine lover (*Kolax*, etc.), and the soldier heartlessly deceived by a hetaira (*Truculentus*), but here (as in the *Epidicus* and differently in the *Hecyra*) the instability of the young man's affections is emphasised and for the soldier the only end is corporal punishment, since he has no father present to marry him off. Here, far more obviously than in the *Curculio*, there may be some reflection of Demetrios Poliorketes' love affairs, and the play is certainly a satire on the kind of soldier to whom he was the beau ideal. The parasite's only function is to display the soldier,

---

[1] Drexler, *Hermes*, 1929, 339 f. ; J. J. Tierney, *P.R.I.A.*, xlix, 167 f.

[2] Ribbeck, *Alazon*, 56, notes also the similarity of Menander, 563K, with *Miles*, 33.   [3] See *Studies in Menander*, 164.

but though he is never seen again he is not completely forgotten, since the soldier tells us on his return that the parasite has been sent to Seleukos (948).[1] The soldier has no part in the wall comedy—only a slave can submit to the running hither and thither which is involved ; therefore he only returns when the escape plan in its first shape has been formed ; the object of a pierced wall is traditionally not escape but reunion, and this is achieved by the defeat of Philocomasium's guard. When reunion is assured, escape is planned, and then the soldier is necessary again because traditionally you can only escape by deceiving your possessor himself. Similarly, in the *Curculio*, reunion is attained by bribing Leaina, but for escape Cappadox has to be paid.

The past history is explained in a prologue which is spoken by Palaestrio (79 f.). There is some Plautine expansion, as has been seen,[2] particularly at the beginning and end. Plautus gave the name of the comedy, and explained at the end what was going to happen in the wall comedy, although the situation which creates the necessity for the wall comedy has not yet occurred. The speaker in the original was probably Palaestrio ; he knows the past history, and as there is no recognition there is no case for a god. In the *Mercator* Charinus speaks the prologue but he speaks it at the beginning. Here, however, a new character speaks the prologue after a dramatic scene (in Aristophanes several times one of the speakers in the opening dialogue pulls himself up to tell the spectators the story, but Palaestrio comes on for the purpose). Palaestrio's recital has various points of contact with other comedies : the method by which the soldier got Philocomasium from the *lena* her mother is paralleled in the *Cistellaria* (cf. particularly 92 ff., 191 ff.). The story of the pirates is like the bogus story in the *Dis Exapaton* (*Bacch.*, 289, cf. also Menander, 15K). The secret passage recurs in Menander's *Phasma* and yet earlier in Euripides' *Protesilaos*. The lovers are helped by the old man, Periplectomenus, with whom Pleusicles is staying because he is a great friend of his father ; he is described as *lepidus senex* ;[3] the detailed character which

---

[1] In the *Epidicus* provision is similarly made that we should not forget the prologue figure Thesprio.

[2] Cf. Leo, *Pl. F.*[1], 194 f. ; Ribbeck, *op. cit.*, 60.

[3] *Studies in Menander*, 53 f., 146.

he is given in this play must be discussed later, but we may note here that he is a comparatively rare figure. The reluctant helper of an elderly lover is known from the *Mercator* and *Casina*, the helpful father (or adoptive father) is known from the *Asinaria* and the *Adelphi* ; the relationship between Pataikos and Polemon in the *Perikeiromene* is a very special case and there is no intrigue ; Chaireas in Menander's *Koneiazomenai* is an elderly helper but is not disinterested ; however they carry out the intrigue themselves. The disinterested elderly helper of a young man only occurs in the *Rudens*, the *Vidularia*, and in the papyrus fragment of the early third century B.C. which we have discussed.[1] The character of Periplectomenus is unfolded at the beginning of the third act ; his first appearance is when he comes out of his house cursing his slaves because Sceledrus, ' chasing a monkey ', has looked over from the soldier's roof and has seen the lovers embracing. The spying slave we know from Euripides' *Protesilaos* ; in Menander's *Synaristosai* (in Caecilius) and a fragment of Diphilos (84K) someone spies from a neighbour's roof.[2]

On the analogy of other comedies the making of a plan to meet this new situation should belong to the second act. It is clear that 210–13, 219–30 are Plautine ; it is at least odd that Palaestrio asks Periplectomenus to send Philocomasium from his house to the soldier's house (182) and then repeats the order (255) ; Periplectomenus' description of Palaestrio thinking (200 f.) has no parallel in Greek comedy and may well be Plautine ; Thierfelder[3] is therefore probably right in regarding the whole passage from 185 (or rather 180) to 235 as Plautine. It covers the act ending. Palaestrio comes from the soldier's house for his prologue speech ; Periplectomenus finds him on the stage ; they go in together at the end of the act to make the plan (180) and come out again to discuss the made plan (235). Philocomasium is to pretend that she has a twin sister. We know the female deceiver in these forms : instructed and active here, later in this play and in the *Persa* ; uninstructed and passive in the *Epidicus* ; initiator herself of the deception in the *Epitre-*

---

[1] There also, as in *Miles*, 624, the slave urges his young master on ; cf. *Trin.*, 454. Zucker, *op. cit.*, 23, compares the friendship between Periplectomenus and Pleusicles with Aristotle, *N.E.*, 1158 b 12.

[2] Cf. Dalman, *de aedibus scaenicis*, 64/5.　　　　[3] *Gnomon*, 1935, 145.

pontes (Habrotonon) and the *Synaristosai* (*Cist.*, 366 f.). The theme of twins is here used in the reverse ; normally as in the *Menaechmi, Amphitruo* (and perhaps one should add wraith and real Helen in Euripides' *Helen*) two different people are mistaken for one, here one person is to be mistaken for two. Periplecto-menus objects that the soldier may return and want to see both (249) ; Palaestrio answers that traditional female excuses can be made.[1] Periplectomenus withdraws to instruct Philocomasium, and Sceledrus comes out. The uselessness of trying to guard women is a theme known from other comedies.[2] Leaina in the *Curculio* is herself a useless guard, but Sceledrus, the soldier's slave, is perhaps developed from a hint in Sosias' failure to keep watch on Glykera in the *Perikeiromene*. The long scene which follows is an immense elaboration of the ' in-and-out ' comedy, used much more briefly by Menander in several plays, notably the *Apistos, Samia,* and *Perikeiromene* ;[3] some of the elaboration is due to Plautus,[4] but the main lines must belong to the original. Philocomasium's dream is in a tradition which goes back over *Rudens* and *Mercator* to tragedy, but this is the first imaginary dream ; her instructions to sacrifice (411) and the comedy of errors (424 f.) are similar twists of old themes. The well-marked climax of Sceledrus' discomfiture is reached when Periplectomenus takes over from Palaestrio.[5] The end (582) raises a difficulty : Sceledrus says he will run away and hide and then says he will go home ; Periplectomenus says Sceledrus has gone from here and then that he is away from home ; in the Lurcio scene (816 f.) he is at home ; in the last act of the play he apparently leaves home with Philocomasium and returns with the news of her escape. This question must be examined later with the Lurcio scene.

Reunion of the lovers is now assured ; escape has to be planned. The plan has to be made on the stage, i.e. in the street ; therefore Palaestrio takes elaborate steps to make certain that the coast is clear (596 f.), and to show the continuity he asks : ' Do we go on with the plan we considered inside ? ' (612). Pleusicles

---

[1] With 251 f. cf. Antiphanes, 148K.

[2] Legrand, *op. cit.*, 191 ; cf. Xenarchos, fr. 4, 10–12K ; Apollodoros, 283/6K.

[3] See *Studies in Menander*, 112.

[4] Jachmann, *op. cit.*, 177 f., notes 319–30 ; 340 is unnecessary anticipation of 378 ; 354 f. is Plautine underlining.

[5] Here again (528) Köhler notices a clear reminiscence of Euripides' *Helen* (559).

objects that Periplectomenus´ should not have to embroil himself
in´ lovers' deceits and this introduces the self-portrait of Periplectomenus, which Leo [1] describes as a flower of Attic characterisation. Only after this does the plan proceed. According
to his self-portrait, Periplectomenus is youthful in body (627),
good in company (639 f.), rich enough to support the burden
(672 f.). The second and third sections have many parallels.
In the second, Periplectomenus distinguishes himself from the
man who does not know how to behave in company ; him
we know from Aristophanes (e.g. Philokleon in the *Wasps*), the
' rustic ' of Anaxandrides (1–3K) and Antiphanes (3K), the
characters of Theophrastos,[2] and Demaenetus in the *Asinaria*.[3]
Periplectomenus' claim (661) to be *adulescentem moribus* is
paralleled in Menander (749K), but when he says he behaves
exactly like a parasite and dances like a *kinaidos* (661/8), we can
reasonably suppose that Plautus has falsified the picture by adding
this passage ; at least the obvious texts on dancing [4] do not suggest
that ' dancing like a *kinaidos* ' any more than playing the parasite
should belong to the portrait of the Athenian gentleman in
company. In the third section Periplectomenus explains that he
does not mind expense because he has neither wife nor children.
The whole passage is closely connected with Theophrastos' work
On Matrimony, with Micio's description of himself in the *Adelphi*,
and the theme is put in brief in a fragment of Menander's *Paidion* : [5]
nuptias abieci : amicos utor primaris viros. It is not clear whether
we should suppose that the author of the *Miles* knew Theophrastos
direct or through the medium of Menander ; [6] the *Adelphi* may

---

[1] *Op. cit.*, 118, cf. 164, n. 1.

[2] Cf. particularly 642 with Theophrastos, XV, 10 (αὐθάδεια) ; 645 with
VII, 9 (λαλία), XII, 10 (ἀκαιρία), and with Menander, 435 Kö. (Pap. Ox.
1803) ; 647 with XIX, 4, 11 (δυσχέρεια).

[3] Note in particular the likeness of *Miles*, 652/3 to *As.*, 814.

[4] e.g. Alexis, 222K ; Theophrastos, *Characters*, VI, 3 ; XII, 15 ; XXVII, 15.

[5] R105, x.

[6] The chief passages to note are : *Miles*, 681, with *Ad.*, 30, Theophr. *garrulae
conquestiones* ; 682, with Menander, 157K ; 685, with Theophr. *quae tamen
rara avis est*, and Diphilos, 115K ; 691 f., with Theophr. *honoranda nutrix eius
et gerula*, etc. ; 705, with Theophr. *Haeredes autem meliores et certiores amici
sunt* ; 718, with *Ad.*, 35 f., cf. Menander, 418K, and Theophr. *(filius) prior te
forte moriatur* ; 727 f., with Theophr. and Menander, 532K (perhaps from
Didymai, produced after 300), i.e. there ought to be standards in assessing humans
as in assessing merchandise. I had written this before I saw that Dietze, *de
Philemone Comico*, 20, n. 2, has collected most of the parallels.

well have been produced about the same time as the *Miles*. In any case the dramatic value of this section is to contrast Periplectomenus with the soldier, who pursues every woman he sees and conforms to the Aristotelian definition of the ἀκόλαστος, the self-indulgent man (*N.E.*, 1146 b 22). The final section on the behaviour of those who ask for a cheap meal seems to be Roman (751 f.) ; the transition to it is good Greek (749/50).[1] In the original perhaps Palaestrio begged Periplectomenus to forget the shopping and consider the more urgent problem of Philocomasium's escape.

Palaestrio sums up the self-portrait (730 f.) with a reminiscence of Euripides (*H.F.*, 656), which has rather different echoes in the *Rudens* (195) and the *Adelphi* (821) : the *lepide ingeniatus* should have a long life and the *scelestus* a short life.[2] *Lepidus* is the word used by Palaestrio when Periplectomenus is first mentioned (135). It presumably translates the Greek χαρίεις, which is used by Aristotle sometimes of intellectual dexterity, sometimes of social superiority coupled with certain moral standards of behaviour. In particular, two passages in the *Ethics* might be texts for the self-portrait of Periplectomenus. When people are friends because of their virtue, no one minds being helped by his friend, but 'if a man is χαρίεις, he takes his revenge by helping him in his turn ' (*N.E.*, 1162 b 10 ; cf. *Mil.*, 660). In the other passage Aristotle discusses leisure and amusement and distinguishes two extremes in behaviour, the vulgar buffoon on one side and the unpolished rustic on the other ; the desirable mean is found in the ready-witted man, who has tact, and he is also called χαρίεις (1128 a 31). The people from whom Periplectomenus carefully distinguishes himself when he describes his behaviour in company could clearly come under these two headings. Periplectomenus is therefore χαρίεις in the Aristotelian sense, and the soldier does not share this characteristic, since, as Menander says (732K), ' a refined soldier is an impossibility even if he were moulded by god '. Another passage of the *Ethics* (IV, 7) brings us nearer still to the soldier ; he is an *alazon* (*Mil.*, 86), ' a boaster ', and his parasite is an *eiron*, ' a dissembler '.[3]

---

[1] Tierney, *P.R.I.A.*, L., 59, n. 39, compares Euboulos, 110K ; Nikostratos, 6K ; Mnesimachos, 3K ; Ephippos, 15K.

[2] Leo, *op. cit.*, 113.

[3] On this pair and on the buffoon see Pickard-Cambridge, *Dithyramb*, 270 ff.

Between these two stand the genuine man ' who owns to what he has, and neither more nor less ' (1127 a 23) : this is a reasonable description of Periplectomenus' self-portraiture. Thus Periplectomenus is carefully painted as a direct contrast to the soldier in sex-life, social behaviour, and self-assessment.

When this contrast has been drawn the planning for escape can continue. The end of this scene makes sense if we assume with Tierney that a new plan develops when the soldier falls for the bait. Epidicus changes his plan in the same sort of way, and in Menander the clever slave can always make use of the unexpected event (e.g. *Dis Exapaton, Andria*). So at this moment Palaestrio suggests the provision of Acroteleutium and Milphidippa as a diversion for the soldier, while Philocomasium is to continue to pretend to be her twin sister Dicea if the soldier finds her with Pleusicles (805 f.). The women are to be dressed up as Periplectomenus' wife and maid, like the parasite's daughter in the *Persa* and Simia in the *Pseudolus*.[1] Acroteleutium lives under the protection of Periplectomenus (compare Thais at the end of the *Eunuch*), and she must therefore be fetched and Palaestrio has to fetch the soldier from the forum. In normal Greek practice both of these intervals would occur between acts, but it is quite impossible to suppose that the scene with Lurcio and the arrival of the women constituted a complete act of the original. Therefore we have to choose between the two alternatives : either Periplectomenus returns with the women at the beginning of Act IV and Palaestrio is not present at that scene or the Lurcio scene is introduced to mask the lapse of time while the women are fetched. For the latter we have an exact parallel in the *Rudens* where the lapse of time while Plesidippus is fetched (1198, 1213) is masked by the introduction of the club tableau (III, 5). This alternative is in fact preferable since the return of the soldier is the obvious beginning for a new act and a scene of slave banter contrasts well with the rather static scene of character drawing which has preceded it, but it is true that it has no relation to anything else in the play except that it shows that Philocomasium has again crossed over to Periplectomenus' house.

The Lurcio scene also accounts for Sceledrus. As we have already seen, Sceledrus' behaviour at the end of Act II is unclear ;

[1] See above, p. 79.

at the very end of the play he apparently brings back the news of Philocomasium's escape (1429) and must therefore have gone with her from the soldier's house to the harbour. If this is accepted, Sceledrus goes home at the end of Act II and hides in the cellar as Lurcio says when Palaestrio shouts for him. Sceledrus' words at the end of Act II (582), *iam aliquo aufugiam*, need not mean more than ' I will find some place of refuge ' ; the passage in which Periplectomenus interprets this as *foris* (593) is probably Plautine as the repeated *senatus* suggests. We can therefore accept the presence of Sceledrus in the soldier's house from the end of Act II and the introduction of the Lurcio scene to mask a lapse of time.

The fourth act begins with the return of the soldier. Palaestrio tells him that Periplectomenus' young wife wants to leave her old husband : several comedies are called *Apoleipousa*, ' leaving her husband ' ; Diphilos certainly and Apollodoros of Gela most probably wrote plays with this title earlier than the original of the *Miles* ; a tragic ancestor for this theme can be found in Euripides' *Hippolytus*, particularly the first version, and Milphidippa plays the part of the nurse (991 f.), although in her actual appeal to the soldier (1054) her flattery reminds us rather of Clytemnestra in the *Agamemnon*. At the end of the scene Palaestrio asks Milphidippa to tell Philocomasium to cross over to the soldier's house, and this may mark his new conception of the escape. He may be inspired to say this by the soldier's wish to get rid of Philocomasium (973) : but it is not certain, however, that the soldier has reached this stage so early, and this passage may be an explanatory insertion by Plautus from the later dialogue between the soldier and Palaestrio, when the soldier has reached this point.[1] Palaestrio quickly invents a seaman (1109) as well as a twin sister and a mother, tells the soldier that Philocomasium has already met the twin sister (this covers anything that Sceledrus may report to his master) and that the seaman is staying with Periplectomenus (because the audience knows that Pleusicles is there) ; the soldier is too interested in their possible physical attractions to inquire further into details.[2] He is persuaded to go and tell Philocomasium that he has been induced by his relatives to marry and therefore must send her

---

[1] Schmidt, *Jb. f. cl. Ph. Suppl.*, IX, 323 f.
[2] 1111 f. is *not* Plautine, cf. *Eun.*, 479.

away. Palaestrio then makes the new plan with Acroteleutium and Pleusicles ; Acroteleutium is to entice the soldier into Periplectomenus' house by saying that it is her dowry ; Pleusicles is to dress up as the seaman and fetch Philocomasium. This escape plan and its execution is modelled on the escape of Helen and Menelaos in Euripides' *Helen*, as Leo has shown.[1]

Where does the fourth act end ? The unreality which allows Sceledrus to return from the harbour (1427) without an act break will trouble nobody, nor is there an act break when the soldier goes into Periplectomenus' house. The slave (is it not really Milphidippa ?) having summoned the soldier to his punishment describes the tableau which the audience then see (1388-94). The break must therefore either come when Pleusicles appears (1281) or after the making of the escape plan (1199). This cannot be certainly decided. Perhaps the later break is more likely. The denouement then hangs together as a single sequence of scenes. There is no clear reason for a break earlier ; the women are ready to play their parts and the soldier has only gone in to talk to Philocomasium. On the other hand, at the end of the scene it is perfectly reasonable that the soldier should take Palaestrio inside. They come out again when Pleusicles has come forward from Periplectomenus' door ; in the original their comment (1281-3) probably followed Pleusicles' opening words. The fifth act then contains the escape and ends with the punishment of the soldier by Periplectomenus.[2]

The architecture is extraordinarily clear in spite of Plautine overlay : portrait of soldier and then wall comedy culminating in submission of soldier's slave to Periplectomenus, portrait of Periplectomenus and then escape comedy culminating in the punishment of the soldier. Soldier and Periplectomenus are contrasted as two opposed types, ἀλάζων and χαρίεις, and the whole play may be regarded as a satire on the contemporary soldier, coloured to some extent by the reputation which Demetrios Poliorketes had won in Athens. Philemon, Diphilos, and an imitator of Menander have been proposed as author. The last is certainly true in the sense that many cross-connections with Menander can be seen, and notably the wall comedy is a development of the in-and-out comedy of Menander, and for the portrait

[1] *Op. cit.*, 150.
[2] Cf. on the form of punishment Fredershausen, *Hermes*, 1912, 215.

of Periplectomenus the author draws on Peripatetic sources either in the same way as Menander or through Menander. But the author of the *Miles* stands in quite a different relation to Menander from Apollodoros of Karystos : he is not working on in the same tradition as Menander. Dietze suggested Philemon because of the violent caricature of the soldier ; this is scarcely sufficient evidence ; there is none of the extemporisation which we associate with Philemon and the moralising is not the flat moralising of late Philemon. In any case Dietze believed that Plautus was using two originals, Philemon's *Alazon* and Menander's *Ephesios* ; we have seen that there is no reason to suppose contamination. The case for Diphilos is stronger and we may remember that he wrote a play called *Hairesiteiches*, an obvious parody of Demetrios' title Poliorketes. Although the minor verbal correspondences noted by Marx do not carry weight, he is certainly right in comparing the end of the *Miles* with the end of the *Casina*. Euripides' *Protesilaos* and *Helen* (and other tragic reminiscences) are used in the *Miles* in the same way as the tragic reminiscences in the *Rudens*. The disinterested elderly helper of the young lover we only know, as we have said above, from the *Rudens*, the *Vidularia*, and a papyrus fragment. The spying slave is attested for Diphilos as well as Menander. The technique of masking a lapse of time by an intercalated scene is known from Diphilos. Above all, the structure with its well-marked climaxes and the black and white contrast between the soldier (with Sceledrus and Lurcio) and Periplectomenus (with Pleusicles and Palaestrio) corresponds to Diphilos' technique as we know it from the *Casina* and *Rudens*. We cannot assert that the original was by Diphilus, but we can say it shows his influence more clearly than that of any other known Greek poet.

VII. MENANDREIA

1. THE NEW MENANDER

THIS section is an attempt to assess what we have learnt about Menander from the *Dyskolos*[1] and the new long fragments of the *Dis Exapaton*,[2] *Sikyonios*,[3] *Misoumenos*,[4] *Aspis*,[5] *Samia*,[6] all published since the Körte–Thierfelder edition (and since the first edition of this book). To put it summarily, we used to have long fragments of *Epitrepontes*, *Perikeiromene* and *Samia* in the original Greek to balance four plays certainly adapted by Plautus and four plays translated by Terence ; we now have the *Dyskolos* complete, the *Samia* nearly complete and long fragments of six other plays, including now the *Dis Exapaton*, which makes a direct comparison with Plautus possible for the first time (see below, p. 208). With long portions of eight Greek originals, it is much less necessary to base our judgment on the Latin adaptations than it was before, and we can correct an assessment which was perhaps unduly influenced by the Latin plays. Briefly, the new Menander seems much lighter in tone and much more varied in incident than Menander as we had assessed him.

The new finds do not tell us much about chronology. The *Dyskolos* is fixed at 317–16 B.C. It has no allusions to personalities, and it has metrical variety, the end of the fourth act in trochaic tetrameters and the end of the fifth act in iambic

---

[1] Ed. E. W. Handley, *The Dyskolos of Menander*.

[2] E. W. Handley, *Menander and Plautus*, 1968 ; BICS, supplement 22.

[3] A. Bataille, *Recherches de Papyrologie*, 3, 1964, 103 ; E. W. Handley, BICS 12, 1965, 38 ; R. Kassel, *Menandri Sicyonius*, Berlin 1966 ; R. A. Coles and H. Lloyd-Jones, *Emerita*, 34, 1966, 131.

[4] E. G. Turner, BICS, Supplement no. 17, 1965 ; *P. Oxy.* 2656 and 2657. Note *P. Oxy.* 2656 gives much of Acts III, IV and V and includes or overlaps the papyri used in Körte, I, 122 f., Körte–Thierfelder II, 284 ff. *P. Oxy.* 2657 gives about 90 fragmentary lines of Act II. It opens with a scene between Thrasonides and Getas, continues with a scene between Demeas and perhaps Kleinias ; Demeas discovers that Krateia is there and seems to enlist Kleinias' help in seeing her, but nothing more can be made out.

[5] R. Kasser, *P. Bodmer* XXV. Cf. E. W. Handley, *B.I.C.S.*, 16, 1969, 102.

[6] R. Kasser, *P. Bodmer* XXVI. Cf. E. W. Handley, *B.I.C.S.*, 16, 1969, 104.

tetrameters. But personal allusions can occur even somewhat later : the reference to the athlete Astyanax in the *Kolax* (*P. Oxy.* 2655) may be as late as 312 B.C. Nor does metrical variety help us much further ; the *Samia* has the whole of the fourth act and the end of the fifth in trochaic tetrameters, and this agrees with the early dating of the personal allusions. The latest trochaic tetrameter that can be securely dated is *Heniochos* (181 Kö.) in 312 B.C. The *Misoumenos* and *Aspis* now join the *Epitrepontes* in showing no trochaic tetrameters over a large number of lines (about 450 lines in *P. Oxy.* 2656 and 2657 ; over 500 in the *Aspis*). Somebody in the *Misoumenos* ' was very successful in Cyprus under one of the kings ', fr. 7 Kö., and this cannot have been later than 310 B.C. if the king was a king in Cyprus, which is by no means certain. But although Demeas apparently arrives from Cyprus (231), this does not say that there was not a gap of years since the time that he (or Thrasonides) ' was under one of the kings '. (The allusion to the murder of Polyperchon in *Aspis*, fr. 68 Kö., is doubtful.) It still seems possible that the plays with metrical variety were early and that the division between early and late comes soon after 312 B.C.

The new Menander gives us new evidence on two technical problems. The five-act structure is now shown to be normal: the *Dyskolos* has five acts, with the climax when Knemon has fallen into the well in the fourth act. In the *Sikyonios* the fourth act contains both the long messenger speech about the arbitration at Eleusis and the recognition scene ; it again was the climax. For the *Misoumenos* we have evidently part of the second act in *P. Oxy.* 2657 and much of the third, fourth and fifth acts in *P. Oxy.* 2656. The brief and expected recognition of Krateia is in the third act. In the fourth act the long recital of Getas about Krateia's refusal of Thrasonides probably leads somehow to the recognition of Kleinias as Demeas' son, so that it also was the climax. In the *Samia* we now know that the expulsion of Chrysis belonged to the third act so that Demeas learns the truth in the fourth act and his superb scenes there with Moschion and Nikeratos may be termed climax.[1] In the

---

[1] *P. Bodmer* XXV presents the act divisions at the beginning and end of the fourth act. Act I ends in the gap after l. 118, and Act II in the gap after l. 205.

Aspis the intrigue is devised in the second act, put into operation in the third act, and has its results in the fourth act, which ends with the return of Kleostratos and a brief recognition scene ; then the dénouement in the fifth act. Thus the five-act structure with a climax in the fourth act, which was already clear in the *Epitrepontes* and *Perikeiromene*, is seen also in the new plays.

Whether Menander used only three actors (with the addition of mutes, who could speak a word or two), as Körte believed, will continue to be discussed, partly because of the patchy nature of our texts and the untrustworthiness of the signs which mark changes of speakers (paragraphoi, double points, or abbreviated names), partly because of the very freedom of Menander's dialogue or monologue, which the ancient editors did not always appreciate themselves.

The only place in the *Dyskolos* where a fourth actor seems desirable (though not strictly necessary) is at the end of the second act (210–19) where Daos observes Sostratos handing the pitcher to the girl and, according to the papyrus, Pyrrhias (who left the stage 70 lines before) breaks in to tell Sostratos to stop lamenting and fetch Getas as he intended. Pyrrhias had no means of knowing that Sostratos intended to fetch Getas, and Sostratos does not answer his intervention. The ancient editor has misunderstood Menander's use of self-apostrophe. The lines run beautifully : ' *Sostratos :* Take the pitcher. *Girl :* Bring it here. *Daos :* What is this man up to ? *Sostratos :* Goodbye, and take care of your father. Oh dear, how unlucky I am. Stop lamenting, Sostratos. It will turn out all right. *Daos :* What will turn out all right ? *Sostratos :* Don't be afraid. As you suggested just now, get Getas and tell him the whole story and come back. *Daos :* What the devil is this all about ?'

A rather similar mistake is made in the *Misoumenos* (269). When Demeas has recognised Krateia, Getas learns what has happened and goes to fetch Thrasonides. Demeas and Krateia go inside before he arrives. We naturally suppose that the actor who has taken Getas comes on as Thrasonides and a mute takes Getas ; then when Thrasonides and Getas go in, one of the two actors who took Demeas and Krateia comes on as Kleinias. But the papyrus breaks Thrasonides' last line with a final ' How? I could wonder ' from Getas. This is nonsense, but the ancient editor wanted Getas to speak. In fact Thrasonides ended his speech : ' I am afraid. But anything is better than guessing, somehow. Yet I should be surprised at this.'

The new papyrus has, however, cleared up an old problem in the *Misoumenos*. At l. 210 Körte's text (l. 12 ff.) gave Nurse, Krateia, Demeas, Getas, Thrasonides. Now the new papyrus names the speakers as Demeas, Krateia, Getas, so that only three actors are needed ; the nurse has already gone inside and Thrasonides has not yet been fetched.[1]

In an interesting paper (*PCPS*, 1967, 40) Professor Sandbach has cleared up two similar passages by denying a speaking part at the end of the *Perikeiromene* (443) to Glykera and to Sophrone at the end of the *Epitrepontes* (759), but has raised a new problem in the *Sikyonios*. At the end of the messenger speech (VIC = 272 Kassel) he sends off the messenger and the old man to whom the messenger has been talking, and brings on Moschion and Stratophanes. The early papyrus gives only paragraphoi and no names of speakers, and it seems to me much easier to continue the dialogue between the messenger and the old man who has listened to him. The debate about the number of actors will, no doubt, continue, but it should be remembered that the only external evidence that we have—the inscription that lists the comic actors at Delphi in the early third century—gives only three comic actors in each troupe.[2]

The limitation to three actors was presumably a rule for competitions ; the five-act shape is rather a codification of the Aristotelian ' complication—dénouement' theory of plot. It is an instance of the influence of peripatetic philosophy ; this, classical tragedy, and earlier comedy have been regarded as the major factors in shaping Menander's comedy. I suggested above [3] that Aristotle's ' combination of probable incidents ' could be interpreted in three ways—with regard to technique of plot construction, with regard to the realities of time and place, and with regard to character-drawing. The *Dyskolos* is

[1] The *Aspis* raises no problems. The actor who leaves as Smikrines in 213 only returns as *trapezopoios* in 233 (if indeed the latter has a part). The speakers at the beginning of Act II are not entirely clear, but at latest Smikrines goes off at 283 and the actor returns as Daos in 299. Similarly in the *Samia* l. 85 ff. Moschion's soliloquy gives time for the other two actors to become Demeas and Nikeratos ; at l. 175 the cook goes in and returns as Nikeratos in 184.

[2] *S.I.G.*,[3] 424, discussed in my *Hellenistic Poetry and Art*, 16 ff., and by G. M. Sifakis, *Studies in Hellenistic Drama*, 71.

[3] P. 114 ff.

interesting in all three ways.   The plot construction is beautiful :
' a play planned as a whole, to progress from beginning through
dramatic climax to light-hearted conclusion '.[1]   The prologue
god Pan is responsible for two of the four threads which inter-
twine : he has made Sostratos fall in love with Knemon's
daughter (and this inevitably involves Gorgias and Daos) and
he has sent Sostratos' mother a bad dream which will bring
her to sacrifice at his shrine.   The third thread is the irascibility
of Knemon.   The fourth is the series of well disasters in Acts I,
III and IV, when Knemon finally falls in.   It is entirely natural
that when Sostratos, daunted by his first meeting with Knemon,
goes to find Getas, Getas should already be on the way to
the sacrifice ; we are not surprised that Getas and the cook
should arrive as an advance party at the end of the second act,
that Sostratos' mother, Plangon, and Parthenis should arrive
at the beginning of the third act and be observed by Knemon,
and that Sostratos' father Kallippides should arrive at the end
of the fourth act so that the double marriage can be arranged
in the fifth.   But this thread also affects Knemon : he sees the
women arrive, he is furious when Getas and the cook try to
borrow pots from him, and this leads up to their revenge on
him at the end of the play.

The only other play which is practically complete is the
Samia, and it is very much simpler : there are two houses on
stage instead of two houses and the shrine of the Nymphs,
and only six characters instead of at least eighteen in the *Dyskolos*,
of whom eleven have speaking parts. In the *Samia* the nerve
of action is the irascibility and successive misunderstandings of
the two fathers, Demeas and Nikeratos, who have returned from
abroad with intent to marry Demeas' son to Nikeratos' daughter
but ignorant of the fact that the young pair have already had
a baby, which Demeas' hetaira Chrysis is protecting until the
marriage.   These misunderstandings are fostered by the fears
of Parmenon and by first the hesitation and then the pique of
the son, Moschion.   Chrysis is not allowed by either of the two
old men to explain.[2]

---

[1] E. W. Handley, *Dyskolos*, 11.

[2] Similarly, in the *Aspis* (on which see below), an initial misconception sets
a story in motion which is essentially a contest between the miserliness of
Smikrines and the cleverness of Daos.

The neatness of Menander's plot construction has, of course, been noticed in the *Epitrepontes* and *Perikeiromene* and has been used as a criterion in recovering Menander from his Latin adapters. It must also be a criterion in restoration. Thus when Demeas in the *Misoumenos* (232) says ' here first I found this girl, of my family ', he is certainly going to find another child ; if he is interested in a sword (178) it is going to be a recognition token ; and if Kleinias, who is surprised by this interest, is made to listen to a very long speech about the negotiations between Thrasonides, Krateia and Demeas, he is going to learn something from it which shows that he is the son of Demeas, and the recognition will follow and cause the reconciliation between Krateia and Thrasonides.[1]

The *Sikyonios* has a large number of characters, at least eleven speaking parts, and a complicated plot. We have one scene of the third act, most of the fourth act, and a little more than one scene of the fifth act. Much of the detail remains unclear. But the messenger speech shows at least that Moschion must somehow have got hold of the girl and brought her (or caused Dromon to bring her) to Eleusis, hoping that an arbitration would get her into his power and away from Stratophanes. Traces of the earlier scene seem to survive in VIII and XII (= 52 ff., Kassel). Similarly, the beginning of the messenger scene in which Smikrines (if that is the name of the father of Moschion and, it turns out, of Stratophanes) comes on talking with the messenger shows that he must earlier have gone out from his house on the stage in order to be able to return now : he may have talked with Moschion but of this we have no certain trace. In the scene before the messenger speech XB (= Kassel 145) the parasite, Theron, prays ' Athena, make Stratophanes a citizen that he may get Philoumene and I may get Malthake '. Here, certainly, is a thread which must have led forwards and backwards. Malthake seems to have been a hetaira living with Stratophanes while he did not feel justified in taking Philoumene : this is why at the end he has Malthake and all her possessions moved from his house, when he knows

[1] In the *Aspis* a friend took Kleostratos' shield in a surprise attack in which he was killed and Kleostratos captured. The friend's body was unrecognisable when Daos recovered the shield and assumed that Kleostratos was dead. The sword which Demeas recognised in the *Misoumenos* must have a similarly complicated history.

that he is going to marry Philoumene. But the actual end, although it may involve Malthake and Theron, is quite unclear (XXI = 411 Kassel) ; the marriage of Stratophanes will start in Kichesias' house, i.e. off-stage, so that the play may have had a farce ending like the *Dyskolos*. Earlier, the first scene after the prologue certainly contained a woman (IVA, 11 and 15) and probably described Theron (IVB 10), but that is all we can say.

The second kind of probability—'the realities of time and place are also carefully observed' (p. 115)—needs comment. Menander works within certain conventions. If the conventions are accepted, it is true that realities of time and place are carefully observed. The *Dyskolos* first made this clear.[1] Pyrrhias is sent to see Knemon at Phyle very early in the morning and Sostratos follows him. Sostratos returns at the end of the first act to find Getas, but Getas has gone not less than eleven miles to Athens to hire a cook for the sacrifice. In the second act Sostratos comes back again and makes his plan with Gorgias to work alongside Knemon, who is still at home ; when they go off, the cook and Getas arrive. The double journey to and from Athens must have taken at least ten hours, but Menander does not mind about this as long as he gets a reasonable sequence of entries. The audience have not seen when Getas left home and do not learn till later (490 in conjunction with 293) that the cook comes from Athens ; what they are meant to appreciate is that after his first return Knemon is prevented from going out again for his day's work by the arrival of the procession at the shrine. They take this point and do not work out the time schedule.

We need not therefore ask how in the *Epitrepontes* Smikrines can go back and forth the eighteen miles between Athens (402), where he lives, and Halai Araphenides, where Charisios lives and the play is set : he arrives in the first act, goes home in the second act, comes back again in the third act, goes home again in the fourth act, and comes back again with Sophrone in the fifth. Nor can we say that the setting of the *Sikyonios* must be near Eleusis because the arbitration takes place there. The convention appears to be that if the play is set in Attica, any other place in Attica can be reached in the interval between

---

[1] Cf. *Rylands Bulletin*, 45, 1962, 237 ff.

acts, even if the on-stage action suggests that the interval between acts is quite short—as, for instance, between the first and second acts of the *Dyskolos*.

As Menander accepts stage time as the prime reality, he also accepts stage space and exploits it. It would be quite impossible to build houses beside the shrine of the nymphs at Phyle,[1] but the stage setting for the *Dyskolos* had three doors, and so Menander gives them to Knemon's house, the Nymphaion, and Gorgias' house. Given this propinquity, Menander uses it. The girl, standing outside the Nymphaion (204), mistakes the noise of Daos opening his door for the noise of Knemon opening his door. Sikon, standing outside the Nymphaion (648), can hear the girl wailing when her father is down the well. When Getas proposes to Sikon that they drag Knemon outside his house and rag him, he explains that they will not be heard because the party in the Nymphaion is making so much noise (901).

He goes a stage further in the *Epitrepontes*. Smikrines and his daughter would naturally discuss her husband's infidelity not on the doorstep but in the women's quarters where they could not be overheard, but the set makes it necessary to use the doorstep. Given this, however, Charisios can overhear the conversation from the doorway of the neighbouring house (563). One mitigation for putting a conversation on the doorstep, when it would naturally take place inside the house, may be that one of the characters is arriving or leaving. In this case Smikrines is leaving. In the *Sikyonios* Theron and Stratophanes do their planning outside because Pyrrhias is going to arrive, and the great messenger speech is delivered outside because Smikrines is on his way home to his house on the stage.

It would be artificial to push this reasoning too far. Getas' great recital in the *Misoumenos* (284) is, it is true, interrupted by Kleinias, and Demeas' great speech in the *Samia* (1 Kö. = 206 B) leads up to the arrival of Parmenon ; but both Getas and Demeas are really outside because they need to give vent to their feelings. In tragedy Medeia or Phaidra could vent their feelings to the chorus. Demeas appeals to the audience, *andres*, twice (54, 114 Kö. = 269, 329 B). Appeal to the audience occurs again in Moschion's doubts whether his defiance is justified (*Samia* 338 Kö. = 683 B), and in the misery of the Moschion

[1] Cf. E. W. Handley, *Dyskolos*, 25.

of the *Sikyonios*, when he is reduced to being his brother's best man (XID = Kassel 405). In the *Dyskolos* it is used twice by Sostratos, first when he is bowled over by the girl's beauty (194) and then when he describes Knemon's rescue (666). Sikon the cook also uses it when he gloats over Knemon's misfortune (659). Finally, in the *Epitrepontes* (567), Onesimos appeals to the audience to convey his horror at Charisios' change of colour when he overhears Sophrone pleading with her father. Moschion's long monologue which opens the *Samia* is more like, for example, the opening speech of the *Andromache*, but he openly addresses the audience: ' I'll tell you our whole story, for I have lots of time.'

Such monologues (to which we must return later) are one of the chief ways in which Menander displays character, whether it is the character of the speaker or the character of the person he describes or both. Aristotle's statement that ' a man of a certain kind performs actions or speaks words of the same kind according to probability' is illustrated again and again by Menander. The persons, acting true to their character, are the force which, given the situation, drive the action along. In the *Dyskolos* Knemon's misfortunes are due to his meanness, Sostratos wins his girl because he is in love enough to disregard the conventions of his class ; the superstitions of his mother, the high-mindedness of Gorgias, the earthy realism of Daos also have an essential part. In the *Samia* we can now see the characters rather more clearly. We know that Moschion persuaded Demeas to have Chrysis in his house to avoid younger rivals, that Chrysis knew perfectly well that Demeas would be furious with her for keeping the baby (which was supposed to be his and hers) but, trusting in a firm alliance with the wife of Nikeratos, she believed that after a period of fury his love for her would produce a reconciliation ; and Demeas on his return was in fact furious and was only restrained by Moschion from turning her out of the house at once—a threat which he carried out when he came to suspect that the child was hers and Moschion's, not his. So the action moves, with, on the one side, the women firmly loyal to each other, and on the other, the men, both the fathers irascible and ready to jump to conclusions, the son day-dreaming and acting only when driven into a corner, the slave so frightened as to be useless.

We know much less of the *Misoumenos* and the *Sikyonios*. Common to both is a soldier in love with a girl who hates him ; this is given by the title of the *Misoumenos* and is a fair inference from *Sikyonios* VIIB (= 97 f. Kassel). In both cases he has not touched her (*Misoumenos*, fr. 5 ; *Sikyonios* XIC (= 372 Kassel)). In the *Misoumenos* it is the persistence of the girl's father which pushes the action to a conclusion, in the *Sikyonios* the intrigues of Moschion to get the girl, and the energy with which Stratophanes intervenes as soon as he finds that he is an Athenian citizen and can intervene (we cannot tell what the earlier plan which he had worked out with Theron was, but there was a plan, XA = 114 Kassel). The fragment of the *Dis Exapaton* at least gives a moment when the young man Sostratos (Mnesilochos in Plautus) assumes without hesitation that his girl has been unfaithful to him with his best friend and pays his father back the money which he had been with-holding to buy her freedom, so that here too an essential twist in the action is entirely due to character.

The *Aspis* is essentially a battle between the greed of Smikrines and the inventiveness of Daos—Daos comes home to report the death of his young master (Kleostratos) in action in Lycia. (The circumstantial report is in fact untrue, and the young man will return, as the prologue goddess Tyche informs the audience.) Smikrines, the young man's senior uncle, sees that if he marries the young man's sister he will gain possession of the booty which Daos has brought back. He proposes therefore to assert his rights as next of kin and stop the marriage which the rich junior uncle, Chairestratos, has arranged between the young man's sister and Chaireas, his wife's son by an earlier marriage. Daos conceives the plan : they will fake Chairestratos' death with a sham corpse and a sham doctor, and Smikrines will promptly assert his right to marry Chairestratos' daughter because she is much richer than Kleostratos' sister and he will be eager to marry Kleostratos' sister to Chaireas. The plan is made in the second act, and in the third Daos announces Chaire-stratos' death to Smikrines and the doctor arrives. Then the text abandons us, but there is certainly mention of betrothal just before Kleostratos returns from captivity, greeting his country and surprising Daos at the very end of the fourth act.

Smikrines is a miser and nothing else. Chaireas is an ordinary

young man in love. Chairestratos is colourless. The chief
interest is that here for once in Menander we see an intriguing
slave in action. Daos' opening speech shows that his affection
for Kleostratos was real as well as realistic. He makes an
immediate thrust at Smikrines' miserliness when he describes the
booty : ' You will not inherit more than that ' (84 f.). He
refuses to have anything to do with Smikrines' proposals (189 ff.)
—that is a free man's business, and a Phrygian naturally regards
Greek customs as strange. As soon as he finds Chairestratos
alone, he tells him to cheer up, and proposes the intrigue very
quickly (in spite of the great complications the scene takes only
90 lines). He then announces Chairestratos' death in the glorious
spate of tragic quotation already known from the part preserved in
the *Comoedia Florentina*. Here alone we see the sort of raw material Plautus had from which to elaborate Chrysalus in *Bacchides*.

Peripatetic literary theory certainly influenced Menander. It
is customary to say also that he was influenced by Peripatetic
ethics. It is certainly true that they gave him his terminology
—the conception of Agnoia (misunderstanding) in the *Perikeiromene*, Anger in the *Orge*, Drunkenness in the *Methe*, as
the force which leads a man to commit an excusable crime, is
thoroughly Aristotelian. The nice discrimination with which
Pataikos defines Polemon's position with regard to Glykera
and Moschion in the *Perikeiromene* (236), or Charisios decides
(*Epitr.* 594 ff.) that his own action in seducing an unmarried
girl is as blameworthy as his wife's in submitting to seduction,
or Demeas forgives Moschion's supposed seduction of Chrysis
as an act of youth and drunkenness unable to withstand her
passion but contrary to his established character (*Samia* 115 ff.),
is certainly peripatetic. In the same way Sostratos in the *Dis
Exapaton* (98) excuses his friend Moschos : ' I am sorry for
the silly Moschos. I am angry, of course, but I don't regard
him as responsible for the crime against me, but her and her
unparalleled audacity.' Knemon's (*Dyskolos* 743) apology, in
which he says that if all men were like him there would be no
law courts, prisons or war, but each would have his modicum
and be content, is true, but the ideal is impossible since it involves
living in isolation. His conception of self-sufficiency runs counter
to Aristotle's definition (*N.E.* 1097b8) : ' by self-sufficient we
do not mean sufficient for himself alone, for the liver of a solitary

life, but also for parents, children, wife, and even friends and fellow-citizens, since man by nature lives in a city '. Menander must have had this text in mind when he wrote Knemon's speech.

There is no doubt that Menander knows his Peripatetic ethics. What perhaps is less clear now is whether he is preaching a Peripatetic sermon, as Michael Tierney put it. It is the word *sermon* that is wrong. Peripatetic terminology is useful, and of course forgiveness of rash acts thus explained is desirable. The disinterested action of Gorgias in saving Knemon from the well or the self-restraint of the lovers in the *Misoumenos* and *Sikyonios* is, of course, admirable, but this is comedy, not preaching. What is clearer now is how carefully Menander told his audience the truth of the situation which his characters may misinterpret. And because their serious speeches are so often misinterpretation, they can be taken more lightly.

The long monologue of Moschion [1] at the beginning of the *Samia* leaves the audience in no doubt that Demeas is utterly wrong in his appreciation of the situation, so that he cannot help appearing funny as well as sympathetic. Similarly, the whole remarkable build-up of Knemon from Pan's opening speech in the *Dyskolos* to his tumble into the well shows what his ideal of self-sufficiency means in terms of behaviour to those nearest to him. The *Epitrepontes* must, it has always been assumed, have had a prologue speech to enable the audience to appreciate the delicious irony of Smikrines arbitrating the fate of his own grandson, and if we had heard this prologue speech in Menander's own words we should have taken rather more lightly Charisios' speech of self-recrimination, particularly after the uncomplimentary portrait of him painted immediately before by his slave Onesimos.

Tragedy is the second great influence. The main lines have long been recognised,[2] and I note here only two new instances.

---

[1] It should have been clear that Quintilian (XI, 3, 91) attests a similar prologue by a youth in the *Hydria*. We now know three forms of prologue : (*a*) opening speech by a god, (*b*) opening speech by a character, (*c*) dramatic scene followed by speech by personification or god.

[2] We see now that Demeas' allusion to the Euripidean *Danae* (*Sam.* 245 Kö. = 590B) picks up an earlier tirade of Nikeratos (495B), who said that Moschion had made Tereus, Oidipous, and Thyestes look small and urged Demeas to blind him as Amyntor blinded Phoinix.

The most startling new example is the messenger speech of the *Sikyonios*. After the purely comic dialogue between the 'democratic' man and the 'oligarchic' man, they seem to be parting (XC = 168 Kassel) when the 'democratic' man suddenly says, 'Old man, stop in the porch of your house,' and the other answers, 'I stop. What reason have you for this urgency?' Tragic metre and tragic language signal that something important is coming—a messenger speech, which is itself a tragic form. Essentially this is the function of the tragic style and reminiscences in the *Perikeiromene* recognition scene, which again is itself a tragic form. The next lines of dialogue are obscure but contain a formal statement of desire to hear and ability to impart information. Then the speech starts with a quotation of the messenger speech of Euripides' *Orestes* (866). As there, the speech describes a trial; as there, the speaker first sees a crowd, then the central figures, then the description goes forward with much direct speech quoted from the participants. Actual quotation of the *Orestes* is confined to the first words of the first two lines and a phrase in the seventh line.[1] The tragic tone of the preceding lines and the echoes of the *Orestes* simply warn the audience that a set piece is coming. The story itself is an entirely realistic account of what happened at Eleusis, just as Smikrines' arbitration in the *Epitrepontes* is entirely realistic and borrows only the general situation from Euripides' *Alope*.

A quite different use of tragedy occurs in Knemon's first speech in the *Dyskolos* (153) : 'Perseus was winged . . . and he had an object with which he turned all whom he did not like into stones.' Knemon could be remembering either the *Diktys* or the *Andromeda* ; the *Andromeda* is more likely because of its great popularity, and he might well have seen a revival before he took to his solitary life. But the audience is surely meant to deduce from the vague terms ' was winged ' for ' was lent winged sandals ', ' an object ' for ' the Gorgon's head ' that it was a long time ago that Knemon saw the *Andromeda*. This may explain the reference in the *Epitrepontes* (150) to Neleus and Pelias as

[1] The general line of the beginning must be ' I was in fact neither walking with raised eyebrows nor behaving like an oligarch (don't suggest that if you are wise : I am very good at damaging others for my three obols and making things a matter of state), but coming from Athens to Eleusis.'

being found by an elderly goat-herd, who gave them a wallet of recognition tokens. The famous play about Neleus and Pelias was Sophocles' *Tyro B* ; they were recognised not by a wallet of recognition tokens but by the *skaphe* in which they had been exposed and which they carried about with them. But in another famous play, the *Antiope* of Euripides, the twins were brought up by a herdsman and the herdsman brought about the recognition. Syriskos in the *Epitrepontes* has got his tragedies mixed ; his education is superficial and the audience is meant to see this point.

The third influence, commonly recognised, is preceding comedy. Here the *Dyskolos* is the obvious example. The beating up of Knemon by Getas and the cook immediately recalls the two thugs molesting the elderly Charinos on a Paestan vase of the mid-fourth century,[1] and the metre—iambic tetrameters catalectic—is traditional in Middle and Old Comedy. The running entrance of Pyrrhias can be traced back to the entrance of Amphitheos in the *Acharnians* (176). The cook carrying his sheep has parallels in Middle Comedy statuettes.[2] The arrogance and loquacity of cooks were established in comedy before the middle of the fourth century.[3] Knemon himself belongs to a tradition which can be traced back to Phrynichos' *Hermit*, produced in 414 B.C. : ' I live the life of Timon, unmarried, unservanted, bad-tempered, unlaughing, unconversable, self-willed ' (18K).

Knemon's misanthropy is not only the chief trait in his character but also the situation to which the other characters, each in their individual way, react. It is the starting point of the sequence of probable incidents discussed above. It is a special situation, and we know its ancestry in comedy. It differs in degree rather than in kind from the special situations of the *Ekklesiazousai* (women take over the assembly) and *Ploutos* (Wealth is healed of blindness). Therefore, whether we can quote a comic ancestor or not, it is fair to say that Menander is working in the tradition of earlier Attic comedy when the whole action or a large part of the action is determined by such a special situation : the special situation starts with the play in the *Aspis* (the untrue report of Kleostratos' death), in the *Aulularia* (Euclio

[1] Cf. pp. 69, 91 on PH 76.   [2] E.g. *MMC*, AT 55-7.
[3] Cf. above, p. 66.

with his pot of gold), the *Samia* (Chrysis' decision to look after Moschion's baby), the *Perikeiromeme* (Polemon cuts off Glykera's hair) and with the second act in the *Epitrepontes* (Smikrines' arbitration) and the *Theophoroumene* (the girl's possession). But whereas Aristophanes shows the effect of the special situation (Dikaiopolis' private peace or the establishment of Cloud-cuckooland) on a large number of unconnected people, Menander restricts its action to a small number of people closely connected with the pair who are going to marry at the end of the play.

Menander was influenced by Peripatetic philosophy, tragedy, earlier comedy, but the more Menander we discover the more varied and alive he seems, and the less influence or tradition seems to matter. The *Dyskolos* is unique in needing to establish a country atmosphere (the admirable picture of the charcoal-burner and the shepherd is only incidental to the *Epitrepontes*) and Menander gives us the whole countryside—the rocks, the thyme, the pear trees, the main road to Phyle, the hardness of the soil, and the olive trees lower down.

His dialogue is incredibly alive. I give two examples : first, the short exchange in the *Dyskolos* (775 ff.) between Sostratos, Gorgias and Sostratos' father. ' *Kallippides :* I am late. They have eaten up the sheep already and gone back to the farm. *Gorgias :* Poseidon, he's starving. Shall we tell him now ? *Sostratos :* Let him have his meal first. He will be milder. *Kallippides :* What ? Sostratos, here ? Have you finished the meal ? *Sostratos :* Yes, but there's some left for you. Go on. *Kallippides :* I will. *Gorgias :* You go in,' then you can talk to your father alone if you like. *Sostratos :* You will stay in, won't you ? *Gorgias :* I am not going out. *Sostratos :* Then after a bit I'll call for you.' This is beautifully simple, and characterises Gorgias' shyness as well as his eagerness, the hurry of the rich Kallippides and Sostratos' skill in dealing with the situation.

The other example is the passage in the *Sikyonios* (XIC = 363 Kassel) where Dromon has just told Kichesias that his daughter is alive. ' *Dromon :* She is alive and is here. Don't fall. Hold up, Kichesias. Theron, water, water, quick. *Theron :* Yes, I will run in and get some and send Stratophanes out to you. *Dromon :* No more need for water. *Theron :* Then I'll get him. *Dromon :* He's coming round. Kichesias. *Kichesias :*

What is it ? Where in the world am I ? And what utterance of omen did I hear ? *Dromon :* Your daughter is alive and safe. *Kichesias :* Is she safe and sound, Dromon, or just safe ? *Dromon :* A virgin still ; she hasn't had a man. *Kichesias :* Good. *Dromon :* And what about you, master ? *Kichesias :* I am alive. This much I *can* tell you, Dromon ; for the rest, when you see a poor and lonely old man, you may be certain all is well enough. *Stratophanes :* I'll come back when I have looked into this, mother. *Dromon :* Stratophanes, the father of Philoumene. *Stratophanes :* Who is ? *Dromon :* He is. *Stratophanes :* Greetings, father. *Dromon :* He has kept your daughter safe for you. *Kichesias :* May he be blessed. *Stratophanes :* If you agree, I shall be, and happy too.' Dramaturgically, the little dialogue covers the actor's change of part from Theron to Stratophanes. The fainting scene is, of course, a reminiscence of tragedy ; the nearest parallel is the collapse of Peleus when he hears of Neoptolemos' death in the *Andromache* (1076), and Kichesias keeps the tragic tone as he revives : ' Where in the world am I ? And what utterance of omen did I hear ? ' But apart from this, which marks it as a moment of real emotion, it is delicious, realistic dialogue.

On a much larger scale the fourth act of the *Samia* (421–615), which we can now appreciate in its full extent, is naturalistic dialogue of the same kind, and like the Kallippides scene in the *Dyskolos* is in trochaic tetrameters throughout. In the third act Demeas had decided to go through with the marriage between his son Moschion and Plangon, the daughter of his poor neighbour Nikeratos, although he believed that the baby (which was in fact the child of Moschion and Plangon but according to their agreed story the child of Demeas and Chrysis) was the child of Moschion and his mistress Chrysis. He had, however, driven Chrysis with the baby out of the house, and she had taken refuge with Nikeratos.

The fourth act begins with Nikeratos leaving his house to complain to Demeas about the bad omen of Chrysis' expulsion. He meets Moschion returning from the agora, extremely bored by the long wait for the evening marriage, and tells him that Chrysis and the baby have been expelled and are now in his house. Demeas enters, speaking back to warn his servants to stop crying for Chrysis and get on with the preparations. He prays Apollo (the altar on stage) to prosper the marriage and to help him get through the ceremony without giving himself away. (This, by stage convention, is unheard by the others.) Moschion asks Demeas why Chrysis has gone. Demeas thinks there is a conspiracy against him between Moschion and Nikeratos, and tells Nikeratos to go in and send Chrysis away. Nikeratos possibly goes in, certainly withdraws at this point.

Moschion struggles on unsuccessfully and even suggests leaving Demeas' house himself. Finally, Demeas charges him with being the father of the child, which he admits but says that this does not mean that Chrysis has wronged Demeas. Demeas asks straight out who is the mother and demands that Nikeratos (who has returned or now comes forward) shall witness the answer—which Moschion in the presence of Nikeratos is naturally unwilling to give. Nikeratos immediately jumps to the same conclusion as Demeas and says that Moschion has surpassed the crimes of Tereus, Oidipous and Thyestes, and demands that Demeas blind him as Amyntor blinded Phoinix. He will not give him his daughter ; if they were his, he would sell Chrysis and Moschion, so that all the barbers' shops would say that Nikeratos had taken a just vengeance. Now he agrees with Demeas that he must turn Chrysis out and goes into his house.

At last Moschion can tell Demeas the truth that Nikeratos' daughter, Plangon, is the mother of the child, and Demeas half believes him. Nikeratos bursts out of his house saying that he has seen Plangon suckling the child. This clinches the matter for Demeas, and he forgives Moschion, who beats a hasty retreat from Nikeratos' fury. (This is perfectly natural, and the actor is needed to play Chrysis later.) Demeas tries ineffectually to persuade Nikeratos that he has not seen what he has seen or that it does not mean what he thinks it means.

Nikeratos dashes in again. (The Cairo papyrus starts again here.) His shouts suggest that he is going to burn the baby. He dashes out and tells Demeas that he will murder his wife, and dashes in again. Chrysis escapes with the baby, and the old men come to blows. At the end Nikeratos says that Demeas is party to the whole story and is wronging him. Demeas, remembering Nikeratos' tragic allusions, answers that Nikeratos is in no worse a position than Akrisios, and there are lots of sons of gods in Athens : ' Pray that it all goes well ; go on with the preparations ; Moschion will come for the girl.' Nikeratos gives in, and Demeas thanks the gods that all his suspicions were untrue.

The long act is superb naturalistic comedy, but what gives it its peculiar flavour is our sympathy with all three characters, who are very distinct but all essentially nice and well meaning. And this sympathy pulls against our laughter at the difficulties into which they get themselves, because Demeas has perfectly naturally misinterpreted one piece of evidence and because Nikeratos is too straight-laced to be told the truth.

But it is remarkable how often Menander gets his most realistic effects by long speeches with sometimes self-apostrophe and often quotation of direct speech. The ancestry lies, as we have said, in the tragic actor's self-presentation to the chorus, in the tragic messenger speech, and sometimes an appeal to the audience (' Men ') takes the place of the tragic address to the chorus. Quintilian (XI, 3, 91) notes the problem that these speeches set the actor when he says : ' The comic actors seem to me entirely wrong when, even if they are acting the part of a young man, they use a trembling or falsetto voice when a quotation of an old man (as in the prologue of the *Hydria*) or a quotation of a woman (as in the *Georgos*) comes into their speeches.' And Choricius (*Spartiates*, 30 ff.) may be referring to the same phenomenon when he says that the comic actor makes Plangon appear when he is acting Daos and Myrrhine : he may be thinking of the *Heros*.

Besides Knemon's opening speech about Perseus (153) and his final apology (708), the *Dyskolos* has three other major speeches. The first is Sostratos' description of his day as an agricultural labourer, hoping to be seen by Knemon and his daughter (522 ff.) : ' I was getting stiff as a board. No one came. And the sun blazed down, and Gorgias came and looked at me swinging up slowly like a well-beam, then swinging down again with my whole body. " I don't think," he said, " he'll come now, my boy." " What are we to do then ? " I retorted. " We'll watch for him tomorrow, and give up now." And Daos was there to take over the digging. That was our first attempt.' So Sostratos relieves himself of the pent-up misery of a day's unaccustomed hard labour, entirely

wasted, as he then thinks, but in fact much later Knemon accepts him as a labourer, and therefore worthy of his daughter,
because he is sunburnt (a beautiful instance of Menander's
economy).

The other two speeches are in parallel, like the pair in the
Epitrepontes (558), Onesimos' description of Charisios' behaviour
and Charisios' apology. In the *Dyskolos*, when Sostratos and
Gorgias rush in to rescue Knemon from the well, the cook
remains outside gloating (639). Like Hekabe in the *Trojan
Women* (888) he sees proof of the gods' existence in the punishment of a criminal : ' No one ever harmed a cook and escaped
scot-free. Our art is somehow hieratic ; but you may do anything you like to a waiter.' Then he hears the daughter's
cries (the equivalent in reverse of the tragic murder shout heard
by the chorus) and concludes that Knemon is not dead. ' What
sort of a sight do you think he'll be after this, drenched and
trembling ? A pleasant one, I think. (To the audience.) I'd
like to see him. (Then to the women in the Nymphaion.)
You, women, pour libations, pray that the old man has a bad
rescue, crippled, lame. So he becomes least tiresome as a
neighbour to Pan and those who make sacrifice. This matters
to me, if anyone hires me again.' He goes into the Nymphaion,
and Sostratos comes out of Knemon's house to give the audience
(' Men ', again) his account of the rescue, in which Gorgias
had done everything and he had done nothing but comfort the
girl and nearly let go the rope. The two speeches beautifully
contrast the malice of the cook and the love of Sostratos.

The fragment of the *Dis Exapaton* has two short monologues
of Sostratos (Plautus' Mnesilochus), which balance each other.
Both of them rather remind us of Demeas' interpretation of
Chrysis and Moschion in the *Samia* (115 ff.). The first (col. ii, 6)
is Sostratos' immediate reaction to the report by the father of
his friend Moschos (Pistoclerus) that Moschos is in love with
his girl. ' Is he gone at last ? When she has had her fill
[ἐμπλησθεῖσα] of Moschos, will she stop ? You took Sostratos
first. She'll deny—that is clear, for she is audacious ; and all
the gods will be trotted out—(that she never did it ? [ποιῆσαι]).
Damn her. But stop, Sostratos. Perhaps she will persuade
you. I shall be the slave of my mistress ; but let me have
nothing when she persuades me. I'll give all the gold back to

my father. For she will stop her rhetoric when she sees, as the proverb says, that she is talking to a corpse. But I must go and find my father. But I see him.' This is very fast-moving and labile, with its swift changes of person ; so is the balancing speech (col. iii, 29), when Sostratos' father has left him, having recovered the gold. ' I really think I should like to see my noble mistress when I go in [εἰσιὼν] empty-handed, see her rhetoric and her expectation of all the gold I bring. She is saying to herself now, " He is really bringing it like a gentleman " (who is more so ?) " and as I deserve." It is a very good thing she has been found out as the sort of girl I once thought she was. I am sorry for the silly Moschos ', etc.

The great speech in the *Misoumenos* (284) is more like Onesimos' description of Charisios' behaviour in the *Epitrepontes* (558). Kleinias has come out of his house to look for Demeas, when he sees Getas come out of Thrasonides' house to vent his fury at his master's treatment by Demeas and Krateia. He goes on talking while Kleinias tries to break in : [1] ' *Getas :* Honoured Zeus, extraordinary and inhuman cruelty of both, by the Sun. *Kleinias :* Did a stranger go into your house just now, Getas ? *Getas :* Herakles. The stubbornness . . .' (The text is broken here, but it is clear that Kleinias tries twice more to interrupt while Getas quotes a dialogue between Thrasonides and Demeas ; then the text gets better.) ' *Kleinias :* I think I had better walk round with him. *Getas :* This one thing he repeats : " I have come and demand that you let me ransom my daughter, being her father." " But I, having found you, Demeas, ask you for her as my wife." *Kleinias :* The man is in the house. He has said the name, Demeas. *Getas :* Herakles, he can't accept what has happened like any other man ? A pig and a mule, as they say. This is not so painful, but she does not even look at him as he speaks. " I beg you, Krateia. Don't abandon me. I took you when you were a virgin, I was called your husband, I first cherished you. I cherish you, I love you, dearest Krateia. What is it that you hate in my house ? You will hear that I am dead, if you abandon me." And not even an answer. *Kleinias :* What *is* this trouble ? *Getas :* A barbarian, a lioness-woman.

[1] Daos' long narrative about the Lycian campaign of Kleostratos takes the first 80 lines of the *Aspis*, but he is conscious all the time of Smikrines' presence so that they must have come on stage together.

Kleinias : Haven't you seen me yet, curse you ? *Getas :* Un-expected. He is completely out of his mind. I would not have set her free, by Apollo here. It's Greek. And we know it happens everywhere. But it is right to pity one who pities you. When you do not pity me, I do not have a thought or a care for you. You don't ? Why ? Nothing absurd, as I think. But he will shout and plan to get up and kill himself. He has fire in his eyes. He rolls on the ground and pulls his hair. *Kleinias :* Man, you'll wear me out. *Getas :* Greetings, Kleinias. Where has he come from ? ' The audience has seen at the end of the preceding act (258), first, Thrasonides extremely doubtful as to what reception he will get from Demeas, and this speech enlightens us about that ; second, Kleinias arriving back with the cook to prepare a meal for Krateia, Demeas and himself so that when he finds neither of them in his house he naturally comes out to look for them at the beginning of the new act and provides the unwilling audience for Getas.

The *Sikyonios* (XC, V–VI = 176 Kassel) has the only preserved messenger speech, just over a hundred lines long. We have already discussed its relation to the *Orestes* and the action which precedes and follows it. The messenger describes how he had gone to Eleusis because it was his deme, and a demesman was going to share out meat. He joined the crowd at the Propylaia. Much is obscure here but it looks as if the demarch starts pro-ceedings about the girl (and both he and the audience use direct speech). Then Moschion intervenes : ' A youth, white-skinned, smooth, beardless, wanted to say something in an under-tone. We did not let him. " Speak louder," someone shouted. " What does he want ? Who is he ? What do you say ? " " This slave knows. I ought to have helped her before," he says, " though you are asking a lover,[1] and I heard him telling the story to his master." Then he turned scarlet and backed out ; he was wholly disgusting, and we did not like him at all, he seemed too interested in sex.' The text becomes unclear again, but Stratophanes arrived—' he looked like a brave man '—and there was a second and a third (Theron and Pyrrhias). Stratophanes apparently ' burst into a river of tears and tore his hair. The people were amazed. " What do you want ? Speak. Speak." " The girl," he says, "—so may the goddess

[1] This is obscure ; possibly the text is κἄν τινος| δέητ' ἐρῶ<ν>τος.

grant you prosperity—I brought up well and justly. My father bought her as a small child." ' When the text resumes after ten lines Stratophanes is still speaking. He is prepared to give Dromon to the girl. ' " Let her find her father and her family. I do not make any obstacle." " Good." " Hear also my view. You are the responsible authorities for her (for she is freed of her fear by me). Lodge her with the priestess and let her keep her for you." Naturally this won him much good will. They all cried " Very right," then all of them, " Speak." ' Stratophanes then tells them that he believes that he can prove he is an Athenian citizen and begs them not to take away his hope of marrying the girl by letting those who are acting against him assume authority over her before her father is found. ' The white-skinned boy suddenly leapt up again. " Does this," he said, " convince me ? He has suddenly found a will somewhere and is your citizen ; he'll carry the girl off in this bogus tragedy and let her go ? Why not kill this shaven-chin ? " [1] " No, but you, whoever you are. Out of the way, gigolo. Many blessings on you all," said the other. " Come, go." The slave stood up and said, " She will go, if you ask her. Ask her, sirs." " Yes, go." She gets up, goes. For so long I was there. The rest I could no longer tell, I went away.'

This is a magnificent piece of realistic narrative. Its object is quite different from the *Orestes* messenger speech, for all its similarity. That is a novelty in putting a modern assembly with all its different speakers into a heroic setting : Euripides almost says that Orestes would have been condemned in contemporary Athens. Here the assembly is the setting for the story, which establishes primarily the character of Stratophanes and secondarily the behaviour of Moschion. But these are seen through the eyes of the speaker, who is a ' democratic ' member of the assembly. For us, with lack of experience and a corrupt text, it is sometimes difficult to establish who says what. For the ancient actor it must have been a great set piece. What is interesting is that Menander uses these narrative speeches as one of his main instruments of comedy.

[1] Stratophanes is clean-shaven as a soldier. Moschion is still beardless.

2. MINOR GAINS

In addition to the major gains since the Körte–Thierfelder edition there are a number of minor additions to our knowledge. Most of them are noticed in Mette's very full bibliographical commentary, *Lustrum* 10, 1965 ; I list here only new information, points of particular interest, and points where I disagree with Mette. The order of plays is that of Körte–Thierfelder, II.

Adelphoi B. Gaiser, *W.S.*, 79, 1966, 194, argues for identification with *Homopatrioi* and shows that fr. 109 Kö. belongs.

Androgynos. The young man dresses up as his sister (cf. *Eunouchos*). See Mette, 47 f.

Apistos. Gaiser, *W.S.*, 79, 1966, 193, argues that this was the original of the *Aulularia.* See Mette, 195 f. C. Corbato, *Studi Menandrei*, 91, attractively suggests that the conclusion of the play is to be found in P. Oxy. 1239.

Achaioi. P. Oxy. 2462 gives the alternative title as *Pelopo* [*nnesioi*]. It was not therefore mythological. The figures on the Oescus mosaic (*MNC*, XM 1) are youth, old man, soldier and perhaps the poet in the background.

Georgos. Barigazzi, *Athenaeum* 34, 1956, 350 attributes P. Oxy. 2329 but on insufficient grounds.

Heautontimoroumenos. A fragmentary hypothesis, P. Oxy. 2534.

Encheiridion. The Mytilene mosaic (*M.N.C.*, YM2 ; Daux, *B.C.H.*, 91, 1967, 474) gives Act IV with two old men, Straton and Derkippos, both holding daggers, and a slave between them. D. del Corno (*P.P.*, 121, 1968, 306) suggests giving *P.S.I.*, 99 (S 9) and fr. 639 Kö. to this play.

Epitrepontes. F. H. Sandbach, *P.C.P.S.*, 1967, 44 (no speaking part for Sophrone in 759 ff.) ; W. G. Arnott, *C.Q.*, 18, 1968, 226.

Ephesios. See above, p. xiv.

Heros. W. G. Arnott, *C.Q.*, 18, 1968, 225.

Theophoroumene. The Mytilene mosaic gives Act II with Lysias (holding clappers), Parmenon, Kleinias, and flautist (small). E. W. Handley, *Menander and Plautus*, 19, n. 4, has noted the connection between this, the Dioskourides mosaic (*MNC*, NM 2), Körte–Thierfelder, I, p. 101, and a papyrus to be published in *P.S.I.*, 15, which is partly iambic speech to bystanders, partly hexameter hymn to Kybele to the accompaniment of flute and cymbals. Cf. now *B.I.C.S.*, 16, 1969, 88.

Karchedonios. P. Oxy. 2654 incorporates fr. 228 Kö. It seems to be about a youth with a Carthaginian mother who proposes to be registered as an Athenian citizen so as to marry an Athenian girl. It seems, therefore, not to be the original of Plautus *Poenulus*, in spite of the parallel between *Poen.* 1086 ff. and *Sikyonios* XI B (cf. H. Lloyd-Jones, *G.R.B.S.*, 7, 1966, 147).

Kekryphalos. See Mette, 145. For the pawning of gold ornaments and clothing in comedy, cf. Caecilius 104R.

Knidia. Probably *Kedeia* (fr. 249 Kö.) should be preferred. Alternative title of *Samia.*

Kolax. P. Oxy. 2655 belongs above P. Oxy. 409 and gives parts of ten lines at the top of 409, col. iii, and the beginnings of eighteen lines of column iv. But very little comes out of it.

Koneiazomenai. If this is *Fabula Incerta*, as Sudhaus suggested, P. Oxy. 2533 may come soon after : Chaireas rejoices in his marriage, but Chaireas and Moschion are common names. I see no link with *P.S.I.* 1176 (61P). See Mette, 73 f., 148 f., 149.

Methe. Fr. 265 Kö. F. Salviat, *B.C.H.*, 88, 1964, 647 interprets.

Messenia. The Mytilene mosaic gives Act V : a young man Charinos being seized by two slaves, Syros and Tibeios.

Misogynes. T. Williams (*Rh. Mus.*, 105, 1962, 193 ff.) argues against the identification by Barns of this play with P. *Antinoopolis*, II, 55, and suggests instead *Proenkalon* as having a legal title. His stylistic parallels suggest that the Antinoopolis fragments are Menander. The order may be : *b* (*verso*), women discuss Moschion's conduct in raping a girl ; *b* (*recto*), a slave Dromon and a young man enter, discussing a report of a tablet being placed on an altar ; *a* (*verso*), they discover on an altar, on which a sacrifice has recently been made, a tablet containing a legal challenge ; *a* (*recto*), Dromon is left to think out a plan. His soliloquy continues, presumably, through *d* (*verso*) to *d* (*recto*). Outside this, *e* (*verso*) gives the arrival of the chorus at the end of the first act and *e* (*recto*) describes a drunken old woman.

Homopatrioi. See above on *Adelphoi B.*

Perikeiromene. F. H. Sandbach, *P.C.P.S.*, 1967, 40 (no speaking part for Glykera in 425 ff.) ; W. G. Arnott, *C.Q.*, 18, 1968, 232 ; *P. Oxy.* 2652 and 2653, second to third cent. A.D., ink drawing of a soldier and ink drawing of Agnoia. Cf. also *P. Oxy.* (forthcoming).

Perinthia. A. Barigazzi, *Hermes*, 88, 1960, 379 attributes *P. Hibeh*, II, 180–1, on no sufficient evidence.

Plokion. The Mytilene mosaic gives Act II with Moschion, Laches, Krobyle. Perhaps the father objecting to the marriage arranged by the mother for the son. On 333 Kö. cf. Camberale, *R.I.F.C.*, 95, 1967, 162. On 339 Kö. Chr. Dedoussi, *Charis Vourveris*, 1964, 290.

Proenkalon. Cf. above on *Misogynes.*

Synaristosai. The Mytilene mosaic of Act I, which repeats the Dioskourides mosaic (NM 1) in reverse, gives the names as Philainis (lena), Plangon (Selenium), Pythias (Gymnasium). Thierfelder has recovered the first line, *Studi Urbinati*, 35, 1961, 113.

Titthe. On fr. 396 Kö. See T. Williams, *Hermes*, 91, 1963, 305, who attributes it to the prologue.

Hydria. W. Kraus, *Serta Aenipontana*, 185 argues that this was the original of Plautus, *Aulularia.*

Hypobolimaios. See G. Zuntz, *P.B.A.*, 42, 1956, 209 ; M. Kokolakis, *Athena*, 66, 1962, 9 ; M. van der Valk, *A.C.*, 37, 1968, 477.

Phasma. The Mytilene mosaic gives Act II with a woman standing in a doorway, and an old man rushing up, followed by a young man. Cf. also *P. Oxy.* (forthcoming).

3. Plautus and Menander

Professor E. W. Handley's brilliant identification[1] of an extremely difficult papyrus as part of the *Dis Exapaton* has for the first time given us a long stretch of a Greek original adapted by Plautus. This confirms all that we had supposed of Plautus' free and easy method of adaptation. The papyrus runs from a little before l. 489 of Plautus' *Bacchides* to l. 561. It was obvious before that Plautus had somehow tampered with

[1] *Menander and Plautus*, London, 1968.

Menander, when Mnesilochus, in the space of four lines (526-9), entered the house of his father, whom he had not yet seen after his return from a long foreign journey, paid him the gold which he had apparently been carrying round with him, persuaded his father not to punish the slave Chrysalus for the first deception, and came out again. Now we know that Plautus cut out sixty lines of Menander here and wrote a new entrance for Pistoclerus (526-9) to cover the gap. The sixty lines of Menander contained first the er trance of Mnesilochus' father and the discussion with him of the gold and Chrysalus' deception. Father and son go off to wherever the son or the slave had deposited the gold, and the act ends. Then a new act opens, with father and son returning after the payment of the gold. They are still discussing the punishment of the slave, and the son finally persuades the father to leave it to him (Plautus preserves a trace of this in 532-3). The father goes off to the Agora, and the son's soliloquy runs for eleven lines before ' Pistoclerus ' enters ; Plautus has cut this to a line and a half (530b-1).

Apart from this change of structure, Plautus has changed some of the names : Lydos remains, Sostratos becomes Mnesilochus, Moschos becomes Pistoclerus, Syros becomes Chrysalus. The papyrus does not give the names of the two old men. Plautus has changed the metre : the papyrus is in iambic trimeters all through, Plautus only uses the equivalent iambic senarii for Mnesilochos' soliloquy after the departure of Lydus and Philoxenus (500-525), but trochaic septenarii for the scene before (475-498) and the later scene between Mnesilochus and Pistoclerus (526 ff.). This kind of variation between scenes in iambic trimeters and scenes in trochaic tetrameters is often found in Menander [1] but not in this stretch of the *Dis Exapaton*. In style, where original and adaptation can be compared, the changes are much what would have been expected, and Professor Handley (p. 18) has well characterized them : ' Plautus likes his colours stronger, his staging more obvious, his comedy more comic.'

The other plays of Plautus which certainly derive from originals by Menander are *Cistellaria* (*Synaristosai*) and *Stichus* (*Adelphoi A*). *Aulularia* can be regarded as certain, whether the original was *Apistos* or *Hydria* or some other play (see above).

[1] Cf. above, p. 184 f.

Miles has recently been claimed (see above under Menander's *Ephesios*). The *Poenulus* does not seem to fit the papyrus fragment of the *Karchedonios* (see above) and therefore may rather derive from Alexis, as Professor W. G. Arnott[1] has argued.

Two plays of Plautus may be founded on originals by Menander although we have no direct internal or external evidence, *Pseudolus* and *Curculio*. The date of the original of the *Pseudolus* is suggested by three passages : (1) the soldier is in Sicyon (995, etc.) ; (2) the soldier is a Macedonian (51, etc.) ; (3) Chrysis is called *anus illa, doliaris, clauda, crassa* (659). Wilamowitz, followed by Hueffner,[2] argued that the Macedonian soldier is a soldier of Cassander fighting against Polyperchon in Sicyon and therefore dated the play 309/8 B.C. This date would fit also the reference to Chrysis, if she is the same Chrysis who is already old fifteen to twenty years before in Timocles' *Orestautokleides* (25K). The original of the *Pseudolus* seems therefore to have been produced early in the New Comedy period.

Before considering its authorship we have to face certain problems in its structure even though we need not discuss in detail the elaborate theories of contamination which have been produced. The most difficult problems occur within the first act. In I, i, the youthful lover Calidorus has received a letter from Phoenicium letting him know that her owner Ballio has sold her to a soldier and the final payment is to be made on the following day ; Pseudolus promises that he will produce the necessary money to buy the girl : in I, ii, Ballio parades his girls, ending with Phoenicium, who, he says, always promises and never pays but she must pay to-day from the estates of her friends (225 f.) : in I, iii, Calidorus and Pseudolus ask Ballio for an extension of time to collect the money (321) ; they are horrified when they hear that she is already sold, although Ballio has sworn to keep her for Calidorus (352) : Ballio says that Calidorus shall have the girl if he brings the money first. Pseudolus claims to have a plan, and sends Calidorus to fetch a friend *astutum, doctum, cautum et callidum* (385) ; in I, iv, Pseudolus soliloquising says that he had promised to get the money from Calidorus' father long ago but the old man somehow got wind

---

[1] *Rh. Mus.*, 102, 1959, 252.

[2] Wilamowitz, *Antigonos von Karystos*, 140 ; Hueffner, *op. cit.*, 11.

of it ; in I, v, the father Simo has heard gossip in the town that Calidorus wants money and interrogates Pseudolus ; Pseudolus persuades the old man to pay if he succeeds in getting hold of the girl (535). The difficulties that have been felt here [1] are that (1) the letter telling Calidorus the whole story of the sale to the soldier spoils the climax in I, iii ; (2) no mention is made in I, ii, of the sale to the soldier ; (3) I, ii, is unlike any other scene in comedy ; (4) Ballio's oath is mentioned in I, iii, but not in I, i ; (5) Pseudolus' plan should not belong to the first act but to the second, i.e. not to exposition but to complication ; (6) Pseudolus' reference in I, iv, to an earlier failure to touch Simo should refer to something within the play ; (7) Simo's reference in I, v, to gossip in the town should also be accounted for by the facts given in the play ; (8) Simo lives in a house on the stage, therefore he should be seen going out before he returns.

It is certain that Plautus has added to his original and may have altered its lines in some particulars as he has in other plays. The early scenes are not unlike the early scenes of the *Poenulus*, which give rise to the same sort of difficulties. There it seems likely that there was a preliminary meeting between Agorastocles and the *leno* in the first act and then in the second act the girls set out for the temple and the plan to get control of the *leno* is formed.[2] The argument that Phoenicium's letter spoils the climax of the meeting between Calidorus and the *leno* does not seem to me important ; the climax has its force because Calidorus now hears this from the *leno's* own lips, and it is this that makes him mention Ballio's perjury now rather than in the earlier scene. The dramatic value of the letter is to show the extreme depression of Calidorus ; his reactions to Ballio come in the later scene. It is of course also possible that the letter is more explicit in Plautus than it was in the original. Respect for the climax may also have moulded the phrasing in I, ii : there is nothing inconsistent in Ballio's demand that Phoenicium should bring him her complete purchase money to-day.

The structure underlying the first three scenes up to Ballio's departure seem to belong to the original. If Simo appeared on his way to the agora at the end of the dialogue between Calidorus

[1] I refer only to the more recent accounts : Fraenkel, *Pl. Pl.*, 144 f. ; Klingner, *Hermes*, 1929, 110 ; Theiler, *Hermes*, 1938, 274.
[2] Cf. *Studies in Menander*, 134 f.

and Pseudolus and threatened Pseudolus (like his namesake in the
Andria), Pseudolus' remarks in I, vi (406 f.), would be intelligible.
If Simo met friends of Ballio in the agora after Ballio's encounter
with Calidorus, Simo's remarks about gossip in I, v (418), would
be intelligible. Then the first act must end between Ballio's
departure (380) and Simo's return (415). The next certain act
break is between Pseudolus' departure in II, iv (764), and his
return with Simia in IV, i (905). On the analogy of surviving
Greek comedy, Act II would begin with the entrance of Simo
(415) and end with the departure of the conspirators (764) ;
Act III would begin with the entrance of Ballio (790), who has met
Simo in the agora (896)—the little soliloquy of Ballio's slave
(767) may be an invention of Plautus. If this is right, Calidorus
must go to fetch Charinus in Act I, so that he may return with
him in Act II (694). Pseudolus' instruction to Calidorus to fetch
hominem astutum, doctum, cautum et callidum (385) means that he
has already made a plan that a friend of Calidorus shall imper-
sonate the soldier, yet in 396 he has not ' a drop of a fixed plan
ready ', in 567 he has no idea how he is going to fulfil his
promise, in 574 f. he is completely confident, and in 601 he
abandons his original plan because he sees the chance of using
Harpax. Fraenkel[1] has shown conclusively that the triumph
song (574 f.) is purely Plautine. The Greek Pseudolus was
nevertheless a supremely skilful manipulator like Chrysalus in the
Dis Exapaton and not a rash extemporiser like Tranio in the
Mostellaria. In other plays, where a chance arrival alters the
original plan (e.g. the arrival of Chremes in the *Andria/Perinthia*
and the arrival of Cleomachus in the *Dis Exapaton*),[2] we are left
to guess the original plan ; here the nature of the original plan
is obvious but may not have been emphasised in the Greek
original. It is much more probable that Callidorus was sent to
fetch a friend in the first act and that the *astutum, doctum, cautum,
et callidum* is a Plautine addition,[3] and that the first plan only
dawns in Pseudolus' mind after the departure of the two old
men and is rejected again as soon as Harpax arrives.

In some such way as this the structure of the original becomes
logical and intelligible. Certain scenes however demand a little further consideration. Fraenkel[4] has urged very strong arguments

[1] *Op. cit.*, 63 f.   [2] Cf. above, p. 193.
[3] Cf. below on *Epidicus*, 314.   [4] *Op. cit.*, 144 f.

that in I, ii, Ballio's orders to his slaves have been greatly expanded by Plautus and that the hetaira parade is an invention of Plautus ; J. J. Tierney [1] has produced evidence from Greek writers for the possibility of the hetaira parade. It is quite impossible that Calidorus and Pseudolus should be on the stage for a soliloquy of 100 lines, and we can point to other instances where Plautus has enormously increased Greek scenes of overhearing. But if, as seems likely, Plautus has suppressed a scene between Simo and Pseudolus after the opening dialogue, Ballio may have had the stage to himself after Simo's departure and until Pseudolus and Calidorus come out again as Ballio makes off to hire the cook. The question then is whether the Greek original had a special display scene in which Ballio reviewed his servants and his hetairai. Fraenkel is undoubtedly right that Ballio's address to his slaves has been greatly expanded, but as a means of showing character abuse of slaves was probably a common element in New Comedy (cf. Euclio in the *Aulularia* and Antipho in the *Stichus*). The junction between the review of the servants and the review of the hetairai is made by Ballio's remark *vel opperire, est quod domi dicere paene fui oblitus* (171) ; this is a good transition for which Tierney quotes parallels from Aristophanes. The fact that *i puere prae* (170) is repeated by *i prae puere* (240) does not necessarily prove that the intervening passage is an insertion.[2] The establishment consisting of four hetairai seems to be perfectly possible for the Greek stage ; such an establishment is implied by several fragments (e.g. Euboulos, 67K ; Philemon, 4K). That each hetaira should have a different class of patrons is a possible idea for Greek comedy and has analogies in the equation of hetairai with different mythological monsters by Anaxilas (22K) ; Euboulos provides different wreaths for different hetairai (104K), and Antiphanes different fish for different hetairai (26K). Fraenkel is however undoubtedly right in saying that the butchers are Roman (196) ; but fishmongers would provide an admirable substitute. For a parade we have no certain evidence : a fragment of Diphilos (87K) in which a *leno* says that ' anything would be better than to have to feed *these* women ' does not necessarily refer to more than

---

[1] *P.R.I.A.*, L, 44 f.

[2] See *Studies in Menander*, 136, 142 ; and cf. Hegio in *Captivi*, 126, *ibo ad fratrem* ; 194, *ad fratrem mox ivero* ; 458, *ad fratrem inviso*.

two hetairai and does not prove even their presence on the stage. The hetairai furies of Timocles' *Orestautokleides* (25K) also may not have appeared on the stage. On the other hand a parade is not impossible and not essentially different from the individual birds who appear to the hoopoe's summons in the *Birds*[1] or from the fishermen in the *Rudens*. On balance it seems to me likely that the parade belonged to the original.

There is however a further curious point. Hedylion is told to bring so much corn from the corndealers that Ballio may be called King Jason in future. Fraenkel[2] interprets this as a mistake in Plautine mythology ; Tierney,[3] however, sees a reference to Jason of Pherae as the great corn supplier of the early fourth century. This is tenable on one assumption which we cannot rule out as impossible. The reference to Jason suggests a date in the 'seventies ; the original of the *Pseudolus* was written about 309. The author must have taken over a description of four hetairai and their customers from an earlier play and adapted it for his *leno* ; we should also have to assume that the *leno* appeared on the Greek stage or at least that his establishment was discussed somewhat earlier than any surviving reference to him. The free use of earlier material is perfectly possible : we need only compare (1) the series Euboulos, 67K, 84K ; Xenarchos, 4K ; (2) Philemon, 123K (= 57P), as enlarged by Straton (1K) ; (3) Mnesimachos, 4K, quoted by Menander, 299K.

Whether this is the right explanation or not, Ballio's brutal treatment of his slaves followed by the parade of four hetairai was a striking showpiece which also gives a clear picture of Ballio. It is balanced by another showpiece which may be conveniently considered here, the scene with the cook. On our evidence the cook appears on the comic stage about the middle of the fourth century.[4] A cook in Alexis' *Lebes* (127K, 340/30) gives a whole long list of herbs which he requires ; our cook is more advanced and scorns those who produce ' seasoned meadows ' (810). The same view of old-fashioned cookery is held by Anaxippos' cook (1K), who gives also a pedigree of chefs ; our cook has not got to this stage yet. He claims,

[1] Fraenkel has recently noted (*Eranos*, xlviii, 83) that these special birds are *not* part of the chorus.
[2] *Pl. Pl.*, 31. [3] *Op. cit.*, 29. [4] See above, p. 66.

however, that his dinners will make people live two centuries and this is out-trumped by Philemon's cook (79K), who can raise the dead and make the living immortal. Other elements are traditional : the savour which flies up to Zeus we know from the *Birds* (1517 f.) ; the rejuvenation (the cook ludicrously and ominously gets his mythology wrong) from the rejuvenation of Demos in the *Knights* (1321) ; and the guests who in their greed eat their own fingers from a fragment of Aristophon (9K). Thus our cook takes his place reasonably in the series of comedy cooks. A third showpiece (largely expanded by Plautus) is the drunken Pseudolus at the end (1246) ; this also is part of a tradition which we can trace from the *Ecclesiazusae* to the *Adelphi*.[1]

The intrigue itself is an accomplished variant of the ' disguise ' comedy. We need not seek an earlier ancestor than the *Persa* where we already find four elements, which recur in a different form in the *Pseudolus* : a message of distress sent by the girl to her lover, a preliminary meeting with the *leno* and abuse of him, a letter brought to the *leno* (in the *Persa* a false letter), and the tricking of the *leno* by a disguise. Three other comedies of approximately the same time as the *Pseudolus* have intrigues of the same general kind but differing in detail, which all however seem to be New Comedy variations of the Middle Comedy theme seen in the *Persa* ; they are the *Kolax*, *Poenulus*, and *Curculio*. It is noteworthy that the first two are by Menander.[2]

This may be a pointer to the authorship of the original of the *Pseudolus*. Diphilos and Philemon have been suggested as authors, but the *Pseudolus* has neither the particular kind of climax structure and grouping about the two chief characters which we associate with Diphilos nor the comedy of extemporisation which we associate with Philemon ; the detailed correspondences which have been noted with these two authors are much too slight to be significant.[3] The general likeness of the

---

[1] Cf. *Eccl.*, 1112 ff. ; *Amph.*, 1021 ff. ; *Ad.*, 763 ; Kunst, *op. cit.*, 164 ; Simon, *Comicae Tabellae*, 202, n. 26 ; *Studies in Menander*, 164.

[2] See *Studies in Menander*, 75, 135.

[3] On Diphilos see Marx, *Rudens*, 308 f. ; on Philemon, Kunst, *op. cit.*, 160 f., the only parallels which are worth noting are 290 ff. with *Merc.*, 209 ; 427 ff. with *Trin.*, 215. Dietze, *de Philemone comico*, 33 ff., notes the likeness of the cook to Philemon, 79K ; his other parallels are insignificant and his comparison with Plautus' *Cornicula* is useless as it is most unlikely that the *Cornicula* is Philemon's *Pterygion*.

intrigue to *Kolax* and *Karchedonios* has already been mentioned, and the slaves most like Pseudolus in readiness to profit from a new situation (678 ff.) are Chrysalus in the *Dis Exapaton* and Davos in the *Andria*. The feeling of the *Pseudolus* is not unlike early Menander as we know him from the *Dis Exapaton*, which like this play is primarily good comedy without any very serious intention or even any very pungent satire. The two show-pieces, the hetaira parade and the cook, are not impossible for Menander ; the girl's dance in the *Theophoroumene* must have been another such showpiece, and the arbitration scene of the *Epitrepontes* is elaborated beyond the needs of the economy of the play. It is therefore worth considering certain details in addition to the more general correspondence already noted. The opening scene between master and slave is typical Menander ; the first scenes of *Phasma* and *Misoumenos* are obvious parallels. I am not certain however that Leo [1] was right in seeing a reference to Menander's *Thesauros* in 412 : *ex hoc sepulcro vetere viginti minas ecfodiam*. It may be significant that Simo says (418) *per urbem solus sermoni omnibus est* ; a very similar phrase in a similar situation occurs in the *Epitrepontes* (408 = 882K) and the *Adelphi* (92 f.). The relation between the two old men, and particularly Callipho's account of Simo's youth (436 f.), has obvious parallels in Menander.[2] Pseudolus' warning to beware of him (517) is like that of Chrysalus in the *Dis Exapaton* (739 f.). The mistaken cleverness of Simo in suspecting collusion between Pseudolus and Ballio (538) is an idea further developed in the *Andria* (469 ff.). The comparison of Simia to a whirlwind (745) is an image which recurs three times in Menander.[3] Ballio's measures in dealing with the cook (855) recall Euclio in the *Aulularia* (90 ff.).

We can, I think, exclude Philemon and Diphilos as authors ; we cannot exclude Menander.[4] It might perhaps be safer to say an imitator of Menander, but if the dating to 309/8 is right the play is very much what one would expect from Menander's own hand at that time. A survey of Menander's fragments suggests that of the plays we know, the *Katapseudomenos* is one of the very few which could have been the original of the *Pseudolus*. It has also perhaps the most likely title.

---

[1] *Hermes*, XVIII, 563.   [2] Cf. *Kith.*, 59 ; *Ad.*, 103 ; *Bacch.*, 409.
[3] *Samia*, 210 ; *Georgos*, 100 ; 536/4K.
[4] Arnaldi, *Da Plauto a Torenzio*, I, 162. Cf. now *Pseud.*, 385 with *Asp.* 374.

The dating of the original of the *Curculio* depends primarily on the reference to Sicyon (395). This has been considered Plautine, but there seems no reason to deny it to the original. Although the parasite's story is a fabrication to account for his disguise, the reference must be to some event which would seem sensible. Wilamowitz [1] thought the siege by Demetrios Poliorketes in 303 B.C. was indicated ; Hueffner [2] referred to an unsuccessful attempt to relieve Sicyon in 313 B.C. and dates the play 310/9. Wilamowitz thinks that his dating is strengthened by the fact that Demetrios ruled Caria in 303 B.C., but Caria as a neighbouring place to which a parasite can go and return in a few days is a Plautine fiction, to which we no longer have the key. [3] Hueffner finds occasions for recent fighting in the places mentioned in the parasite's account of the soldier's victories but omits India (439) ; but surely the subjugation ' of half of all the nations in twenty days ', including India, Persia, and Libya, can only be a reference to Alexander's campaigns, just as in Menander's *Kolax* (produced soon after 312) the soldier agrees that he has not drunk less than King Alexander (293K).

We have therefore the certainty that the play was written after Alexander's conquests and the alternatives 313 and 303 for the references to Sicyon. Elderkin [4] has argued very elaborately for 303/2 and believes that the play was written by Philippides as a satire against Demetrios Poliorketes. His article raises both the general question of whether it is reasonable to suppose that the *Curculio* is political satire as well as various detailed points of some interest. The only political reference in Philippides which we know is the attack on Stratocles (25K), which is clear and direct and was apparently part of a speech in a comedy. We are asked by Elderkin to believe that Therapontigonus = servant of Antigonos = Demetrios, that the old woman Leaina is one of Demetrios' hetairai, and that Planesium is another, Lamia. If the identifications could be accepted, where is the satire ? Therapontigonus does not know of the existence of Leaina, and when he returns he finds that Planesium is his sister and marries her off to Phaedromus. In fact the two chief identifications are untenable. Therapontigonus is a Plautine

---

[1] *Isyllos von Epidauros*, 37, n. 8.   [2] Hueffner, *op. cit.*, 20 f.
[3] Cf., however, Leo, *Pl. F.*[1], 200, n. 2 ; Kunst, *Szenische Studien*, 165.
[4] *A.J.A.* 1934, 39.

fabrication, and we cannot guess his name in the original. The identification of Planesium depends on *noctuinis oculis* (191) being a translation of γλαύκωπις (Demetrios introduced Lamia into the Parthenon as a substitute for Athena) ; there is no evidence that γλαύκωπις could be used as a term of abuse in Greek, and passages in Plautus where the young man's slave abuses the girl are always much exaggerated if not entirely invented by Plautus. Sometimes certainly the comic poets were much more direct in their allusions to Lamia.[1] Leaina, even if the name comes from the original, is too common to be significant. To take the more detailed points, Phaedromus' claim to be a god when he sees Planesium (167) has nothing to do with the deification of Demetrios ; it is an exaggeration used by other lovers in comedy.[2] Cappadox' dream of Asklepios' indifference (260) does not refer to the hymn to Demetrios, which was in any case written ten years after Elderkin's date for the *Curculio* ; the same idea, god's dislike of the wicked, recurs in the *Poenulus*, where Aphrodite refuses the *leno's* sacrifice (847). Lyco's suggestion that the disguised parasite belongs to the *Coculitum prosapia* (393) may derive from an allusion in the original to Antigonos Monophthalmos as Cyclops, but apparently we do not know when Antigonos lost his eye, and the allusion may be to Philip who evidently was called Kyklops after he lost his eye.[3] Summanus (413), which for Leo [4] is a name invented by Plautus for the sake of a Latin pun, for Elderkin is an adaptation of *Kataibates*, a divine title given to Demetrios, when ' he descended ' from his carriage in Athens in 307 ; Plautus may have understood and adapted this allusion, but Leo's suggestion is certainly as likely. The soldier's ring (424) shows him carving up an elephant with his sword ; Elderkin interprets this as meaning that Demetrios will easily cut up Seleukos, the commander of elephants, who used elephants as a coin type. The use of elephants was not confined to Seleukos and his elephant coins were issued after 302 when he received the spectacular present of elephants from India.[5] If a parallel must be sought it may be remembered that Alexander fought against elephants and

---

[1] e.g. *C.A.F.*, III, 463/303.   Cf. above, p. 106.
[2] Cf. below, p. 223.
[3] Didymos, *in Dem.*, 12, 59.   [4] *Gesch.*, 147.
[5] Seltman, *Greek Coins*, 227 f.   *Miles*, 25, refers to Seleukos' campaign in India.

issued coins on which he was shown charging an elephant ; [1]
as the imaginary conquests seem to be based on Alexander, a
reference here also to Alexander is possible. A reference to
Seleukos is impossible as the soldier has owned the ring for at
least ten years (629) ; it is his father's ring, and I do not feel
certain therefore that its device has not been invented by Plautus
for this particular scene. Finally, the golden statue (440) is as
likely to be Alexander as Demetrios.

The case for intentional satire of Demetrios and therefore for
the authorship of Philippides seems to me not to have been made
out. The parasite's invented picture of the soldier seems to be
based on Alexander and his own disguise may be based on
Antigonos. The allusion to Sicyon suggests a date in the last
fifteen years of the fourth century, but Plautus has not left us
any other evidence ; the scene is Epidaurus and presumably
Phaedromus is a citizen of Epidaurus ; the soldier on the other
hand (and therefore his sister) apparently came from elsewhere
(429, *hospiti*). If the play were satire of Demetrios and Demetrios was to be identified with the soldier, we should expect a
soldier like Pyrogopolinices who combined boasting with amours.
Therapontigonus as a braggart is largely a fiction of his rival's
parasite ; the only other evidence is Lyco's remark (452) : ' I
certainly believe you come from him, you talk such rubbish ',
and two remarks of Therapontigonus himself (533) : ' *non ego
nunc mediocri incedo iratus iracundia sed eapse illa qua excidionem
facere condidici oppidis*', and (555) ' *quid refert me fecisse regibus ut
mi oboedirent, si hic me hodie umbraticus deriserit*'. These, and
especially the second, recall the two lines preserved by Arrian
from the prologue of Menander's *Misoumenos* (338K) : ' a cheap
little girl has enslaved me who never yet yielded to any foe '.
Thrasonides in the *Misoumenos* was sympathetically treated but
nevertheless had a considerable veneer of the braggart soldier.
Similarly Polemon in the *Perikeiromene* (43) is led by Ignorance
into *non mediocrem iracundiam*, *etc.*, but in the course of the play
is shown to be essentially different from the braggart soldier.
Therapontigonus even in the original was probably not a study
of this kind and was not treated in the same detail ; but though
he is gullible (337 f.), irascible, and to a certain extent boastful,
as befits the successful soldier, his behaviour in the recognition

---

[1] Seltman, *op. cit.*, 213.

scene wins sympathy and certainly unfits him for a caricature of
Demetrios Poliorketes : Pyrgopolinices in the *Miles* shows us
what such a caricature should be like.

Judgement of this play is the more difficult because it is clear
that Plautus has cut a great deal as well as elaborating what he
has left of the original.[1]   Thus a recognition play requires a prologue speech to warn the audience of the recognition and this
has been omitted.   We are not in fact told anything about the
soldier until the parasite reports having met him (337), and the
situation there is obscure ; the meeting is described as a meeting
between two acquaintances, cf. particularly *rogat quid veniam
Cariam* (339).   Perhaps then the parasite had met the soldier
before and approached him on this occasion because he was likely
to have money and to prove an easy prey, but having elaborated
the parasite's entrance (280 f.) Plautus has shortened his narrative,
and has not explained at the end that Phaedromus and Curculio
have not only to forge a letter (365) but also to disguise Curculio
with eyeshade, *causia*, and *chlamys*, because Lyco knows him (342).
The preceding scene with Cappadox has probably been shortened ;
the *leno* must surely say something about Planesium and probably
something about Phaedromus and the soldier ; much more also
was probably made of his dream which Plautus turns aside with
a Roman joke (266 f.).   In the original the scene performed the
same function as the hetaira parade of the *Pseudolus*.   It looks as
if the original had a very long first act (for which there are
parallels in Menander), consisting of (i) Night walking ; (ii)
temptation of Leaina ; (iii) Planesium scene ; (iv) prologue
spoken by Asklepios ? ; (v) Cappadox and his dream ; (vi)
arrival of Curculio.   The making of the plan should belong to
the second act and may very well have been a first scene between
Phaedromus and Curculio before the arrival of Lyco, and Lyco's
opening speech may have covered the time while Curculio put
on his disguise.   When Lyco is satisfied that Curculio comes
from the soldier because he talks such rubbish (452), he says,
' Come this way and I will pay you since that is why you came.'
Then goes straight on :

' There he is.   Good morning, *leno*.'

CAPPADOX : ' God bless you.'

LYCO : ' What of my reason for coming to you ? '

[1] See Fraenkel, *op. cit.*, 153, n. 1.

CA. : ' Say what you want.'

LY. : ' Take the money and send the girl with him.'

CA. : ' What of my oath ? '

It is quite clear from what follows that the *leno* is in fact paid thirty minae at this moment (cf. 520, 530, 535), although for a reason that is never explained the balance of ten minae for frocks and jewellery remains with the banker (cf. 342, 525). Therefore Lyco and Curculio must have gone to get the thirty minae before they meet Cappadox. As Lyco does not live on the stage, this means that the break between the second and third acts must come here. Legrand [1] is no doubt right in saying that Cappadox soliloquised when he came out of the temple and no doubt in this soliloquy (if not also in his earlier scene) he said something about the oath which comes in without any preparation (458) : the simplest explanation is that Cappadox had sworn to Therapontigonus to give him the girl personally and claims afterwards that he has done this (566) ; in that case 346b–348 is an addition to Plautus to shorten the plot. Cappadox must also have said something about the possibility of Planesium being a citizen, which Lyco suddenly mentions (490) and which had in fact been previously discussed with the soldier (667). Plautus has inserted the Roman monologue of the Choragus, but something must have covered the brief interval while Planesium is fetched ; a monologue by Lyco is perhaps most likely. In the next scene Fraenkel [2] is probably right in regarding the abuse of Cappadox and Lyco as Plautine invention (495–514). What happens at the end of the scene (which must also be the end of the third act, since Lyco has time to get home before Therapontigonus arrives) is not entirely clear. Curculio cannot take Planesium into Phaedromus' house before the eyes of Lyco and Cappadox and the final speech of Cappadox seems to be a soliloquy ; yet they come out of Phaedromus' house in the next act (591, 599). The simplest solution would be for Planesium and Curculio to go away and return to Phaedromus' house by the back door, which is used by Tranio in the *Mostellaria* [3] (1043 f.) to rescue the party from the house and for which

---

[1] *Op. cit.*, 377, following Bosscher, *De. Pl. Curc.*, 65 ; but the monologue cannot, as he thinks, have covered a journey to get money.

[2] *Op. cit.*, 114 f.

[3] Cf. Dalman, *de aedibus scaenicis*, 86, 93, 95.

there is evidence in other plays.[1]   In the scene between Therapontigonus and Cappadox, Fraenkel thinks that Cappadox should have described the parasite (583) ;   in the *Pseudolus* (1218 f.) Harpax's description of Pseudolus enlightens Ballio and Simo as to the trick ;   here this is impossible because Curculio is disguised, but Cappadox must describe the seal on the letter which he had accepted as genuine and this reminds the soldier of his ring ; Cappadox' joke about the weevil in the corn comes from the original, since Anaxilas (33K) calls flatterers the weevils of the rich ; Curculio was presumably called *Skolex* in the original.[2] Cappadox goes off at the end of the scene to fetch his ten minae from Lyco (588 = 559) and should not therefore return until the next act, but it seems quite possible that V, iii (679 f.), represents a short last act of the original, which was not unlike the final scene of the *Poenulus*.   The intervening scenes are more difficult, and it seems unlikely that the whole double recognition was crammed into a single scene in which four people had speaking parts.   Curculio's monologue (591) certainly comes from the original and is not unlike Onesimos' monologue in the third act of the *Epitrepontes* (243 f.), and Planesium bursts out after him rather as Habrotonon there ;   the struggle for the ring also recurs between Syriskos and Onesimos in the *Epitrepontes* (218). Phaedromus follows and Planesium tells her story at greater length than in Plautus.   Then perhaps Therapontigonus, who has been searching elsewhere for Curculio, comes back (610, *salvos sum, eccum quem quaerebam*) and sees Planesium as she goes into the house ;   Curculio after preliminary bluster goes and sends Phaedromus and Planesium out to him and the recognition follows.

The cross-threads which bind this play to the *Kolax*, *Poenulus*, *Pseudolus*,[3] *Perikeiromene*, and *Misoumenos*, all produced in the last twenty years of the fourth century, are so numerous and intricate that a common authorship seems likely.   We have already noticed that Therapontigonus has some affinity with the soldiers of the *Perikeiromene* and *Misoumenos* and we do not know of any other writer except Menander who represented soldiers at all sympathetically.   Therapontigonus turns out to be the brother

---

[1] Cf. *Studies in Menander*, 89, 141.

[2] The parallel between *Curc.*, 228, and Menander, 937K (possibly *Sikyonios*), is not sufficient to identify Curculio with Menander's Theron.

[3] Note also (perhaps too slight to be significant) *Curc.*, 144 = *Pseud.*, 405 ; 213 = *Poen.*, 360 f. ;   520 = *Pseud.*, 1038.

of the girl he wants just like Moschion in the *Perikeiromene* ; Phaedromus (51) has exercised the same self-control as Thrasonides in the *Misoumenos* (336K) and Agorastocles in the *Poenulus* (98). Like Agorastocles also he fears at the beginning (46) that the *leno* is going to make the girl into a common prostitute. The intrigue depends on impersonation as in the *Kolax, Poenulus,* and *Pseudolus,* and the disguised man pretends to be a soldier as in the last two plays. He has won the confidence of the real soldier as in the *Kolax* and *Pseudolus.* The relation to the *Kolax* is worth a moment's attention. There too (as also in the *Pseudolus*) the *leno* knows that the girl may be recognised (121 f.). There too the parasite Gnathon is not merely a traditional figure of fun but the active helper of the young man ; he wins the confidence of the soldier by playing the part of the flatterer Strouthias, thus making a new use of the traditional *alazon/kolax* [1] scene ; this scene was acted on the stage in the *Kolax* but in the *Curculio* (337 f.) the confidence trick is narrated. We only have the shortened narrative of Plautus ; the original was no doubt more convincing because the *Kolax* scene was known, just as in its turn the *Curculio* narrative ending with the loss of the ring gives verisimilitude to Habrotonon's doubts in the *Epitrepontes* (326 f.) : ' Who knows if some one else lost the ring after taking it from him as a pledge. Perhaps he was dicing and gave it as security for an agreement. Perhaps he made a bet and then lost and surrendered the ring.' Here we seem to have a series : *Kolax—Curculio—Epitrepontes.* *Curculio* shares with *Kolax* the new conception of the parasite as an active helper which we only find again much later in Terence's *Phormio,* based on an original by Apollodoros, an imitator of Menander. (We can add now parallels with *Sikyonios* : Theron the active helper, Stratophanes the chaste soldier, Moschion the thwarted brother.)

So far we have been chiefly concerned with parallels between an interconnected group of contemporary plays, but we have also noted the development of the short scene between Curculio and Planesium (591 ff.) in the *Epitrepontes.* The setting of two houses and a shrine was used also in the *Apistos* and the *Dyskolos.* Several points in the first act also have parallels in Menander.

[1] I have noted above that ' Strouthias ' compares Bias to Alexander and Curculio's fictitious picture of Therapontigonus is based on Alexander,

The lover wandering outside his house at night recurs in several plays.[1] The lover is restrained by an old slave as in *Dis Exapaton*, *Phasma*, *Eunuch*. The old slave notes the deterioration in his conduct as in *Eunuch* (225). Phaedromus' claim to be a god because he sees his girl recurs in the *Poenulus* (275–6), *Heautonti-moroumenos* (693), and *Andria* (959, transferred by Terence from *Eunuch*). The bibulous old woman and the song before the door are traditional comedy,[2] but we also know the bibulous old woman from the prologue of the *Synaristosai*.[3] We know that there was song in Menander's *Theophoroumene* (and probably in other plays [4]), and the vestigial remains of a song before a closed door is preserved by Persius (V, 165) from the prologue of the *Eunuch* : *dum Chrysidis udas ebrius ante fores extincta cum face canto*. The parallels with Menander are therefore numerous and far outweigh the correspondences with the *Rudens* noted by Marx,[5] which are normal turns of phrase such as might occur in any comedy ; the structure of the *Curculio* has close affinities with Menander and none with Diphilos as we know him. Again it is the light-hearted early Menander but with a touch of seriousness and sympathy for three figures who normally only meet with mockery on the Greek stage, the soldier, the parasite, and the sickly *leno* who has guarded Planesium carefully (like Melaenis in the *Synaristosai*).

[1] Cf. on *Pseudolus*, above, p. 216.
[2] Cf. Prehn, *Quaestiones Plautinae*, 40 ; Wehrli, *Motivstudien*, 23 ; Oeri, *Typ der Komischen Alte*, 46.
[3] It is perhaps worth noting that the *improba lena* occurs in Ovid's short summary (*Am.*, I, xv, 17) of Menander's characters and is omitted from the similar summary of Philemon's characters by Apuleius (*Florida*, xvi).
[4] The fragments in metres other than iambic and trochaic (collected in *Studies in Menander*, 107) were presumably sung.
[5] *Rudens*, 315.

VIII. APOLLODOROS AND HIS COMEDY

THE identification of Apollodoros of Gela with Apollodoros of Karystos, which Kaibel maintained in his Pauly-Wissowa article, was dropped when a new fragment of the list of victors at the City Dionysia [1] showed Apollodoros after Poseidippos, i.e. about 280, whereas in the Lenaia list Apollodoros appears between Philemon and Diphilos soon after 320. Kaibel [2] himself admitted that the gap of forty years between City and Lenaia was too long and that we must assume two poets. Suidas distinguished Apollodoros of Gela, who was ' a contemporary of Menander ', from Apollodoros of Athens, who wrote 47 plays and won 5 victories. There is no reason why we should not identify Apollodoros of Karystos with Apollodoros of Athens and assume that like Philemon and Diodoros, Diphilos' brother, he obtained Athenian citizenship.

The identity of name inevitably led to confusion in the fragments. Suidas gives Apollodoros of Gela the following titles : *Apokarteron, Deusopoios, Hiereia, Grammateidopoios, Pseudaias, Sisyphos, Aischrion.* Our authorities quoting the *Apokarteron, Apoleipousa, Grammateidopoios,* and *Hiereia* ascribe these plays to both poets. Identity of title is so common in Greek comedy that both poets may have written plays with the same title ; but the fragment of the *Grammateidopoios* (281/5) which describes the mutual hatreds of Greek states, a fragment of the *Hiereia* (287/24) which mentions the marriage of Ophellas as a recent event, and a fragment of the *Sphattomene* (288/26) with a reference to Chairephon dates these plays to the last quarter of the fourth century and they therefore must have been written by Apollodoros of Gela although Athenaeus attributes them to Apollodoros of Karystos.[3]

Apollodoros of Karystos clearly obscured the memory of his earlier namesake, but his own meagre fragments do not give us much idea of him. If we can assume that quotations of an unspecified Apollodoros are more likely to belong to the

---

[1] *I.G.*, 2325. [2] ap. Wilhelm, *Urkunden*, 182.
[3] Cf. Capps, *A.J.P.*, 1900, 48 f.

Karystian, perhaps when he had become an Athenian, then his dependence on Menander is clear.[1]   Menander's influence is also very clear in the *Phormio* and *Hecyra* of Terence, and this in itself makes it likely that the Apollodoros who wrote their originals is the younger rather than the older.   Moreover, one version of the Donatus Life of Terence known as the *Vita Ambrosiana* describes Apollodoros as *Caricio* where the manuscripts of the full life give *comico* ; it seems therefore that the Donatus Life originally had *Carystio* and that this had become corrupted to *Caricio* before the *Vita Ambrosiana* branched off and was further corrupted to *comico* by the time of the extant manuscript of the full Life.[2] There is no other external evidence [3] for the poet's identity, but in any case there is a strong probability that it was the younger and more famous poet who was inspired by the later plays of Menander and provided Terence with his originals.

Apollodoros of Karystos started to produce not long before 280.   The original of the *Phormio* can be dated by the references to Lemnos.   If Lemnos was lost to Athens between 286 and 279,[4] a comic poet is unlikely to make his characters travel there freely in a play produced between those dates ; on the other hand, this dead period would make it impossible for Chremes to visit Lemnos for some time (569 f.), and the visit recorded in the play may well be his first visit when communications are re-opened.   The play may then have been produced soon after 279.   There is no reason to suppose that Terence has made any major alterations.   He changed the name of this play from *Epidikazomenos* (or *-e*) to *Phormio* ; but Phormio was a character in Apollodoros' play (Donatus on l. 26).   Donatus [5] notes minor changes of phrasing to suit Roman taste, and Demipho in the original undoubtedly saluted the Agyieus outside his house instead of the Penates (311), which involves an awkward entry

[1] Cf. 291/13 with *Sam.*, 57 f., 128 f. ; 16 with Menander, 128K.

[2] See particularly Sabbadini, *S.I.F.C.*, 1894, 26 f.   I am much indebted to Professor E. D. M. Fraenkel for help with this problem.

[3] A possible indication, however, is given by the name Phormio : Phormio was a character not only in the *Epidikazomenos* (Donatus on *Phormio*, 26) but also in the *Diabolos* which is ascribed to the Karystian (283/7) ; he is likely to have been named after the parasite of Seleukos (Ath., VI, 244 f.) : references to Seleukos in comedy date from the early third century (see above, p. 108).

[4] Ferguson, *Hell. Ath.*, 155 f.   This excludes the date 285 given by Dziatzko-Hauler, 78, n. 3.

[5] On 49, 91, 482, 647.

into the house in the Roman adaptation. The present division into acts is impossible : Geta goes to the harbour and back between Acts I and II, therefore Act II must start at l. 153 and not at l. 231 ; similarly an act break is necessary to give Geta time to fetch Phormio (308–15) and Demipho to fetch the *advocati* (312–48), therefore Act III must start at l. 315 and not at 465 ; finally there is no break where Sophrona comes out (729) but a clear break when she goes in with Chremes (765), which must be the end of Act IV.[1] For these mistakes the responsibility lies not with Terence but with his early editors.[2] Terence himself, however, as in his adaptations of Menander, probably omitted a divine prologue at the end of the first act because he preferred surprise to suspense.[3]

This comedy has much in common with other comedies :[4] Phormio's betrayal of Chremes is like Peniculus' betrayal of Menaechmus in the *Menaechmi*, and the discovery of Chremes' misdemeanours by his wife has parallels in the *Casina* and *Mercator*. In both cases the laughter is less uproarious in Apollodoros ; the betrayal is a device to bring about the discovery and the discovery leads to a conclusion which emphasises the solidarity of the family, perhaps the real value which Apollodoros wants to display. The tone is much more like Menander than Philemon or Diphilos or the author of the *Menaechmi*, and Menander provides parallels for characters, situations, ideas, and to a certain extent technique and style. To take the most obvious instances : Phormio, the ' confident, dark ' flatterer, as Cicero calls him, who engineers the whole intrigue is a development of Gnathon in the *Kolax* [5] (the other instance, Curculio in his name play, may also be a creation of Menander) ; Geta stands in the same relation to the two sons as Parmeno in the *Eunuch*. Recognition of an elderly father by his daughter's nurse we know from the *Misoumenos* and the *Poenulus*, but Apollodoros gives it a new twist here. Nausistrata's decision at the end to

[1] So Legrand, *op. cit.*, 375.
[2] According to Legrand, *op. cit.*, 371, they date from the time of Varro.
[3] So Kuiper, *Two Comedies of Apollodorus of Carystus*, 52.
[4] *Servus currens* (179 ff.), the play with the two-sided mask (210), the forgetting of the name (386), the rough and tumble (982 f.), are traditional and used in the traditional way. The *leno* scene (485) is much like the *Pseudolus* (250).
[5] Cf. *Studies in Menander*, 74 f. In the *Kolax* (as here Geta at the beginning, 122) the young man's paidagogos mistrusts the parasite.

refer the verdict on Chremes to their son is a reminiscence of the *Epikleros* in which ' a man and his wife went to law and their son gave the verdict ' ; [1] Nausistrata also is an heiress and treats her husband with contempt. In these and other instances [2] Apollodoros borrows a situation from Menander and either develops it or reduces it according to his needs at the moment. Sometimes he seems to quote Menander directly,[3] although where the quotation can be traced a stage further back it may be safer to say that such a sentiment belonged to the common stock of the educated Athenian.[4] But even so we may note that Apollodoros uses his brief gnomes in much the same way as Menander and draws on high literature for the same purposes as Menander : the conflicting views of the *advocati* (450 f.) recall the useless chatter of the Aeschylean chorus after the murder of Agamemnon, and Phaedria appeals to Dorio (496) : *tu mihi cognatu', tu parens, tu amicu', tu* . . . in language which derives ultimately from Andromache's appeal to Hector. Demipho, in stating his philosophy of life (241 f.), quotes Euripides (fr. 964N[2]) in just the same way as Demeas in the *Samia*.[5]

At first sight the characters seem also to derive from Menander. We have already spoken of Phormio, Geta, and Nausistrata. The two young men are loyal to each other in their difficulties like the two young men of the *Heautontimoroumenos* and the *Adelphi* ; Antipho (153) has a very real respect for his father like Pamphilus in the *Andria* (262). Demipho is the hard business man who would never allow his son to marry a girl without a dowry [6] (120) and Chremes is his foil. The quartet of young and old men is known from several plays of Menander, but here the interrelations, the qualities, and the emphases have been changed. The contrast between Demipho and Chremes is a contrast which we do not know in quite this form in Menander. It is summed up in two statements : Demipho (quoting Euripides,

---

[1] Cf. *Studies in Menander*, 97.

[2] Cf. also 84 ff. with *Andria*, 71 ff., *Heautont.*, 285 ff. ; 682 ff. with *Andria*, 607 ; probably also 865 ff. with *Hiereia*, 56, and a lost scene of the *Perikeiromene* (cf. *Studies in Menander*, 13) ; 110 f., 422 with *Com. Flor.* (Wehrli, *Motivstudien*, 34).

[3] e.g. 162 with *Phasma*, 42 ; 168 with *Heautont.*, 225.

[4] e.g. 77, 203, 405, 705, 790.

[5] Minor instances : 587 with E., fr. 1005N, 726 with E., *Hel.*, 830. For Demeas, cf. *Studies in Menander*, 158.

[6] Cf. 301, 311 (with Donatus' note), 358, 371, 664.

as we have said) : 'When things go best, then above all you should consider how to bear disaster—danger, losses, exile' (241 f.) ; Chremes : 'How often things happen by chance which you would not dare to pray for' (757). Demipho is shrewd and calculating and as far as possible protects himself from the blows of fortune. Chremes hopes that something will turn up and meanwhile pursues the easy path as long as he can preserve appearances. Demipho in the original had exposed his legitimate daughter ; [1] Chremes preferred to adopt a false name and rob his wife in order to bring up his illegitimate daughter in Lemnos. Before the recognition of Phanium, Demipho is only anxious to get rid of her but Chremes wants also to save appearances (719). In Menander the contrast between the old men is echoed by a contrast between the young men even when, as in the *Adelphi*, one son takes after his adoptive instead of his real father. He is interested in the son's behaviour as a problem partly of heredity and partly of education, and he is concerned to show that many of the difficulties between the young and the old arise from the old adopting conventional instead of true values. These problems do not arise in the *Phormio*, perhaps because Menander had stated them once and for all. The point can be put in this way : in the *Heautontimoroumenos* it is convenient that Antiphila should turn out to be Chremes' daughter because Clinia is in love with her ; in the *Phormio* it is convenient that Antipho should have married Phanium because she turns out to be Chremes' daughter. Here is possibly the real value which Apollodoros is stating. According to Demipho's standards, Chremes has been a fool to bring up his Lemnian daughter, but he has done it and therefore she must marry Antipho. The family must stick together and this is also Nausistrata's feeling when she asks Phaedria to judge between her and Chremes.

Family solidarity is stressed in the *Hecyra* too, and will be discussed later. We can also see stylistic resemblances : in both plays special characters are introduced for the exposition and do not reappear (in the *Hecyra* Philotis and Syra are fixed for the original by Donatus' quotation of the Greek of l. 58) ; they are enlivened by naturalistic detail such as the account of slave

---

[1] This is, I think, implied in Donatus' note on 647 : 'in the Greek play the old man said " what do I gain from not having raised a daughter, if I have to give a dowry to someone else's daughter ? " '

contributions at the beginning of the *Phormio* and of Philotis' experiences at the beginning of the *Hecyra* [1] (and later Sosia's account of his life on the sea (416) makes a similar lay figure interesting). Once in the *Hecyra* (452) the action is speeded by giving a character rather more knowledge than he might have been expected to have—at least it is not clear how Laches knew that Pamphilus had returned—and the same method of saving time and repetition on the stage is used twice in the *Phormio* (231 : Demipho knows that Antipho has married, 577 : Chremes also knows).[2]

The only indication of the date of the *Hecyra* is the mention of Imbros. Journeys to Imbros would have been unlikely between 288 and 279 B.C.[3] But this only provides us with a top date. Terence seems to have handled this play more violently than the *Phormio* and it is more difficult to detect exactly what he has done. He certainly omitted a divine prologue which would naturally come after the first act (198) ; Donatus (*ad* 318) points out that the audience know more than the characters, which they do not unless they have been given information. Donatus also has three important notes on Bacchis' speech when she has visited Myrrhina and Philumena (816 f.) : on her opening line (816), *reliqua pars argumenti per monodiam narratur* ; on her description of her earlier conversation with Pamphilus (825), *brevitati consuluit Terentius nam in Graeca haec aguntur non narrantur* ; on her summing up (833), *conclusit narratione fabulam more suo ne haec in actu futuro exspectaremus.* The second note makes it certain that Terence has shortened the original here and there has been much speculation about this.[4] We cannot know the extent of Terence's alteration ; I do not feel certain that the third note implies a general clearing up with the parents at the end : Pamphilus' conspiracy of silence is in character and the final words of Parmeno express a leading idea of the play (880) : *equidem plus hodie boni feci imprudens quam sciens ante hunc diem umquam.* Therefore Apollodoros rather than Terence underlined the novelty of the conspiracy of silence (866), just

---

[1] Cf. perhaps Phoinikides (334/4) for her experiences and Adespota (471/340) for the opening.
[2] Cf. below, p. 242.
[3] Ferguson, *Hell. Ath.*, 155 f.
[4] e.g. Stavenhagen, *Hermes*, xlv, 580 ; Leo, *Röm. Lit.*, 241 ; Legrand, *op. cit.*, 377 ; Kunst, *Studien*, 97 ; Kuiper, *op. cit.*, 26 f. ; Legrand, *R.E.G.*, 1949, 49 f.

as he underlines other novelties in this play and in the *Phormio*.[1]
It is at least possible that Donatus' three notes mark first the
beginning, then the chief subject, and then the end of the
narrative which Terence substituted. If this is correct, the
attachment of the second note to the words *quid exanimatus aut
unde* can only mean that, as Legrand in his latest article says, in
the original Bacchis played confessor to Pamphilus and made
him give a full account of the night when he had violated
Philumena ; before he had only given her a vague account,
as she says. For this kind of interrogation a parallel can be
seen in the papyrus discussed below.[2] Donatus never suggests
that Bacchis and Myrrhina met on the stage and therefore we
must assume that in Apollodoros also Bacchis related to the
audience or to Pamphilus that Myrrhina recognised the ring.
Kuiper has constructed an ingenious hypothesis that in the
original there were twin rings of which one belonged to
Philumena and never left Pamphilus' possession after he had
taken it from her and the other belonged to Bacchis and brought
about her recognition as the daughter of Phania and Myrrhina.
Apart from other difficulties the fatal objection to this theory is
that the whole complication of the plot depends on the mutual
ignorance of raped and raper, and this in turn depends on Bacchis
holding Philumena's ring from a time before Pamphilus and
Philumena married ; it is essential for the story that Pamphilus
should have both stolen Philumena's ring and given it to
Bacchis.

Terence seems to have substituted a narrative for a considerable
scene between Pamphilus and Bacchis, of which he has preserved the end (856). Parmeno can hardly listen to this scene
if he is to remain in ignorance to the end (880). Either he
returns after it or Bacchis sends him into the house to call out
Pamphilus (815), and he only comes out again after the con-
fession. Pamphilus himself had taken refuge in the house when
Laches tried to force him to accept the child (703). There
seems therefore to be no break in the action between Bacchis'
reappearance (806) and the end of the play, but it is difficult
to believe that Bacchis and Myrrhina could have got the situation
clear in the short time allowed by Terence ; an act ending must
separate Bacchis' entering and leaving the house. An act ending

---

[1] Cf. 573, 756, 834 ; *Phormio*, 972. [2] See below, p. 239.

need not be assumed before Bacchis' arrival because Bacchis is
a neighbour (720, 98) : the only difficulty here is the speed
with which Phidippus fetches a nurse (726/768). Before this
the next clear break in the action is when Myrrhina follows
Phidippus into his house after his discovery of the child (576) ;
from there all runs smoothly until Bacchis goes into the house
(795/8) and this will have been Apollodoros' fourth act. The
next break before this seems to be after Pamphilus' great monologue (408), since an act end should separate Parmeno's mission
and return (360/415). For the second act we have two choices :
we may assume with Kuiper [1] that it begins after the divine
monologue (198) and that Sostrata's prayer for her son's return
is immediately answered by his appearance (280/1) ; or, as
seems to me more likely, Apollodoros may have followed
Menander's practice of continuing Act I after the divine monologue and have started his second act with Pamphilus' arrival.

In any case the influence of Menander on this play is very
strong. It is true that Syra's advice to Philotis (64) is paralleled
in the *Mostellaria* (165 ff.) and the *Asinaria* (504 ff.) as well as
in Menander's *Synaristosai* (*Cist.*, 7 f.), and some other incidents
are part of the traditional comic stock,[2] but the birth of a child
during the action (317 f.) can be traced in fourteen plays of
Menander,[3] Pamphilus' soliloquy (361 f.) with its long narrative
followed by the taking of a resolution is very like the first speech
of Demeas in the *Samia* (1 f.), and the decision of the old men
to beard Bacchis recalls the similar decision of the old men in
the *Dis Exapaton*.[4] The old men are themselves a contrasted
pair of stern father and mild father like Chremes and Menedemus
in the *Heautontimoroumenos* and the brothers of the *Adelphi*, but,
as in the *Phormio*, Apollodoros is not concerned with the problems
of heredity and education which interested Menander. The
study of Pamphilus, who loved first Bacchis and then his wife,
may have been suggested by Aeschinus in the *Adelphi*, whom
we see devoted to Pamphila but of whom Micio says : *quam hic
non amavit meretricem ?* (149).

In particular, Apollodoros remembered the *Epitrepontes*, and a

[1] *Op. cit.*, 13.
[2] e.g. Parmeno's advice to Pamphilus (292), the drunken nurse (769).
[3] *Studies in Menander*, 59, n. 3.
[4] *Bacch.*, 1116. Minor parallels are : 552 ff., with *Ad.*, 734 (conscious contrast) ; 734 with *Eun.*, 865 ; 843 with *Andria*, 960.

comparison with this play shows both his indebtedness and his divergence ; [1] he notes both debt and divergence, when Myrrhina laments that the girl took nothing from her assailant by which he could be recognised, whereas he snatched her ring (573/4). The situation is the same and the token is the same but here the man instead of the woman takes it. Charisios' abstinence from Habrotonon (256 f.) becomes in this play Pamphilus' abstinence from Philoumena at the beginning of their married life (136). This abstinence and his love for Bacchis Philoumena (164 f., 302) endures as loyally as Pamphile defends Charisios to her father (600/1). Bacchis herself is a development of Habrotonon, but her action is almost entirely disinterested, while Habrotonon hopes to win freedom. Bacchis' account of her meeting with Myrrhina (830 f.) is inspired by Habrotonon's meeting with Pamphile (544), and Bacchis' scene with Pamphilus is a development of Charisios' scene with Habrotonon (632). Parmeno, who does little but run, is a paler edition of Menander's Onesimos, himself far less active than for instance the slave of the *Dis Exapaton*.

So far we have spoken of likeness and development ; the difference in casting is obvious. Smikrines in the *Epitrepontes* is a valuable irritant and the youthful Chairestratos is a light-hearted foil. He has vanished, and Smikrines is replaced by both parents of both the principals. The *Epitrepontes* is a play of reconciliation, and the essential factors are the wife's ideal of sharing her husband's life and the husband's definition of his act and hers as ' unwilled misfortune '. Pamphile's attitude is the same as the wife of the papyrus Didot in her rather different situation, but Charisios' acceptance of the same standard for judging male and female conduct is new and Pamphilus in the *Hecyra* fails to reach it (403). As in the *Heautontimoroumenos*, the discovery that Antiphila is Chremes' daughter is a con-venience which makes a neat ending, so in the *Epitrepontes* it is convenient that Pamphile's assailant was Charisios, but the essential reconciliation is complete in Charisios' mind before he discovers this. Pamphilus in the *Hecyra* refuses to reach this point ; and he is only prepared to keep silence as long as he can also remain loyal to his mother (447). He is saved finally by the discovery that Philumena's child is also his own.

[1] See particularly Stavenhagen, *Hermes*, xlv, 1910, 578 f.

Menander shows Charisios making a difficult and new decision. For Apollodoros Pamphilus is only one element in a complicated situation in which, as in the *Phormio*, the leading idea of the principals is family solidarity. Laches and Phidippus return again and again to this theme (263, 466 f., 721–4) ; Pamphilus himself has given up Bacchis because his father wants him to marry, has found a new content in marriage but is prepared to give up this too rather than do something which is against the honour of the family (403) ; his mother Sostrata gives her name to the play because she is a *good* mother-in-law and does not therefore run true to comic type ; the girl's mother Myrrhina first takes her away before her condition has been observed and then is prepared to expose the child to avoid discovery ; the girl has silently and uncomplainingly allowed Pamphilus to visit Bacchis.   The loyalty and affection between the members of the family and the readiness to sacrifice personal pleasure, convenience or rights to this end is the real value which the principals pursue through a maze of misconceptions.

But the maze of misconceptions is also interesting in itself, and Parmeno speaks for most of the other characters in the play when he says at the end (879/80) : *equidem plus hodie boni feci imprudens quam sciens ante hunc diem umquam.*   False interpretation and misconception run right through this play.   There are two main misconceptions : that Pamphilus is still in love with Bacchis and that Sostrata, like the normal mother-in-law of comedy, hates her daughter-in-law.   Parmeno in the first scene introduces variations of both : Bacchis had become grudging and proud when Pamphilus tried to visit her in the early days of his marriage (158), the truth is given by Bacchis herself in her scene with Laches (750 f.—she had refused to see Pamphilus because she wanted his marriage to be a success) ;   and Philumena had taken an extraordinary dislike to Sostrata (178, elaborated by him to Pamphilus, 288 f.).   Laches of course assumes that his wife is responsible for Philumena's withdrawal and that Sostrata has acted as the typical mother-in-law (198 f.).   When Pamphilus discovers that his wife is having a child, he finds the theory of the quarrel a convenient excuse for leaving Philumena where she is (470 f.), and Sostrata although she knows that she is innocent herself accepts the theory when she offers to withdraw to the country (577).   The other misconception, that Pamphilus is still

in love with Bacchis, becomes important in the later part of
the play ; Phidippus (530 f.), remembering that Myrrhina had
objected to Philumena marrying a man who was in love with a
hetaira, assumes that she has withdrawn Philumena to break
up the marriage and now wants to expose the baby because it
spoils this scheme. When Pamphilus shows his unwillingness
to take back his wife or to accept the baby,[1] Laches in his turn
assumes that Pamphilus wants to be rid of Philumena because
he is still in love with Bacchis (675 f.). The two old men then
pool their improvisations and agree to tackle Bacchis, which in
due course leads to the solution.

On a much smaller scale we can see the same sort of misconception in the *Phormio*, but there it is confined to a single question : Chremes' relations with the woman in Lemnos.[2] The
truth, which can be deduced from the statement of Chremes
himself (569 f.) and the Nurse (740 f.), is greatly exaggerated for
his own purposes by Phormio (1004 f.) and equally minimised
by Demipho (958 f.). But in the *Hecyra* the misconceptions are
held by most of the principal figures and provide to some
extent the motive force of the plot. We can see beginnings of
this in Menander in the deliberate deceptions or false assumptions
of slaves on which their masters act and in the misinterpretations
of the masters themselves : Demeas in the *Samia* assumes that
Chrysis is the mother of the baby and acts on this assumption
until he is fairly quickly disillusioned ; Sosias in the *Perikeiromene*
assumes that Moschion is Glykera's lover and tells his master ;
Simo in the *Andria* regards everything that happens in Glycerium's
house as an attempt by a greedy hetaira to capture Pamphilus
(834 f.). Menander is interested primarily in the Aristotelian
problem of the relation between knowledge and action, and we
are reminded of Apelles' picture in which Slander is the result
of Ignorance and False Assumption. In Apollodoros, on the
other hand, such false assumptions have become part of the
dramatist's stock-in-trade. His scenes are natural and lively
because many characters make these false assumptions, and the
action moves because of the conclusions that they draw from

[1] Schadewaldt has shown (*Hermes*, 1931, 1 f.) that the baby is a nine months
child, the old men accept it as a seven months child, Pamphilus at this stage
believes that it can only be his if it is a five months child.
[2] See Fredershausen, *Hermes*, 1912, 209.

their false assumptions ; underlying the maze are a good Fortune, which makes everything turn out right because this is comedy, and certain real values of which affection and family loyalty are the most obvious ; in these the characters believe, and no other comic poet emphasises them quite so clearly.

Modern scholars are apt to sum Apollodoros up as an obscure imitator of Menander, but this judgement needs qualification. The author of the *Hecyra* can hardly be called obscure, and if he imitated Menander, he also went beyond him.   In a genus like New Comedy where situations and characters are freely borrowed, it is necessary to define what we mean by imitation. It is clear that the tone of the two Latin plays and of the Greek fragments remind us more of Menander than do the remains of any other poet of New Comedy.   The naturalism, which we have noticed in several passages and which recurs in the charming fragment about arrival at a friend's house (293/14K), can itself be paralleled in Menander.   Menander's idealisation of stock characters such as parasite and greedy hetaira is continued by Apollodoros, developed and perhaps extended, since to us at any rate the good mother-in-law is new.   He is not merely an imitator, because what he takes from Menander is not in the foreground but becomes part of the background, which obtains an exact significance just because it recalls a more elaborate treatment by his predecessor ;   such themes for instance are the account of the trial at the beginning of the *Phormio* and at the end Nausistrata's submission of her quarrel to the judgement of her son.   Bacchis in the *Hecyra* is not a foreground figure like her ancestor Thais in the *Eunuch* but a background figure, who is more intelligible because we already know Thais.   With her help he opens up a new area in human psychology, and gives a possible answer to those who feel that the marrying-off of Clitipho, for instance, in the *Heautontimoroumenos* is unsatisfactory and unlikely to lead to happiness.   Is it possible for the young man who is in love with a hetaira to make a success of marriage ?   Pamphilus shows that it is ;   after his preliminary difficulties he speaks of his wife in as warm terms as any of Menander's young lovers : *amor me graviter consuetudoque eius tenet* (404), and his love for Bacchis changes into a warm friendship : ' You have your old charm, and your words and your coming, whenever you come, are always pure pleasure ' (858). Bacchis herself has made this

possible and her character is summed up in her own words :
' While it could be, I found in him a friend, charming and kind.
That it should end in his marriage was displeasing, I admit. But
I think my actions never deserved such an ending. But it is
reasonable that I should endure displeasure on his account who
brought me so much pleasure ' (837). Pamphilus' relation to
Charisios in the *Epitrepontes* we have already discussed, but
though he fails to make the new decision which Charisios makes
in similar circumstances, he has this other side to his nature which
Charisios lacks and in this respect Apollodoros has produced a
new character. Derivative from Menander Apollodoros certainly is, but he has developed a further stage of naturalistic
comedy.

Besides the two plays of Terence some papyrus fragments
deserve mention. The first is undoubtedly by Apollodoros ; [1]
one man tells another (Kleainetos ?) that he is wrong to rate
wealth more highly than goodwill between man and wife,
because this mutual goodwill is the means of preserving life.
The man works outside and the wife stores what he brings in
like the queen bee. But if two disparate people are forced to
live together, they cannot reasonably be expected to save. The
parallel between home and hive is worked out at length in
Xenophon's *Oikonomikos* (VII, 17), from which Apollodoros
has borrowed it. The context of this fragment is easy to supply.
A father wants to marry off his son to an heiress for whom the
son has no affection. A friend argues with him in terms that
he can understand, the economic basis of love between husband
and wife. In character the two old men stand to each other
rather as Demipho and Chremes in the *Phormio*. The mutual
goodwill between husband and wife is a real value, as in the
Latin plays.

Another fragment [2] is worth quoting here because of its likeness to the *Hecyra*. A young man with the rare name of
Kantharos opens an act.[3] He says that no one in Athens has

---

[1] 58P.   [2] *Antinoopolis Papyri*, no. 15. Fourth century A.D.
[3] The list of characters at the top of the page is too long for a scene and too
short for a whole play ; possibly the ϱο to the left belong to μέϱους ' act ' (cf.
Ox. Pap., 2086, l. 12). It is neither alphabetical nor in order of appearance.
Perhaps therefore it has been copied in the same order as the dramatis personae
at the beginning ? The page is numbered 60/61, which suggests that it is far
on in the second play of the volume.

suffered worse than he : he married four months ago at his
father's bidding.   Since then he has not slept a night away from
home.   The generosity and sincerity of his wife constituted a
tie which kept him entirely happy in her love.   Now he has
been shown something by a woman which ' grieves his heart '.
The woman who shows him must be the maidservant since she
is the only female in the list of characters and she presumably
comes out with him.   The situation reminds me of Pamphilus'
speech in the *Hecyra* (361) when he has discovered that his wife
has given birth to a child which he believes cannot be his, and
Kantharos' marriage seems to have been not unlike Pamphilus'
marriage.   He married to please his father ; he has been faithful
since his marriage and he has fallen in love with his wife ; so Pamphilus *huc transtulit amorem postquam par ingenium nactus est* (169).
We cannot say, although it seems likely, that Kantharos also was
married off to keep him from a hetaira.   It seems certain, however, that his protestation of fidelity is caused by his wife's supposed
infidelity which has been demonstrated by the maidservant.

   What is the relation between this act beginning and the end
of the preceding act ?   There two persons discuss recognition
tokens (one certainly a man).   The tokens themselves are normal
—a bit of a cloak, necklaces, anklet, and a piece of inscribed
clay [1] (cup ?) ;   necklaces and anklets are the gifts of the mother
but do not necessarily prove that the baby is a girl.   They are
taken out of a box which was sealed and it is then resealed.   ' The
mother was preserving them.   Put them back as they were.   I
will seal them.   It is not convenient now to try to solve the
riddle ' ;   then something about the present confusion and getting
control of oneself.   It is certain that the owner or carrier of the
box is not present.   For this the *Cistellaria* (Menander's *Synaristosai*) provides a parallel : there the servant Halisca is given the
box of Selenium's tokens by Melaenis, drops it in her agitation
when she goes into the house, and it is found by Lampadio and
Phanostrata (637, 655).   There Phanostrata recognises the tokens
as belonging to her daughter ; here one speaker recognises the
seal, but the tokens themselves apparently mean nothing to either
of them and they do not guess the identity of the child's mother

---

[1] l. 10 must read τί δέ ; κέραμος.   The lamp is required for reading small
letters as in Aristophanes, *Nub.*, 18.   For the ' inscribed clay ', cf. the ' lettered
cup ' of Euboulos (188/69).

or father. The probable interpretation of the scrappy first lines [1]
seems to me to be : ' (the seal) of my wife's (ring) . . . If she
gave it to the woman and *she* used it for sealing the box, has it
anything to do with my wife ? ' If this is right ' the woman '
is not the speaker's wife but has deposited the box before she went
into one of the houses. We must assume that the child will
prove to be the child of Kantharos and his wife : therefore one
of the speakers may be Kantharos' father-in-law since the tokens
must reveal the father of the child and Kantharos himself would
recognise them. As in the *Epitrepontes* and *Hecyra*, the young
husband violated his wife before his marriage without recognising
her ; he has now either to accept a five months child (cf. *Epitr.*,
758) or to believe her unfaithful. Some trouble has already
arisen between the two households since the ' present confusion '
is mentioned ; perhaps the young wife had gone home to have
her child and left Kantharos ?

A papyrus newly published by Schubart [2] may come from
the same codex. It only contains ends of lines on one side and
beginnings on the other, but on the recto Kantharos is addressed
in the vocative and there is talk of a male (child), this sword,
violation, and a nurse. This seems to put it somewhere near
the Antinoopolis leaf which we have been discussing. On the
verso a woman (perhaps a servant) and two other persons discuss
something which she apparently had and which they claim and
are to keep until the rightful owner, who is somehow connected
with them, is found. If the sword is a recognition token as in
the *Rudens* (1156) and Menander's *Encheiridion* the following
reconstruction is possible. The two persons who looked at the
box of tokens and probably by now have discovered that the
baby belongs to Kantharos' wife meet the servant, who is probably also the girl's nurse ; the little sword was among the recognition tokens and (verso) they now drag it out of its sheath
into which it has rusted ; the blade is clean and reveals a name
(Kantharos' father ?) ; they then interrogate the maidservant
who reappears. She tells them that someone violated the girl
nine months ago, leaving the little sword with her. The inscription implicates either Kantharos or his brother ; they accordingly
interrogate Kantharos (recto).

---

[1] In l. 3 something like διὰ τήνδε γ᾽ ἐπεβέβλητ᾽ ἐκεῖ.
[2] *Ber. Sächs. Ak.*, xcvii-5, no. 23. Cf. *C.R.*, 1952, 57.

The sequence of events that we can see is as follows : (1) Kantharos' wife flies to her mother's house to have her child and Kantharos finds her gone ; hence the estrangement between the houses ; (2) the nurse instead of exposing the baby takes it to Kantharos leaving the tokens outside ; (3) the father-in-law finds the tokens and goes into his house to find what this means ; (4) *New Act*. Kantharos is told by the nurse that his wife was violated before her marriage ; (5) the father-in-law discovers that the sword may implicate Kantharos and extracts the story of the rape from the nurse ; (6) he interrogates Kantharos himself and so identifies him as the father of the baby. As we have seen, the play owes much to the *Cistellaria* and *Epitrepontes* and, as Mr. Roberts says, Menander is a possible author. But the likeness of Kantharos to Pamphilus in the *Hecyra* and the behaviour of the father-in-law (I cannot help thinking that his associate is Kantharos' father) suggests to me Apollodoros and that is the justification for including it here.

The third papyrus cannot be ascribed with any certainty to Apollodoros but it seems at least to have more affinities with him than any of the other writers whom we know. It is a papyrus of about 200 B.C. from Ghoran [1] with fragments of six scenes from which a good deal of the play can be reconstructed. The reason for including it here is that its likeness to the *Phormio* first suggested to me its probable interpretation. There we have a trio of conspirators, Phormio, Antipho, and Phaedria ; here a trio, Nikeratos, Phaidimos, Chairestratos. Nikeratos takes the place of Phormio ; in Menander's *Samia* the name is given to an elderly man, and Nikeratos might therefore belong to the class of elderly helpers like Chaireas in two plays of Menander.[2] But names were not absolutely fixed : Nikeratos in another fragment (K., iii/361/1) seems to be young, and Philinos is old in Menander (*Perik.*, 448) but young in Apollodoros (290/7). Nikeratos may therefore be a helpful young friend. His rather effusive greeting of Phaidimos, ' dearest of friends, embrace me, please', suggests that like Strepsiades in the *Clouds* (81) he has to explain something to Phaidimos that Phaidimos will not like.

---

[1] 65P ; 22–3D ; 4S. Schroeder and Demianczuk number the line on the assumption that ϱ against l. 15P signifies l. 100. Prof. E. G. Turner informs me that there is no parallel for this method of enumerating lines ; and no play could reach the middle of the intrigue in 100 lines.

[2] *Koneiazomenai* and *Heauton Penthon*, cf. *Studies in Menander*, 53 f., 146.

Phaidimos, however, believes that Nikeratos has married the girl whom he loves ;[1] over fifty lines is occupied with this quarrel, which is finally resolved by Chairestratos. A quarrel between friends of this kind we know from Menander's *Dis Exapaton* (*Bacch.*, 534). The loyalty of friends is a real value and Phaidimos thinks that to wrong your friend and look him in the eyes needs more courage than to fight ; there is a double reminiscence here of the young Neoptolemos in Sophocles' *Philoctetes* (110) and Phaedra's description in the *Hippolytus* (415) of women who wrong their husbands. Phaidimos has made one of those false assumptions which are common in Apollodoros ; Nikeratos has no intention of marrying the girl but is trying to make it possible for Phaidimos to marry her.

With the help of the *Phormio* we can at least make a probable suggestion of how part of the play runs. At the beginning Phaidimos told Nikeratos that he loved (and had violated ?)[2] the daughter of X, who, however, had promised to give her to someone else when he returned from abroad. Nikeratos lives in one of the stage houses (179S ; 86P) ; X in another (why else should he return here ?) ; and Phaidimos in a third (at the end of the preserved act according to Jouguet's very probable restoration[3] Chairestratos and Phaidimos go in together and clearly at this moment they can visit neither X nor Nikeratos) ; three houses on the stage are also needed for Apollodoros' *Hecyra*. The third conspirator, Chairestratos, is not the brother of Phaidimos (165S ; 72P) and therefore he is probably the son of X with his own troubles to conceal from his father ; Chairestratos in Menander's *Epitrepontes* and *Eunuch* was in love with a hetaira and this may be traditional. News then came that X was arriving at the harbour. Probably X's slave brought it to Chairestratos and Phaidimos was also told. Phaidimos begged Chairestratos to go to the harbour (22) and plead with X, but Chairestratos missed him (as he tells us when he returns (160S ; 67P)). It seems likely that Phaidimos, like Antipho (218) in the *Phormio*, then ran away and left Chairestratos and the slave

---

[1] Page's reading ἠξίωκας (from Schroeder and Sudhaus) seems to me essential in 149S, 56P.

[2] Cf. the Vienna papyrus 29811 ; Oellacher, no. 22.

[3] Körte (*Hermes*, 1908, 44) says that 180S = fr. 23D cannot join on here because Phaidimos has to hear Chairestratos' explanation ; but if the audience already knows, the friends can tell each other off the stage.

to solve his problems : this is the meaning of Nikeratos' later remark ' as I did not meet Phaidimos anywhere, he has turned back and stood his ground '.[1] When Phaidimos had gone, Chairestratos and the slave worked out the plan perhaps with Nikeratos himself : the details are unclear but it seems certain that the story for X was that Nikeratos had violated X's daughter and was prepared to marry her (100S ; 15P with 149S ; 56P), so that the girl is assumed to be in Nikeratos' house by the time X arrives ; whether she actually is, we cannot say, but perhaps it is more probable that she is concealed in X's own house. When the plan had been made, Chairestratos went on his fruit-less errand to the harbour, Nikeratos also fruitlessly went to find Phaidimos to tell him the plan, the slave probably went into X's house to tell his mistress to hide the girl. Here the act should end.

Our fragment begins soon after the beginning of the new act with the slave speaking back to his mistress through the door ; he has evidently told her the story. The story has got out ; we need not ask how ; we have noticed in Apollodoros that char-acters sometimes know more than they should to save repetition before the audience ; Phaidimos arrives knowing it and is furious with the slave, but the slave cannot explain because X arrives. Phaidimos overhears the short dialogue—at most 20 lines—between X and the slave. This must have been very like Demipho's entry in the *Phormio* (231) ; the tone of *iniussu meo* is exactly repeated by τίνος κελεύσαντος ; how the intrigue develops and what further complications are involved we cannot say.

Another play which may possibly be ascribed to Apollodoros is the original of Plautus' *Epidicus*. The date is fixed by the allusion to Thebes (206) : *a legione omnes remissi sunt domum Thebis.* Thebes was destroyed by Alexander in 335 B.C., rebuilt and resettled by Cassander in 316 B.C., captured by Demetrios Poliorketes in 293 B.C., revolted from him in 292 B.C., and

---

[1] 106S, 20P : μεμένηκα can hardly be right here ; if Jouguet's original reading μεμένηκεν is palaeographically impossible, there may be some further corruption. I have assumed that τὸ διὰ χρόνον (113S) means ' the length of our friendship '. Körte, *loc. cit.*, took it as ' our long separation ' (cf. Menander, 13K ; Telekleides, 38K) ; if that is right, Nikeratos presumably returned with X and must have been told of Phaidimos' love before he went away and have made his proposal during the voyage.

was besieged by him and fell in 291 B.C. Wilamowitz [1] therefore
suggested 290 B.C. and Hueffner fixed the limits as 292/289.
Demetrios is likely to have had Athenian help, as on the second
occasion the younger Antigonos actually went from Athens to
quell the revolt. Stratippocles served Demetrios, though apparently ingloriously (29 f.). His father, Periphanes, won great
riches in his youth by fighting for ' the kings ' (450). Perhaps
neither the plural nor the title should be stressed, but the reference
might be to Antigonos and Demetrios in the years before Ipsos.
Periphanes met Philippa in Epidaurus, but their daughter Telestis
was born in Thebes (636) ; it seems possible that Periphanes was
serving with Cassander when he took Epidaurus in 317 B.C.,
and that Philippa, described as at that time *virgo paupercula*
(555), was a Theban exile who returned in 316 B.C. when
Cassander rebuilt Thebes.

The dates seem to support each other. Menander died in
292 B.C. and can therefore almost certainly be excluded as an
author ; Diphilos is unlikely as we cannot trace him long after
300 B.C.[2] and the *Epidicus* shows none of his characteristics. The
possibilities therefore are Philemon, Apollodoros, or another.
The problem is not soluble. But an examination of the *Epidicus*
may show something of its relation to other comedies and
therefore something of its own quality. The play opens with a
dialogue of two slaves : Epidicus, the old slave of Periphanes
who had brought Periphanes' birthday gifts to Telestis in Thebes
(639), and Thesprio, the young slave who has been to Thebes
with Periphanes' son Stratippocles. Thesprio takes no further
part in the action, although he is once named later (657 f.), but
(unlike Grumio in the *Mostellaria* or Davos in the *Phormio*) he
provides essential information : Stratippocles has fallen in love
while abroad and has brought the girl back (like Charinus in
the *Mercator*), and proposes to send her to his friend and neighbour's house (so Clinias in the *Heautontimoroumenos* uses Chremes'
house on his return). The girl turns out to be his half-sister
Telestis, and this fact must have been communicated to the
audience in a divine prologue. During his absence Epidicus has
secured for him his former love the harpist Acropolistis by

---

[1] *Antigonos von Karystos*, 242.
[2] The correspondences noted by Marx in his edition of the *Rudens*, 315, are
too slight to be significant.

R

persuading Periphanes to buy her under the impression that she
was his daughter, Telestis. Epidicus acted on the assumption
that Stratippocles would remain loyal, again like Clinias in
Heautontimoroumenos ; Epidicus' deceit can hardly have been acted
as Kunst [1] thinks, but may very well be a reminiscence of an
earlier comedy like the law-suit similarly narrated in the first scene
of the *Phormio* ; this is one of the marks of the later comedies.
Epidicus' final appreciation of the situation (81) belongs to a
well-known type of slave monologue,[2] although here recast by
Plautus into lyric form. Pseudolus similarly soliloquises when
Calidorus leaves him (394 f.), and Megas in the papyrus fragment
attributed above to Philemon passes through the same stages
but with elaborate imagery ; [3] Epidicus' soliloquy is more like
Menander than Philemon.

A papyrus fragment [4] of which the authorship is unfortunately
uncertain shows us a similar situation. A young man is talking
to his slave. He has apparently decided not to marry a girl
who is already living with him although she is the daughter
of a respected citizen and he has already received part of the
dowry. He leaves the slave to deal with the situation, and
then the father arrives from the country to hold the marriage
ceremony. Like Stratippocles the young man has changed his
love since it seems clear that his marriage was a love match.
The slave, like Epidicus, is left to think out a stratagem and decides
that he cannot abandon his master : like Epidicus, he addresses
himself : ' Now, Daos, it is no good lying down and giving up.
That's funk. But you must try everything first that he may
recognise how rare a prize you are. It is a big enough job. To
deceive a master and get hold of a flute girl is the job of a new
arrival. I have done that once or twice but this needs no small
thought.' There is here a clear echo of Menander's *Perinthia*
(393K) where Daos speaks with scorn of the slave who cheats
an idle and light-witted master ; and Plautus remodelled a
similar sentiment of a Menander slave in the *Bacchides* (649)
when Chrysalus says : *non mihi isti placent Parmenones, Syri,
qui duas aut tris minas auferunt eris.* The papyrus is clearly in

---

[1] *Op. cit.*, 168.
[2] Cf. *Studies in Menander*, 37, 189, and above, p. 143, on Philemon.
[3] Cf. Theiler, *Hermes*, 1938, 288.
[4] 62P. Another example is 68P.

the tradition of Menander and Epidicus' soliloquy belongs to the same tradition.

The two young men, Stratippocles and Chaeribulus, then arrive. Stratippocles, having been in love with Acropolistis until he went away, is now in love with Telestis. This kind of fickleness is perhaps implied in Moschion of the *Perikeiromene* and Clitipho in the *Heautontimoroumenos* and stated of Aeschinus in the *Adelphi* (149) but is not portrayed on the stage. The only other actual presentation of a shift in love is the picture of Pamphilus in Apollodorus' *Hecyra* and perhaps also in the Antinoopolis papyrus which we have already discussed. It is inevitable that we should ask how this story worked out in the end. Stratippocles, like several young men in Menander, has respected the innocence of Telestis because he wants to marry her ; he finds himself in the position of Moschion in the *Peri-keiromene* [1] when she turns out to be his sister. It is true that marriage with half-sisters was possible in Athens but we have no instance of its happening in comedy and no reason to suppose that it was regarded as desirable.[2] The echo of Moschion's cry ' if she is my sister, I am utterly ruined, poor wretch ' (*Perik.*, 348) by *perdidisti et repperisti me soror* [3] (652) suggests that the same end awaits both young men and that neither Epidicus' solution that Stratippocles can satisfy himself with Acropolistis nor the modern opinion [4] that after his distress he is nevertheless married to Telestis is tenable. Plautus has shortened the play considerably, particularly at the end. The second act starts with the entrance of Apoecides and Periphanes (166) and ends when Epidicus sets off to the agora after handing over the money to Stratippocles (381). The third act starts with the return of Apoecides from the forum (382) and ends with Periphanes' departure to the forum to look for the real Telestis (606). Plautus has therefore compressed the fourth and fifth acts of the original into two short scenes. We cannot be certain of the sequence of happenings, but that the soldier returned and paid Periphanes for Acropolistis seems likely, since this has been so

---

[1] Cf. Therapontigonus in the *Curculio*, and the instances noted above, p. 222 f.

[2] Cf. Fredershausen, *Hermes*, 1912, 202, and most recently Keyes, *T.A.P.A.*, lxxi, 217.

[3] Cf. Fraenkel, *op. cit.*, 317.

[4] e.g. Mesk, *W.S.*, xlvii, 65 ; Wehrli, *Motivstudien*, 37, n. 1.

carefully forecast (153, 300, 492). Periphanes marries Philippa, or at least takes her as his *pallake*. Menander's *Hiereia* ended with a triple marriage, and here Chaeribulus may have married Telestis and Stratippocles may have been given a sister of Chaeribulus. Stratippocles, who moves lightly from one love to another, was thus finally settled like Moschion in the *Perikeiromene*, and marriage had been planned for him from very early in the play (190).

The scene between the two young men (104 f.) opens with a line which echoes the two young men in the *Pseudolus* (694). There are some points which are worth noting in this scene. The type is common and we know the *sodalis opitulator* from Menander, Philemon, and Apollodoros. In Menander the firm basis of friendship may be broken by a passing jealousy arising from misunderstanding as in the *Perinthia* and *Bacchides*, but there is nothing in Menander or Philemon like the ingratitude of Stratippocles, who accepts Chaeribulus' home as a refuge for Telestis and taunts him because he does not also provide her purchase money (117, 330). Nor is there anything quite like the coolness with which Stratippocles tells Epidicus that his labours have been wasted and threatens him with hard labour if he does not produce the price of Telestis before the moneylender demands it (132 ff.).

The scene between the two young men is linked to the scene between their fathers, as Duckworth has noted, by a common criticism : 107 CHAERIBULUS, *idne pudet te* ; 168 APOECIDES, *quid est quod pudendum siet*.[1] If the date accepted for the *Epidicus* is right, we know four other plays of the early third century with similar quartets, Menander's *Heautontimoroumenos* and *Adelphi* (the adopted son clearly takes after his adoptive father rather than his real father there), Philemon's *Trinummus*, and Apollodoros' *Phormio*. Menander is concerned with the problem of education in both plays, but particularly in the *Adelphi* where the issue between repression and freedom is clearly stated.[2] Neither of the other two plays raises this question. Menander's sympathy lies with freedom rather than with repression and therefore with the milder, more idealistic and less conventional father, and his son turns out the steadier character who makes a love match with every prospect of success. In Philemon and

---

[1] 165 f. recalls *Andria*, 638.   [2] See *Studies in Menander*, 65 f., 209 f.

Apollodoros, however, the steadier son is the son of the steadier father and vice versa. Philemon does not develop the contrast between the fathers; in Apollodoros' *Phormio*, Demipho is shrewd and calculating while Chremes is an optimistic opportunist. In the *Epidicus* also the father of the wild son has had a wild youth behind him (386 f.), which he himself recalls like Laches in Menander's *Kitharistes* (59) and introduces his description with an image borrowed with variation from Menander (*Ad.*, 415). Apoecides was perhaps a member of the Areopagus in the original (292, 522) like Kleainetos in the *Koneiazomenai* (*Fab. inc.* 11) ; [1] he is a *polypragmon* and he goes off to help a friend in the agora (422) like Chremes in the *Heautontimoroumenos* (498 f.) ; he advises Periphanes to get his son married (190) ; Periphanes is as grateful for his help as Menedemus in Menander's play (425 = *Heauton.*, 502) and like Menedemus also takes a certain delight in his efficient friend's later discomfiture (522 = *Heauton.*, 874). He also like Menedemus had been to the wars in his youth (433, 450 = *Heauton.*, 111). The likeness of the *Heautontimoroumenos* to this play is very clear and extends further to the formula with which Epidicus insinuates himself into the confidence of the old men (255 = *Heauton.*, 585) and perhaps even to the complication of the intrigue itself. But although the two old men are a contrasting pair of the same kind as Menedemus and Chremes, the contrast between the sons simply repeats in less detail the contrast between the fathers as in the *Phormio*, and this is emphasised by the common criticism already quoted (107 = 168), whereas Menander was at least as much interested in the sons as in the old men, but was particularly concerned with the relations between the sons and the old men and its effect on the sons. This question does not arise in the *Epidicus*, and it would be unreasonable to suppose that Plautus was responsible for suppressing all reference to it. It is much easier to suppose that the original was in this respect more like the *Phormio* than the *Heautontimoroumenos*. There Chremes is intent on finding his lost daughter and Demipho on marrying her to his son in the interests of family solidarity. Here Periphanes is intent on finding his lost daughter and her mother, and prepared probably, as we have suggested, to cement relationships by cross-marriages with the family of Apoecides. Menander's

---

[1] Demipho in the *Synaristosai* was a member of the *Boule* (*Cist.*, 776).

Hiereia has already been quoted as a parallel ; there the old man marries the mother of his children and the children are married into the neighbouring family. In his *Georgos* it is extremely probable that Myrrhine marries the father of her children ; and the subsequent marriage of the girl raped in youth to her raper recurs in his *Heros* and *Synaristosai* ; in the *Synaristosai*, as in the *Epidicus*, the father has had another wife who dies before he returns to the mother of his children. As far as we know, the mother of grown-up children who finally marries her ravisher only occurs in the Menander plays and the *Epidicus* ; in the *Phormio*, Chremes' wife is very much alive and so the mother has conveniently to die. Only the *Phormio* and the *Epidicus* give evidence that the father made some provisions for his child in the early stages of its life.

The first dialogue between the two old men (166 f.) is almost unintelligible as it stands. They are not named ; Apoecides starts by discussing Philippa and then they lapse into conventional denigration of Periphanes' dead wife ; Epidicus arrives and Apoecides suddenly says, 'He had better be married at once,' referring to Stratippocles. Plautus has embroidered the conventional denigration and preserved the minimum of the original chain of thought, which runs :

PERIPHANES : 'I want to find and marry Philippa but I feel some shame before my legitimate son.'

APOECIDES : 'You can get him out of the way by marrying him off.'

PERIPHANES : 'That is a good plan because I do not like the stories of his being mixed up with a hetaira.'

If two old men arrive talking, they should come from somewhere else, and it is difficult to believe that Apoecides was at home when Thesprio arrived (67 f.) and Chaeribulus brought Stratippocles to his house (102). Neither have they been to the agora, because they both accept Epidicus' news as news (206). The simplest solution would be to suppose that Apoecides arrives from the country and goes straight to visit Periphanes who has been at home all the time. Apoecides probably entered soliloquising, summoned Periphanes out and the dialogue about Philippa then developed.

When Periphanes accepts Apoecides' suggestion that Stratippocles had better be saved from Acropolistis by matrimony,

Epidicus seizes on this situation as the basis of his intrigue. His immediate objects are to have money to pay the Theban money-lender for Telestis and to keep Apoecides away from his house for as long as possible. Periphanes wants Acropolistis out of the way because on his premises she is the chief obstacle to Stratippocles' marriage. So Epidicus pretends to arrive with the news that the soldiers are back from Thebes, Acropolistis is waiting at the harbour, and Stratippocles has borrowed money in Thebes to buy her freedom. The *servus currens* has a long ancestry which goes back to the messenger in the *Birds*[1] but is only used here to support a fiction ; the fiction is a blend of false and true—Stratippocles has returned and has borrowed money in Thebes ; but Acropolistis is in Periphanes' house and Stratippocles has no intention of buying her—rather like the first deceit of Chrysalus in the *Dis Exapaton* (*Bacch.*, 243 ff.). The old men believe it and therefore go on to accept Epidicus' advice to buy the imaginary Acropolistis at once ; she will agree if Periphanes pretends to be in love with her and therefore to be buying her freedom (275 ff.)—here there is a clear reference to the *Mercator*, and as in the *Mercator* Periphanes is not to appear but the transaction is to be carried out by Apoecides. The plan is the more acceptable because the girl can be sold to a Rhodian soldier ; here again is an element of truth because a soldier (Euboean not Rhodian) is in love with the real Acropolistis.

The plan will achieve Epidicus' two immediate objects, but to carry it out he must produce a bogus Acropolistis. But here we have a series of statements which do not cohere. When both old men have gone, Epidicus remains on the stage and considers how he can produce a bogus Acropolistis. 'I know ; in the morning the old man told me to hire a harpist to sing for him while he sacrificed ; she shall be hired and indoctrinated so that she can deceive the old man' (314 f.). The whole monologue is suspicious as the first six lines are Plautine in imagery. We cannot, however, say that it must be Plautine because Epidicus fails to go in when summoned ; that can be paralleled from many comedies, but it is against all the conventions that Epidicus should quote an order of which we have never heard and for which there is no reason ; Periphanes has shown no signs of

[1] Cf. above, p. 143.

wanting a flute girl and will accept the girl when she comes as Acropolistis. Next, in the scene with the two young men (363 f.) Epidicus says that he will persuade the *leno*, who had owned the real Acropolistis, to say that he has been paid 50 minae (this is an insurance in case the careful Apoecides tries to make sure that the girl has really been bought; it is not used and is probably a reference to a deceit in an earlier play which has not survived); Epidicus will hire a harpist and indoctrinate her so that she can trick the two old men, who will assume that she has been bought; the indoctrination theme alone survives from the earlier monologue and is again a back reference to a deceit of the type which we know from the *Persa*.[1] Later, Apoecides, when he returns with the flute girl, says (410 ff.) that Epidicus had told her she was being hired for the thanksgiving sacrifices which Periphanes was going to offer for the return of his son; finally the flute girl herself (500) shows no sign of having been indoctrinated but simply says that she was hired to sing while the old man made his sacrifice. She is speaking the truth and this was the reason given to her by Epidicus. Apoecides assumed that it was a fiction to persuade Acropolistis to come (and therefore also assumed that Epidicus had dropped the earlier fiction that Periphanes was in love with her?) and adds the detail that the sacrifice was to be a thanksgiving for Stratippocles' return, which would be particularly attractive to Acropolistis. It follows that the reference to Periphanes' morning command for a harpist is Plautine preparation for Epidicus' ultimate fiction; we have a parallel in the *Pseudolus* where Plautus introduces words which suggest that Pseudolus has made his plan before in fact he has made it (385). The Greek Epidicus had three ideas, all probably from earlier comedy: (1) Periphanes as his son's rival; (2) *leno* insurance; (3) indoctrination; and dropped them all, merely telling the girl that she was to help the thanksgiving sacrifice, which Apoecides accepted as a brilliant bait to lure Acropolistis into Periphanes' clutches.

The intrigue is brilliant and complicated and ensures at least a respite. Epidicus has no reason to suspect that Telestis is Periphanes' daughter; it is reasonable to hope that Periphanes' daughter will turn up soon after Stratippocles is established with

---

[1] Cf. Wehrli, *Motivstudien*, 37.

his girl and then in the general rejoicings the real Acropolistis, who has been impersonating Periphanes' daughter, can be sold off to the soldier and everybody will be forgiven. Events turn out differently ; the soldier refuses to accept the flute girl as Acropolistis and Philippa refuses to accept Acropolistis as her daughter, but all is saved because Epidicus recognises Telestis. The breakdown in the plan does not mean that Epidicus is a bad planner like the extemporising Tranio of the *Mostellaria*, who is only rescued by the eloquence of his young master's friend ; many of Menander's master-intriguers fail in their first attempts and have to try another way (e.g. *Andria*, 670) and they may be saved by chance rather than by design. The actual revelations by the soldier and Philippa recall the pair of scenes in Philemon's *Mostellaria* in which Theoropides first learns from Phaniscus what his son has been doing in his absence (933 ff.) and then from Simo that there has never been any question of buying Simo's house (993). The arrival of Philippa (526) is very like the entrance of Sophrona in the *Phormio* (729) and Crito in the *Andria* (796 f.) and the actual recognition is paralleled many times in Menander. The two final scenes of the play, as we have suggested, probably represent two acts of the original, and we cannot tell in detail how they worked out.

Our examination has shown us points of contact with Menander (particularly the *Heautontimoroumenos*, and the *Hiereia*) and with Philemon and Apollodoros. Menander seems to be excluded by the date, but the author must have been very strongly influenced by Menander. To argue that it is inconceivable that the original of *Epidicus* could have been written by Philemon at some date between the *Trinummus* and the *Captivi* would be rash ; yet in the three plays which survive Plautus has reproduced both the imagery and the moralising which we know from the Greek fragments of Philemon, and here both elements are strikingly absent as a comparison of Epidicus' monologue (81 f.) with the papyrus fragment attributed to Philemon shows. No such obstacles stand in the way of attributing the play to Apollodoros, whom we know to have been an imitator of Menander. Phormio is as formidable an intriguer as Epidicus ; the only parallel outside Menander for the relations of Periphanes, Philippa, and Telestis is in the *Phormio* ; Stratippocles is a ' double lover ' like Pamphilus in the *Hecyra*. The old men

and their sons form a quartet more like that of the *Phormio*
than of any other play. The evidence is not conclusive : the
play is certainly by an imitator of Menander and may be by
Apollodoros. *Paralogizomenoi*, 'Drawers of false conclusions',
might be the title.

APPENDIX ON 'ASINARIA'

HUEFFNER [1] suggested a date after 294 B.C. when Demetrios Poliorketes became King of Macedonia, since the references to Arcadian asses and merchants from Rhodes and Pella (333, 499) imply peace on the sea and in the North ; he also notes that *Salus* (712) may represent the title *Soter* assumed by several of the Diadochi. Fraenkel [2] has, however, suggested that the *Salus* passage is Plautine, and the other indication would fit many years between 294 B.C. and Plautus' play. As long as Demophilos himself remains undateable, we have no safe external evidence to give us a closer date than 294/190 B.C. We can then only ask what are the peculiarities of this play and on what originals does it depend.

The father Demaenetus appears at first sight to be a new figure, but closer inspection shows him to be a combination of elements in preceding figures into a not very convincing whole. In the first scene he appears both as indulgent father and henpecked husband. For the former we can see three ancestors in the preserved comedies. The theme of heredity running through three generations (68 f.) has already appeared in the *Heautontimoroumenos* [3] (111). The father who helps his son to 'achieve his love' is already known to Euripides (*Hipp.*, 465, etc.). The story of the father who disguised himself as a sailor to get his son the hetaira (68 f.) [4] is founded on the original of the *Miles*, by conflating the elderly helper Periplectomenus with the young lover, Pleusicles, who actually carries out the trick ; *neque puduit eum id aetatis sycophantias struere* (71) in particular recalls the *Miles* [5] (618 f.). Demaenetus' behaviour to his son (74 f.) reads

---

[1] *Op. cit.*, 69.   [2] *Op. cit.*, 116.

[3] Perhaps from this play also the use of a slave to help the son in his love affair (*Heautont.*, 470 f., 330 ff.).

[4] I do not think it is necessary to suppose that this theme comes either from an earlier play of Demophilos (Leo, *Hermes*, xviii, 564 ; Kunst, *op. cit.*, 156) or from the *Naukleros* of Menander (Dietze, *op. cit.*, 79). Dietze argues ingeniously that Strato (348K = *As.*, 344) the father of Demaenetus dressed up as a *naukleros* to steal D. the hetaira from the other brother Theophilos, whom he takes to be a *nothos* (350K). 350K refers to a father's hatred for his son rather than a quarrel between brothers ; the name Strato may be a coincidence and we have no evidence that Plautus is not responsible for it rather than Demophilos. The Caecilius fragment (Ribbeck, 55/III) suggests that a hetaira was stolen but not that a father stole her.

[5] Another echo of this part of the *Miles* at 814 = *Miles*, 652.

almost like a parody of Micio in the *Adelphi* (50 f., 147 f., 821 f.) because Micio's indulgence is due to a theory of education, while Demaenetus indulges his son to win affection for himself. Micio and Periplectomenus are unmarried, and Periplectomenus discourses at length on the disadvantages of matrimony (678 f.) ; Demaenetus has married an heiress and so belongs to the succession of henpecked husbands after Strepsiades of the *Clouds* ; in particular he reminds us of the husband in Menander's *Plokion* (403K), whose wife is ' master of the house and the fields . . . cruel to all, not only to me, much more to my son, and to my daughter '. Artemona does not, however, use her husband to look after her estates like Nausistrata in the *Phormio*, but has a slave, Saurea, whom she has brought with her from her father and whom Demaenetus is perfectly prepared to cheat ; this also is probably traditional. At least the picture on a South Italian vase of the early fourth century [1] is most easily interpreted as an heiress wife with her bailiff checking the accounts brought by her old husband from the farm. Later on (734), we find surprisingly yet another traditional theme included in Demaenetus' character, although it is scarcely compatible with his desire to help his son—rivalry between father and son for the same girl, which had been the central interest of Philemon's *Emporos* and Diphilos' *Kleroumenoi*.[2] Here it comes in irrelevantly and unexpectedly for the sake of the later scenes of the play. Demaenetus is compounded of traditional elements. Two further points in the first scene may be more individual. Kunst [3] explains the fact that Demaenetus knows that Argyrippus needs 20 minae before Argyrippus knows it himself by Demophilos' looseness of structure. It is, however, possible that Plautus is responsible ; we have noticed similar difficulties in other plays.[4] Secondly Demophilos likes to give realism to his dialogue by naming people who will not appear on the stage : Artemona's bailiff is Saurea (85), the banker Archibulus (116), Leonida when he is pretending to be the bailiff mentions Stichus, Exaerambus, Dromo, Philodamus, Periphanes (435 f.), Artemona names the people with whom Daemaenetus says he dines : Archidemus, Chaerea, Chaerestratus, Clinia, Chremes, Cratinus, Dinia, Demosthenes (865). It is more artificial here than in the cook fragment which can probably be attributed to Philemon ; [5] there the list of guests is necessary for the joke, the host's inability to understand δαιτυμών. Here Demophilos is trying to make his scene more real.[6]

[1] Apulian bell krater, Leningrad : Heydemann, r ; Bieber, *H.T.*, fig. 383.
[2] Wehrli, *op. cit.*, 57, traces it back to the Old Comedy : of his instances Pherekrates, 71, 73K, are certainly relevant.
[3] *Op. cit.*, 155.   [4] Cf. above, p. 212, on *Pseudolus* (385).
[5] 57P. Cf. above, p. 145.   [6] Cf. also Euphron, 10K.

The excluded lover of the next scene is also traditional ; we know him best from Phaedria at the beginning of the *Eunuch*. The description of the *lena* as a sea (134) is one of the several links between this play and the *Truculentus* [1] (350). The impossible threat to reduce the *lena* to pristine poverty (139) recalls Demeas' genuine threat to Chrysis in the *Samia* (177). The scene between Cleareta and Argyrippus also reminds us of the scenes between Phronesium (or Astaphium) and her lovers in the *Truculentus* and of scenes between a young man and *leno*, e.g. in the *Pseudolus*.[2] Here we have the *improba lena* (attested for Menander by Ovid) behaving exactly like a *leno* ; so we can imagine the *lena* of the *Cistellaria* behaving, whereas in the same play Melaenis' conduct is justified by her suspicion that Alcesimarchus is going to be married. Argyrippus leaves to seek money from his friends in the agora. Here is the first mention of the 20 minae for a year's hire (230) and Cleareta suggests that Argyrippus may bring back a written contract if he wishes (238). This anticipates the later scene when Diabolus brings his contract (746) and Legrand [3] has therefore suggested that this whole scene should be given to Diabolus rather than to Argyrippus. This solution is impossible in this form. Traditionally we should see the young lover in the first act of the play. We must therefore suppose that either Demophilos or Plautus wanted to prepare for the later scene by mention of a contract here. We may also suppose that the actual mention of Diabolus is withheld just as Demaenetus' private desires are withheld until the poet wants a new theme. The difficulty does not end here. Argyrippus departs to the forum ; Libanus arrives from the forum without having met him and informs Leonida that he is 'here inside' (329). At the beginning of the Plautine third act (504) Cleareta flies out at Philaenium apparently because she has admitted Argyrippus since he comes out of her house soon afterwards (591) : he then knows that Diabolus has promised to give her 20 minae for a year's hire of Philaenium (634). A possible solution of the difficulties seems to me that, in the original, Cleareta goes out in search of customers after her first scene with Argyrippus (242) ; Argyrippus goes to the forum, meets Libanus and his father and tells them about his need of 20 minae ; at the beginning of the second act Argyrippus returns with Libanus and Libanus sends him in to Philaenium while he thinks out a plan—his opening monologue (249) has been slightly changed by Plautus and was in the original a link monologue between the departure of Argyrippus and the arrival of Leonida ; Cleareta

---

[1] Cf. above, p. 148.
[2] Cf. also 203 with Xenarchos, 4K ; 215 f., with Theophilos, 11K (Oeri, *Komische Alte*, 51).
[3] *New Greek Comedy*, 376.

returns at the beginning of the (Plautine) third act, and it seems to me quite possible that she comes on with Diabolus and that Plautus has in fact preserved the end of their brief scene together in the words about the contract in the first act (229-42) ; in this modified form Legrand's solution was right ; then Cleareta enters her house and sees Argyrippus, hence her fury with her daughter.

The scene between the two slaves (267) is full of traditional ideas. Leonida enters as a *servus currens*. The dialogue has parallels in the *Epidicus, Stichus, Persa*, and ultimately in the opening scene of Aristophanes' *Knights*. In the original Libanus was probably the white-haired slave and had been the paidagogos of Argyrippus ; Leonida is red-haired (400). The intrigue (350 f.) is borrowed partly from the *Truculentus* and partly from the *Pseudolus*. In the *Truculentus* (647), Strabax gives Phronesium the money that an unexpected and unsuspecting visitor has given him for his father's sheep ; here the money for Artemona's asses is diverted. In the *Pseudolus* (607) Pseudolus gets the essential document by pretending to be Ballio's major-domo ; here Leonida pretends to be Saurea and so diverts Artemona's money to Demaenetus. Leonida has to be got out of the way so that Libanus can confirm to the ass-dealer his identity as Saurea ; Demaenetus also has to be warned of the plot. Therefore an act break separates the departure of Leonida and the arrival of the ass-dealer. The ass-dealer accepts Leonida as Saurea because he recognises the description given by Libanus (400). Recognition by description we know from the *Pseudolus* (1218),[1] which Demophilos must have remembered, but he gives it a further twist by making it a false recognition. Presumably at the end of the scene in the original Leonida and Libanus accompany the merchant to the forum to meet Demaenetus. The rest of this act, the third of the original, was occupied by the return of Cleareta and her meeting with Diabolus.

The fourth act of the original (504) begins with the scene between Cleareta and Philaenium (a traditional clash reminiscent of the *Synaristosai* and ultimately of Sophocles' *Electra*), and continues with the farewell scene between Argyrippus and Philaenium (591) ; it seems to me at least possible that this was modelled on the name scene of Diphilos' *Synapothneskontes* (cf. particularly 606). The intervening slave dialogue (596 f.) is largely Plautine, and Plautus has also greatly extended the scene between the slaves, Argyrippus and Philaenium. We cannot now say how this was managed in the original ; possibly only Libanus came back from the agora and arrived in the scene between Argyrippus and Philaenium. But there is much more that is difficult to understand in the later scenes of the play. The announce-

---

[1] Cf. also *Poen.*, 1111 f. ; *Capt.*, 646.

ment of Demaenetus' demand is, as Wehrli [1] says, a well-thought-out comic effect : all seems to be clear for Argyrippus when this new obstacle is interposed. The arrival of the old man by the garden is surprising but not impossible, [2] and we cannot say that a scene has been suppressed here ; Prehn's note [3] that the need for secrecy is forgotten at the beginning of Act V is irrelevant because the first scene of Act V is in theory played indoors. The rigmarole of Diabolus' contract reminds us of the oracles, etc., in Aristophanes. Probably an act break separates his entry into Cleareta's house and his return (809/10). At the end of this scene the parasite plays the part of informer as in the *Menaechmi* (518, 560 f.) and in the *Phormio* (985 f.). When his master goes home, he must go into Demaenetus' house (827). His absence is masked by the banquet scene, which is not a genuine banquet scene but an interlude in which father and son appear outside Cleareta's house while the banquet is being prepared (828 f.). Then the parasite reappears with Artemona. The scene recalls the scene in the *Bacchides* (830 f.) where Chrysalus shows Nicobulus the banqueters and may well have been played in the same way : Artemona looks through the partly opened door and the voices of the banqueters are heard off. Suess [4] rightly compares Diphilos (73K) for dicing at a banquet. Then Artemona goes in (910) ; the parasite goes off with a hint that Diabolus may share Philaenium—a reminiscence of the *Eunuch* (1072). The final scene is probably played between Artemona, her husband, and her son.

The moral at the end—'the old man has done nothing extra-ordinary '—may well be the moral of the original. It certainly suits the whole tone of the play, which is uninterested in moral problems. Argyrippus and Philaenium are genuinely in love, but how little this interested Demophilos is clear from his introduction of the father's rivalry, which is the chief interest of the end of the play. Demaenetus is not a new character but a new mixture of old elements and for almost everything in the play we can point to an ancestor. The originals of the *Miles*, *Adelphi*, *Heautontimoroumenos* all probably belong to the beginning of the third century and the original of the *Truculentus* to the end of the fourth. These plays give the top date for Demophilos' *Onagos* ; how much later it is we cannot say.

[1] *Op. cit.*, 59, n. 1.

[2] Cf. Kunst, *op. cit.*, 155 : and on the use of the garden way above, p. 221 ; *Studies in Menander*, 89, 141 ; Beare, *Roman Stage*, 251.

[3] *Op. cit.*, 6.

[4] *Rh. Mus.*, 1910, 458 f.

CHRONOLOGICAL TABLE

(Dating of Middle Comedy plays is discussed in *C.Q.*, 1952, 13 ff., of Menander in *Studies of Menander*, 103 f.: see also heading 'Chronology' in the index. The table contains plays quoted in the text which can be approximately dated.) [1]

400–390 Aristophanes, *Pelargoi, Gerytades*. Plato, *Hellas*. Strattis, *Zopyros, Perikaiomenos, Kinesias, Makedones*. Theopompos, *Althaia, Stratiotides, Medos*.

394 Aristomenes, *Dionysos*.

393/2 Plato, *Presbeis*.

391. Plato, *Phaon*. Aristophanes, *Ekklesiazousai*.

390–80 Antiphanes, *Kyklops, Omphale*. Aristophanes, *Second Aiolosikon*. Nikochares, *Galateia*. Philyllios, *Anteia*. Plato, *Laios*. Theopompos, *Theseus, Aphrodisia*.

388 Aristophanes, *Ploutos*. Aristomenes, *Admetos*. Nikophon, *Adonis*. Alkaios, *Pasiphae*.

387 Aristophanes, *Kokalos*. Plato, *Women after Sacrifice*.

380–370 Anaxandrides, *Protesilaos, Herakles*. Antiphanes, *Anteia, Philometor*. Ephippos, *Homoioi*. Epikrates, *Antilais*. Euboulos, *Dionysios*. Philetairos, *Atalanta*. Strattis, *Atalanta*. Theopompos, *Admetos, Hedychares, Pamphile*.

374 Anaxandrides, *Io*.

373 Theopompos, *Eirene*.

380–360 Antiphanes, *Dyspratos*.

370–360 Alexis, *Ponera, Eisoikizomenos, Phaidros*. Anaxandrides, *Odysseus, Poleis*. Antiphanes, *Sappho, Stratiotes, Philothebaios, Antaios, Kleophanes*. Ephippos, *Geryones, Nauagos*. Euboulos, *Antiope, Sphingokarion*. Theopompos, *Nemeas*.

360–350 Alexis, *Galateia, Meropis, Milkon, Olympiodoros, Parasite, Traumatias*. Amphis, *Amphikrates, Dexidemides, Dithyrambos*. Anaxandrides, *Gerontomania*. Anaxilas, *Kirke*. Antiphanes, *Knoithideus, Plousioi, Didymai, Athamas, Kitharode, Korykos*. Aristophon, *Plato*. Axionikos, *Phileuripides*. Ephippos, *Peltast*. Kratinos, *Pseudhypobolimaios*. Philetairos, *Kynagis, Asklepios*.

360–340 Anaxandrides, *Amprakiotis*.

---

[1] Many of these plays are dated by G. Schiassi, *R.I.F.C.*, lxxix, 217 ff. This was only published when my list was already in proof. For the most part his datings are near mine. He, however, dates Timokles' *Orestautokleides* 345–4 (but Autokleides may well have been notorious for 15 years, and the hetairai are all old, Chrysis is at least a memory in *c.* 312 B.C., and Sinope is omitted and therefore is probably dead) and Philemon's *Neaira* to 324–3 (but the title need not be the name of a living *hetaira* and the absence of the royal title for Seleukos does not give a safe bottom date).

360–330 Antiphanes, *Hydria, Arkas.*
350–340 Alexis, *Adelphoi, Stratiotes, Sorakoi, Isostasion, Pankratiastes.* Amphis, *Kouris.* Anaxandrides, *Agroikoi, Tereus, Anchises, Nereus.* Anaxilas, *Euandria.* Antiphanes, *Neottis, Kares.* Axionikos, *Chalkidikos.* Euboulos, *Nannion.* Mnesimachos, *Philippos.* Sotades, *Paralytroumenos.* Timokles, *Kaunioi, Heroes.*
350–330 Euboulos, *Pornoboskos, Stephanopolides, Plangon.* Timokles, *Neaira.*
350–320 Alexis, *Thesprotoi.*
340–330 Alexis, *Lebes, Epidaurios, Agonis, Titthe.* Anaxilas, *Neottis.* Antiphanes, *Kitharistes, Halieuomene.* Euboulos, *Anasozomenoi.* Heniochos, (?) *Poleis.* Timokles, *Sappho.* Original of *Persa.*
340–20 Alexis, *Spondophoros, Dorkis, Mandragorizomene, Pontikos, Syntrechontes, Phaidon, Apokoptomenos, Milesia, Poietai, Demetrios, Olynthia, Odysseus Hyphainon.* Antiphanes, *Gorgythos.* Aristophon, *Pythagoristes.* Euboulos, *Kampylion.* Heniochos, *Polyeuktos.* Kratinos, *Titans.* Theophilos, *Iatros.* Timokles, *Polypragmon, Epichairekakos.*
340–310 Alexis, *Kouris.*
330–20 Alexis, *Tarantinoi, Krateuas* (i). Dionysios, *Thesmophoros.* Diphilos, *Enagismata, Synoris,* (?) *Kleroumenoi* (=*Casina*). Euphron, *Muses.* Philemon, *Babylonian, Lithoglyphos, Metion,* (?) *Emporos* (*Mercator*). Theophilos, *Boiotis.* Timokles, *Delos, Dionysos, Ikarioi, Lethe, Orestautokleides, Epistolai, Demosatyroi.* Original of *Amphitruo.*
321 Menander, *Orge.*
320–310 Alexis, *Synapothneskontes, Phryges.* Antiphanes, *Skythai.* Apollodoros (of Gela), *Hiereia, Sphattomene, Grammateidopoios.* Diphilos, *Gamos, Apoleipousa, Theseus.* Menander, *Kolax, Paidion, Apistos* (*Aulularia*), *Dis Exapaton* (*Bacchides*), *Samia, Pseudherakles, Androgynos, Kekryphalos, Perinthia, First Adelphoi* (*Stichus*), *Halieis, Heros, Synaristosai* (*Cistellaria*), *Perikeiromene, Aspis, Sikyonios, Georgos, Leukadia, Misoumenos.* Nikostratos, *Tokistes.* Philemon, *Phasma* (*Mostellaria*), *Philosophoi.* Theophilos, *Philaulos.* Timokles, *Philodikastes.*
320–300 Menander, *Theophoroumene, Hiereia, Karchedonios* (*Poenulus*), *Hydria, Hypobolimaios, Phasma.*
310–300 Diphilos (*Rudens*). Originals of *Curculio, Pseudolus.* Menander, *Thesauros, Andria, Eunuch.*
307 Alexis, *Hippeus.*
306/5 Alexis, *Krateuas* (ii).
302 Menander, *Imbrians.*
300–290 Alexis, *Pyraunos.* Antiphanes (ii), *Parekdidomene.* Demetrios, *Areopagite.* Menander, *Second Adelphoi, Heautontimoroumenos, Didymai, Epitrepontes.* Philemon, *Thesauros* (*Trinummus*), *Neaira.* Original of *Miles, Truculentus.*
300–270 Damoxenos, *Hauton Penthon, Syntrophoi.*
291 Antiphanes (ii), *Didymoi.*

290–280 Phoinikides, *Auletrides.* Original of *Epidicus.*
280–270 Alexis, *Hypobolimaios.* Apollodoros (of Karystos), *Epidikazomenos*
(*Phormio*). Philemon, *Panegyris.* Baton, *Synexapaton.* Original
of *Captivi.*
270–250 Baton, *Androphonos.*

INDEX LOCORUM

(This index includes references to lines of plays, fragments in Kock (K), Ribbeck (R), papyrus fragments in Page (P), Demianczuk (D), Schroeder (S), and elsewhere. Menander fragments are given the Kock numbers with the numbers of the Körte – Theirfelder text in brackets ; the new papyri are indexed under the plays in the General Index. Plays by Plautus and Terence are recorded under their names, not under the authors of the Greek originals.)

270

Index Locorum

GENERAL INDEX

(Except for Menander, plays are only quoted here when mentioned without reference to particular lines or fragments, for which see Index Locorum. Figures in *italics* denote chief passages.)

Academy : 6, 35, 51 f., 54 f., 105, 111.
actors, number of : 186 f., 199, 200.
Adaios : 64, 116.
Aeschines : 26, 39, 43, 45, 59, 80.
Aeschylus : 9, 50, 59, 82, 132, 168, 181, 228.
Aetolia : 146.
Agathokles : 104, 107, 154.
agriculture : 14, 32 f., 47, 49, 76.
Agyrrhios : xi, 25, 27.
Aisimos : 24, 27.
Aixone relief : 63, 75, 120 f.
Akragas : 154.
alazon : 53, 54, 57, 64, 66, 158, 179, 223.
Alexander : 42, 52, 91, 95, 121 f., 217, 223, 242.
Alexandria : 125.
Alexis : xii, 6, 39, 44 ff., 48, 53, 55, 57, 60, 62, 64 ff., 67, 72 ff., 76, 83, 105, 108, 111, 113, 125, 146, 210.
plays :
 Adelphoi : 72.
 Gynaikokratia : 62, 67.
 Lebes : 66, 214.
 Mandragorizomene : 76.
 Milesia : 77.
 Odysseus Hyphainon : 57.
 Pannychis : 83.
 Parasite : 6, 65.
 Ponera : 66.
 Stratiotes : 77.
 Tarantinoi : 53.
Alkaios : 12, 18, 22, 88, 161.
plays :
 Komoidotragoidia : 88.
 Palaistra : 22, 161.
Amphis : 39, 48, 50 f., 67, 75, 83.
plays :
 Dithyrambos : 83.
 Gynaikokratia : 67.
Anaxandrides : 6, 18, 30, 32, 39 f., 51, 56, 65 f., 72, 77, 83 f., 88, 146, 178.

Anaxandrides—plays:
 Agroikoi : 56 f.
 Amprakiotis : 77.
 Anteros : 83.
 Helen : 84.
 Herakles : 18.
 Io : 18.
 Kanephoros : 77.
 Komoidotragoidia : 88.
 Nereus : 6, 66.
 Samia : 77.
 Phialephoros : 77.
 Protesilaos : 18.
Anaxilas : 39, 44 f., 47, 61, 63, 75.
Andokides : 25, 29.
Anteia : 23.
Antidotos : 60.
Antigeneidas : 30.
Antigonos I : 105, 173, 218 ff.
Antigonos II : 108, 243.
Antiochos III : 109.
Antipater : 101, 103, 160.
Antiphanes : 6 f., 18, 20, 22 f., 39 f., 43 ff., 47, 49 f., 53 f., 56, 58, 60, 62, 64 ff., 68, 75, 77, 80, 83, 108, 132, 178.
plays :
 Agroikos : 56.
 Didymai : 68, 77, 178.
 Drapetagogos : 80.
 Dyspratos : 80.
 Parasite : 6.
 Philothebaios : 39.
 Poiesis : 56, 58, 83.
 Stratiotes : 6, 83, 174.
Anytos : 24, 27.
Apelles : 136.
Apollodoros (of Gela) : 104, 115, 181, 225 *ff.*
plays :
 Apoleipousa : 181.
 Pseudaias : 115.

272

Apollodoros (of Karystos) : 4 f., 39, 73, 100, 108, 110, 113, 115 ff., 123, 152, 183, 223, *225 ff.*
plays :
  Amphiareos : 115.
  Epidicus : see Plautus, *Epidicus.*
  Epidikazomenos (= Terence, *Phormio) :* 6, 65, 103, 110, 118, 203, *226 ff.*, 236 ff., 240 ff., 243, 246 f., 251.
  Hekyra (= Terence, *Hecyra*) : 103, 118,138,174,*223ff.*,239f.,244.
Apuleius : xiv, 135 138 f., 142.
Apulian Vases : xii, xiv, 77.
Archedikos : 103.
Archippos : *Nyx,* 95.
Argas : 30.
Aristippos : 35, 53.
Aristogeiton : xi, 45.
Aristomedes : 45, 127.
Aristomenes : 17 f.
plays :
  Admetos : 18.
  Dionysos Asketes : 17, 82.
Aristonikos : 46.
Aristophanes : 3 ff., 6, *10 ff.*, 23 ff., *32 ff.*, 49 f., 51, 58, 62, 70, 77, 96, 101, 175, 178, 197 f., 213
plays :
  Acharnians : 10, 13, 14, 24, 64, 80, 110, 132, 197 f.
  Aiolosikon : 15, *18.*
  Birds : 28 f., 41, 82, 92, 161, 198, 214 f., 249.
  Clouds : 15, 17, 33 f., 52 ff., 110, 136, 238, 240, 254.
  Ekklesiazousai : xi, 3, 5, 8, *10 ff.*, 15, 22 f., *32 f.*, 48, 51, 57 f., 69, 198, 215.
  Frogs : 4, 10, 17, 19, 26, 28, 34, 62, 67, 80, 160.
  Georgoi : 19.
  Gerytades : 10, 19, 28.
  Knights : 13, 15, 31, 80, 110, 130, 215, 256.
  Kokalos : 17, 77, 126 f.
  Lysistrata : 161.
  Peace : 4, 14 f., 161.
  Ploutos : xi, 3, 8, *14 ff.*, 23, 28, *32 f.*, 49, 58, 71, 80, 140, 198.
  Storks : 10, 19.
  First Thesmophoriazousai : 19, 135, 161.

Aristophanes—plays :
  Second Thesmophoriazousai : 17.
  Wasps : 178.
Aristophon (comic poet) : 50, 53, 65.
plays :
  Iatros : 68.
  Plato : 6.
  Pythagoristes : 6.
Aristophon (politician) : 39, 45.
Aristotle : xi, 4, 7 f., 13, 22, 25, 27, 38, 50, 54, 56 ff., 63 f., 71, 77, 84, 88, 113 ff., 123, 137, 141, 150 f., 160, 179, 187, 194.
  Ethics : 8, 38, 56, 137, 176, 179, 194.
  Poetics : 7 f., 21, 56 ff., 117, 141, 151, 187 ff.
  Politics : 56.
  Rhetoric : 56.
Aristyllos : 29, 35.
Arkesilaos : 111.
Arnaldi, F. : 216.
Astydamas : 126 f.
Attic terracottas : xii, 76, 85, 121, 132, 135, 161, 197.
Attic vases : xi, xii, 10 ff., 18, 29, 85, 121, 123.
audience : 101 ff., 139, 141, 191, 201.
Axionikos : 61, 66.

Barry, E. : 25.
Bataille, A. : 184.
Baton : 111.
Beare,W. : 160, 257.
Beazley, J. D. : 18, 41, 85, 87.
Bieber, M. : xii ff., 11, 69, 76, 77, 80, 85 f., 91, 119 ff., 135, 160, 184.
Bignone, E. : 113.
Blass, F. : 142.
bomolochos : 54, 56.
Bosporan kingdom : 41.
Bosscher, W. : 221.
brothel-keeper : see leno.
Bryson : 51.

Caecilius : 73, 99, 207.
Caldera : 86.
Campanian vases : xii, xiv, 77, 86 f., 161.
Capps, E. : 104, 225.
Caria : 217.
Cassander : 106, 210, 241.
Celts : 41 f.
Chabrias : 40, 43, 48, 153.